For the Record

For the Record

Felix Morley

Regnery/Gateway, Inc.   South Bend, Indiana

Foreword

Some justification is needed when a person of restricted fame, and even less notoriety, presents an autobiography. Why should anybody, outside the narrow circle of intimates, be interested?

In this case a partial answer is that my life has been both observant and long, spanning the wide gap that now separates us forever from the Nineteenth Century. Over much of this period I have kept careful diaries, with honest delineation of the passing scene as it appeared to me. This documentation has enabled me to revive the whole as it transpired, in comprehensive and at least generally objective manner.

Furthermore, my journalistic career has been adventurous, giving me contact with many individuals, in many countries, who have been associated with great events. They have repaid discretion on my part with sometimes unpublished disclosures. To tell these now is to assist historical research. Truth crushed to earth does not rise again unaided.

Finally, the reactions of any well-informed individual to critical contemporary problems is of potential value. That can be more the case with controversial opinion, as mine has often been. In the protection of reasonably critical individuals against their government lies much of the glory of Anglo-Saxon political tradition and of this Republic, founded thereon. Because it has been good to me I naturally hope for its continuation, and am sensitive to often unappreciated dangers.

Heredity counts, as well as environment. Therefore, even at the expense of brevity, I have broadened this review to give my forebears and family some consideration. Additionally, I owe gratitude to many friends, living or dead, who have given encouragement and/or assistance to this conscientious undertaking; especially: Ivan Bierly, Vera Brittain, Huntington Cairns,

Lambert Davis, Marion Doenhoff, David Franke, Edith Hamilton, Bertrand de Jouvenel, Joseph Lalley, Leonard Liggio, Archibald MacIntosh, Elsie Redstone, Edmund Stinnes and Kenneth Templeton. In final preparation Shirley Bawden and Ann Otto have been invaluable. Any political misjudgments, or unconscious factual errors, are entirely my own.

Particular appreciation is owing to Henry Regnery, my publisher, who also produced my study on *Freedom and Federalism*, a quarter-century ago. It is probable that he personally disagrees with some of my argument. Yet, like Voltaire, he upholds its claim to presentation. Also without prejudice, he has made helpful suggestions for improvement.

Some parts of this book have been previously published: a section of Chapter I in the *Johns Hopkins Magazine*; two sections of Chapter V in *Modern Age*; part of a section of Chapter VIII in *Reason*. Thanks are extended to the editors of these publications for their advance permission to reprint. Gratitude is also owing to Harcourt Brace Jovanovich, who have allowed me to quote from T.S. Eliot four lines for which they hold the copyright.

Felix Morley
Gibson Island, Maryland
Jan. 1, 1979

Contents

Just as the twig is bent, the tree's inclined.

POPE, *Essay on Man*

◀Chapter 1

As the Twig Was Bent . . .

Was it by accident, or by design, that the old tree stretched its length along the ground, just back of the college library? Some thought that William Carvill, the English landscape gardener who planted the campus in its early days, was responsible for this arboreal contortion. Henry Scattergood, who for a Quaker had a puckish wit, avowed that some serious founding father had forced the unnatural alignment with ulterior purpose. Certainly it was frequently referred to in Haverford Meeting, to point the moral that "as the twig is bent the tree is inclined."

In any case, the outcome provided a marvelous outdoor gymnasium for small children. A four-year-old could easily scramble onto its sturdy trunk and then hoist himself along the branches that angled thickly upward. There one could admire, and even occasionally detach, the rough-skinned globular fruit, as big as croquet balls, which made it known as the mock orange tree. None knew, or cared, that this is really the colloquial name for what should properly have been called an Osage Orange.

Ordinarily there were few children to play among the branches, since the faculty was small and not compensated in a manner conducive to large families. Nonetheless, for me the tree was a transplant from Paradise. It was especially gratifying to be conducted there by my older brother, nearly four years senior, when the latter's schooling permitted. Kit, as this deity was

1

familiarly known, would then disappear in the library to indulge his voracious reading tastes. Sometimes the nursemaid, pretty Irish Lizzie, would be in charge, pushing my younger brother in the pram well-worn by his two predecessors. But usually she was wanted at the house so I would be left to my own devices, in the company of favorite Kitty Sharpless and two or three other campus children. Even if one slipped off the rounded trunk the distance to the ground was short and nothing more than slight damage to pride and clothing was involved.

Had it been otherwise I would not have been allowed to enjoy myself unsupervised, since the mother of this trio was particularly solicitous for me. She and my father were both English, but in her background there was none of the Quakerism which bridged the Atlantic for him. Her girlhood, scarcely behind her at the time of emigration, had been passed in the mid-Victorian comfort of a solidly Anglican family almost as extensive, interwoven and prosperous as the Forsytes. But wealth had vanished, along with formal church affiliation and easy uppercrust environment. Consequently this gentle expatriate lavished on her American children more than a normal amount of maternal attention. I was especially favored because, at the age of four, I had suffered a severe attack of appendicitis from which recovery was slow and none too sure. In 1898 an operation for this ailment was regarded as the last recourse, as hazardous as the peritonitis likely without it.

Though not indifferent, my father was less habitually concerned about his sons. As an unusually gifted mathematician his primary loyalty was to the denationalized world of abstract science. Moreover, as a small-town East Anglian Quaker, whose father's early death had left the family saddled with a failing business, there was no socially pretentious loss to be regretted. By his own ability and on borrowed funds he had put himself through Cambridge University and was lastingly grateful to the small American college whose president, in 1887, had appointed him to a promising position.

My mother, on the other hand, felt more than a trace of alienation in the separation from England. There was a crest on the family silver she had brought to the New World but nobody paid attention to that fading distinction and her remarkable

2

musical talent, especially as a violinist, was viewed mistrustfully by the then predominantly puritanical Quakers. Socially adept and with well-developed artistic and literary tastes she undoubtedly found life at Haverford somewhat cramped and solaced herself by giving constant stimulus to her sons. All three learned reading and writing early, at her knee. If accused of matriarchy she would laughingly reply that this was because her husband had a Mistress—Miss Mathematics.

"Kit," to use the nickname which suited him far better than Chris, was the one who profited most from this maternal guidance. He was a natural romantic, though of a swashbuckling rather than pallid type. Blessed with a quick intelligence, a lively imagination and boisterous humor he easily dominated me and, in due course, Frank, who followed me by five years almost to the day. This baby, who called himself and thus became known as "Toto," was also quick minded and destined to show much intellectual stature. He was the only one who inherited my father's mathematical talent. Kit was more than competent in every subject of study, but leaned unswervingly towards literature. I was the plodder, who in years to come would listen with half-irritated amusement as my brothers monopolized a conversation adorned with sparkling thrusts and miserable puns. But I was not without an intuition for essentials and a stubborn tenacity which were to serve me well.

No such appraisals, of course, passed through the mind of the little boy who climbed contentedly among the branches of the mock orange tree. When taken there by Kit I would also be collected by the elder brother to return home at lunchtime. Between the tree and the professor's house there was then an open meadow, where violets bloomed profusely in the spring. At Kit's instigation the two would linger to pick bouquets for mother, who loved flowers. His posy always had long stalks whereas to me the blooms were all-important and these I crumpled in my small hands. This brought fraternal reproof to which I replied, or so the family legend says: "I'se only a baby awhile, Bubby."

Even so I was sufficiently observant to recall vividly, after many years, the now vanished house in which both Toto and I were born. Close to the northern edge of the campus the western

3

exposure looked past the college observatory over an open, undulating countryside which, in the 1890's, was almost devoid of any but a few farm buildings. There were beautiful sunsets over the long ridges between Haverford and Darby Creek so it was natural for my mother to call this rented dwelling "Westward Ho!" But the romantic name did not ameliorate the icy blasts that swept through its ill-built frame in wintry weather, when the coal furnace could scarcely cope and drifts of snow prevented access to the mock orange tree and all other college amenities.

It was not the first home of my English parents in this country. After their European honeymoon, in the summer of 1889, they had initially occupied the small apartment at Bryn Mawr College which the Woodrow Wilsons had then just vacated for Princeton. With Benjamin Harrison serving his first year in the White House nobody anticipated that Professor Wilson would eventually follow him there. But what had cramped the political expert was also straitened quarters for the immigrant couple who knew nothing of American politics. Shortly before Kit's birth, on May 5, 1890, they daringly moved to "Spring Cottage," a small stone farmhouse north of Bryn Mawr, now long since submerged under the spread of suburbia. There was no telephone, of course, but the doctor nevertheless got there by horse and buggy in time for the baby's arrival. Rural charm did not offset the long "bike" ride to Haverford, so the next parental move was to the campus of that college.

The second floor of "Westward Ho" was bisected by a well-remembered corridor, down which a penetrating draft would seek the dark back stairway to the kitchen. To keep that sanctum relatively warm the nether door was always closed by Irish Lizzie, better to entertain the "company" graciously allowed her when the parents attended an evening function. This made the back stairs a pit of Stygian darkness, prompting one of Kit's ingenious and, to his small brother, not far from fiendish impositions. The first ploy was to tell the latter, very casually, that two dreadful creatures, known as the Champlong and the Minnie-Whee, had been reported in the Haverford neighborhood. Then, when I was tucked snugly in bed and father and mother departed, Kit planted himself at the foot of the black

4

back stairs. Soon thereafter a piercing cry of Minnie-Whee-ee-ee-ee would mount crescendo to where I huddled trembling beneath the covers. Then Kit's intentionally noisy footsteps would be heard on the front stairway, coming to inquire whether his small brother was "all right." When I admitted to disturbance from the Minnie-Whee I was informed that the voiceless Champlong was actually far more deadly.

Of course these figments were shortlived, slain by Lizzie as soon as she realized they were not harmless leprechauns. But their final appearance gave further evidence of Kit's unfailing ingenuity. The victim had told him that the parents should be informed and at that moment they were heard below, returning unexpectedly early from a college party. "I don't think so, Felix," replied the thoughtful brother. "You know that mother doesn't like this house much anyway and we shouldn't say anything that might worry her more."

Such exuberant incidents have little in common with the introspection of Henry Adams, who brooded over "the mere accident" of his birth "under the shadow of Boston State House." The problem of starting life in "a nest of associations so colonial—so troglodytic— . . . was so queer as to offer a subject of curious speculation to the baby long after he had witnessed the solution. What could become of such a child of the seventeenth and eighteenth centuries, when he should wake up to find himself required to play the game of the twentieth?"

Nevertheless, although unrealized until much later, similar psychological problems surrounded the three Anglo-American brothers who arrived on the famous "Main Line" during the last decade of the nineteenth century. Already social unrest was making the current turgid, along this plutocratic river that had its source at Paoli, flowing along the Pennsylvania Railroad into Philadelphia at Overbrook. Sixty years earlier the Unitarians on Beacon Hill had rightly feared submergence by the rising tide of cosmopolitanism. Now the Quakers, in their strongholds at Haverford and Bryn Mawr, were equally threatened. Into this confusion the young English mathematician and his wife brought an unwavering Victorianism, in her case the more resistant to change because of

5

loyalty to a sentimental image of the Old Country. It would indeed be interesting to see how those three lively brothers assimilated.

But nothing of this was in their minds as they unconsciously savored the tranquility of the Haverford campus. Its more than 200 park-like acres then harbored fewer than that number of resident students, so there was little institutional flavor for these boys, none at all for Toto, just beginning to toddle when the family left. Kit, always gregarious, was naturally the best integrated. The most vivid memory taken away by Felix was of the mock orange tree, from which eyrie he absorbed a seemingly unpolluted atmosphere.

Yet pollution of a kind was already creeping in. As the century closed three wars were raging, mere brushfires by modern standards yet highly significant in their imperialistic overtones. It was interesting, but very puzzling, to a little boy who was just beginning to read the newspapers. His country had liberated Cuba and the Philippines from Spanish tyranny only to find that the faraway Asiatic people did not like their liberators. Similarly his mother's beloved England was finding it extremely difficult to dominate some troublesome African upstarts called Boers. Chinese "Boxers" were using more than their fists against good Christians. From the Quaker viewpoint all of this ugly business were better ignored. To me, however, it was disturbing.

Among my associates at the mock orange tree was a somewhat older and quite sophisticated lad who, as the saying went, "knew his way around." One day he broke into a treble chanty, to the tune of a bugle call which later always recalled the words:

> See a Spaniard in the grass;
> Stick a bay'nit up his ass.
> Stick it up; Stick it up;
> Stick it up, Uncle Sam!

Thus it transpired that the mock orange tree became confused with the tree of knowledge in this Quaker Eden. "Boys never see a conclusion;" to quote again from *The Education of Henry Adams*, "only on the edge of the grave can man conclude anything; but the first impulse given to the boy is apt to lead or

6

drive him for the rest of his life into conclusion after conclusion that he never dreamed of reaching."

As the twentieth century dawned, I was ready to leave the quiet beauty of Haverford. I knew, though I could not have put it into words, that I needed broader horizons, regardless of the scenery thereby displayed.

◐

◀Baltimore in 1900 was not a beautiful city. In spite of much face-lifting it can scarcely be called beautiful today. But then, more so than now, it had a definite character and charm, together with an intellectual vivacity for which the Johns Hopkins University was to no small extent responsible.

Since its establishment in 1876, Daniel Coit Gilman, one of America's most gifted educators, had been president of the Hopkins and later of its adjunct medical school. His concept of a university was a scholarly center devoted to postgraduate professional training, undisturbed by athletic competition and wholly free from the political interference which had so hampered him as president of the University of California. Without either campus or dormitories, with laboratories and lecture halls housed in modest downtown buildings, the endowment was adequate to fulfill these ambitions. By the turn of the century both university and medical school possessed faculties of international renown. One of President Gilman's last appointments, before his retirement in 1901, was to the vacant chairmanship of the department of mathematics, which he offered to Professor Frank Morley, of Haverford College.

It was a promotion which my father could not reasonably refuse. The opportunity to teach only graduate students, already well versed and deeply interested in their subject, was itself persuasive. Although Baltimore, as a city, was more provincial than Philadelphia, the Hopkins at the height of its fame offered a circle more cosmopolitan and dynamic than the introverted Quakerism of Haverford. There would be opportunity to collaborate with the Carnegie Institution in nearby Washington, which Dr. Gilman was to direct after relinquishing the reins in Baltimore. There would be good and easily accessible schools for the three Morley boys. Finally, the salary offered, though it was never to exceed the $5,500 per annum then tops for a full professor, was above anything Haverford could pay. So, coincident with my father's fortieth birthday, there was an arduous cleanup at "Westward Ho" and the Morley family moved south, only a hundred miles in distance but across the Mason-Dixon Line with all that it then symbolized in sharp division.

Undoubtedly the uprooting was a wrench, especially for the oldest son who, at the age of ten, had established himself as a popular Haverford figure, with a sensuous delight in the beautiful campus domain over which he roamed at will. For baby Frank, not yet two, the transplantation made no discernible psychological difference. For me, approaching seven, the change was profoundly stimulating. For the first time and at the right time I found opportunity to emerge from the closeknit family circle and establish an identity of my own.

With kindly assistance from well-posted Baltimore Quakers, my parents selected their place of residence. It was an outwardly handsome brick and brownstone front in what was then the last block on Park Avenue, only a five-minute walk through cleared but unbuilt land to the wide open spaces of Druid Hill Park. This group of solid three-storey houses had been built a few years earlier and vacancies were obtainable at moderate rental because they stood three squares distant from the nearest streetcar line. In front of these dwellings Park Avenue broadened to embrace a long central grassplot containing two large flower beds which in season were planted with flaming canna lilies. This was an attraction for my mother, who loved flowers and was now offered only a meager backyard with small opportunity to grow her own.

Like the sidewalk the street paving was neatly laid red brick, on which the hooves of passing horses sounded a very agreeable clop-clop. While hazardous when icy it was advantageous that the droppings could be easily swept up by the "white wings" and not left odorous as between the cobblestones of adjacent blocks. There were no houses directly opposite but across and a little to the south was the steep elevation of Bond's Hill, crowned by a picturesque stone residence which had been used by the "Yankees" as a battery site during the Civil War

8

occupation of the city. From the wall around this hilltop down to Mount Royal Terrace a block below was excellent sledding and the vacant lots made good playground for small boys. While the section was not modish it had eminent respectability and was authentically Baltimorean, except that the front steps were not white but brown, mounting parallel to the sidewalk with a right-angled jog to the porticoed entrance.

A generation after Appomatox memories of "the war" were still vivid in Baltimore, partly because of the large number of Southerners who had moved there during the reconstruction period. Next door to us lived an elderly lawyer who had fought for the Confederacy and when there was family singsong my mother would always turn the page on "Marching through Georgia" and "The Battle Hymn of the Republic." "Mr. S———— would not like to hear those," she would say. On the other hand the Baltimore Quakers, with whom the newcomers from Haverford naturally associated, were prone to forget their neutralism where politics was concerned. Mrs. Simon Flexner, in her charming story of *A Quaker Childhood* (in Baltimore from 1871 to '88) tells of the "outrage" felt by her distinguished father, Dr. James Carey Thomas, when one of his sons decided to cast his first vote for Grover Cleveland, candidate of "the rebel party of the Civil War." The Morley parents had no such partiality so I easily associated myself with the leanings of my friends and contributed a squeak for Democratic candidates around the fringes of neighborhood election night bonfires. One must, I thought, take sides in such tremendous issues.

Indeed, the lingering emotions of the Civil War were for me the first instance of a profound political cleavage, where convictions differed sharply and in which one necessarily made somewhat arbitrary choice. Responsibility was sharper because there was no direction in the matter at home. There my scientific father viewed all political problems with philosophic detachment. And my mother throughout her life remained too English in sympathy to be deeply interested in purely American concerns. Once when I sought at the supper table to start discussion on "The War between the States" it somehow moved into a parental argument on the seventeenth century struggle between Crown and Parliament. Here my father, a free-thinking

9

Quaker puritan and protestant to the core, was fundamentally at odds with my Anglican and royalist mother. This left me puzzled as to the antagonistic loyalties which could divide people so decisively. Could both sides in a civil war, I wondered, be equally patriotic?

A local event emphasized the political mystery. On Mount Royal Avenue, close to the handsome Maryland Institute of Art, stood (and stands) a small but beautiful Confederate war memorial, a life-size statue of a wounded and exhausted youth, supported and sheltered by a ministering angel. It was directly on the way to the apartment of a schoolmate, "Ferdy" Turnbull, in which, between steel engravings of Lee and Jackson, was a faded photograph of the family home at Petersburg, Virginia, as gutted by Union troops after the capture of that last redoubt. Incredulously I heard that the "Yankees" had thrown the family dog into the flames.

Early in these Baltimore days I went to watch the ceremonial unveiling of another Civil War memorial, to the Union cause. This was also placed on Mount Royal Avenue, at the vantage point where it joins Park Avenue to form an entrance to Druid Hill Park. The more recent monument, much more heroic and imposing than its Confederate predecessor, represents a Northern officer on a high pedestal, striding forth to battle in the direction of his dying adversary, a few blocks away. And behind this warrior, urging him forward, is another angel, arrogant and flamboyant by contrast with her colleague attending the dying Southerner. With the coming of the automobile this monument by its very size became a traffic hazard and was later removed to a less provocative location.

But the original juxtaposition of memorials to opposite sides in the same war, both on the same street and each invoking at least semi-divine alliance against the other, made a lasting impression on my opening mind. Long before I had even heard of Thomas Aquinas these contrasting statues disposed me to agreement with his conclusion that "the good angels do not entirely restrain the bad from inflicting harm." Skepticism was strengthened by my mother's distress over school-book references to the "Boston Massacre" and other perfidious British actions against the liberty-loving Colonials. Quaker influences

10

supported a dawning conviction that wars should never be allowed to shake a perhaps childish faith in fundamental human decency. While I was destined to witness ample evidence of viciousness and cruelty, I have never believed that these are special characteristics of one class, condition, color or country.

Fortunate, as my name optimistically suggests, I was certainly so in the boyhood friendships formed in Baltimore. The first was to prove one of the firmest. Soon after the Morleys arrived at 2026 Park Avenue a family named Davis took occupancy of 2040, next to the other end of the block. The father, E. Asbury Davis, was a rising young merchant in the wholesale tobacco business, with four small children—a second daughter came later—of whom the oldest, Francis Asbury Davis, was six months my senior. We soon chummed up and found that in spite of surface differences we had most of the fundamentals in common.

The two families were wholly dissimilar. The Davis clan, with roots in the lower Eastern Shore of Maryland, was keenly alive to commercial opportunity, which could not possibly be said of the Morleys. The latter were a literary family, the house always cluttered with books of all varieties, in several languages. The architecturally identical Davis home had a scrupulously tidy "library," but the standard sets behind glass-fronted bookcases gave the impression that the contents were infrequently disturbed. This family was as orthodox in its Baptist faith as the Morleys were casual in their Quakerism. Francis in particular had strong spiritual qualities, the more impressive because he lived and did not preach his Christianity. Though destined for the family business, which he eventually directed with habitual efficiency, he was at heart a scholar and would have been happier and no less influential in the Ministry. A very modest person, both as boy and man, his natural dignity was mellowed by a dry and pleasing humor. He and I went to different schools and colleges, married very different women and followed very different walks of life. But always, after a separation, we came closely together again. Damon and Pythias had no stronger association.

In this juvenile relationship a subtle alchemy was at work. I instinctively wanted to break from my English background to

11

become authentically American. Yet because of that background I could supply the greater cosmopolitanism which Francis unknowingly sought. And I could indeed consider myself fortunate in acquiring Americanism from one who had the very best of that amorphous quality to offer.

It is difficult, in the current environment, to realize how much small boys were thrown on their own resources for development, in the early years of this century. There was, of course, no radio, no television and only the crudest sort of "phonographs." There were no movies worthy of the name; no automobiles and, in the Morley circle, no private horse and carriage to encourage visiting. When the telephone came in its use for juvenile conversations was most severely discouraged. On the other hand primitive household arrangements built up a list of chores almost as extensive as those of a farm. The coal furnace required constant attention and the removal of its ashes was no easy task. Kindling to light the kitchen stove had to be constantly chopped. Bicycles had to be taken to and from the cellar. There was a choice between boiling all tap water or trudging with a wagon to Druid Hill Park to bring it home in bottles from a communal spring. Because screening was deficient, mosquito netting had to be hung over beds and folded away every morning. The family employed a cook, and for Toto a colored Mammy, "Wizzie" to him, who was also a seamstress and outstayed numerous kitchen drop-outs. Nevertheless there were plenty of household duties for the older boys, especially sturdy Kit whose constant query was: "Why can't Felix do that?" It often happened that I did because at first my assumed delicacy kept me from school, taking regular lessons from my mother.

These were adjusted so that on Thursday mornings I could accompany her to Lexington Market which sprawled its open, dirty and fascinating length over three full blocks in the heart of the business district—a long "parallelogram of plenty" as Kit was later to describe it. One traveled on the bouncing little John Street trolley, where passengers sat facing each other on the two long benches. Getting off at Lexington Street there were a couple of crowded blocks to walk, under mysterious festoons of overhead wires, to the Great Atlantic and Pacific Tea Store. In spite of its name this was a very modest shop where customers selected tea and coffee from gaily colored bins defined by exotic names like Oolong and Pekoe, Mokka and Java. When coffee was ordered the obliging clerk, in spotless white apron, would shovel the selected beans into a marvelous electric grinder, from which the resulting mixture would be deftly bagged and tied. It was usually the first package popped into the capacious string bag which I carried as we entered the market proper and made the familiar rounds from stall to stall. That of Mr. Plitt, the butcher, was particularly impressive, not only for its great sides of refrigerated meat but also because it had as background a lovely painted scene of sheep and cattle in a luxuriant meadow from which protruded the long curving horns of what once must have been a most magnificent steer.

Always there was a round of amiable conversation, as vegetables were weighed on shiny scales or meat sliced off with glistening knives on well-scrubbed tables. Generally, also, there were unexpected meetings with family friends, and tiresome adult conversations which the little boy endured with roving eye and ill-concealed impatience. But there was compensation, especially in frosty weather, from the habitual stop at the stall of the stout old German baker, whose wife presided with a shawl around her ruddy face and fingerless mittens on her hands. She would call me *"Liebchen"* and present me with a fragrant bun as, laden with weekend provender, the shoppers turned homeward. On the streetcar again I would pay the nickel fares and ask the conductor for transfers. He would punch the blue slips solemnly and hand them over with a wink, knowing they were wanted only to swap for more unusual collector's items, such as the Pennsylvania Avenue variety, surcharged with green stripes and hard to come by because that line traversed a "black belt" which was well understood to be out of bounds.

But there was no prohibition on unescorted visits to the old Pratt Library building, on Mulberry Street, and therefore the residential side of the business district. Thither Francis and I made pilgrimages at least weekly, usually via the pleasant municipal gardens of Park Place where we would likely meet up with Francis' grandfather, a fine old patriarch with flowing white moustache. It was his wont to present us with carfare home, never used for that purpose but happily exchangeable for paper soldiers at a penny per cardboard sheet at the intriguing little stationery shop on McMechen Street. That transverse thoroughfare was also notable for its Chinese laundry and for the "Stepping Stones" which carried pedestrians dryshod over the always odorous and frequently brimming open gutters. A little further along Park Avenue came the two old country houses on Lanvale Street, long since engulfed by the city but still keeping substantial grounds, in one of which lived our friends the Howells. Then, from its well-tended hollow, there loomed the gothic clocktower of Mt. Royal Station, where the big B. & O. engines came with clanging bells out of the black tunnel and seemed to gasp for breath as they halted and blew off clouds of steam. Still another landmark for lingering was the Parisian beauty and charm of Mount Vernon Place, at that time unspoiled in its symmetry around the stately monument to Washington. Indeed, this walk was in itself well worthwhile, even without the objective of the excellent library.

On the return, physical surroundings were almost dangerously ignored, since we would habitually read our books as we walked, the idea being to see who could get through the most pages in a block. The practise must have been annoying to other pedestrians but was perhaps commendable for developing speed in comprehension. Nor were the texts exacting, being mostly straight adventure fiction of the Conan Doyle, Rider Haggard, G. A. Henty, H. G. Wells or Jules Verne types. At home, however, this lust for reading was skillfully directed for me into the Victorian classics. During a winter when my mother was suffering from protracted eye trouble I read aloud to her all of *David Copperfield*, who thereby became almost as real a person as some of my friends. This interest in transference carried on into imaginary conversations with my favorite characters in bed at night, not so much in adventurous situations as in travels, discussions or even arguments together.

Thus the two circles of my English background and American environment began to merge. There was no friction because I simply absorbed from each what pleased me most. And synthesis was forwarded by exciting direction from my masterful older brother. Somehow there were no boys of Kit's age in the immediate neighborhood, so he condescended to cultivate the

14

society of Francis and me, forcing us at a great pace to keep abreast. Even baby Frank, always precocious, was soon admitted under tutelage to imaginative activities, some so unusual as to deserve separate recollection. Perhaps the close family association could justify the belief of E. V. Lucas that: "No study about three brothers with different character can go far wrong."

I was certainly not the most brilliant of the three, but was in some ways the most reflective. Even as a small boy I was prone to listen to the observations of others, a characteristic which made me a good reporter in later years. Because of this attentive quality I was admitted to the informal teas which were periodically given for my father's graduate students. Although often socially awkward young men they seemed very mature beings to me and I strove hard to understand what they were saying. On one occasion a recent Yale graduate referred to a teacher of his there who had given a provocative lecture titled "The Conquest of the United States by Spain." I ventured an inquiry since I knew, of course, that the outcome had been gloriously the other way round.

A few days later a big envelope addressed to Master Felix Morley was delivered by the friendly Park Avenue postman. It contained a reprint of the lecture, by someone named William Graham Sumner, with a red circle around his prediction that "the democratic republic, which has been, will stand in history, like the colonial organization of earlier days, as a mere transition form."

This made no sense. But I kept it, out of pride at having had a printed pamphlet sent through the mail. And this was appropriate, since I was destined to live through that transition.

◀From the outset, in the Park Avenue home, Kit had his private sanctum on the third floor—though only in one of two tiny servants' rooms of which the twin was occupied by whatever cook might be temporarily in residence. Toto slept under the watchful eye of his beloved "Wizzie" in the second floor back, next to the only and often over-pressured bathroom. When 2026 is finally demolished housebreakers may discover the small hoard of Indian-head pennies which he collected and profligately pushed through the poorly-laid pinewood floorboards. I was installed, because of alleged delicacy, in a windowless "dressing room" adjacent to the second-floor front bedroom of my parents. It gave no scope for the arrangement or disarrangement of personalia so dear to the heart of any growing boy. Consequently, whenever the weather was bad, I would seek admission to my older brother's hideout. And, at a price, this intrusion was graciously permitted. The *quid pro quo* was usually obedient cooperation in production of "The Family News," a file of which in the publisher's rounded handwriting is now among the Morleyana in the Haverford College library.

This weekly paper, issued with spurts of remarkable continuity over a span of several years, was the channel through which Chris Morley first steered his literary talent toward open seas. The graceful little craft was run as a tight ship, under the absolute dictation of its editor and publisher, with Francis Davis and I listed somewhat crudely as Ass. Editors on the decorative cover. Here brother Frank also obtained his introduction to the publishing business, though in accord with the Horatio Alger formula his apprentice duty was to take the finished product to neighboring subscribers who paid five cents apiece for the privilege of reading it. There was first an editorial and then an installment of a major continued story by the editor-in-chief. After a layer of rather uncomplex riddles and puzzles ("solution in our next issue") followed tales and articles by the docile Ass. Editors, evenly compensated at the going rate of one cent per thousand words. Original art work was encouraged and a well-compressed series on "The Kings of England" was completed through Victoria by Francis Davis after literally encyclopedic research. It was doubtless intended as a delicate tribute to the nativity of the Morley parents who were also solicited for occasional contributions. With notable foresight my mathematical father once took two lady astronauts on a trip to the moon. My more mundane mother contented herself with amusing notes on the peregrinations of what she aptly termed "The Traveling Morleys."

This was a fertile field since every summer, after much consideration and planning, the family would close house and

16

depart for some modest vacation site, whether near or far depending on the current budgetary situation. The practise was not only unique in the Park Avenue neighborhood but also made the advent of mid-June as exciting as that of Christmas. Parental *Wanderlust* meant that these often complicated journeys always broke new ground, except when modified by the powerful magnet of a return to England. The summer of 1901, the first after the move from Haverford, was necessarily one of enforced economy. And so it happened, at a modest boarding house at Deer Park in the mountains of Western Maryland, that I heard of President McKinley's assassination. The sense of an ending era was made more pronounced by the sequence of McKinley's passing to that of Queen Victoria, a few months earlier.

More personally fateful was the connection between this Deer Park summer and my eventual marriage. As fellow "paying guests," at the Droege home, were a Washington couple by the name of Tweedy, with their two children, Temple and Gertrude, of approximately the same ages as Kit and I. The two mothers became great friends and for some years exchanged visits between Baltimore and Washington, as did Kit and Temple. Neighboring the Tweedys, on the 3400 block of Thirteenth Street, N.W., lived Jefferson Middleton, a colleague of Mr. Tweedy in the then modest U.S. Geological Survey. The Middleton family, of old southern Maryland stock, had two sons and two daughters, the younger of whom—Isabel—was a close friend of Gertrude Tweedy. In the summer of 1917, when I was in camp near Washington, Mrs. Tweedy invited me to bring a friend and enjoy a weekend leave. The rendezvous, with Gertrude and Isabel, was at the old Willard Hotel and the result, tracing directly back to Deer Park, was that before the end of 1917 the latter and I were married and so remained through the vicissitudes of more than sixty years.

Though with less notable consequences most of the boyhood summers went further afield, involving exciting overnight trips on the now vanished sidewheel steamers that regularly plied Long Island Sound and the majestic Hudson. Perhaps they were even then becoming popular for extra-marital excursions, but if so this never occurred to me. I found excitement enough in the cream and gold decor of the big dining saloons, the rhythmic motion of the walking beam, the splash of the great paddles and the coziness of the little cabins where, to Kit's disgruntlement, I was always awarded the greater security of the lower bunk. Whenever possible, in later years, I would travel by these great inland waterways, twice making the leisurely two-night steamer trip from Baltimore to Washington. There, loading and unloading frieght at lower Potomac landings, it was easy to imagine a century swept away. But with the coming of the automobile, and great diesel trucks, the water-born economy of the Chesapeake languished. For years the Old Bay Line struggled on, with the holds of its fast propeller ships converted to carry cars and thus permitting as delightful a weekend expedition, to tidewater Virginia and return, as anything the world could offer. Now they are all gone and driving by congested highways is a sorry substitute.

The summer of 1902 must have found the Morley family in funds for in that year we journeyed, perhaps to touch down on British soil, to a Quebec village called Knowlton, on a small lake close to the headwaters of magnificent Lake Champlain. This trip was memorable because it involved no less than three of those delightful side-wheelers—up the Hudson to Albany, then up scenic Lake George and finally a second overnight ride on elongated Champlain, with the Green Mountains to starboard and Adirondacks to port, all the way to Rouse's Point on the Canadian border. From the well-remembered names of the steamers one could immediately identify the waters they traversed. The *City of Norfolk* and *City of Richmond* on the Chesapeake; the *Pilgrim*, *Priscilla* and *Puritan* on the Fall River and Providence lines; the *Hendrick Hudson* and *Washington Irving* between New York and Albany; the *Mohican* and *Horicon* on Lake George; the *Chateaugay*, *Vermont* and, after 1906, the queenly *Ticonderoga* on Lake Champlain. The last is now permanently grounded as a feature of the Shelburne Museum near Burlington, Vermont.

For me, in the early summers of this century, what is now lost was being absorbed. In 1903, the vacation choice fell on Nantucket Island, at the then primitive settlement of Wauwinet, where a cottage was rented with the pleasing innovation of outdoor stairs to the attic where Kit and I slept. Along with the windswept moors and lonely beaches this somehow ✳ emphasized the independence for which the nine-year-old was unconsciously yearning. I became a good swimmer and began to assert a zest for modest adventure under the watchful eye of my still solicitous mother, who was herself far from being a sissy.

Indeed, those long vacations were very largely under her management. When the location was chosen, after much correspondence and careful budgeting, time came to pack the trunks, sent off by "express" two days in advance. This permitted travel with a minimum of hand baggage and economy was emphasized by streetcar to the station and sandwiches for lunch on the train. Timing was arranged to reach either the Hudson or Fall River steamer well before its departure from New York, and from then on juvenile boredom was impossible.

Not only in domestic matters but also as an educator my mother's ability was outstanding, even though her own schooling had been limited to the curriculum of a Victorian Seminary for young ladies. The atmosphere of the home was decidedly bookish and in the winter evenings, with the baby asleep upstairs, my parents would often read aloud by an open fire, with the older boys listening. To this ear training both attributed a facility in public speaking which, in our separate fields, was to make us much in demand in years to come.

Only in the field of music, and there primarily because of her own proficiency, did my mother fail as an instructor. Herself as a girl a concert violinist she sought to teach me to play that beautiful instrument, selecting me because of my long and delicate—termed by Kit "quabbly"—fingers. But, though well able to keep a tune, I lacked both the ear and the desire to fiddle, so the effort was abandoned. Even with the piano none of the brothers achieved more than a very modest ability in reading music, the more surprising because my father liked to "strum," as he called it, and had a good bass voice which kept him in demand with the Baltimore Oratorio Society and other amateur singing groups. Skipping the Morley brothers this musical talent was to reappear, in very advanced form, in one of Frank's children.

Musical deficiency, which never implied a lack of appreciation, seemed of small moment to me amid the excitements of

19

those early years in Baltimore. That numbered 1904 was particularly memorable because my tenth birthday, on January 6, was practically coincident with its dawn; because of the great fire which swept the downtown district a month later; and because of the long visit to England undertaken that summer, with "the little Tote," at five considered old enough to enjoy his three living grandparents over there. For him, excepting the Canadian summer two years previous, it was the first trip abroad.

Not so for Kit and me. In 1897, Professor Morley had more than earned sabbatic leave from Haverford and had decided to devote it to study in Germany. His *Treatise on the Theory of Functions*, written in collaboration with Professor James Harkness of Bryn Mawr, was already accorded widespread recognition in mathematical circles. He wanted to confer with some of the leading German thinkers in this field before publishing an even more advanced study which was to prove instrumental in bringing him to the Johns Hopkins. Consequently the family was overseas from June, 1897, to September, 1898, part of the time with relatives in England, but during the winter of 97–98 in Göttingen, where I celebrated my fourth birthday.

From this sojourn the two of us acquired, if not a speaking knowledge of German, at least a sense of its complicated structure and a good *Aussprache* which later was to serve me well. And three clear recollections stuck with me from the Reich of Bismarck's time. One was of the *Weihnachtsfest* and the caroling of "*Stille Nacht*," so vivid that I have always felt a sense of impropriety on hearing the lovely hymn sung to English words. A second recollection is of an old hilltop castle breaking into view from a steep and winding road up which the family were driving by carriage. Finally, a memory of soldiers—many soldiers—drilling in the picturesque spiked helmets (*Pikkelhaube*) of the period. The trio of vignettes was characteristic.

There is much evidence to show that the Morley foursome had a delightful time in their Göttingen lodgings and that my mother, with her violin, was quickly accepted into the informal musical life of the famous old university town. When I revisited it, shortly after the first World War, a sense of familiarity broke through the barrier of intervening years and I quickly found my way to the Weendestrasse where, in the flat of Fräulein

20

Schultze, over Postamt 2, we had lived nearly a quarter of a century earlier. Stories of that mature *Studentenleben* were often recalled and not long before my mother's death, in 1939, she wrote to me, recalling that: "On those far-off nights in Göttingen there would be watchmen on the church towers on the lookout for possible fires, a disastrous matter in that picturesque huddle of buildings where so much was of wood." Against the blockbusters, a few years afterwards, that watch availed nothing.

In the spring my father proceeded to Leipzig, for further study, while my mother unaided took her two small sons back to England. Their destination was Woodbridge, the little market town on the river Deben, in Suffolk, where the Morleys, now extinct there, had lived for generations. There, until summer, the trio stayed in the large old building, half store, half dwelling, that housed the family business. An authentic picture of this house, its inmates and its rambling garden is found in the opening pages of Kit's novel *Thorofare*, where he identifies Woodbridge as Wilford. That is written from his sharp recollections at the age of eight but all that I remember of the ancestral home from this period is the walled garden, running down toward the river, with its stone animals which Kit did all possible to animate in his partially autobiographical story.

However, I have often revisited Woodbridge and on what would have been our father's eighty-ninth birthday (September 9, 1949) circumstance permitted the three brothers to hold a sentimental reunion there. Together we went over the old house, then converted as the local outlet of an English grocery chain. And shortly afterwards I assembled genealogical notes which reconstruct an era as well as a family.

◀While Morleys had probably lived in or around Woodbridge for centuries, the first of whom we find comprehensive record is William M. Morley, my great-grandfather, who was born there in 1790. A business directory of 1830 shows that since 1818 he had been conducting a china and glassware store on the town's main street—the Thorofare—though whether he founded or inherited this business is uncertain. At the close of 1848, "gratefully acknowledging the liberal support received for the last thirty years," William "declined his share of the business" (i.e., retired) in behalf of his son, Joseph Roberts Morley, my father's father.

Joseph R. Morley was unquestionably enterprising. He added furniture to the existing lines of merchandise. He took advantage of the newly opened railroad to develop wholesale as well as retail trade. He imported what he called "fancy articles"—porcelain and bric-a-brac—to attract the neighborhood gentry. He built a warehouse for his extensive inventory and cannily rented space therein for private storage. And for Woodbridgians ready to abandon the discomfort of outdoor privies he acquired, as his early handbills show, the exclusive local agency for the indoor installation of "Moule's Earth Closets," then the latest thing in urban sanitary progress.

At first the economic climate favored my grandfather's activity. During the Napoleonic wars Woodbridge, though ten miles from the sea on the tidal Deben, had built numerous small ships for the Navy. Nearby military camps had brought temporary prosperity to the area, as was to happen in future wars. Unlike most of England, Suffolk was a county of peasant proprietors, tilling their own land. So the farmers prospered directly from the high price of meat and the protection of the Corn Law of 1815, forbidding the importation of wheat. The county was not industrialized and during the general postwar depression had little unemployment or labor unrest. With this stability the Morley store did well, making it possible for William to retire before his sixtieth birthday.

But by the beginning of 1849, when my grandfather took over, all that had changed. Famine in Ireland had forced the final repeal of the Corn Laws. The Chartist movement had spread to threaten the open revolution that flared up in much of continental Europe. The turn toward Free Trade was expanding industry but dislocating the inelastic agricultural economy. The banking system was unstable and credit hard to come by in rural areas. And the over-expanded railroads were making it easy for the better financed London merchants to skim off the hitherto lucrative retail trade of country towns. In the autumn of 1847

22

an acute business crisis pushed interest rates to ten per cent.

It is doubtful that Joseph Morley had more than a superficial realization of what was happening. Certainly only a very intuitive reader could tell from contemporary newspapers that the great days of agriculture were over in England and that wealth was now flowing to the grimy industrial cities. With this shift the importance, and even the population, of small market towns like Woodbridge declined. But the china merchant had been married, on October 3, 1848, to Elizabeth Muskett, daughter of another Quaker tradesman in the Norfolk town of Attleborough, from whom my middle name of Muskett (a corruption of Norman French *émouchette*, or Falcon) is derived. Like many another, Joseph Morley believed that he could counter "recession," as we would call it now, by expansion. He had already enlarged the store, to make it the imposing three-storey building that still remains. Now, in the eighteen-fifties, he established branches in Ipswich and Norwich, respectively the largest cities in Suffolk and Norfolk and, either one, with twenty times the population of little Woodbridge. The Ipswich branch, incidentally, was only two doors from the Great White Horse Inn, already made famous by the nocturnal adventures of Mr. Samuel Pickwick in that labyrinthine hostelry.

All this enlargement, however, brought more problems than profit, and most of the latter was drained off by the family of five daughters and three sons whom Joseph and Elizabeth Morley successfully raised to maturity. Only two of these girls married and only one of the boys, my father, in turn had sons to maintain the family name, far from its source of origin. For Morley is simply a derivative of Moor-lee, the sheltered parts of the East Anglian terrain on which my Angle ancestors settled when they stormed over from what is now Schleswig-Holstein, after the collapse of Roman rule in Britain.

In this petit bourgeois, provincial Quaker family my father, born in 1860, was indubitably a curiosity. His deep affinity for mathematics was obvious at an early age; chess was his favorite recreation and he had no interest whatsoever in the business, into which his brother Walter, senior by ten years, had been rather unwillingly inducted. It was a bad time to be apprenticed to any but the most solid commercial undertaking. The Crimean

War and the Sepoy Rebellion had brought economic disruption in their wake. To this was added strangulation of the textile industry by the cotton embargo during the American Civil War. In 1866 another financial crisis shook the over-extended British banking system to its foundations. Like many small concerns the Morley business reeled under these successive blows.

Studying the history of the period I confess to admiration for the manner in which Joseph Morley confronted outrageous circumstance. In 1868 he was selling, and offering licenses to manufacture, a patented desk "combining Cabinet and Bureau, the best, most useful, commodious and cheapest that can be made." He was also "sole wholesale agent" for the "Sandringham Chair" described as "a very clever and simple contrivance for combining chair and steps in one" and so named because it was supplied "to Sandringham, the Norfolk seat of His Royal Highness the Prince of Wales." For all his sturdy Quakerism Joseph was evidently not averse to a commercial connection with Potiphar.

It is a family legend that in his closing years Joseph Morley became slack, deserting his business for the pleasures of the neighboring pub and growing grossly fat to an extent attested by an old photograph. But I would caution that this story came to me from a strongly teetotal maiden aunt, whose "Band of Hope" excluded even the most temperate drinker. Certain it is that my paternal grandfather entered my father at the best school in the neighborhood, the Seckford Grammar School, where the lad distinguished himself in a way that is still remembered. No Suffolk ancestor of record had previously gone to a university, but the young mathematician was already accepted by Cambridge when Joseph Morley, in 1878, died suddenly, leaving his affairs in confusion. To enter King's College, where he lived penuriously, it was necessary for my father to borrow money, at six per cent. By a quaint crotchet, in later life he was always uneasy if unable to obtain as high a return on his own savings.

My grandmother, with the aid of her unmarried daughters, pluckily undertook reorganization of the business. The two metropolitan branches were closed and the whole operation cut down to a modest retail trade. Even so the end was in sight. At the turn of the century Elizabeth Muskett Morley, a diminutive but dignified Quaker lady whom I remember clearly, sold out and moved to much smaller "Barton House," named after Bernard Barton, the Quaker poet who, with far more famous Edward Fitzgerald, was the chief literary celebrity of nineteenth century Woodbridge. For the Morleys of that town, as for their once flourishing business, it was closing time. But the name is still remembered there and in 1963 I attended, and spoke, at the dedication of Morley Avenue, one of the few new streets to be opened in Woodbridge since the death of Queen Victoria.

In the carefully stratified society of Victorian England my mother's background was of superior tone to that of the provincial Morleys, or certainly was so considered. For instance, the Birds and the Clays, which were the families of my mother's grandparents, were London people. Moreover, they were both very well "fixed," as the picturesque though often highly inaccurate phrase related. My Great-Grandfather Bird had been active in the development of England's large-scale iron industry. My Great-Grandfather Clay was of the family which managed the Cambridge University Press and profited from the spread of literacy as did his neighbor Bird from the expansion of industrialism. In the days of George IV, the two families had adjacent estates in the environs of London, both now long since cut up into suburban streets. There were also big "town" houses near each other in the Marble Arch district, where my mother was born in 1864. So when her parents, James Bird and Elizabeth Jane Clay, were married in the early eighteen-fifties it was, as my brother Frank has written, "a very prosperous amalgamation."

In addition to being city folk and wealthy, whereas the Morleys and Musketts were provincials of modest means, the Birds and Clays were Church of England. Only someone personally associated with Victorianism can appreciate the Anglican sense of superiority to religious "non-conformity." It was matched by a similar arrogance toward those engaged in "trade," though by some occult semasiology trading with foreign countries, or on the stock exchange, was held free from this plebeian taint. My father, by gaining admission to Cambridge and making a professional career, also escaped the stigma; but rather narrowly.

I do not think, however, that there was any trace of snobbishness about my maternal grandfather, James Bird. He was a charming dilettante who early abandoned the travail of the iron industry to toy with publishing and other gentlemanly occupations. I still recall his courtly, gracious manner, his merry laugh, the venerable long white beard of his old age. He was well informed and enlarged my economic horizons by telling me that British steel could never cope with that of the United States as developed by the Civil War, or even with that of Germany after the seizure of Lorraine. But he himself, I am sure, did not have the pugnacity to make a fight of it.

Retiring early from uncongenial business my maternal grandparents, before the turn of the century, settled in the little town of Royston, some thirty miles north of London and known to history as a Roman depot on their Ermyn Street (the Great North Road) and because James I, a monarch of dubious grandeur, maintained a lodge there for hunting and other virile sports. Of the four daughters of James and Elizabeth Bird, the oldest, my sprightly Aunt Florence, never married, and after showing capacity by managing a large commercial laundry— perilously close to "trade"—returned to live at home. She was, until the first World War, rather proud of having been born in Berlin, where my grandfather lived for a time after his marriage, enjoying Prussian society and giving secondary attention to the Continental connections of the Bird business. Aunt Florence had a very lively mind and showed a particular affection for her American nephews, except when they failed to reply to her long and invariably crossed-over letters.

A second sister, my Aunt Margaret, lived at Cambridge, only nine miles from Royston, where her husband was for many years the highly-respected Bursar (treasurer) of Trinity College. Their two sons were both killed in action as mere boys, a few months apart, during the closing year of World War I. Their only daughter, Christina McLeod Innes ("Biddy") in 1926 became the wife of my brother Frank who stayed in England, in publishing, after he obtained his doctorate in Mathematics at Oxford in 1923. Frank's major contribution to this science is delicately adumbrated in his little book entitled: *My One Contribution To Chess*. But he says little therein about our mother's family. Kit is more explicit in the few pages of *Thorofare* which he devotes to

26

Kneesworth, the pseudonym selected for Royston because our grandparents' home there was on a street so named. His verbal picture of "Uncle Kneesworth," who is our grandfather Bird, rings true in my memory. This I find doubly interesting, because while Kit drew his fictional characters from real originals he never hesitated to adapt them to the exigencies of the tale. Indeed he prefaced *Thorofare* with a supporting quotation from G. K. Chesterton, saying: "The past is always present; yet it is not what was, but whatever seems to have been." With this I disagree, or would not be writing as I am. Of course we see the past through the glasses of the present. But I think this makes it possible to focus it more accurately. It is the present which is so frequently not what it seems to be.

The third Bird sister, Katharine, was married to Dr. Lovell Drage, a busy physician at Hatfield, also only a few miles from Royston. So "Cranbrook," the house on Kneesworth Street, was a logical center during the summers we spent in England. In addition to my mother's three older sisters her only brother, Clement, an Anglican priest with a "living" in distant Yorkshire would also come for these occasional reunions. Although the Bird family had its full share of internal dissonance these rare visits were naturally precious to mother, not less so because her husband was always eager to look up old friends at nearby Cambridge. To me, as a child, the contrast between the polished urbanity of the aunts at Royston, and the prim simplicity of those at Woodbridge, was striking, though I cannot recall that I much preferred one to the other. It was more a matter of adjustment to get the best of both, as was also the case in the overall variations between the English and American ways of life. Certainly the shifting among different environments did much to develop social adaptability.

Of my several visits to Royston, that in the summer of 1904, at the impressionable age of ten, was the longest and most memorable. And from it I derived a sense of the desirability of style in living. While the Bird fortunes were by that time sharply attenuated, my grandparents were still surrounded by luxuries unfamiliar to me. "Cranbrook" was a substantial semi-detached "villa," with a handsome living room opening through French doors on a big and beautifully tended garden.

There were cabinets filled with what my other grandfather would have described as "fancy articles" and a number of fairly good paintings, for James Bird had shown himself much more active as collector than as industrialist. A less favored oil that particularly attracted me was of my grandmother's favorite thoroughbred from the back of which, with characteristic individuality, she had years earlier painted out the girlish figure which she had lost, leaving a most intriguing wraith at which a formalized King Charles spaniel gazed in not unnatural bewilderment. In the house were three servants, in addition to the gardener and boy. The correctly pretty waitress, in spotless cap and apron, is not forgotten. After late dinner, served by candlelight, James Bird would raise his glass of Port, imparting little lozenges of richest color to the linen tablecloth. To this ritual my senses responded as they never have to the temperance sections of the Quaker Discipline. It was the cue for Kit and me to make polite excuses and depart.

I was to learn later that Grandfather Bird was living in state on almost the last reserves of inherited capital. Little, even in those days of trivial "death duties," was left for his children when he and my grandmother died a few years later. To James Bird, born to a fortune and reared in luxury, this closing chapter in the mediocrity of Royston perhaps seemed a sad decline. But to his scrubby-headed grandson, familiar with genteel poverty, the ordering of "Cranbrook" seemed almost regal. One day I accompanied the old gentleman to the local bank where, in return for his check, the cashier took a little wooden trowel and scooped what seemed to me a fortune out of a drawer apparently filled with golden sovereigns, counting a number of them over. Those lovely and now hoarded coins, with the fascinating imprint of St. George spearing the dragon on the reverse, were intrinsically seductive. To see that my grandfather need only write his name on a slip of paper to get as many as he wanted was miraculous. Reading my thoughts he handed one to me. But when I showed it to my mother she shook her head sadly. "He always found them so easy to give away," she said.

That memory was still vivid on the day, 27 years later, when Great Britain finally junked the gold standard. What I had seen, in 1904, was an illustration of the financial confidence on which

28

a great people had built a free and basically stable economy. Their confidence did not rest on the often ill-judged extension of governmental power. On the contrary, its basis was the almost automatic control of governmental spending provided by having the currency convertible at a fixed ratio into gold. Regardless of the rise and fall of families, or individuals, society as a whole could be secure so long as, but only so long as, its paper money remained "as good as gold." When that ceased to be, Pandora's box was opened.

◆That episode of the sovereigns had a sequel with importance for the three brothers. It led directly to the origination of our imaginary countries—Christophalia, Musketty and Totoland. Of course other families, perhaps most notably the Brontës, had developed the same pastime. But few ever carried it as far as we Morley brothers, in whose hands it became an unconscious satire on the immaturity of the nationalistic age.

The beautifully tended garden at Cranbrook, with its great elms, its close-cropped turf, its rosebeds, potting sheds and gravel walks, was an invitation to adventure. But my grandfather's health was failing that summer and my grandmother demanded both reasonable quiet and protection of the horticulture which she devotedly supervised. So my mother asked Kit, always inventive, to think up some quiet game in which five-year-old Toto could join.

Without much cogitation Kit took me, together with my treasured sovereign, to the marts of Royston. We returned lacking money but laden with rolls of beautiful white cardboard and practically every other offering of a well-equipped stationery store. The idea, said my older brother, was for each of us to have a country of his own, to create and manage as he pleased, and the obvious first step was to make maps, in peaceful consultation.

Desire, thus awakened, ran riot under the Cranbrook elms. Not even Roosevelt and Stalin ever gained so free a mandate to mold provinces and peoples in accordance with individual fancy. Tables were found, the virgin cardboard sheets tacked down and coastlines sketched in forthwith. Cleverly, I waited to see the

29

modest proportions of Christophalia take shape and then made Musketty a good deal larger. "And what is your scale?" inquired Kit when this triumph was drawn to this attention. At first the question mystified me, but I fastened on the explanation that a mile to the inch was the accepted scale for the best professional maps. If this was the best, I said, it would do for Musketty and was so recorded. "My scale," Kit then observed, "is fifty miles to the inch."

At the outset Christophalia was designated a Republic, with a President named Justin Forrett. To avoid the stigma of "copycat" Musketty therefore became a kingdom. But as its ruler groped haltingly for the names of national dignitaries he was anonymously known as K.O.M., which stuck through life. Totoland knew nothing of political variations and was satisfied with a Governor, who fluctuated from Christophalian to Muskettian control as these greater powers alternatively coerced his under-developed sovereignty. The first wars, and these came soon, were naturally waged for the liberation of Totoland, though its hapless spokesman was too immature to understand why this necessarily involved the planning of campaigns for freedom across his speckled map. There was real fighting, between Russia and Japan, that summer and the obvious resemblance of Manchuria and Totoland as battlegrounds was apparent to everybody except the unfortunate Governor of the latter.

Both the actual and the simulated conflicts were stimulating to a ten-year-old's expanding mind. Grandfather Bird was keenly interested in world politics and from his residence in Berlin, during the sway of the Iron Chancellor, had absorbed a sense of the dynamics of national power which opened up a wholly new field of thought for me. The old gentleman, then approaching 76, must have been pleased to have so receptive a listener. He would talk of mysterious background forces, such as the "Balance of Power" and the "Open Door." Then there was a visit by a relative named Geoffrey Drage, an authority on Russia brought to the fore by the war in the Far East. It dawned upon me that the whole world was not grouped around the North Atlantic; that there were countries other than Britain and America to be understood.

30

All this gave impetus to the newly created sovereignties, a game aptly described by Kit as involving "stroke and counterstroke of invention." Returning to Baltimore in the fall I introduced the pastime to my particular circle of friends, and soon Francis Davis, Gideon Stieff and Eddy Requard had their own countries also. Christophalia, whose president was soon to wrestle with College Entrance Boards, to become interested in girls and otherwise experience the distractions of the middle teens, lost national power. Totoland, on the other hand, began in time to assert the right of self-determination and, having fought enough wars to be definable as "peace-loving," was duly admitted to a forgotten forerunner of the League of Nations.

This, for reasons which none can now recall, was known as The Poughkeepsie. Derivation from the term "powwow" is not improbable. Anyway, it was an international Council of our five sovereign States, with Christophalia self-excluded, meeting periodically on upper Park Avenue. The accredited delegate of each participating nation had full power to bind his government and problems of modern internationalism were avoided by establishing majority rule and denying veto privilege. In this manner childish ingenuity showed itself able to cope with difficult issues, such as arms limitation and currency stabilization, which nowadays often leave professional diplomacy frustrated.

Our national armies, for instance, were built up with paper soldiers, often Indians and cowboys, then obtainable as vivid cutouts at a penny a sheet. Mounted on matchboxes these contingents maneuvered against each other on any floor-space available, while the rival marksmen sniped with marbles. Rapid expansion of these obedient levies sustained national dignity but also involved a cumulatively disturbing drain on the slim resources of the respective potentates. Moreover, logistics became complicated in transporting shoeboxes packed with warriors on those rainy afternoons which were appropriate for battles. Therefore Francis Davis, a very pragmatic ruler, proposed at a Poughkeepsie meeting that each country limit its recruitment to one sheet a week and that for each such addition there should be honorable discharge of the same number of veterans, with scarce matchboxes removed to support the replacements. After appropriate debate this limitation of armament was unanimously adopted and thereafter scrupulously observed. In later years, watching the SALT negotiations drag fruitlessly on, I have thought that delegations of American and Russian schoolboys might handle the problem more conclusively.

Regular schooling and that supplied by our imaginary countries seemed to complement each other. In the mornings, at supervised lessons, one was subjected to strict though kindly discipline. In the evenings, or on stormy afternoons, a form of self-organized play took over. This meant well-rounded education, since each channel of experience tended to strengthen the other. And there were distinct advantages for parents. These could testify that no Poughkeepsie member was ever at a loss for innocuous activity. The opiate of TV was not merely unavailable. Its stultifying indoctrination was not even unconsciously desired. Learning came from an active participation that was much more broadening than any precise form of vocational training. At the age of ten the figment of Musketty was already arousing what was to become my lifelong interest in national and international politics.

There was, of course, a shadow side to the absorbing game of countries. It made participants vigorously resentful of such amenities as music lessons or dancing classes. It was overly monastic. But the pastime folded automatically as the 'teens took over. By then each individual had learned to "do his own thing," cooperatively with others. Nor were there any pitfalls along those pleasantly wandering paths. They did not lead Francis and Gideon away from the merchandizing over which these friends were destined to preside. They did not consciously affect my drift into journalism. Probably the most general result of these imaginary sovereignties was to build an aversion to nationalistic vainglory based on the defamation of other peoples.

It would seem that the Park Avenue Poughkeepsie held its final meeting in the spring of 1907. By the autumn of that year the demands and interests of formal schooling had taken over. The memory of Musketty and its sister states, however, remained to form a lifelong bond among their diverse rulers.

◖◗

◗The Old Friends School in Baltimore, at the corner of Park Place and Laurens Street, was only four blocks from the Morley home and in 1902, at the age of eight, I was entered there. I could walk the distance alone, carrying my lunch, in five minutes and did so for nine years, until graduation in 1911. Admitted to the third grade I proved sufficiently advanced by my mother's training to skip the fourth and so was ready for college at the age of 17. Even so this was more than a year behind brighter brother Kit, who was graduated with honors from Marston's University School a month after his sixteenth birthday. It would be difficult to say which of these two good private schools was then the better, or how they compared with the rival Boys' Latin School, attended by Francis Davis.

Certainly I was well satisfied with the educational establishment chosen for me, though I did not at first recognize one of its notable distinctions. There was at the time no school in Baltimore catering primarily for Jewish children and Friends had more than its share, probably a quarter of the entire enrollment, largely from the families of the merchant princes who tended to cluster on nearby Eutaw Place. Not until I heard this referred to as "Jewtaw Place" did I realize that there was such a thing as Semitic prejudice, pro or con. What I did notice was that my Jewish classmates for the most part had keen and inquiring minds, together with stimulating cultural interests. There were, in keeping with the time and place, no Negro students and nothing which even by courtesy could be called black studies at the school. The Baltimore Quakers were not that liberal.

For its upper middle-class clientele the school provided good teachers who for the most part remained year after year, though few of them received an annual salary of over $1,000. This continuity led to better mutual acquaintance and eliminated, for better or worse, most aspects of a "generation gap." I cannot recall that any of my teachers ever so much as hinted that an era of civilization might be drawing to a close. The training was for peaceful continuation of unquestioned and almost unquestionable social stability.

Among the faculty the most picturesque figures, though either would have resented the adjective, were "Cousin Eli" Lamb and his sister "Cousin Petty." The former had been headmaster of the school in its earlier days but when I entered had as his major duty control of the big "Intermediate" study hall. These were the classes from the fifth to eighth grades inclusive and to be their disciplinarian was no sinecure. But the natural dignity and kindly austerity of the old gentleman usually sufficed to keep perfect order.

If this pedagogue did not anticipate he could at least look back to give his charges a vivid sense of the history he taught. As a young Quaker, during the Civil War, Cousin Eli had taken alternative service with the Union Sanitary Commission, like his older friend Walt Whitman whose *O Captain, My Captain* he once recited in place of the customary Bible reading. It was, as I recall, the fortieth anniversary of Lincoln's assassination and was coupled with an even more vivid recollection of that martyred President. After the battle of Gettysburg this eventual teacher had been one of those assigned to bury the dead and identify the graves of the thousands who had fallen in that holocaust. Thus it was that, on November 19, 1863, young Eli Lamb found himself stationed at the speakers' platform erected for dedication of the National Cemetery. And there, by the feet of Abraham Lincoln, he listened to the delivery of the immortal Gettysburg Address. A consequence was that all the older intermediate students were required to memorize and declaim this brief but deeply moving message. This was instruction at its best.

When asked to prepare a memo on teachers that had influenced me, I placed Cousin Eli first, not merely for chronological reasons. "Memory of the old gentleman," I wrote, "cuts cleanly through the mist of years. Thin, spare and upright he invariably dressed in sober black on which, for all his neatness, professional chalk marks were toward the end of the morning obtrusively apparent. Like his costume, Cousin Eli's voice, even when irritated, was a quiet monotone, clearly and evenly articulated. Neither brilliant nor consciously inspirational, he was nonetheless a link with the simple, well-grounded education of the past and I know that he was loved, as well as respected, by all his exasperating little wards. He died during my school course and most of us came to say farewell at the funeral service in the Meeting House adjacent to the school. His was the first corpse that I had ever seen and unforgettable is the remembrance of that withered face against the white lining of his coffin, like a russet apple that has survived the early frosts and then fallen gently on the snow."

Baltimore Friends School was controlled by the dissident Hicksite branch of the Society, meaning that it pointed toward Swarthmore College rather than to Orthodox Haverford. This once bitter doctrinal division is now all but forgotten, but in the early years of the century made it the more desirable that the Morley boys should attend the Orthodox Sunday School, located downtown. Under Kit's somewhat grudging custodianship the mile-long walk would be taken nearly every fine "First Day" and always through the municipal gardens of Eutaw Place. Scattered amid the shrubbery were impressive life-size Italian statues of the Four Seasons placed there through the munificence of Judge Calvin Chesnut, an outstanding citizen of the day. If time allowed, Kit would stop at one or other of these classical landmarks, appropriate to the time of year, and give his brothers one of those whimsical declamations at which he was even then adept. Years later, as the genteel elegance of Eutaw Place decayed, the statues were removed because of growing vandalism. Two of them found refuge on the woodland Magothy River property of Wilson K. Barnes, the equally notable son-in-law of Judge Chesnut. Visiting there, after my older brother's death, these mute links with the past suddenly loomed up. Both Winter, in his voluminous cloak, and Spring, in an early conception of the mini-skirt, shed a flood of memories from their chiseled draperies.

I enjoyed Sunday School largely because in Frank D. Watkins I had a teacher who awarded handsome prizes of adventure books to those with good attendance records. Also there were memorable gala picnics at Tolchester Beach, traveling across the Bay in the excursion steamers *Emma Giles* or *Louise*. Austere Sunday Meeting, for which the boys would remain when their parents attended, was far less appealing. The premises, later converted into the headquarters of a labor union, lacked

35

the simple dignity and mellow beauty of the Haverford Meeting House. I responded poorly to that mystical apprehension of the eternal which is the essential value of the silent Quaker communion. Moreover the influence of the great Quaker families in Baltimore, such as the Careys, Thomases and Whites, was waning and with it the quality of the speaking. Lesser figures were too easily moved, not necessarily by the Spirit, to elaborate what sharp young minds could recognize as tedious banalities.

Day school, though equally well disciplined, was much more exciting and teachers younger than Cousin Eli were equally stimulating for inquiring minds. One of the best was little Mr. Pike, in elementary physics and chemistry, whose rotund, Pickwickian form belied any piscatorial likeness. On the last day before every vacation he would always beguile his classes with the reading of a Baron Munchausen story. Many years later he told me that he hoped to show how easily absurd conclusions can be drawn from imprecise observation. While this was probably wholly ineffective the happy informality certainly developed a bond between teacher and pupils. Equally friendly, in every sense of the word, was Mr. Harry in mathematics, who labored patiently to implant that intuitive faculty so important in the subject. As the predisposition of my mind was literary and historical this scientific emphasis gave healthy balance and I acquired the habit of working resolutely at tasks for which I had no natural enthusiasm. In short, nothing could have been further from my early intellectual training than what is now called Permissive Education.

It was by no means habitual, in the first decade of this century, to proceed from private school to college. Because the high school diploma was often an end in itself, children were called upon to develop at least a nodding acquaintance with many subjects and I never regretted that, in addition to compulsory Latin, I was exposed to both French and German at Friends School. In languages I had the "ear" which I lacked in music and mathematics. This proficiency was to prove of great practical use in later years. Indeed I have often wished that I had also studied Greek, and a quarter-century after leaving school, when I was editor of the Washington *Post*, I startled the Dean of a new

36

school of journalism by advising that its curriculum should concentrate on mathematics and the Classics.

There was nothing haphazard in that extraordinary advice. Mathematics, I argued, would train an embryonic newspaperman in the importance of observation, accuracy and intuition. Latin and Greek are basic to that precise understanding of the English language which is the essential tool of the journalist's trade. And I went further by asserting that the New Testament would be a valuable study for moral guidance and that the debility of Western Civilization in the face of the Communist challenge is perhaps largely a consequence of the antecedent collapse of classical education. The Dean came hotfoot to Washington to see if I were crazy, I recalled later. He talked a lot about the importance of what he called "relevance" in education and didn't like it when I said that what he meant was vocational training, which will never maintain a threatened culture.

But that is anticipation. It should be mentioned that another teacher did much for me at Friends School. This was Theodore Kistler, the gymnasium instructor, also physically a little man, prone to impress on his pupils that he had been a sickly child. But he had achieved a muscular development and precision of athletic execution which made his demonstrations on the horse, bars and flying rings fascinating to an awkward boy. This I undoubtedly was, but under "Teddy" Kistler's direction set myself seriously to the development of a strong physique and, in the course of time, attained it. I was naturally a good swimmer and when the school installed a pool it was a thrill to be chosen a member of the team.

So *Mens sana in corpore sano* was added to *Palma non sine pulvere* (the school motto) as Latin tags of which I am still childishly fond. They acquired a deeper meaning when, for the summer of 1909, my parents decided to send me to a boys' camp near the Canadian border on Lake Champlain. Two of Professor Morley's postgraduate students were counsellors there and, to clinch the case, after some family conclave the parents of Francis Davis decided to enter him also. Furthermore, Kit had a meal ticket that summer taking care of a small boy at Essex, farther down the lake on the New York side, where the whole Morley

37

family had spent an earlier summer. So all portents were favorable and the two chums excitedly traveled to northern Vermont together on this great adventure. Its success was such that both returned the following summer and in 1912, after my Freshman year at college, I had a third spell at Kamp Kill Kare as a part-time counsellor. It celebrated its fiftieth anniversary in 1958 and again the two old boys from Park Avenue went up for the occasion, touring by automobile far more of the lovely countryside than they had learned to know on foot at age 15.

One can imagine no more perfect paradise for growing boys than was well-named Kill Kare during the early years when it was located on Ram Island, in St. Alban's Bay. This was a well-wooded outcropping of rock, surrounded by deep water, perhaps a quarter of a mile in length and twice that distance from the nearest shore. Thus it combined insular romance with ample accommodation for the thirty or so boys, the five counsellors and the fat old German cook who together composed the summer population of this Eveless Eden. At the northern end of the island, where the rock shelved away to a sandy, sheltered beach, was the roughly carpentered "lodge," adjacent office and storeroom, and the motor-boat dock. The swimming raft was anchored in twenty feet of water on the side away from this beach, close to the channel used by the majestic *Ticonderoga* on her daily passage to the dock for St. Albans, the French-Canadian town located a short and bouncing streetcar ride inland. Along the ridge of the island were the dozen tents of the campers and at the southern end the kitchen and open-air dining room. There was level space for a primitive tennis court in the middle of the island, close by "Mary's Rest," a popular three-holer cleverly built out over the rocks of the south shore.

Socially as well as physically, I thrived on the insular environment of Kamp Kill Kare. Like a fish in its then limpid water I achieved my first newspaper publicity when, accompanied by a counsellor in a rowboat, I swam the two full miles to the steamer dock at St. Alban's Bay. Nearly every evening after supper, as the sun was sinking beyond the noble Adirondacks across the lake, Francis and I would run a canoe down into the unruffled water, let out our lines until the glimmering trolling spoons sank from sight, then paddle quietly around the rocky shore of our island waiting for the swift strike which was almost sure to come before darkness. If we would clean the fish ourselves the genial old cook would fry them for our breakfast and nothing tastes better, at any age, than the firm white meat of a pickerel caught by yourself.

Francis and I were almost inseparable at this idyllic camp, both on the water and during the gruelling hikes which were taken up Mount Mansfield in Vermont and even more formidable Whiteface on the New York side of Lake Champlain. There are well engineered roads up both of these now, but in pre-automobile days the ascent was a pioneering struggle by ill-marked trails. This was the climax of long tramps under July or August sun, since every mile was laboriously trudged, with scathing counsellor comment for any lad who begged for an unscheduled rest. Getting our own roadside meals and sleeping under the stars—or in the rain—was the better experience because of the coddling I had received at home. I would have a good deal to endure and was learning how to take it.

Most of the other boys, including two likable Cubans, were from a well-known New Jersey boarding school with which the camp director was connected. A few were quite sexually advanced by the standards of the young Baltimoreans, and tales told in the tents after taps were sometimes more enlightening than enlightened. As Francis cogently observed, however, much was probably concocted to impress the innocents, and it is doubtful that the dirt did either of us any harm. Moreover, the most ribald talker committed the folly of getting drunk in St. Albans and the next morning departed from camp with a celerity which a complaint from the mayor of that municipality did nothing to diminish. This outraged dignitary was Warren R. Austin, destined to be a Senator from Vermont and our Ambassador to the United Nations, of whom I saw much in later years.

There was further healthy experience at the close of my second summer at Kamp Kill Kare. Brother Kit had graduated from Haverford College that June (1910), had been awarded a well-merited Rhodes Scholarship from Maryland and was proceeding to Oxford at the end of September. He was spending that summer with our parents and young Frank in Nova Scotia, where he remained until his sailing date. This left me at a loose

39

end for September and it was arranged that I should go for that period with Joshua Tracey, my favorite counsellor, to the family farm of the latter in Carroll County, Maryland. It was real dirt farming and I supposedly earned my keep cutting corn, watering the stock and doing other unskilled chores. Often since I wished that this agricultural experience had been deeper but even from that month I learned to love the land and to sense the mystery of its fertility. Here, to my utter confusion, the Methodist Minister called upon me to "testify" at service in the little church. And here Mr. Tracey, also a good teacher, humiliated me in healthy fashion by an order to lead a young bull calf to the drinking trough. I was stubborn and growing strong but in both qualities the calf excelled.

Nevertheless, two summers away from home had taught me much, not least a deepening appreciation of the grandeur and beauty of this country. Amid the New England mountains, on the waters of Lake Champlain, in the cornfields of central Maryland there was quickening within me a sense of what America means in the long history of civilization. Imagination lavished on the Kingdom of Musketty began to focus more realistically on the Republic of the United States. The opening of my last year at school found me eager to make the most of it. Changes were taking place before my eyes. Mr. Davis had brought the first automobile to our block on Park Avenue, and in the spring of 1910 the pupils were all given time off from school to watch the first airplane ever to fly over Baltimore, piloted by a French aviator, Hubert Latham, whose name was as famous then as that of Lindbergh a quarter-century later. That wavering flight a few hundred feet above the roofs was by no means a matter of course to me and in my diary I wrote: "Maybe I shall see the day when the aeroplane will be considered a real necessity."

But most of the remaining childhood records show more interest in physical accomplishments. Soon after the exhibition flight of Latham's plane—the *Antoinette*—two classmates and I decided to walk from Baltimore to Washington, over the pretty and unpaved country road which was destined to be overlaid by the hideous striptown length of U.S. 1. We noted that we were passed by 40 automobiles during the 12 hours of this exacting march, one for each mile of the dusty journey. I was also proud of

40

jogging, on winter nights, once and occasionally twice, around the mile and a half circuit of nearby Druid Lake.

I know that my parents, anyway, were impressed by this change from a rather sedentary to a very active physical life, and were happy that they had sent me away to camp. "You might be rather good at distance running, Felix," said my father one night at the dinner table. "You can leave the sprinting to Kit."

"But Kit's too fat to sprint," commented Toto, who had yet to acquire that taste for double meanings which he savored in later years.

My trouble was that I had no clear idea of the direction in which I wished to run. Most of my friends knew where they were headed—Francis Davis and Gideon Stieff into the family businesses; Lawson Wilkins, who became a world-famous endocrinologist, to follow his father's footsteps into medicine. I knew that I could never be a mathematician and while I liked composition my older brother's much greater flair in that direction was discouraging. When I asked Kit for an opinion on some verses I had written the reply was devastating: "If I were you, Felix, I'd stick to chemistry."

My mother, well acquainted with her middle son's argumentative nature, shrewdly suggested the law, but I thought the training too lengthy and too expensive. I had a strong liking for ships of every kind and from the Muskettian navy, composed of neatly mounted photographs of warships, had acquired familiarity with the fighting craft of many nations. My plan was to go to Haverford for a year, then proceed to M.I.T. to study naval architecture. "Of course you realize," said my father diplomatically, "that this will take a lot of Math and Physics." The thought was unwelcome, for these were not my best subjects by any means.

To enter any college, however, a scholarship was necessary, not less so because Kit for four years at Haverford had achieved the best of the competitive prizes, paying both tuition and board, awarded to the four leading students in each class. So, in addition to editing the school magazine, I studied hard during my last year at Friends School. No girls distracted me and I did nothing to bother them. College Board exams were both obligatory and stiff but were attacked without stagefright. A few days after graduation I heard that I had been graded fourth in the entering class of fifty boys at Haverford. My English paper, as I delightedly wrote to Kit at Oxford, had been labeled "excellent."

◀Chapter 2

Toward Wide Horizons

So far as the grim realities of life are concerned, I was almost wholly innocent when, after eleven years, I returned to the Haverford campus as a Freshman.

Although I had traveled and read more than most of my new classmates, my experience as a whole was sharply limited. I had never visited a factory of any size, had been shielded from slums and was wholly unaware of the shadow side of a capitalist society. I knew well the difficulties and strategems of a cultured family living in mildly straitened circumstances. I knew that I would have to supplement the fifteen dollars monthly which was all my father could allow for pocket money. But the desperate problems of unemployment, the wage earners' haunting fear of insecurity, were known to me only through the pages of fiction. Strikes, which were becoming frequent, were to my unstretched mind an essentially unhealthy phenomenon, and the theory of class war was absurd.

The college curriculum contained nothing that would now be called "relevant" for a civilization drifting toward the brink of inexorable disaster. In chemistry we were taught that the atom was indestructible. History was prescribed in nationalistic capsules so that one did not realize the identity of the forces urging the European countries into suicidal conflict. Latin was a purely linguistic exercise with no parallels drawn for the ease with which a republic can degenerate into dictatorship. Indeed it must be said that during the first decade of this century Haverford, like many other small liberal arts colleges, was practically static. Isaac Sharpless, who had brought Professor Morley to the campus in 1887, was still its ageing but able president. The faculty was still largely composed of those who had been my father's colleagues. The entire student body, in 1911 as in 1900, was still slightly under 200.

An enrollment of that number is certainly on the small side and Haverford has now quadrupled it. But the advantage was that every student got to know all others on the campus and thus made more friends than is likely for anyone at an educational factory where 30,000 are being processed. And there was stimulating diversity in the tiny class of 1915 at Haverford. It counted only one Jew, but two very different Syrian boys; no Negroes but a Chinese and a Japanese with both of whom I fraternized; no paupers but a number who could attend college only because of very real family sacrifice. Among these was a romantic young Quaker from Westtown School, Eugene M. Pharo, whom I was fortunate to draw as roommate. Pharo was already planning to go into newspaper work and as our friendship ripened, showing a strong similarity of taste, he began to urge me to do the same. "What fun is there in designing warships?" was his persistent question.

Autre temps; autre moeurs. Not one member of the class of 1915, at Haverford, was planning to enter government service, national, state or local. About one-third were heading for business careers and the balance for professional work, medicine, teaching, law, the ministry, architecture and journalism in that order. For a Quaker school there was surprisingly little interest in social work, with the strong exception of one classmate, Cyrus Falconer, whose mother was the superintendent of a girls' reform school in the vicinity. It was quite an experience when Cy took me and some other friends to Sleighton Farm for a weekend, to see how the "wayward girls" were handled. Apart from some feminine whistling and posturing the young visitors were carefully protected. The experience, however, led to the formation of a small "social science club" among boys who found the college atmosphere oppressively conservative. One evening

44

we had Scott Nearing, in those days regarded as a dangerous radical, out from the University of Pennsylvania to speak. As a result I found myself reading Thorstein Veblen's *Theory of the Leisure Class*, which started me thinking along lines hitherto completely unexplored.

Not so curiously it was another girl, anything but wayward, who did most to focus my mind on the social problems which, even in 1911, were pushing to the fore. Helen W. was, indeed, the first of the opposite sex with whom I established any real rapport. I had no sisters, and my father had frowned upon children's parties at home. At school there were no dances and the two sexes kept rather rigidly apart. So, at college, I was more than ready to explore that form of companionship which is now commonplace among adolescents. The trouble, as the pendulum has swung, is that the overtones always latent in boy-girl friendships have crowded out much of the light-hearted comradeship which the male animal enjoys with his own sex. He has a better time at a college that is not co-educational.

Helen W., almost exactly my age, was certainly a serious as well as an attractive girl. We met at a YMCA playground in the slightly proletarian area between Haverford and Bryn Mawr where both of us had separately volunteered to teach basketball to what would now be called underprivileged children. Helen was of Scottish extraction, not a college student but the daughter of a small-scale builder whose office, following her graduation from public high school, she was managing with characteristic efficiency. She was athletic, vigorous and well proportioned but a rather shy girl with a strong social conscience which was soon to take her into training as a nurse. Her influence on me was such that before long I agreed to teach a Sunday School class at her Presbyterian church, in which I was able to put my compulsory Biblical Literature course at Haverford to immediate practical use. After this duty the two of us would frequently go off for long rambles in the then open country around Bryn Mawr, discussing the many problems which complicate the instincts and aspirations of both sexes at age 18.

Had this been half-a-century later we might well have slipped into the ultimate sexual experience, for something more forceful than puppy love developed between us. However, I was

45

either too immature, too cautious or too chivalrous to seize what sometimes looked like carnal opportunity. What I really wanted was a receptive and sympathetic listener who believed me destined for notable accomplishment and would assure me that my many uncertainties were merely growing pains. Helen did this and more, always emphasizing that the talents which she was generous to see should not be put to merely mercenary use. With ups and downs, breaks when "Felix" slipped back to "Mr. Morley" and reconciliations the more emotional for that aloofness, this friendship lasted a full five years. By then the girl was a full-fledged hospital nurse while I, though legally a man, was still stumbling.

At Haverford, I was certainly not thinking of marriage. Indeed I argued to the point of acrimony against the early engagement made by my roommate. For me the question of what to do in life was much more to the fore than any prospect of such a contractual relationship. Moreover I was inclined to savor variety in female as well as male friends. Before I had taken many walks with Helen I somehow met a rival, almost as appealing, from the top echelon of Main Line society. Still at one of the local "finishing schools" Frances L. had all the advantages, and disadvantages, of a single, wealthy and carefully nurtured child. When I could scrape up the money for theatre tickets I would first walk from my dormitory a mile or more to the big house back of the Merion Cricket Club, for family dinner. Then the young couple would be chauffered into Philadelphia, picked up after the performance and returned by the luxurious Pierce-Arrow to the parental mansion for late supper. I had nice manners and was deferential, without being unduly shy, towards older people. Somehow I made a hit with the parents of modish Frances and this bilateral entertainment was repeated whenever I could save enough from my regular chore of tending faculty furnaces. It did occur to me that a father-in-law in a position to dispense agreeable jobs would be an asset. But I was really not interested in the financial background of my friends, of either sex. I liked or disliked them as individuals and it is a fair surmise that I gravitated toward Helen and Frances, who never knew each other, in part because of their sharp contrast.

Equally contrasting, and fundamentally more stimulating,

46

were the political problems which began to impinge on me as a Haverford undergraduate. In Baltimore childhood adherence to the Democratic Party had been taken for granted and it was something of a shock to find the college atmosphere dominantly Republican. This, I realized, was not due to any deep political affinity for the GOP, but rather to lingering mistrust of the pro-slavery "rebel party" of the Civil War. Philadelphia Quakerism also owed a debt of gratitude to Pennsylvania Republicanism because it made no encroachments on the cherished independence of the sect. And while political activity was shunned by many Quakers as "worldly" some, especially President Sharpless, had not hesitated to participate in what today would be called the liberal wing of the GOP.

The furious political campaign of 1912, when I was a Freshman, brought this rather tepid brew to boiling point. A generally placid student body grew excited as "Teddy" Roosevelt moved to break away from the regulars under President Taft. And there was also keen interest in the rising political star of Woodrow Wilson, known to some of the faculty when he had been a professor at neighboring Bryn Mawr. At Princeton, President Wilson had argued that: "The American college must become saturated in the same sympathies as the common people. The colleges of this country must be reconstructed from the top to the bottom." All this was argued in countless "bull sessions," further enlivened by the contemporaneous ratification process on two obviously important Constitutional Amendments. Of these the Sixteenth, permitting the federal income tax, was rejected by the Pennsylvania Legislature while Maryland took no action on the Seventeenth, providing for the popular election of Senators. I found this churning of absorbing interest and, with Wilson as Governor of New Jersey, looked up his political writings for material in the lively class in public speaking. My Freshman year was over when the Democratic nominating convention met in Baltimore, in June, 1912. Somehow I wangled a ticket and was happily in the Fifth Regiment Armory when William Jennings Bryan dramatically transferred his allegiance from Champ Clark, the Democratic Speaker, to Governor Wilson, leading to the latter's nomination on the 46th ballot. So the virus of American politics entered my

47

bloodstream. That campus intellectual ferment was greatly promoted by Woodrow Wilson seems to me unquestionable.

As these new considerations impinged on my awakening mind I became increasingly doubtful about the wisdom of the college course which I had chosen. Engineering as taught at Haverford then was in any case pitifully elementary, and I found the hours spent in the primitive machine shop dreary, excepting those devoted to mechanical drawing. More disturbing was my inadequacy in physics and mathematics, though with some idea of loyalty to my father I stuck with the latter right through differential and integral calculus, neither of which I really ever understood. Teachers were patient, perhaps over-lenient, and I got by in all my studies, but with grades which in Freshman year dropped me from near the top to the middle of my class. Only because of facility in the humane studies did I remain that high. I soon realized that my interest in ships was much more aesthetic than architectural; that neither applied nor theoretical science was my cup of tea. But I enjoyed Haverford greatly and soon abandoned my idea of leaving it to proceed to M.I.T. After that the natural sequel was to shift my sights from the B.S. to the B.A. degree, not too difficult because I had in any case loaded myself down with most of its required courses. In an old copy of *Middlemarch*, which I was reading at this time, the following parenthetical observation by George Eliot is heavily underscored: "And certainly, the mistakes that we male and female mortals make when we have our own way might fairly raise some wonder that we are so fond of it."

That this struck home throws light on my undergraduate character. I was well aware that I was prone to make mistakes and there would be plenty of them. But I also had self-confidence and believed that eventually I would find the right road. Meantime, a wrong turning should not be regarded as a disaster. "A primary function of a good liberal arts college," I wrote years later, "is to reveal to its students where they are deficient as well as where they are efficient. This minus side may be in manners, in teamwork, or in intellectual interest. Whether the consideration be social, athletic or curricular the undergraduate, even the very occasional genius, should not let himself become one-sided. If his tastes are literary or philosophic he will learn to think

more clearly from some rigidly scientific application. If his leaning is mechanistic he will be a more responsible engineer for
some exposure to abstract ideas. Either way his critical faculties
will be sharpened and that achievement is the essence of good
education."

In writing this I certainly had personal experience in mind.
But to turn thumbs down on naval architecture was not to
discover the desirable alternative. For this broader experience
was necessary and the initial stimulus came from my roommate.
Pharo had spent the summer after Freshman year selling
Neverspoil Aluminum Kitchen Ware in Lancaster County,
Pennsylvania. He returned with a couple of hundred dollars in
unspent commissions, with a fine fund of first-hand stories
about the Amish farmers and with a determination to repeat the
experience. I had rather unprofitably idled that summer away
as a junior counsellor at Kill Kare. With imagination fired I also
applied to Neverspoil for an area to exploit and, for some unknown reason, was awarded Cleveland. By the census of 1910
that Queen City had forged ahead of Baltimore in population, to
the latter's great humiliation. It was said to be a wealthy metropolis and to work there would for the first time take me across
the Appalachians. "Westward Ho!" I wrote to mother, in telling
of this decision.

Before close of the college year I signed up and paid the
deposit on my case of samples, to be collected at the Cleveland
"Y." Eager to grasp this opportunity I traveled direct from
Philadelphia, upper berth on a P.R.R. sleeper. There had been a
final dinner at the home of Frances L. that soft June evening.
Then together we attended a D'Oyly Carte performance of
"H.M.S. Pinafore," finding a somewhat strained analogy in the
enterprising seaman whose unadvertised lineage finally entitled him to wed the captain's daughter. That night the Pierce-
Arrow left me and my well-worn suitcase at Broad Street station. Behind the chauffeur's back we kissed farewell and it was
permanent.

◗▮

◀Woodrow Wilson was firmly in the White House; Warren Gamaliel Harding was being groomed for the U.S. Senate, and the then fledgling Cleveland Museum of Art was just getting started when I arrived in that city to make my fortune. Of its half million or so inhabitants I knew just one—my Haverford classmate Selim Totah. That youthful Syrian had gone out to assist a relative, a local rug dealer, for the summer, and he took me to an exotic Armenian restaurant the night of my arrival.

On the narrow bed in my cell-like room at the "Y," I opened my big suitcase of samples, containing every sort of kitchen utensil: double boilers, frying pans, colanders, egg poachers and whatnot. Each piece was light but in the aggregate they made a formidable load. A salesman's manual advised that a good way to get established was to secure the cooperation of a church for a demonstration at a parish "sociable." A lower middle-class district was suggested for urban operations—one in which the housewife herself would probably answer the doorbell. Behind Selim were generations of shrewd mercantile experience, so with his help, and that of a city map, a promising plan of campaign was soon worked out. A few telephone calls turned up a friendly Baptist Minister willing to allow my brief participation in a scheduled church affair. "We don't have any other amusement on the program," he observed a little ominously.

June can be hot in Cleveland and certainly seemed so to the young pedlar that summer. Day after day I dragged my bag of samples through torrid streets until the wares seemed not of aluminum but lead. Perhaps I was too polite, or timid. Certainly I seldom gained admission to the modest homes selected, and even when inside few deals were clinched. With earnings on a commission basis this was serious. By the Saturday of the church engagement I no longer had the three dollars needed for next week's rent. It was a virtual Waterloo that loomed and a report of the engagement was written contemporaneously.

I am afraid that I had given the kindly pastor the impression that I too was a Baptist. Anyway, he received me cordially, placed my sample case beside a small gas stove in the rear of the big room and said he would "put me on" immediately after the opening prayer. When the meeting was over I could collect any orders. I noted optimistically that about two-thirds of the sixty persons present were women, for the most part comfortably stout and matronly.

My manual had said that to open such a demonstration effectively the salesman should intentionally scorch some vegetable in a saucepan, proving that this would not damage the utensil. So putting it empty on a blazing burner I filled the container with overripe tomatoes which I had obtained gratis from a neighboring corner grocer. Every housewife present, I said, must frequently have been called to the door or telephone while preparing dinner. During such an interruption water in the saucepan could easily boil away, with ruinous results.

To emphasize my point I strolled ostentatiously through the room, turning at the door to note apprehensively that a dense volume of smoke, with sickening odor, was pouring from my experiment. With an ordinary saucepan, I announced bravely, this would portend calamity. But with the brand which I had the honor to represent one need only scrape out the charred vegetable and proceed afresh. Vigorously I scraped—and the bottom of the saucepan gave way depositing the entire witches' brew on my shoes and trousers. I must give Cleveland Baptists credit for a lively sense of humor. Those present rocked and howled with mirth while some vociferously cried "Encore." I was the success of the evening. The travelogue of the Holy Land which followed was pallid by contrast. But the only order obtained was for an egg-poacher, from a sweet old lady who said that she was sorry for me.

I was sorry for myself. I had abandoned the project of naval architecture and now that of salesmanship had also failed. The next morning I shipped my samples back to the factory and examined my resources. For the previous two days, excepting the free supper at the "sociable," I had lived entirely on powdered cocoa, mixed with hot water in the "Y" lavatory. I had only to send a wire to my parents, but such confession, following sanguine predictions of a profitable summer, could not be faced. After some cogitation I walked to the lake front and in an hour was hired as a stevedore on the *See and Bee*, a grotesque four-funnelled leviathan which that summer was the last word in comfortable travel between Cleveland ("See") and Buffalo ("Bee"). The ship appealed to me as a monstrosity of naval architecture, quite as unique as was the *Great Eastern* in an earlier day. And thirty years later I would see her again, transformed into a training flattop renamed *Wolverine*, though Hippopotamus would have been more appropriate.

After the dust of Euclid Avenue the ex-salesman was happy to be aboard any ship and though the pay was poor, the work was easy. The roustabouts started loading freight at 3 p.m., mostly small stuff which was run aboard on hand trolleys and stored on the capacious waterline deck. This was noisy and exciting exercise, with a big banging and clanging as one trundled the truck over the steel gangplank, and much shouting and swearing if anyone faltered. When the ship pulled out the gang, both black and white, had supper together and then nothing but crap shooting and sleep until arrival in Buffalo early next morning. Unloading and cleaning up then took another three hours, after which there was freedom until time to ship cargo for the trip back to Cleveland. So it was only a six-hour day, but during the busy summer season a seven-day week. As the boss stevedore told me in a metrical phrase: "You must wait for winter when you wanter go to church."

Lake Erie, however, soon began to pall. In Buffalo harbor I saw and loved a beautiful white steamer, small but with the clean lines of an ocean-going liner, very different from the clumsy pretentiousness of the huge side-wheeler where I was working. This other ship was the *Northland* which with her sister the *Northwest* ran weekly from Buffalo to Chicago, with stops at Cleveland, Detroit, Mackinac Island and Milwaukee. They were operated by the Great Northern Railroad and at its office innocent Felix was told that he could have a job on either—in the stokehold. It was even agreed that I could join the ship in Cleveland, where all possessions not carried in my pockets still rested at the "Y."

The *Northland* left Buffalo every Wednesday evening, which soon coincided with a departure thence on the nightly shuttle of the *See and Bee*. This was perfect because the more delectable ship, taking it easy on a cruising schedule, reached Cleveland a couple of hours after the glorified ferryboat of which

I wearied. This allowed ample time for me to get to the "Y" and back except that the foreman of stevedores, seeing me about to jump ship, said sourly that since I had taken breakfast aboard I would "damn well help with the unloading." And so, with simmering rage, I did, watching the lovely *Northland* steam in and out again before dumping my final crate. Somebody told me that if I really wanted "that lousy job" it would doubtless be obtainable when the white ship returned to Cleveland, eastbound, the following Monday evening. But, with the few dollars in my pocket, that left the problem of the next four days unsolved. I got a good lunch, studied the want-ad columns in the *Plain Dealer* and soon was installed as elevator boy in a distinctly second-class hotel close to the then decrepit railroad station. In spite of my engineering training there were some shockingly abrupt starts and stops, but I got by.

On boarding the *Northland* through the freight entry that Monday evening, I soon learned why a stokehold job was so easily available. The "blackhole" conditions on those beautiful ships were simply so bad that an unorganized boycott was in operation against them. There were no picket lines and I think not even a seamen's union on the Great Lakes at that time. So I did not need to reproach myself as a scab, though something of that nature unwittingly I was.

A deck above, the bellhops were ceremoniously showing the passengers who embarked at Cleveland to their staterooms. An assistant engineer, no older than myself but a lot more tough, took me in charge without any expectation of a tip. Before I knew what was happening I was booted down a long and treacherously greasy ladder; pushed through a steel door into what seemed a veritable outpost of Hell. Facing me was a huge furnace with blue flames licking avidly over a great bed of molten coals. "Shuck your clothes and feed it, you bastard," said my cicerone, leaving me to my own devices.

Back in the shadows was a huge coal bunker and on either side, facing furnaces adjacent to mine, two older men, half-naked and streaming with sweat, were tossing fuel into their fiery caverns. What had to be done was obvious and for the next four hours I did it, lurching and sliding over the slimy floor plates while the lovely *Northland* smacked merrily ahead

53

through the tricky cross-sea which is characteristic of Lake Erie. Not until later did I learn that by rights every stoker should have a trimmer, to pull the coal from the bunker and pile it within easy reach of his shovel.

At midnight a bell clanged and one of my neighbors, a huge Negro, flexed his big shoulders and addressed me cheerfully. "For Chrise sake," he bellowed, "whyn't you have the sense to stay in jail?"

I had no ready answer but, as our relief lumbered in, went gladly under his guidance to the washroom and then to the firemen's mess, where plentiful pails of beef stew and loaves of bread were set out on a linoleum-covered table. Thence Sam took me to the section of the foc'sle allocated to the "black watch." It was below the waterline in the very bow and my bunk was actually within the cutwater. Lying on the foul-smelling mattress I could stretch out my hands and touch both sides of the ship as they narrowed to form her shapely prow. For a moment I wondered about my fate if we should collide with anything. But I was too exhausted to worry about this, or even the obvious fact that my bunk swarmed with vermin. The next thing I knew Sam was shaking me by the shoulder. "Hey, kid," he said, "you got two hours in the hellhole before we docks in Buffalo. Jeese, them bugs bitten you proper. You must be sorfe!"

From head to foot the bedbugs had indeed played havoc with me. But there was a shower available and Sam had some ointment which relieved the itch. That good soul insisted on taking me to breakfast and over the fried eggs, which were cold storage and livid, and the coffee, which was abundant and excellent, he showed the depth of his concern.

"I watch you heavin' coal las' night," he began. "You aint no stoker. You hannle yo' shovel like a preacher hannle a Bible. What you all doin' on this stinkin' job anyhow? You get yo' girl in trouble or what? You tell old Sam. He won't give you away."

I may confess that I felt close to tears. Why should this battered bum, for that was what he looked and was, give even a thought to my troubles? By what intuition did his dull mind divine that he could help me? And why should he want to do this, for someone so obviously more fortunate in life than himself? Often these questions have recurred to me but at the moment I felt only that I had gained a friend and there in the confusion of the dirty messroom I summarized my story, watching with fascination the skill with which he spat tobacco juice into an empty cup across the table. When I was finished he sat for a moment in silence. Then; "Has you all got a white shirt?" he inquired.

I told him yes, in the bag under my bunk. The salesman's manual had emphasized the importance of a neat appearance.

Sam scratched his grizzled wool thoughtfully, spat again and spoke decisively. "I think you all make a goddam good fuck detective."

I was, of course, familiar with the then ostracized Anglo-Saxon word, so economically utilizable as noun, verb or adjective. But as descriptive of this particular occupation I was perplexed. "What's that," I asked?

"Cabin Watchman they calls it," responded Sam. "He has to see that folks doan git in the wrong beds. Ef they does they pays extry an' they pays it to you. You'se a detective when you detects 'em gettin' in the wrong bed. See?"

I saw, but was not sure that the activity fitted my Quaker background. "What are the other duties," I inquired, "and how do you know the job's vacant?"

"Heard in Detroit yestiday," said Sam, "that the Cabin Watchman's quittin' right now. Of cose they's some formularities. You wears a uniform an' a white shirt an' sometimes you has to answer bells. But where you rides home is on that detecting. You'se got to be smart there, an' talk smooth. Ain' no job for no old no-account nigger but you'se got a college edication! I tell you, Flix, you make good quick."

Anything seemed an improvement over the stokehold. As we docked in Buffalo I sought out the purser and in ten minutes had signed the articles as Cabin Watchman. His description of the duties was less graphic than that of Sam and he admitted that the wages were not spectacular. "But," he added, "there may be perquisites."

So I moved up the ladder from the stokehold, receiving my predecessor's uniform with a gold stripe on the cuffs and the name (official) of my new post embroidered on the lapels. I even received a key to a semi-private cabin which I shared with the junior wireless operator. To my relief the work proved far more

respectable than Sam had pictured it. Once a bibulous gentleman slipped me five dollars for not turfing him and his lady off
the promenade deck at the hour when all steamer chairs were
supposed to be stacked and roped. Perhaps I sometimes closed an
eye to stateroom assignations. Otherwise "perquisites" were
confined to occasional bellhop tips for when not on my rounds I
shared with the Assistant Purser, a Cornell undergraduate
named Russell Bean, the duty of answering any cabin calls.
Bean, who labored all night with passenger accounts, was putting himself through college and made it plain that additional
small change was vital to that objective. So I surrendered most of
the night calls, the more willingly because a lingering interest
in ship design made it agreeable to wander round the vessel and
speculate how I would have planned arrangements differently.

Intimacy develops from companionship in working all
night, and in the few weeks that our paths twined "Old Bean"
and I became close friends. Together we explored those sections
of Chicago which could be reached during the Saturday afternoons when the *Northland* was moored in the river there. Together we swam in the then clean lake off the Buffalo break-
water, during the full day of idleness that came weekly in that
city. Together we tramped from Buffalo to Niagara Falls, with
wayside adventures such as come naturally and happily to lads
of nineteen. Together we discussed our problems and aspirations, as youth will always do.

I made other friends during this formative period. There
was an old Swedish Quartermaster who would give me the
wheel to steer the steamer, under the summer stars, across great
Huron and elongated Michigan. There was a Yankee bosun who
advised me to put my money into Postal Savings. There was an
English deckhand about my age, who had already wandered
round the world and was a bit contemptuous of seafaring on the
lakes. One morning, as the *Northland* approached Mackinac
Island in a golden dawn, he spoke with unconscious artistry of
watching St. Helena rise from the ocean during another sunrise.
And there was Sam, who kept a fatherly interest in his stokehold
neophyte and twice abandoned the habitual weekly debauch in
Buffalo to savor the innocent amusements which "Old Bean"
and I so obviously preferred.

The blue pencil is lenient with this summer of 1913, the last one in which—aside from the faraway Balkans—there was no war or obvious threat of war to disconcert. In some respects this workout clearly meant more to me than all of my formal studies. I read practically nothing, but learned much. I learned that in America as it was almost anyone willing and able to work could find it. I learned that kindliness and decency are innate qualities, quite independent of birth or breeding. I learned that the instinct to help others is strongest among the humble, who have best reason to know the meaning of a friend in need. I learned also that many men are altogether lacking in ambition and that the problem of aiding them will doubtless outlast every conceivable refinement and revision of political and social practise.

The nights grew longer and more chill. Amid the crew was talk of what to do when the *Northland* was laid up for the winter months. The senior Morleys, with blossoming brother Frank, were closing the summer on Prudence Island, in Narragansett Bay. Kit was there, returned from Oxford and about to start work with a New York publisher. All signed a letter urging me to join them. On Labor Day the ship docked at Buffalo to complete my seventh roundtrip from there to Chicago. I had tapped the Middle West and in my pocket was nearly one hundred dollars in hard-earned savings. Not without pride I took sleeper to New York and traveled thence, in all the luxury of a passenger, by steamer to Providence. Three weeks later, with refurbished wardrobe and feeling quite adult, I was once more at Haverford.

◑

◖Four years as an undergraduate, I would argue in later years, is too long a stretch for ardent youth to loll in classrooms. Everything taught there could be learned better if compressed into a more continuous three-year term. Until the colleges realize this I would advise any alert student to break this often debilitating period with a trial of some wholly different way of life, logically after his Sophomore year. That is when he should take his military service, if there must be such, though any occupation in which he gets kicked around will serve as well.

The boy who returns to campus after facing rigorous external pressures will really appreciate what his college has to offer. And he will be immunized from that boredom which is a large element in the phenomenon of campus demonstrations.

In this I was speaking from personal experience and there is plenty of evidence that, after the summer described, I blossomed during my Junior year at Haverford. Now much less introverted, and an active participant in most sports, I was to my surprise elected class president. Of more significance was a growing desire to write which, suppressed during long hours of shop and laboratory, now burst forth with almost volcanic force. The literary lava was crude, but it was also in places molten with vitality. Soon after my return from the Great Lakes I won a short-story contest conducted by the college magazine and was elected to its board. Gene Pharo and I divided the awards in the competition for undergraduate verse.

Realizing how little I knew of style and form in composition, I entered as a candidate for the much-respected Garrett Reading Prize, making my subject "The English Novel." That great teacher, Francis B. Gummere, helped me to outline and integrate this plan and, in due course, I received the award—fifty dollars worth of books to be chosen by the successful candidate. Several which I then selected at Leary's famous bookstore in Philadelphia are still in my library.

Probably there is no pastime which arouses keener interest among neophytes than a companionable analysis of the art of writing. At Haverford, in those last months before the war broke out in Europe, a group would gather weekly to discuss the subject. In this I attached myself the more enthusiastically because I had earlier pushed aside that type of bull session. Occasionally there would be an expedition to Philadelphia, for the fifty-cent *table d'hôte* at Lauber's, with a half-bottle of domestic Riesling included. Sometimes meetings would be in a backroom of the old Red Lion tavern in Ardmore, with a tankard or two of beer to lubricate the conversation. Usually, because money was always short, it would be a dormitory gathering, scrupulously devoid of alcoholic beverage since the possession of that on college property could then bring expulsion. But always these talks would focus on the various forms of literary expression and the craftsmanship appropriate to each.

I soon found that the short story and the set verse form were the types of writing which appealed to me most strongly, primarily because they applied standards and rules to an imaginative or emotional effort. While I had dropped science as such, I had become deeply impressed by the value of the scientific method. Order and precision, both in theme and choice of words, seemed to me as essential for good writing as in any laboratory experiment. With instinctive conservatism I argued that literature should be as disciplined as mathematics, and I fell back on eighteenth century essays to prove that such self-control implies no lack of either tight reasoning or stylistic beauty. Indeed, it was a study of *The Federalist* from a literary angle which first stimulated my interest in the theory of American Government, as it was originally.

It is also revealing that I should have steeped myself in *vers de societé*, suggesting that I was sensitive to fragile as well as enduring beauty. The *triolet* and *villanelle*, the *rondel*, *rondeau* and *ballade* are pallid and generally unsubstantial products of molds which easily become tiresome. But through their controlling rules they all relate to the sonnet, which in every Western language has become the vehicle of sublime poetry. From my first attempt during Junior year I periodically resorted to this form as an emotional or even merely recreational outlet, deriving from the effort the same creative satisfaction that many get from more conventional "do-it-yourself" activities. And I also discovered that even the most jejune sonnet, if addressed to a particular young lady, could have much the same psychedelic effect as is today more injuriously sought through drugs. Years later, in Paris, I would have a long discussion with Edna St. Vincent Millay on the question of whether the sonnet adapts itself better to emotional or intellectual expression. Naturally she maintained the former, but Milton, Byron, Wordsworth and many others could be cited to the contrary. As I saw it: The sonnet is a set pattern, into which the thought must be compressed with rhyming skill. Whether that pattern takes the form of hearts, flowers or philosophy is a secondary matter.

Philosophy, as a study, was becoming for me of primary importance. Under the kindly tutelage of Rufus Jones, it threatened to displace literature as my favorite subject. The metaphysical genius of Plato had a strong appeal and perhaps more so its political application. Still at hand is the well-worn copy of *The Republic* which I used, with much underlining and often marginal comment on the sometimes tortuous track of this quest for justice in human society. *"Fiat Justitia Ruat Coelum"* I wrote on the flyleaf, hoping to make my own life conform to that high principle.

I was much impressed by the Platonic thesis, implicit in all Greek thought but in *The Republic* directly applied to politics, that in excess is found the element of decay. The American republic had been aristocratic in conception, but to young eyes in 1913 had clearly become oligarchic, defined by Plato as "A government resting on a valuation of property, in which the rich have power and the poor man is deprived of it." In the Eighth Book of *The Republic* is the graphic description of the manner in which oligarchy is replaced by democracy, and with the Sixteenth and Seventeenth Amendments ratified I could sense that the tide was running toward "One man, one vote." But, Plato warned me, don't expect democracy to last. By "excess of liberty" it will pass into tyranny, and the transition will be the more rapid the more complete the democratic form. To hold his power, Plato concluded, "the tyrant must be always getting up a war." The predictions sank in, and I annoyed many of my friends by quoting them when, in a few years time, President Wilson set forth on his crusade "to make the world safe for democracy."

Although the political aspects of philosophy intrigued me greatly I was far from indifferent to the ethical side and here, with gentle prompting from Rufus Jones, I did quite a lot of collateral reading. A book which I found difficult to understand was Thomas Hill Green's *Prolegomena to Ethics* and this I confessed to Rufus Jones. "Then thee should read it again," observed my mentor. I did so, summarizing the rather involved thought in notes of my own wording as I went along. Gradually the pattern fell into place, like the pieces of a jigsaw puzzle, as I reported to Rufus with some pride. "Now it might be well for thee to read it once more," he observed.

60

It was a lasting lesson in the value of concentration, nicely balanced five years later when, as a Rhodes Scholar at Oxford, I was reading English Constitutional history under the tutelage of Ernest Barker. At our first session this great scholar assigned an essay, reeling off the titles of some eight books which "might be useful." "But," I protested, "you want this essay in a week. I can't read eight source books in that time. That's as many as I read in a year at Haverford." Sir Ernest (as he was to become) looked quizzically at me from under shaggy eyebrows. "My dear chap," he said, "it seems high time you learned how to read. Of course I don't want you to absorb every word in those references. Just run through them and pick out what is cognate to your theme."

So the importance of reading both judiciously and quickly was driven home, to prove of great value when I would scan a dozen newspapers and skim through a voluminous government report before writing editorial comment. "Did you ever take one of those rapid reading courses?" my secretary once asked me. "No," I replied, "I was just fortunate in having a lot of severely impractical education, under good teachers."

But as my Senior year at Haverford opened I had not reached any smug conclusions. I was more aware of the fact that philosophy, literature and languages, delightful though they were, led to no very precise goal. To become a teacher myself, at college grade, would require graduate study, for which I had neither funds nor any keen desire. Attentively I hearkened to the eloquence of my roommate, who had definitely decided to enter newspaper work. One autumn night, by the open fire in our cozy room, Gene handed me *The Street of Adventure*, by Philip Gibbs, a good story of Fleet Street and English journalism. "Put down Plato and try this," said Gene, and burst into enthusiastic prediction. Together, he averred, we would storm the editorial sanctums, bringing a new note of philosophic certainty to the American press. Gene would even postpone marriage so that we might leaven the shallowness of journalism with logical thought. We would live as bachelors in a book-lined apartment, combining the amenities of college with the not necessarily prosaic business of making a living. We even discussed optimum income, deciding that no rational person, mar-

61

ried or single, would need or desire more than $6,000 per annum.

For the youth with no very positive bent, an anxiety before the first World War, and probably more so today, was worry over the way in which he would make his living. This can still be an anguish because in adolescence many boys are both sensitively conscious of their immaturity and simultaneously anxious to justify great expectations. The distress of mind is largely unnecessary because under any economic system—capitalistic, communistic or in between—there will be constant demand for those who can prove reliability rather than for those with a smattering of some technical skill. The world has always a variety of important work at hand and most of it is well within the average capacity and available if an excessive wage is not expected. Consequently, though perhaps after one or two false starts, the apprentice in any line is likely to find his natural level, learning the necessary technology as he moves along. Character counts most and in its emphasis on character-building is the enduring though often unrecognized advantage of the liberal arts over vocational training, of the small independent college over the huge educational factory and, one may add, of private over public schooling.

This is how I reasoned it out later, and might have done so more quickly except for the dislocation of the war in Europe. For the summer of 1914, at the close of my Junior year, I had utilized my Kill Kare training to take a job as counsellor at a camp in New Hampshire. This was not very enterprising but, as a result of my change of course, I had some arrears of classical reading to make up in which the camp director, who taught Latin at the Gilman School in Baltimore, was an admirable cicerone. Hamlet Philpot, shy and scholarly, tall and shambling, was almost a stage Englishman and around an old stone farmhouse, in the hills above Lake Winnepasaukee, he had gathered a quaint group of paying guests who together made a sort of Brook Farm community. I was away with the younger male members, actually on the summit of Mount Washington, when the papers headlined the sweep of the Kaiser's armies across the Belgian frontier. For several days the small party of hikers had been isolated in the wilderness. A shattering earthquake would not have been more unexpected.

62

To me, as to Woodrow Wilson at the time, the conflict seemed a European civil war in which the United States, with ties of inheritance to all the belligerents, should maintain strict neutrality. I was confirmed in this opinion by a letter from my usually unemotional father, speaking of American responsibility for keeping the torch of civilization alight. But stopping on Long Island, to visit brother Kit and bride as the summer closed, I grew a little doubtful. During his Oxford sojourn Kit had traveled widely on the Continent and was disposed to think the balance of power so even that American intervention would be needed to decide the outcome. This was a shrewd appraisal, which made me the more attentive to a fraternal criticism of my writings. Already Kit was in publishing, had brought out one slim volume of verses and was getting acceptances for stories and other poems. What he told me sank in: "Your descriptive writing is good, but I don't see that you have as yet shown any creative genius."

In effect, this was a directive towards journalism, which accidentally became more persuasive through another college friendship with Eddy Rice, now like Gene Pharo long departed. Eddy, known as "Puffed Rice" for his round and deceptively cherubic countenance, was a year ahead of me, but in so small an undergraduate community this made little difference and we were drawn together by mutual interest in ships. When I worked on the Great Lakes Eddy had a job on a coastwise tanker and we had fun swapping yarns. Both of us had been favored students of Rufus Jones and both had vied for the same position on the soccer team. So there was much in common.

As I entered Senior year Eddy was working as a riveter's assistant, in a Camden shipyard expanding with the naval preparedness program. But he often came to Haverford for weekends, where we discussed nautical aspects of the war together. For anyone in the know there were many sea actions of great interest during the early months of World War I: the flight of the *Goeben* and *Breslau* through the British Mediterranean fleet to internment by Turkey; the catastrophic destruction of three British cruisers within a quarter-hour by a single North Sea U-boat; the victory of Germany's Asiatic fleet over a British squadron off the coast of Chile and, soon afterwards, the obliteration of von Spee's ships by superior British metal near the Falkland Islands. Both of us knew the particulars of all these vessels and no two admirals could have argued the strategy and tactics involved more ardently.

From this militaristic interest, paradoxical in view of the Quaker background of both, evolved the idea that we might go to the front in Red Cross work of some kind. Aside from humanitarian feeling I had an aspiration to try my wings in some sort of war correspondence. Anyway, we discussed the project with Rufus Jones, shortly before the sinking of the *Lusitania* sent reverberations through even the placid foundations of Haverford. Our mentor was sympathetic and cabled immediately to Quaker leaders in London about enlistment as members of the Friends' Ambulance Unit, organized in England early in the war. Two Seniors at Earlham College, in Richmond, Indiana, had made a similar application and word came that the four of us would be accepted.

Before this decision could become operative, however, there were college duties to be completed. For the last half of Senior year I had been elected president of the College Association, with responsibility for developing a rather advanced system of student self-government which the trustees, even at that early date, had been sufficiently far-sighted to permit. I was running the campus "Y" and was on the editorial board both of the college magazine and the 1915 *Record*, which did not underrate these small achievements. My pen still spouted literary fragments of which one—a war poem entitled *Byzantium*—was awarded first place in the annual Browning Society Verse Contest for students at Pennsylvania colleges. My grades had again brought me well up in the scholastic running and my Senior Thesis, on "The War and the Socialist Movement," was completed on time. The argument was that the failure of European socialism to prevent the war should not be over-stated. The fighting, especially if protracted, must lead to ever greater extension and centralization of governmental power, itself the essential feature of socialism. It would be much easier to scorn the name than to prevent the growth of this political development. I had done not only some reading but actually some serious thinking on the subject. I fear, however, that in this exciting period modest success was coming a little too easily. I was in danger of self-conceit.

One more sharp question of choice confronted me as the sands of undergraduate days were running out. Shortage of shipping caused by the war was bringing old sailing vessels out of moth balls and one day Loring Crosman, a classmate from Saco, Maine, asked me if I would like to visit a square-rigger just docked in Philadelphia, her skipper being a fellow-townsman and old friend of Loring's father. No invitation could have been more persuasive and together we sought out the beautiful four-master. She was completing the loading of a mixed cargo for Buenos Aires and the captain, a typical "Down-Easter," hospitably pressed his visitors to stay for supper in the after-cabin. There was purpose in his mind for as we ate he told of losing his cabin boy overboard during a gale off Cape Cod, and offered me the job. I was enthralled by the suggestion. Everything about the ship, from the curves of her shapely hull to the pattern of spars on the towering masts, was more seductive than any feminine beauty I had discovered. That night I could not sleep, for thinking of this opportunity to roll down to Rio and beyond. But the commitment to the ambulance project had been made. The road of destiny was chosen.

A fortnight later President Sharpless handed out the diplomas at Commencement and the Haverford class of 1915 was scattered forever. I had a couple of days at home, to note that Frank, now about to enter Haverford in his turn, had become a well-poised and obviously thoughtful youth. Then to New York, to meet up with Eddy Rice and the two tall Earlham graduates, H. L. Carey and Earl Fowler. On the rattletrap *St. Paul*, of the old American Line, the foursome shared a crowded cabin. With the neutral flag illuminated by searchlights on its sides the ship slipped by the Statue of Liberty, headed for flaming Europe.

◀London always fascinated me, above any other except Peking, in the long array of cities I came to know. And this was never more true than during that climatically beautiful summer of 1915.

The Western Front had then settled down to virtual stalemate, along the double network of trenches and barbed wire which scarred the Continent from North Sea to the Alps. In consequence the casualties returned to Britain were not for the moment numerous and it was a good time to stimulate patriotic fervor. The national lassitude to be expected when young manhood is bled white was still to come.

Conscription was not yet imposed, although the preliminary of a National Registration Act had just been adopted by Parliament. So the streets were bright, not only with flags of all the Allies, but also with huge posters of flamboyant exhortation. One, quite effective, depicted a pretty little girl asking her obviously embarrassed father: "What Did *You* Do In The Great War, Daddy?" Less successful was one of a broadly grinning Tommy Atkins in full war kit, over the caption: "He's Happy And Satisfied. Are You?" This became a subject of bitter jest among front-line fighters who admitted satisfaction only in the literal sense of having had enough.

Piccadilly, Regent Street, Haymarket, the Strand and other thoroughfares resounded daily to the blare of Tipperary, Fritzy Boy, Rule Britannia and other martial airs. Nobody denied that the route marches through main streets were carefully planned and the propaganda was the more successful because of the great variety of manpower the Empire was rallying to its cause. Tall Australians with their jaunty sombreros alternated with bearded Sikhs in spotless white turbans. Canadian regiments were always in line and generally neat companies of Negro troops, in tan shorts, from African or West Indian colonies. But always the British regiments, with their charming designations, were in the foreground. A battalion of the famous Koyli (King's Own Yorkshire Light Infantry) would be followed by one of the Sussex Borderers, or Artists' Rifles. The beardless cadets of the Royal Flying Corps were sure of a big hand and perhaps even more so the kilted Scottish troops—The Black Watch especially—as they swung by behind their skirling bagpipes.

I was thrilled by all this pageantry, and happy to be getting into uniform so that none would murmur "slacker" when I stopped on a street corner to watch the glamorous scene. But I could see that, beneath the dolled-up surface, all was not well.

Winston Churchill was being called "the bungler," *sotto voce*, for his leading role in the disastrous effort to save Antwerp and, later, storm the Dardanelles. Ireland was in sullen mood and the United States showed no disposition to get involved. In spite of skyrocketing debt, the supply of munitions was clearly inadequate. On the Western Front the German armies held the British and French in check while in the east they hammered the Russians closer and closer to collapse. Even the magic name of Kitchener, soon to die on a mission to bolster the Czarist regime, was getting tarnished. Through the courtesy of a Quaker M.P. I obtained entry to the House of Commons and listened to sharp criticism of that courtly Liberal leader, Herbert Henry Asquith, then still Prime Minister. The star of demagogic Lloyd George was clearly rising.

The ambulance unit to which the four Americans were attached assembled in London a couple of days after our arrival. It consisted of some 40 men, from 18 to 30 in age, for the most part English Quakers who had volunteered for this service ahead of conscription. Socially they were a mixed lot, some from the universities, others run-of-mine employees of Quaker industry, notably the great chocolate firm of Cadbury, located near Birmingham. The group, enrolled as part of the Royal Army Medical Corps, was destined to take over one of the hospital trains which transported the sick and wounded from the then stabilized front to the base hospitals already established at the French channel ports. Here those diagnosed as permanently incapacitated would be separated and returned to England by hospital ship. It soon became clear that to be thus ticketed with a card for "Blighty" was a widespread ambition. Already, because of malingerers, there was a ruling that none suffering from "trench [or frozen] feet" would be so favored.

For two weeks the young Quakers were billeted in London lodgings, attending lectures on first aid, sanitation and hygiene which proved of little practical value. I can remember only a couple of cases in which I alone actually bandaged wounds though I was rather proud of being called on several times to build outdoor incinerators for the disposal of discarded dressings and other waste. Then, after perfunctory examinations, the trainees moved to a beautiful country estate, at Oxhey Grange in Kent, where we were joined by another unit, lived in tents, studied the workings of two ancient Fords, learned the rudiments of drill and practised on each other the handling of various types of injuries. Here the group got acquainted, noncommissioned officers were chosen and a few of the volunteers weeded out for physical or other reasons. On August 14, in British uniform but with a Red Cross brassard and "dog tag," I found myself embarking with hundreds of fighting men at what was then known only as "a Channel port." A vivid memory, as the ship left Dover, was the stationing of two soldiers with fixed bayonets in every lifeboat.

Ambulance Train No. 16, finally located by the unit in the railway yards of Abbeville, was one of two donated and equipped by the Flour Millers Association of Great Britain and placed in charge of the F.A.U. on the justified assumption that the Quakers would handle this valuable rolling stock carefully. Most other British ambulance trains and decidedly those of the French, were makeshift by comparison.

A.T. 16, and No. 17 its twin, were each composed of fourteen standard English railway coaches of late design, remodeled for their wartime purpose. Of these, nine were designed to transport patients, four of them for stretcher cases with double doors to pass men in on either side of the car and fitted with 18 narrow spring beds in three tiers on each side of the broad central aisle. Five other cars, regular corridor coaches with eight separate compartments each holding six men easily, were for sitting-up cases, whether sick or ambulant wounded. Between the two types was the dispensary car, with a registered pharmacist and an emergency operating room in which an occasional amputation or other essential surgery was performed during transit. In this car was also a small isolation ward and the train office where all the rather complicated book-keeping was handled.

This was the middle section of the train. At the front end, back of the big Nord engine that was hooked on for travel, was a stores and kitchen car, the latter part including a big coal stove, ice compartment (when ice was obtainable), sinks and service equipment as well as bunks for the regular army cook and his two F.A.U. scullions. Next to this was the staff car, with relatively plush accommodations for the three medical officers and three nurses, including a private dining room spacious enough to accommodate one or two VIP visitors. At the rear of the train was another stores car with supplementary kitchen and mess room just big enough to feed the unit in two sittings. This was followed by the personnel coach in which the orderlies lived and had their being, crammed four into a standard compartment with two bunks transverse to the car's axis superimposed on either side. Finally, at the end of the train, was attached a French *fourgon*, or brake van, filled with stretchers, spare blankets, cleaning materials and tools as well as the compartment for the French brakeman who had telephonic connection with the crew of the locomotive. The circuit of the whole train was almost a quarter-mile, as we soon learned from jogging round it on frosty mornings as a compulsory setting-up exercise. Prepared accommodation was for 384 patients, with 29 orderlies to care for them in transit since the pharmacist and the cook's two assistants, though provided by the unit, had no direct connection with the hapless passengers.

"The night of our arrival," I wrote in a letter, "was fortunately warm and we stowed ourselves higgledy-piggledy in the personnel coach, sleeping in our underwear and without blankets. The next morning our sergeant made permanent assignments. We arranged our scant possessions in the least possible compass and then democratically sought the formula whereby thirty men can in the briefest possible time make their toilettes with a single small washbasin and adjacent water closet. The system adopted was a simple Solomonic decree. Both shaving and bowel evacuations must be managed during evening hours. Except in transit, bladders must be emptied directly onto French soil. Under this program the unit found itself able to prepare for 6 a.m. reveillé in a scant ten minutes."

After our first mess room breakfast—tea but no coffee—we were paraded to receive instructions from our commanding officer, a snappy young doctor named Walker who was by acclamation rechristened "Johnny." He was recruited from civilian life but nevertheless outranked his regular army medical aid, Captain Tebbs. There was also a third medic, a young intern who was continuously being replaced, and for our debut was present a majestic staff officer, Colonel J. Stuart Gallie, Director of

69

Medical Services for Ambulance Trains, who told us frankly that many had advised him not to entrust any of this work to "undisciplined Quaker personnel." Therefore it was up to us to prove our admission justified. The "Galley Slaves," as of course we promptly named ourselves, were duly impressed and it is a matter of record that at the end of the war Colonel Gallie handsomely declared that "no personnel worked better, more conscientiously or with more success than did that of No. 16 Train."

From Captain Walker came precise, close-clipped instructions. We must always address all officers as "Sir." Our primary duty was to keep the train spotless, inside and out, and to give the sick and wounded whom we carried every reasonable consideration. Any case beyond our resources must be immediately reported to one of the medical officers or nurses who would be constantly circulating throughout the train during its passage from the Casualty Clearing Stations, just back of the trenches, where we would load. There would be a rollcall every morning and a minute inspection of the train at an unspecified hour at least once daily. Except when otherwise informed we would be continuously on duty but could be on our own during hours that would be posted. To miss the train without good reason, however, would mean immediate and dishonorable discharge. Captain Tebbs said nothing then, or more than brief medical orders at any time afterwards that I can recall. This extreme taciturnity, indeed, was basic to the much-discussed "Tebbular Hypothesis."

In cautious language this was first aired in the columns of *The Orderly Review*, a handwritten train magazine reminiscent of *The Family News* of Park Avenue days. In camp at Oxhey Grange I had been attracted by a young Scot, James E. Miles, who had joined the unit at the close of his first year at Baliol College. Miles was a delicate, retiring youth, son of an eminent Edinburgh surgeon, a devout Roman Catholic, humorous and with pronounced literary ambitions. He was to Celticize his given name as "Hamish" and thus known became later a writer of repute and a lifelong friend of all the Morley brothers. As medically unfit he would have been draft-exempt but found entrance to non-combatant service for reasons not dissimilar to those which had prompted me.

70

By alphabetical chance Miles and I were bunked in the same compartment and during the first week of relative inaction decided that an informal train publication, its columns open to all on any permissible subject, might relieve boredom and encourage *esprit de corps*. The interest of two others was aroused and on August 26, 1915, at the mining village of Blendecques, the first issue appeared, charmingly illustrated with sketches by a talented young architect in the unit. Throughout the war this sprightly periodical continued to appear and the complete file was somehow preserved by Cyril A. Harrison, one of the original editors who, in 1919, arranged publication of *A Train Errant*, being the story of A.T. 16, with many reprints from *The Orderly Review*. Considering the circumstances, the quality was high.

Indeed those first days in Flanders had an almost idyllic quality. For a time there were only one or two trips weekly to the front and more slightly ill then seriously wounded to convey. There was opportunity for eccentric soccer, in fields where the wheat had been harvested, or for wanderings along poplar-lined canals, already kissed by the poignant beauty of approaching autumn. Frequently the train lay overnight at Saint-Omer, an ancient provincial capital then headquarters of the British Expeditionary Force, where the soaring tower of St. Bertin brought home the inspiration of medieval religious architecture. There, as in the village *estaminets*, spartan diet could be supplemented by an evening omelette, with *vin de pays* and colloquial French for the often over-friendly mesdemoiselles from Armentières and other German-occupied towns who picked up a living as best they might. The country back of the lines was alive with troops with whom the young Quakers fraternized and, if it rained, impromptu debates and even crude theatricals were staged in the crowded messroom. Always for background was the constant rumble of the guns. Sometimes a railway station, or a section of quickly-repaired track, would be hit by the Luftwaffe. But the risk was small, the environment full of interest, the companionship stimulating. It almost seemed a phony war until, without any warning, came Loos.

This battle, all but forgotten in later carnage, was the first massive attempt by the British, coordinating with a French

71

attack at nearby Arras, to break the northern German lines. The immediate objective was the important mining center of Lens and, with good luck, it was hoped to smash through to the big industrial complex around Lille, the loss of which had been a serious blow to the French economy. But Lille, precisely because of its importance, was firmly held by the Germans until their final retreat in 1918.

What went wrong I never really ascertained, though I looked up conflicting professional accounts of the battle, both English and German. In the opinion of the rank and file, the artillery preparation was inadequate. The enemy deliberately let the British infantry through the front-line trenches, then closed the gap to trap them with machine-gun fire from all sides. Anyway, to quote the historian J. A. R. Marriot, "the losses were terrible." There is no question about that.

On September 25, when the attack at Loos was launched, A.T. 16 was "garaged" at Calais, having just transferred a small load of casualties to a hospital ship there. Suddenly all absence from the train was cancelled and rumors started flying—Ostend had been captured, the German lines cut from behind, their troops were in full retreat and the unit's next destination was the Rhine! So went the stories as, after filling all water tanks, coal bins and medicinal storage, the big locomotive was hooked on and No. 16 slowly headed southeast, amid an obstructive medley of troop and ammunition transport. There were aerial dogfights overhead and several jarring halts where the bombed right-of-way required immediate repair.

By our route Calais was only some forty miles from the front, yet the jolting journey took all night. At five in the morning I was roused to find us at the village of Lapugnoy—"Pug" to the Tommies—just back of the trenches from which the British attack had been launched. There was heavy artillery fire from gun emplacements round the village and, as dawn broke, responding German shells threw up great spouts of earth from the surrounding fields. Directly beside the railhead were the big tents and Red Cross flags of a C.C.S., from which stretcher bearers poured out with their loads of human breakage. There was no breakfast for the orderlies who immediately began the grim task of loading. This time there were no "sitting up" cases

72

and, after all beds were filled, stretchers were placed in the dispensary, mess room, stores and finally all the aisles. A high proportion of the wounded were officers, in surprisingly good spirits because of the early reports that a significant victory had been achieved. By noon the train was fully loaded and started slowly westward by what was called the southern route to Rouen, rail lines to the closer Channel ports being too congested for passage. Here my diary becomes vivid.

"Outside," I wrote, "was beautiful autumnal weather. But in the crowded confines of the train, the scene was very different. We were by then well trained in our humble duty of caring for the wounded, each with his own quota. It was a new difficulty, however, to make one's way through crowded aisles, to the kitchen for food or to summon medical assistance in the more grievous cases. So we improvised a system of calling our requests, each for his nearest neighbor to pass along, which worked quite well through the long afternoon and night. There were numerous halts on sidings, to let troop trains by, and a couple of times for emergency amputations when the limbs removed were grimly placed in the big garbage cans. All night we plodded on, of course sleepless, rolling into Rouen at dawn. As we passed through the suburb of Darnétal I was holding a coffee cup for an officer with both arms broken. Sitting up on his stretcher he noticed the station sign. 'Should be Damn-it-All,' he muttered.

"At Rouen's *Gare Centrale* ambulances were waiting. Unloading proceeded expeditiously, the last to leave being two who had died during the night. Ordinarily we were allowed two days to load drinking water, coal and stores; give the train a thorough cleaning including window polishing; shake and fumigate blankets and rid our own persons of parasites at the base delousing station. This time orders were to return to 'Pug' immediately, and by nightfall we were rumbling slowly east again, now through dreary autumnal rainfall. This became steadily stronger and when we reached the railhead, the following afternoon, the whole dismal scene was a sea of mud.

"In this quagmire the overburdened stretcher bearers slipped and slid, as they carried their helpless burdens from the clearing station up the sharp rise to the railroad tracks. Arc lights had been rigged to illuminate the vicinity as darkness fell, but their glare served only to emphasize an Inferno more dreadful than anything ever imagined by Dante. My incredulous eyes kept turning to the burial party at work in the field beside us. A long and deep trench had been dug into which uniformed bodies were being sunk by ropes slipped under shoulders and knees, the heads and feet dangling grotesquely downwards. Over each corpse, before interment, a Union Jack was reverently drawn while a chaplain made the sign of the Cross and said a brief prayer. Then the flag was quickly transferred to the next victim while his predecessor was lowered onto the body below. It was the termination of the parades which had so thrilled me, a few weeks earlier in London.

"The pressure was heavy and we did what we could to assist the exhausted bearers, some of whom had obviously been drinking heavily. Occasionally one would tumble, dumping his moaning burden in the mud. Other wounded were almost equally filthy, plastered with dirt and their own excrement, with hastily bandaged wounds often still oozing blood. Pitilessly the rain poured down and the stream of broken bodies seemed as endless. Again we were soon placing them in the aisles, across the seats of the sitting-up coaches and wherever room for a stretcher could be cleared. The mingled smells of ether, vomit, suppuration and incipient gangrene soon filled the wards, almost overpoweringly so when, towards midnight, the train pulled out, with windows closed against the chill and driving rain."

That was, indeed, a night to remember and some incidents were indelibly etched into my memory. There was a boy with both legs amputated at the hips, so light that he could be lifted unaided into an upper bed. The lad was feverish but coming out from the anesthetic. "Cover up me feet, chum," he whispered. "They're perishing cold." But the poor remnant, who did not survive the night, possessed no feet. Another youngster had a bayonet wound in the stomach, which one of the nurses thought should be redressed, calling on me for assistance. As we worked, a great gush of blood poured out on both of us, something which curiously was to have a significant future influence. And there was a German prisoner, a young officer with a bullet through his lungs who was handled, with characteristic British magnanim-

74

ity, exactly like their own wounded. Because I could speak the language, I was called in to translate for this boy, a first-year student at the University of Bonn. His scarcely audible concern was that a letter should be sent to his mother, saying falsely that his wound was not serious and truly that he was now out of the war for keeps. This, in due course and dubious German, was accomplished and chivalrously passed through censorship by Captain Walker. But I doubt that it got through neutral Holland for I never received a reply and never knew whether the youth lived or died.

That trip was the worst of the five loads, nearly 2,000 wounded in all, carried by A.T. 16 during the eight days of what was called the losing battle of Loos. The British pins on the big war map in the train office were advanced a couple of millimetres, and trench warfare resumed its course of slow attrition. A residual worry for the unit was that all its members had become infested with lice, not less disagreeable associates because of their romantic designation by the *poilus* as "papillons d'amour." All were required to shave their heads and bodies, dismantle and thoroughly fumigate the beds and seats and patronize delousing stations whenever "garaged." Typhus was epidemic on the eastern front and had ironically brought fighting to a halt in Serbia. But both the British and French medical services were alert to the threat and the only serious illness among the train personnel that winter was tuberculosis, two cases of which were sent back to England.

Autumn faded into winter. The cars, unheated except when en route, grew bitter cold and as much time as possible was spent outdoors or in unventilated village inns where a warming "fug" and convivial companionship could be expected. There were subdued celebrations of Christmas and of the dawn of 1916. After Loos, as one can tell from the file of *The Orderly Review*, a rather serious mood prevailed, intensified by the reluctant adoption of conscription in Britain. Members of the unit felt their position somewhat anomalous, since their relatively safe war service would in effect send an equal number of draftees into the trenches. A very interesting debate was held on the issue after which a few conscientious objectors proved their convictions by returning to England to serve jail terms while about as many resigned to enlist in fighting regiments. It was a dilemma that I did not need to face and anyway other plans were in store for me.

The American quartette had kept in touch with Rufus Jones and, in the late autumn, Eddy Rice went home to report on our work. It was suggested to the London Quakers that I be allowed to survey all other F.A.U. activities in the war zone, then return to Philadelphia to describe and raise money for the entire undertaking. The Earlham boys would do something of the same in Indiana. Consequently, early in February, I said farewell to A.T. 16, traveling with my kit bag in an army lorry to the Flemish village of Poperinghe, near Ypres, where a small F.A.U. detachment was engaged in evacuating civilians from the devastated area around that shattered town.

I had mixed feelings as I said good-bye to friends who had become the firmer because of the circumstances in which those bonds were forged. While completely undistinguished, the work I had been doing was the more satisfying because purely humanitarian and unaffected by any alloy of narrow patriotism. I had no feeling of duty to the allied cause, no hostility towards Germany, and was indeed now certain that the war was for all a horrible blunder. European civilization focussed in Britain, France and Germany—three countries with the language, literature and history of which I was at least fairly familiar. These three belligerents had close economic, financial and cultural ties, yet nationalism had driven them into a basically suicidal conflict in which all, except in a meaningless militaristic sense, must necessarily be losers. The best solution of the mess would be a negotiated peace, making some rational adjustments but with the spirit of revenge powerless on both sides. If the United States remained neutral, that seemed the probable outcome and another, even more enlightened Congress of Vienna could be anticipated. That, at least, was what I intended to argue when I got home.

Meanwhile, I felt that my time had not been wasted, and while some of the experience had been gruesome, the horrors of the war disturbed me less than its insensate stupidity. I was quite decided now that I would become a reporter and had no doubt as to my ability as a descriptive writer. Some "Wartime

Vignettes," of life in the French villages just back of the lines, had cleared the censor to be strategically placed by brother Kit. I was no longer worried about getting a job on my return. If there had been adolescent prudishness about me at Haverford, that had been swept away, yet without injury to the strong critical faculty I had consistently sought to develop. That would remain.

◀ Ypres, called Ieper in Flemish and always Wipers by the Tommies, was the only sizable town in the tiny corner of northwest Belgium unoccupied by the Germans during World War I. It had been saved by the British in the early fighting and held by them in the face of furious enemy attack in the spring of 1915. These hostilities had completely wrecked the medieval stronghold, and most of its inhabitants had fled westward into the villages along the French border. To relieve the misery of these pauperized fugitives was the more of a problem because they were predominantly Flemish, speaking a Germanic tongue which the neighboring French peasantry seldom understood and generally mistrusted. The F.A.U. had volunteered to do what it could in the matter and had received a green light from the Belgian Government-in-Exile. Some assistance also came from Herbert Hoover's Commission for Relief in Belgium, though this gallant organization was already overtaxed by the enormous civilian need in its focus behind the German lines.

Into this undertaking I was now temporarily plunged. The work was of two kinds. Food kitchens, with some distribution of clothing and small necessities, were established in the Flemish villages, and simultaneously there was continuous effort to provide safer habitation for those whose dwellings had been wrecked by shell fire, or were in constant danger of being thus destroyed. In both activities I participated, working out of the F.A.U. headquarters in Poperinghe. I was quartered in a badly damaged *petit manoir*, in a former servant's bedroom of which one outer wall was missing. Though chilly, it was agreeably spacious and well-ventilated after the crowded compartment on A.T. 16.

My halting German was of assistance, because more understandable by the Vlamands than the quite fluent French of my co-workers. In one battered farmhouse it was even instrumental. The scene was close to the enemy batteries on the low ridge of Passchendaele, soon to be drenched with Canadian and German blood but then relatively quiet. Here the old peasant proprietor, gnarled and arthritic, had refused to be moved, because of the regulation that only essential belongings could be transferred. On the parlor table stood an old-style phonograph with an enormous horn, and hearing that I was American, the old boy told his withered dame to put on "the American music." From a closet she produced a wax cylinder, and soon the strident tones of Sousa's "Stars and Stripes Forever" echoed through the ruin. "Your people," said the old man as the music died away, "will soon be marching to that."

I said I hoped not, but the Flemish farmer shook his head. The war, he said, was a contagious disease affecting the minds of men. Long ago, he had been told, there had been a plague called the Black Death which had spread all over the known world. Now there was a Red Death, which was also spreading and bringing great changes though he would not live to see them. This plague was caused by governments, and you could not escape it. Nevertheless, he and his wife would move to a safer place, if they didn't have to go to France and could take the phonograph with them. And it was so arranged.

From Poperinghe, towards the end of February, I proceeded to Nieuwpoort, also known as Nieuport-les-Bains, a small seaside resort on the Belgian side of the French frontier. Here the F.A.U. sustained and operated a hospital for invalided French and Belgian soldiers, located in a former hotel right on the *plage*, or beach. In accordance with Quaker convictions, maintained more strictly here than on the ambulance train, all patients were beyond return for further military service. Consequently they were a depressing lot, mostly advanced tubercular cases for whom it was surmised that the North Sea air would be beneficial. Actually, the late winter atmosphere was perniciously damp, chill and gloomy. I promptly came down with flu, my only spell of sickness in the war zone, and for a week did my observing as a patient. But upon recovery I was set to work, one memorably

78

disagreeable chore being the collection and cleansing of the *crachoirs* (spittoons) for my tubercular comrades.

Curiously, I cannot recall a single individual from this Nieuport stay, perhaps because of concentration on reading while there. From London I had brought a copy of Goethe's *Dichtung und Wahrheit* and had endeavored to read it on the train. But conditions were adverse and I had no German-English dictionary. By good fortune there was one at the Nieuport hospital and I made good progress with the fascinating autobiography, sharing with its author at least something of Goethe's appreciation of solitude.

Moreover, the forlorn surroundings encouraged introspection. All the gimcrackery along the ocean front was faded, shops were boarded up and the promenade was pitted with shell craters. Many buildings had been demolished, and just east of the town the trenches ended in machinegun nests from which barbed wire was strung in tangles across the beach and on steel posts sunk in the seabottom to far beyond low water mark. A hundred yards farther on the German lines ended in similar fashion and in the No Man's Land between gulls foraged with raucous cries that seemed derisive of the human race. In Goethe's words I "began to feel complete incarceration irksome." So, in March, I obtained military transport to Dunkirk and thence to Paris.

Here, in the small Hotel Britannique, close to the Ile de la Cité and the somber majesty of Notre Dame, the F.A.U. maintained an office for the coordination of its activities. And from this base I richly enjoyed every minute of my first visit to the beautiful city, so far as wartime conditions and my very modest financial resources allowed. I was still an enlisted man, drawing the same meager pay as any British "ranker." And while Paris will always give much pleasure at small cost, there was particular savor in the chorus that rolled forth nightly in the taverns where the Tommies congregated:—

> We are but little soldiers meek,
> We get just seven bob a week.
> The more we do, the more we may.
> We get one bloody bob a day.

79

But the plaintive "I Want to Go Home," which had been popular at the front, was heard no longer. It had been banned as "inconducive to good morale," not surprising if one recalls the mournful words: "I want to go over the sea, where the Allemand can't get at me. Oh my, I don't want to die. I just want' to go home."

The doleful ditty was of no moment to one who was going home himself. Spring had already touched the Tuileries when I crossed back to Blighty on a hospital ship. There were formalities in London and I was given two weeks leave to visit relatives, which I had been unable to do when outward bound. Then demobilized, but still wearing British uniform, I traveled down to Somerset for a stay with my A.T. 16 bunkmate Andrew Morland, who had been invalided home after being diagnosed tubercular. Of course, I should have changed back to civilian dress but my one suit, none the better for nine months storage in London, had been crammed into my kit bag and forwarded to the Holland-America office in Falmouth, from which port and by which line I had secured passage to New York. So I took a chance on the unauthorized military dress, and had reason to regret it.

The immediate objective was Glastonbury, where I was met by Andrew and conveyed to the Morland home at Street, a picturesque village a couple of miles from the old Saxon town, formerly called the Isle of Avalon because then completely surrounded by branches of the tiny river Brue. The Morlands, I was pleased to see, were wealthy as well as devout Quakers, a combination by no means rare in the Society of Friends, whether in England or the United States. There were morning and evening prayers, attended with no exceptions by both family and servants. I enjoyed these the more because recent experience had done a good deal to encourage religious thinking, if not observance. Also Mr. Morland senior conducted the informal service in lively and memorable manner. I recall one that focused on a reading of the 33rd Psalm.

"Now," said the stout old Quaker, "let us review some of that. Take verse 13: 'The Lord looketh down from Heaven and beholdeth all the children of men; from the habitation of his dwelling he considereth all them that dwell on the earth.' Does this mean, Andrew, that the Lord is currently as considerate of the Germans as of the English?"

"I don't see how it can mean anything else."

"And what does thee think, friend Felix? Does it suggest that every Black in thy country is as worthy of consideration as any White?"

I replied that I couldn't argue otherwise.

"Good," said the kindly leader approvingly. "Now Alice"—addressing the cook—"we move on to verse 15: 'There is no king that can be saved by the multitude of an host.' What does that mean to thee?"

"It means," said Alice firmly, "that with God's help our lads will soon do the Kaiser in. And now, Sir, may Mary leave to brew the tea?"

It was a delightful change from the atmosphere of the front. With Andrew, an amateur archaeologist, I explored the ruins of Glastonbury Abbey and relished the legend of the flowering thorn that first sprang up where Joseph of Arimathea is said to have planted his staff. Together we cycled to nearby Wells, where the unsurpassed cathedral is also one of the least known to Americans. And it was good to see that Andrew's tuberculosis was steadily yielding to home care. Indeed he lived to become a well-known specialist in that field of medicine.

But I had a walking trip through the West Country minutely planned and after the allotted stay in Street set forth blithely across the forgotten Sedgemoor battlefield, where Monmouth's ill-managed rebellion was crushed in 1685. From Bridgwater I tramped by country lanes to Nether Stowey, at the foot of the Quantock Hills, stopping in the village inn close to the cottage where Coleridge wrote *The Ancient Mariner* and *Kubla Khan*. That poet's young admirer from America reveled in surroundings unspoiled by either time or war. It was well into England's lovely month of April, and I was deep into one of the most appealing of England's charming rural areas. Lingering at Nether Stowey, I steeped myself in the volume of Coleridge's poetry carried in my knapsack. I wrote a long letter to Gene Pharo, then a reporter in the grotesque Xanadu of Atlantic City, reminding him that at our age Coleridge and Southey had concocted the unfilled ambition of establishing an ideal "pantisoc-racy" on the banks of the Susquehanna. Once I had obtained a job, why should we not carry this through from Philadelphia?

Romantic imagery was equally influential at my next stopover, in the heart of Exmoor. *Lorna Doone*, which I later claimed to have read ten times over a span of seventy years, had been a boyhood favorite, and I wanted to savor at first hand the bucolic beauty that lingers so caressingly in the pages of Blackmore's famous book. By good luck I found a secluded farm, close to John Ridd's fictionally exaggerated waterslide, and was welcomed almost as a substitute for a son of the family who had recently enlisted. For several days I stayed there, dreaming amid the bracken-buried foundations of the Doone cottages and pampered with rich Devonshire cream and other homemade delicacies. But time was passing, and with reluctance I took the road again, through Simonsbath and Barnstaple and Bideford to Cornwall.

In that fabled county a proper retribution overtook me. I had spent a night at Clovelly, a rather "arty" fishing village at that time distinctly improved by inclusion in a prohibited area for visitors. There, while climbing the hill that rises steeply from the sea, I was summarily haled from behind by a stout police-man, pushing his bicycle. Surprisingly I found myself in the toils of the law and was shown a telegram saying: "Arrest Felix Morley American in British uniform and send him to Exeter for questioning." This curt message I was able to obtain from the quite friendly Bobby, who at first protested that it was his evidence for making the arrest. "But you've got me," I said, "which is much better evidence."

I was not at ease, however, knowing well that with or without uniform I should not have been where I was, lacking permission to that effect. At Clovelly police station I was thoroughly searched, then taken back to Bideford by army lorry and locked in a compartment on a slow train to Exeter. It was luxurious privacy, after A.T. 16, but rather too much so as was the prison cell into which I was politely ushered at the end of this disturbing journey.

Next morning, after a decent breakfast, the young romantic was taken before an imposing official whom I believe, though without any proof, to have been the Lord Lieutenant of Devon. Anyway this impressive figure gave me a stiff examination under which I sensibly told nothing but the truth. That I had served in the British army was in my favor, also to some extent the steamer ticket found in my slim wallet. But what proof did I have that this was not all the elaborate cover of an Irish-American spy? Did I not know that rebellion was plotted in Ireland, with German and Fenian connivance, and that any foreigner found in disguise on the coast across from Ireland was therefore automatically suspect?

The poor innocent knew nothing of this and suggested a contact with the F.A.U. in London to clear him. It was made, but what helped most, I gathered, was the content of my battered pocket diary. "Apparently," said the dignitary judiciously, "you are much more interested in Coleridge than in the Kaiser."

In the upshot I was sent on to Falmouth by train, after pledging myself to report to the police on arrival and to remain in that town until I boarded the *Ryndam*, due to sail in two days' time. I would not reach the western seaport until late at night and readily agreed to stay at a designated hotel where room and bath were courteously, if peremptorily, reserved for me. After ten days of hiking, I badly needed immersion in hot water and had just enough money to cover the cost. And I was truly grateful to the even-handed magistrate, who could unquestionably have clapped me in jail for the duration.

The adventures of this sentimental journey were not yet ended. Bathed, shaved and brushed, I reported at the police station early next morning, to be greeted with stunning news. Because the U-boats were unusually active the *Ryndam* had been re-routed away from the Channel and would be coming around the north of Scotland, reaching Falmouth five days late. I knew that after paying my hotel bill I would have only a few shillings left. How would I live, unless as a guest in jail, during this unexpected delay?

The jovial police inspector, more amused than sympathetic, had a solution. There was a dearth of agricultural labor, just as it was urgently needed for spring planting. Even though unskilled this curious American would be a welcome farm hand and would be rewarded with bread and board for his efforts. As a "land worker" I could even continue to wear my now palpably disintegrating uniform. As to staying within the confines of Falmouth, the term was elastic and would be stretched to nearby acreage. So, before lunch, I was installed on a nearby farm where for five days I inexpertly did the work assigned me, feeding well but without any Devonshire cream or other tidbits. Then a police car graciously brought me back to town where I retrieved my kitbag, changing into that neglected and now too spacious civilian suit. Finally, in a gesture where cordiality certainly concealed suspicion, I was seen aboard the steamer tender. It was Easter Eve, which seemed a happy augury as the Netherlands' ship steamed out past the rocky headlands of Falmouth's beautiful harbor.

Next day, with the coast of Ireland in view, the radio brought news which amply explained why I had been in trouble. A German auxiliary, masquerading as a Norwegian freighter and convoyed by a submarine, had been intercepted with a cargo of arms near the mouth of the Shannon. Among the prisoners taken was Sir Roger Casement, returning from Berlin where he had been arranging aid for the revolt. On Easter Monday it flared out prematurely in Dublin, and for long hours the Irish Republican Army held the general post office, the law courts and other vantage points. British troops were rushed in and the abortive rebellion was soon crushed, though not without heavy casualties on both sides. Aboard the neutral *Ryndam*, crowded with German as well as Allied sympathizers, there was disquieting tension. But for me, as I told a new acquaintance among the former, the main thing was that the uprising had been delayed until I was out of custody.

This confidante was a girl a little older than I, a schoolteacher from the Hartz mountain town of Goslar, emigrating with her widowed mother to join an uncle who farmed in southern Illinois. There she hoped to resume her profession and therefore welcomed the chance to practise her quite good English, while I was equally eager to improve my German. So our conversation, each in the language of the other with reciprocal correction of mistakes, was mutually amusing. I learned much of the worsening conditions in Germany, where the British blockade was now really pinching, with the non-productive encouraged to get out, if possible. Mathilde's *Verlobte* had been killed on the Eastern Front and her only brother had fallen at Loos. The German newspapers were certain that the United States would remain neutral, and she looked forward to a haven of peace where she might rebuild her broken hopes.

I could only tell her that I knew southern Illinois to be rich farming country, its population including many of Teutonic origin. The *Ryndam* docked in New York, on May Day of 1916.

Chapter 3

Under Apprenticeship

"There are few biographies," observes Goethe in his preface to *Poetry and Truth*, "which can represent a genuine, undisturbed and steady progress on the part of the individual. Our personal life, like the universe in which we move, is . . . a compromise between freedom and necessity."

The pressure of this compromise weighed heavily on me as I considered the state of the nation in the summer of 1916. During my eleven months of absence there had been a pronounced shift from neutral to pro-Ally sentiment. Generally this was attributed to the loss of American lives, some 200 in all, on torpedoed merchantmen. It was more than a counter-balance to the originally resented infringement of "freedom of the seas" by the British blockade. Search and seizure unquestionably violated the hitherto accepted code of neutrality and had brought U.S. trade with the Central Powers to a standstill. But the loss of commerce was less deplorable than the loss of life, still less so because the soaring Allied purchases were more than compensating for any economic slack.

A few days in New York convinced me that the Allied loans floated in this country would alone bring us into the war. The United States had become a very profitable "Arsenal of Democracy" but the huge bills being run up by Britain and France would be waste paper unless they were victorious. Few had the prescience to suggest that these accounts would never be settled, no matter who won. So a vested interest in the defeat of Germany was lessening the efficacy of Woodrow Wilson's continued efforts for a negotiated "peace without victory." Public sentiment, however, was still too divided to permit any candidate to advocate belligerent action prior to the approaching Presidential election. Moreover, on May 4, the German government agreed to sink no more merchant ships without warning, thus insuring protraction of the wobbly American neutrality.

I was pessimistically certain that the war would have neither quick nor constructive outcome and that eventually I would be in uniform again. "If eventually why not now?" I asked myself, and seriously considered enlisting in the Canadian army, which would at least mean that I wouldn't be sent to the Mexican border. On the other hand I had made a definite commitment to the F.A.U. and was also deeply anxious to make at least a start in journalism. In Philadelphia I inquired at the *Public Ledger* about a job, choosing that paper because of its superior international coverage and because I knew and liked the city. The City Editor offered me employment "right after Labor Day," which was just what I wanted. During the interim I could work under the direction of the Philadelphia Quakers, telling the story of what their English colleagues were doing and incidentally helping with preparatory work for what was to become the American Friends Service Committee. So I filled a schedule of small gatherings from Washington to New York, with most attention to the wealthy environs of Philadelphia. The hat was never passed, for the Quaker way is to reflect on charitable opportunities and send in generous contributions later. Therefore I never knew how much money I raised but Rufus Jones, whose outward eye was never blinded by the Inner Light, told me that: "Thee has been a good investment, Felix."

I hoped so, but was well aware that there had been an unsettling side to my war zone experience. When I resumed contact with my old friends in Baltimore, I noted that all were forging steadily ahead in their chosen lines. Gideon Stieff was already carrying a large responsibility in the family business. The same was true of Francis Davis, who had met "the one and only" and was about to set his marriage date. Lawson Wilkins

87

was completing his second year at medical school and was well on his way to becoming an outstanding physician. Even "Ferdy" Turnbull, who like myself had shown no early bent, was now demonstrating that he could bring salesmanship to strengthen his training as a chemist. In comparison I was getting nowhere and it worried me.

Also, at home again, I soon became restive. For the first time I found myself out of sympathy with my deeply loved mother, who had dropped all pretense of neutrality and was deeply engaged in various pro-Ally activities. She really believed in such alleged German practises as boiling down bodies to make soap and cutting off the hands of all Belgian male babies—fantastic fables which I had never heard while at the front. It further seemed to me that my brothers had been sucked in by the anti-German propaganda so sedulously fed to Americans by Allied agents. Kit's generally charming poetry was getting into the better magazines, but on a visit I reacted sharply against some which heavily satirized the Hohenzollern cousins of Britain's royal family. He did not like my observation that genes were unaltered by giving the name of Windsor to the House of Witten, or by transforming Battenberg into Mountbatten. Petty irritations were aggravated by my own dissatisfaction with a Quaker pacifism which pallidly ignored all differences between the warring camps and often seemed to view political aspects of the struggle as immaterial. What distressed me most was the indifference to the gathering clouds of nationalistic hatred. I very much doubted that "militarism" and "frightfulness" were unique characteristics of the German people. I could agree that Germany must be beaten to its knees, but not in accord with the secret treaties that were already rumored, nor in the vindictive manner that Lloyd George and Poincaré seemed to want. My taciturn father, I think, was one of the few who understood what I clumsily sought to express. He certainly realized that the cleavages which politics exploit can be disastrous for the unity on which progress in abstract science depends.

A great help, during this period of spiritual confusion, was Helen W., the girl with whom I had enjoyed close companionship as an undergraduate. She had written to me regularly, sensitive letters, and after my monastic life abroad I was eager to renew the contact. Helen was now entering her last year of training as a nurse at the big Pennsylvania Hospital in downtown Philadelphia. It was easy for me to see her while filling speaking dates in that area. She did much to keep me stable at a time when scarcely anybody thought of professional psychiatric help. She was professionally advanced and dedicated, while I was still floundering in a way which made eventual separation inevitable.

Before starting work on the *Ledger* I had arranged to spend the last half of August vacationing with my parents on Nantucket Island. Always fond of ships, and with a little money remaining from my slim compensation as a fund-raiser, I took passage from Philadelphia to Boston on one of the old Merchants and Miners coasting steamers—the *Persian*. She had few passengers, since many were scared of the U-boats supposed to be prowling along the seaboard. Indeed, Germany had just won a minor propaganda victory by slipping the commercial submarine *Deutschland* up the Chesapeake to Baltimore with a cargo of chemicals. German sympathizers had given its courageous crew a big hand.

As the *Persian* steamed slowly away from Philadelphia I left my cabin to watch activity at the busy League Island navy yard. Beside the starboard rail was a slim young girl, with a white beret rimmed by her dark brown curls, who drew me like a magnet. Dorothy A. was only 18, pretty as a picture and, for her age, socially poised. She had only just graduated from high school and was that fall entering a New Haven school to train as an athletic instructor. Meantime she was heading for a New Hampshire camp to fill out a vacancy as junior counsellor there.

Appropriate to the name there was a Rubaiyat atmosphere about the *Persian* on that short voyage. For the 40-hour trip to Boston the young couple was inseparable. We ate together, in the nearly empty dining saloon, and until far into the night lingered in adjacent deck chairs under the romantic August moon. Close to the coast, seagulls followed the lumbering little vessel in effortless flight. Perhaps they were so numerous, I suggested, because embodiments of those lost at sea, a number greatly augmented by the then recent naval battle off Jutland. But there was nothing morbid about this wartime idyll.

I was, moreover, far too pre-occupied with the newspaper work into which I plunged enthusiastically on return from Nantucket. My salary, $15 for a six-day week from noon to midnight—if assignments were then concluded—certainly did not encourage philandering. And the nature of the work was of itself absorbing.

There were eight daily newspapers in Philadelphia in September, 1916. Half a century later the population of that metropolitan area had doubled, but the number of papers serving it as a whole was reduced to two. Attrition was not due to any lack of variety in the original company, for each of the five morning and three evening papers had a distinctive character of its own. The *Public Ledger* was then being expensively developed by Cyrus H. K. Curtis as a rival to the New York *Times* and therefore had some formidable opposition to overcome. The *Inquirer* inquired into nothing which might seem to sully Philadelphia's dominant Republicanism. The *North American* crusaded valiantly against the abundant municipal scandals. The *Press* had real flair behind its "human interest" flamboyance. Finally, the *Record* was a typographically conservative sheet with feeble Democratic leanings. For homebound reading Philadelphians could choose between the *Bulletin*, voluminous and uninspiring; the *Evening Ledger*, hopefully designed to make up the deficits of its sober senior partner, or the *Telegraph*, which I recall as a sporting and theatrical journal largely indifferent to other news. It is noteworthy that the eventual survivors of this galaxy, *Inquirer* and *Bulletin*, were in 1916 its dullest members.

For all their differences these eight papers were on many subjects sharply competitive, which made Philadelphia an excellent locale for a fledgling. My City Editor, Mike Kelly, a brisk young Irishman with a shock of prematurely gray hair, was a driving force from whom I learned much. Under him was a small staff of excellent reporters, well-informed on city life, cheerfully cynical and helpfully friendly to a greenhorn with enough sense to realize that nothing in his experience gave him any immediate journalistic advantage. None of my particular friends in the City Room had more than a public high school education. But they all possessed the sense of drama, the gift of colorful writing and the ability to question searchingly which in those days were essentials of the reporter's trade. Of these three attributes the last is the one that has most completely succumbed, giving way to the often personalized opinions of the columnist or radio commentator. The *Ledger*, at the time of which I write, had two august columnists of its own, in the persons of William C. Bullitt and Lincoln Colcord. In the former I was somewhat interested, not for any anticipation of his eventual diplomatic prowess, but because his then wife was the beautiful Ernesta Drinker of the talented family which had been neighbors and friends of the Morleys during the early days at Haverford. These social giants would occasionally stalk through the City Room, on their way to confer with the Managing Editor, and this superior status was resented. "They're not newspapermen," said my colleague Sam Dashiell scornfully. "They don't report. They just tell you what they think you ought to think. Don't ever fall that low, Muskett [as he always called me]."

Mike Kelly, certainly, saw to it that I did not get my head up prematurely. I well recall my first assignment, to cover a lecture on the Virgin Islands, which had just been purchased from Denmark by the United States, at the University of Pennsylvania. The speaker had the improbable and unforgettable name of Toothaker and as the meager audience filed out I went up to ask him some carefully concocted questions. So did another young reporter from the *Press*. He was Joseph Michael Lalley, a shy and appealing Irishman whose interrogations seemed to me as intelligent as my own. This meeting opened a lifelong association of mutual esteem and we were later co-workers on both the Baltimore *Sun* and Washington *Post*, where Jo' came into his own as a brilliant literary critic. Our friendship was founded when he and I returned to our respective offices by subway, for in those days a taxi fare on the expense account required meticulous justification.

I was enthusiastic about my story, which seemed to combine military, political and social significance, so was distressed when told by Mike to give it "two sticks," meaning twelve lines of type with a total of about 100 words. To boil my copious notes down to this residue was a heroic task, but finally I accomplished a miracle of compression. That evening I hung around for the early "bulldog" edition in order to relish my opus in print. It was disappointing not to see it boxed on the first page and more so not to find the little gem anywhere. In some embarrassment I asked Mike where I had goofed. "The piece was okay," he said magnanimously. "I never intended to use it; just a dry run to give you practise."

Aside from such trifling afternoon assignments, my first "beat" was the Germantown police station, where I was on duty from 8 p.m. to midnight, with instructions to phone in any news of moment. It was not a flattering post and no other paper troubled to place a representative at this decorous suburban location. As Dashiell put it: "You'll have plenty of opportunity to relax. There's been no news from Germantown since George Washington fought a battle there."

For some weeks this estimate was justified and I divided my time in the police station between whatever book was crammed in my pocket and quiet gin rummy with the old German night sergeant. The war was bitter to him, but he thought that Germany had asked for it. From him I learned, much better than in any classroom, about the abortive democratic revolution of 1848. Following its failure old Otto's father had emigrated from the Rhineland to Philadelphia, bringing him as a child. Such expansion of textbook history is one of the unsung compensations in newspaper work.

There was to be a sharp break in the monotony of this assignment. Close to midnight one stormy November evening a phone call made Otto jump to unaccustomed activity. An excited stranger was telling him that a huge branch had broken from a tree in Fairmount Park, crushing the roof of a roadster standing beneath and pinning the two persons therein. The park police, if any, were not around so a sleepy patrolman was summoned from the station-house bunkroom. Here my friendship with Otto paid off as he let me go to the scene of the accident in the police car.

We swept rapidly through deserted streets down to the park, that night of lashing wind and pouring rain. A couple of cars had stopped at the scene of the tragedy and all of us joined in pushing the huge fallen limb over onto the engine hood. The roof had been smashed like cardboard and from their distorted positions it was clear that both the occupants, a man and woman, had broken necks. Having seen death in many disagreeable forms I was less horrified than anxious to learn the identity of the victims. The bodies could not be extricated but the policeman reached in to obtain the man's wallet and the woman's handbag, with results which increased my professional interest. He was a well-known Philadelphia socialite and she, though also married, was not his wife. By flashlight I jotted down the particulars and, since there was then no police radio, one of the bystanders agreed to drop me at a drugstore where I could phone Otto for the necessary assistance. And this I did, but not until after calling the *Ledger* to report my scoop.

As I learned next morning this story, with all its titillating implications, raised perturbation in the City Room. The managing editor was roused from bed to decide whether or not it should be published. His judgment was that the account phoned in by this cub reporter should be checked with the police and at the homes of both victims; then, if substantiated, utilized. Verification took a couple of hours but in the final edition, as I recall, the sad little tragedy got display heading.

The net result for me was a promotion in status, though not in salary. I was brought back from Germantown and assigned to "Hotels and Clubs," with the further favor of being made stringer to the dramatic critic to cover such secondary theater openings as he did not wish to attend. This included excellent seats, enabling me to play host to a girl friend if she didn't mind inattention culminating in my hasty departure for the office as the final curtain fell. Hotels and clubs provided a fertile field, with responsibility to pick up information from visiting celebrities and to cultivate the "fat cats" at places like the Union League. In that sanctuary of rock-ribbed Republicanism I first met Senator Boies Penrose, who taught me that a much-criticized political boss can also be an erudite and gracious gentleman. On this beat also I gained my first by-lined front page story, when Herbert Hoover, in January, 1917, came over from London to arrange further financing of his Belgian Relief Commission. I was a natural to cover his speech at the

93

Bellevue-Stratford on this trip, and it began an acquaintance with that great humanitarian which ripened into close association as the years rolled by.

In November of 1916 I had cast my first vote, for Woodrow Wilson, largely because "he kept us out of war." But as the New Year dawned, with the Mummers parading on Broad Street, it was apparent that we were nevertheless being rapidly drawn into the maelstrom. Sitting around the City Room we young reporters discussed what each would do when the tocsin sounded. On February 1, the German Government announced resumption of unrestricted submarine warfare, and two days later our Ambassador was recalled from Berlin. Morale was low. On Washington's Birthday Sam Dashiell got drunk, garbled his story on the memorial parade of the elite First City Troop, and was fired. Promptly he joined the Naval Reserve and visited the office to flout his uniform under the indignant nose of Mike Kelly.

I was the more affected by Sam's nifty service attire because my own clothes were literally wearing out. Even in those days $15 was a niggardly wage. One of the three crisp fives in my weekly envelope went immediately to pay room rent. By eating only two meals a day, a big breakfast before going to work and a post-midnight dinner of hot cakes and coffee at the all-night Child's, I could hold my nourishment to a dollar per diem. The remainder did not permit much patronage of the romantic bar in Green's Hotel, at Eighth and Chestnut, where the big-name reporters refreshed themselves. There was no opportunity to moonlight and the idea of asking assistance from home was repugnant.

Yet my penniless condition had some then unappreciated assets, such as making any idea of marriage absurd. My roommate at Haverford, Gene Pharo, had taken this step soon after graduation and, with wife and baby, was marking time on an Atlantic City newspaper. Hearing from Lalley of an opening on the Press I phoned Gene to come up and strike for it, which he did successfully. Because of greater experience he received a salary considerably larger than my own. After three months employment I asked Mike for a raise and was gently rebuffed. "Bide your time," he advised, "you're still serving an apprenticeship."

94

In retrospect I realize that each day was then too agreeable to bother about the morrow. The streets of the drab old city were full of adventure and often I walked them not merely to save carfare but rather for ringside observation of the *Comedie Humaine*. I enjoyed my friendly colleagues, all poor in pocket but rich in zest for living. The desultory nature of the work gave opportunity for long discussions which at the time seemed much more sophisticated than college bull sessions. Every assignment was a challenge and I must have met them to the generally unexpressed satisfaction of my superiors. Occasionally there was the thrill of having a clipping of my copy posted on the bulletin board, meaning that it was judged a superior piece of reporting. I wanted to do each job, no matter how trifling, as well as possible. That was characteristic of all my friends and, I think, of the period in which we were stretching our muscles.

One payday, when I had been with the *Ledger* not quite six months, something was added to my weekly envelope—a one dollar bill and a fifty-cent piece to be exact. That curiously coincided with an invitation from the local United Press correspondent, whose office was in the *Ledger* building, to assist him at a salary of $35 a week, or more than double my enlarged compensation. Without hesitation I accepted, to be summoned "up front" by the austere managing editor and given a lecture on the ingratitude of resigning right after receiving a ten per cent raise. To this I ventured to respond by saying that I believed in free enterprise for employed as well as for employers. Then I celebrated, rather wildly, by immediately purchasing for $80, payable in four monthly installments, a second-hand Harley-Davidson motorcycle on which I had been casting envious eyes. For those days it was a powerful brute, though with the sizable defect that when throttled below ten miles an hour the engine would generally stall. But I thought that Nujol, as I named the acquisition, would help me in getting about and also had the vague idea that it might qualify me to become a dispatch rider, like those I had admired weaving through military traffic in France.

My principal activity for the U.P. is now archaic. I was placed in charge of the "pony wire" to a number of small daily papers in towns within a fifty-mile radius from Philadelphia.

95

Since these could not afford, or obtain, direct wire service from the press associations, the arrangement was to call them at scheduled times, dictating over the phone a precis of late afternoon stories which they might want for their morning editions. It was an exacting job, since each client got only five or ten minutes of phone time. Therefore, to cover several items, each had to be severely compressed and clearly enunciated. Years later, when I did regular broadcasting, this experience served me in good stead.

For the short time I was at it, the new work proved fascinating, aside from the much larger wage which now came in by check. It compressed a twelve-hour day of spasmodic effort to a much shorter period of really intensive labor, although unless by special arrangement this was every day. Ordinarily I merely recomposed my reports from the longer ones that streamed into the telegraph desk of the *Ledger*. And it was a maturing thought to realize, in those pre-radio days, that on my discrimination depended what thousands of small-town readers would know of current events. I had barely mastered the procedure when, early one March afternoon, a flash came telling of a disastrous explosion in a munitions factory at Eddystone, just south of Philadelphia. Evidently this tragedy, with its implications of German deviltry, called for something more than a rewrite and I vainly sought to reach my easy-going boss to tell him so.

Failing in this, I took Nujol from its garage and rode hazardously to the scene. There I visited the crowded makeshift morgue, interviewed some of the supervisors and slightly injured girls, then phoned an eyewitness account to our client papers, arranging to have photographs available for those who wanted them. With this accomplished I chugged back in some trepidation, uncertain as to whether I would be fired or commended for this unauthorized foray. The results were pleasantly dramatic. My initiative was reported to New York headquarters and a few days later came word that I was assigned to the Washington Bureau of the U.P., starting immediately.

That was on a Friday. I sent off my last "pony express," placed Nujol in cold storage, was given a farewell party by my pals, packed my one suitcase, spent the Saturday night with my parents in Baltimore and by Sunday evening was located in a decent boarding house on Washington Circle, in a capital bustling with the anticipation of immediate war. In little over six months I had made it, from cub reporter to Washington correspondent.

❰❱

❰Although brief, time spent on the Washington Bureau of the United Press was significant. I had joined a small but harddriving organization, since the U.P. was then of recent origin and had an uphill fight to make progress against the well entrenched Associated Press. Emphasis on wholly objective reporting, so as not to offend the prejudices of any subscribing publisher, was salutory. The local manager, "Pete" Yoder, was an overdone embodiment of energy, who would fairly throw himself across his desk merely to answer the telephone.

I was assigned to the State, War and Navy building, that massive Victorian pile just west of the White House and now joined to it as part of the Presidential establishment. In early 1917 this one structure easily housed the cabinet offices of Secretaries Lansing, Baker and Daniels, together with all their numerically modest aides. My job was that of assistant to Carl Groat, a Washington veteran who covered all three of the departments named, giving me particular responsibility for State Department news. Carl himself seemed to hibernate in the pressroom, playing endless pinochle with other older correspondents and waiting for the occasional releases brought in personally by the then solitary public relations officer of each department. But I soon realized that my new boss was far more alert than appearance indicated. One piece of advice received was never forgotten: "When you're onto a story," said Carl, "always go to the top. Milk what you can from any underling but don't let him put you off. For confirmation check with the all-highest. And always respect a confidence or you'll be sunk."

This instruction was the more feasible because official doors swung open easily for recognized reporters in those days. In a short time I made acquaintance with the Secretaries named and established more friendly relations with minor State Department officials, with some of whom I kept contact for many years.

97

All the news, of course, focussed on the hostilities with Germany now become imminent. Control was about to pass out of the hands of the diplomats into those of the military, which explained why I was assigned to the former sector. But with less pressure the State Department officers had more time to discuss how matters should be settled at the close of the war. The League of Nations had already been sketched in outline and there was sharp difference of opinion about the capacity of Colonel House, emerging as the President's *eminence grise*, to carry this project through to fruition. I revelled in this *haute politique*, very different from the provincial gossip of the *Ledger* City Room.

Because of my strategic position, I heard of the Declaration of War, coming ironically on Good Friday, April 6, as soon as any one. My immediate reaction was one of relief. After long months of painful indecision, at last the die was cast. I doubted that any good would come of it, but neither was I a doctrinaire pacifist. I believed in the democratic process and would loyally follow the decision of the Congress. The next week I applied for admission to one of the newly-forming officers' training camps and was accepted. On May 8, I was sworn into the military service at nearby Fort Myer.

Like many others, I was resigned about the interruption in what I had hoped would be my life work. So, while camp life seemed on the whole boring and meaningless, I nevertheless derived some satisfaction from it. Choosing the field artillery as my form of service, I enjoyed the unaccustomed association with horses. Mostly they were elderly, broadbacked, stolid creatures already well-broken to standard evolutions with the out-moded guns provided for the trainees. I knew that these Civil War tactics had no relation whatsoever to the mechanized operations I had seen in France, but found the grooming and care of my allotted horse moderately interesting. On weekends it was permissible to ride at will through the then open country around Fort Myer, and it was fun to amble with slack reins across the old battlefields of Manassas, imagining that one was a Confederate scout surveying the terrain. Map-making, also, was a natural extension of the mechanical drawing I had studied at Haverford. Another pleasing pastime was supervised boxing, in which I was fairly proficient because my reach was above average for my weight class. The life was healthy, the food good, and I made new friends, notably Emory H. Niles of Baltimore, a then recent Rhodes Scholar who would become a distinguished jurist and who, at Fort Myer, had the bunk over me in the hastily erected wooden barracks.

I fulfilled my military duties adequately, but unquestionably talked too much, and too controversially, about the war. I felt, not unnaturally, that my experience in ambulance work had given me superior insight and had not changed my opinion that a reasonable settlement would be more durable than one based on *force majeure*. That was argued for industrial disputes, so why not also for conflicts between nations? Russian resistance to the Germans was collapsing, with the Czarist regime finished and Prime Minister Kerensky helpless before rising Communist strength.

One hot July afternoon the day's schedule called for bayonet practise in a meadow on the spacious camp grounds. Man-size bundles of hay had been piled up in irregular rows on the rough terrain. On top of each pile was grotesquely placed a German soldier's forage cap, either from captured stores or, more probably, turned out by some local manufacturer in response to War Department order. Each pile also had a circular cardboard disc in front, roughly corresponding to what would be cover for the vital organs of the simulated enemy. The drill was to charge at these straw men, halt to make a few defensive passes in the empty air, then plunge the bayonet into the center of the target. This weird operation was supervised jointly by the company commander, a West Point "shavetail" and a rawboned Scottish sergeant in British uniform, brought over to give expert instruction to Americans in the art of "pig-sticking."

It all seemed supremely silly and in the mess that evening I emphasized this opinion to an older trainee who had expressed a wish to sit with me. That this man was an informer, assigned to report on the personal viewpoints of his fellows, never entered my head. When he asked my opinion on the bayonet drill I said heatedly that I considered it both ridiculous and obscene. It was absurd, because in case of close combat an artillery officer would use his revolver and would not have a bayonet available. And the exercise was obscene because these piles of hay represented

99

human beings who should be killed mercifully, if at all, and not by methods that would be considered crude and vicious in a slaughterhouse. I recalled the bayoneted boy on A.T. 16.

This iconoclastic position was undoubtedly reported to the camp commander. So I should not have been surprised when, at the close of the three-month course, I was informed by him that I would not receive a commission. "Your attitude toward the war," said the Colonel pleasantly, "does not encourage the belief that you are desirable officer material. I can, however, recommend you for a sergeancy at Fort Meade."

This denouement was a deeply humiliating shock, the more so because my quick advance in newspaper work had undoubtedly made me a bit presumptuous. Furthermore, my strong personal choice had been for the Navy. Only because the war at sea was virtually over had I decided to go "where the action is," as later jargon put it. From this came my distorted idea that I had personally favored the U.S. Army by volunteering to serve therein. For this a commission was only a fair return, more so because in the ambulance work I had already served my term as an underling. I knew that one of my friends would have to repeat the officer training course and inquired whether I could do the same. The Colonel answered in the negative. "My reports," he said, "define your deficiency as in attitude, not aptitude."

While I admired the neat phraseology, it further irritated my bitter resentment. Not even for the President of the United States could I change my conviction that the war was a hideous blunder, not less so because Woodrow Wilson now thought differently. Morosely I declined the offer of a non-com rating, saluted and returned to the barracks to pack. There was a letter from Dorothy A., saying that she had just become engaged but hoped that she would always be able to regard dear Felix as a friend. "To Hell with the whole lot," I thought. "If they can do without me I can certainly get along without them."

However, I had met Isabel Middleton during this Fort Myer period, and had been much taken by her. She had agreed to dine with me, at the romantic old Ebbit House, on what I had thought would be the eve of my commissioning. Some change in arrangements was necessary. I had to doff my uniform and get a modest hotel room for the night. But I wisely decided against

100

cancelling the date and in favor of telling Isabel my lugubrious story, before admitting shame to anyone else.

Somewhat to my surprise the girl—she was not yet 21—made light of the whole affair. I knew that she also was strongly opposed to the war but had not expected congratulations on obtaining an honorable discharge so easily. Before the evening was over, we had reached an understanding that was close to formal engagement. Isabel was already entered as a special student at Barnard College for the Fall Semester, having laboriously saved money for that end. Meanwhile, I would re-enter newspaper work in Washington and we would see how matters evolved. Next day I took a room on G Street and, with equal ease, obtained a reporter's job on the Washington *Post*. As often after my boxing bouts I felt bruised rather than fundamentally shaken.

An active courtship lessened the sense of bitterness, though this lingered a long time. Relations with Isabel were not always smooth since, though companionable in many ways, she had a stubborn will with which mine often clashed. In particular, she had a circle of strongly socialistic friends, whose beliefs were highly suspect by her new admirer. The Bolshevik gains in Russia were bringing this issue sharply to the fore and I was sympathetic with their announced intent to stop the slaughter on the eastern front. But, as I saw it, extension and centralization of governmental power would prove a far greater threat to human freedom than the much-maligned capitalist system could ever be and socialism, whatever its humanitarian pretense, necessarily pointed towards authoritarian government. We argued at length about this and other issues rather beyond the grasp of either. Isabel had an advantage in her stable job as principal researcher for an information service which answered queries on all sorts of subjects as submitted by subscribers to supporting newspapers throughout the country. Her salary was as large as mine and her position more assured, for though I was out of the army the threat of conscription was in the background. I was not pleased when she said that her employer had characterized me as "an experiment."

Moreover, my initial accomplishment with the *Post* was not auspicious. One early assignment was to cover an equal suffrage demonstration, staged by the National Women's Party in Lafayette Square, directly opposite the White House. For this objective I had no particular sympathy and indeed I have never regarded any mere extension of the franchise as being automatically a gain for good government. But I disliked brutality and a good deal of this was employed by self-styled patriots against the resolute women activists. While I was observing the scene, close to the statue of Kościuszko, a burly man beside me seized the banner carried by a girl demonstrator and tore it roughly from her hands. Without reflection, and probably prompted by my frustrations, I instinctively shot an uppercut to the man's chin, knowing from boxing experience just how and where to hit. The fellow went to the ground but the next second a heavy hand fell on my shoulder and I was hustled to a patrol wagon. The National Women's Party, I thought optimistically, would bail me out. They did not, and while I was released on payment of $25 collateral, in time to write a report for the *Post* featuring my own arrest, the episode took a large slice of my army savings. I reflected that I now had a police record in two countries, which scarcely made me a hopeful experiment in any respectable calling.

However, I was not fired and the affair served to fulfill the newspaper adage that any publicity, good or ill, is helpful to its subject. Angus McSween, the benign and elderly correspondent of the Philadelphia *North American*, read the account with relish and heard that I had a Pennsylvania background. Angus was a Scot of antique mold, receptive to passion as well as prudence in his fellow-men, and phoned me to come to his office in the now long-vanished Wyatt Building, at 14th and G Streets, N.W. We liked each other and the interview ended with my taking a post as McSween's assistant, with special responsibility for covering the Pennsylvania delegation in Congress. The pay was good and Isabel was pleased.

Again an accredited Washington correspondent, I found life far more interesting than it had been in the army and soon the urge toward voluntary re-enlistment faded. I loved the labyrinthine Capitol and explored its utmost recesses, often stopping to brood in the old Supreme Court room, vacant during the summer recess. This small chamber had once housed the Senate and I looked up the great speeches with which Calhoun, Clay, Webster and others had electrified its walls. With many of the other reporters, and with Jim Preston, the genial superintendent of the press galleries, I attained firm friendship. The Pennsylvania solons, generally anxious to be quoted, for the most part met my advances more than half way. A forgotten Congressman whom I have always remembered was Louis T. McFadden, of Canton, Pa., formerly a small-town bank president who was highly critical of inflationary potential in the newly established Federal Reserve System. This forced me to inform myself on the reasons for, as well as the arguments against, central monetary management, one of many financial subjects in which, as I began to realize, my ignorance was profound.

Equally educational, in the political field, was Senator Penrose, who graciously remembered me as a reporter in Philadelphia. In his comfortable office, cigar alight, "Big Boies" would receive me as an honored guest and fill me with anecdotes which must have paid off in the customarily critical columns of the *North American*. Once I asked why, as acknowledged Republican boss of Pennsylvania, the Senator did not extend himself to exercise control in adjacent Delaware and New Jersey. "Son," replied the scholarly politician, "this is a big country, built as a Federal Republic. I've got all I can do to keep on top in Pennsylvania. If I start messing into other states I gain enemies there and lose friends at home." I remembered this when Huey Long, and later George Wallace, sought with indifferent success to extend local political dominance across state lines. The federal system evidently had proved a valuable safeguard against attempted dictatorship.

Now, there was plenty of circumstantial evidence to indicate that war strain was undermining federalism from the center. Largely autonomous agencies, loosely grouped under the Council of National Defense, were using clearly dictatorial methods to mobilize the nation's resources, industrial, agricultural and intellectual. First of these was the War Industries Board, directed by Bernard Baruch, which applied minute supervision to all kinds of production—one of its claims was the saving of 8,000 tons of steel by simplifying and standardizing the manufacture of corsets, though I noted that these were

103

rapidly going out of fashion anyway. Under the Secretary of the Treasury, William G. McAdoo, the railroads were nationalized. Ship construction, some with unsuccessful concrete hulls, was controlled by Edward Hurley, chairman of the War Shipping Board. Perhaps most immediately successful of the emergency agencies was the Food Administration, where Herbert Hoover was empowered to fix prices, license distributors and direct consumption. As this directive complexity ballooned Angus McSween told me to cover the spreading network of new executive agencies. It was, of course, impossible to do this adequately, but I learned enough to wonder whether all this bureaucracy, thrown together for war purposes, would ever be wholly demobilized.

What concerned me more, however, was the parallel development of governmental control over public opinion. A week after the declaration of war, Congress had established the Committee on Public Information, to which George Creel, a Western newspaper man and longtime Wilson partisan, was promptly named as chairman. Several acquaintances, notably Arthur Bullard and W. L. (Bill) Chenery, joined the staff of this agency, and I was asked if I would be interested in doing so.

My reply was negative. The whole idea of governmental propaganda was distasteful to me, and as the flood of official venom against "the Hun" spilled over I was appalled by the poisoning of popular thought. Even my emotionally pro-Ally mother was perturbed when any public rendition of Beethoven was prohibited in Baltimore, while my father shook his head sorrowfully as schools and colleges dropped the teaching of German. Nevertheless, the means by which George Creel produced such ends were clever. He claimed to be opposed to censorship and in a circular on "What the Government Asks of the Press" said that enforcement of these requests, ostensibly concerned only with secrecy in military activities, "is a matter for the press itself." Naturally, this made most newspapers lean over backwards, in both reporting and editorializing, since almost every governmental action now had a military aspect and any critical comment could be called disloyal. Rather than take chances the Fourth Estate in general preferred to be guided by the propaganda that poured in torrents from Mr. Creel's prototype of Dr. Goebbel's Ministry of Public Enlightenment.

The pressure for conformity increased as the Communists took over in Russia. To explain the Treaty of Brest-Litovsk it was effective to assert, in Creel's words, that "Lenin and Trotsky had been, and were, German agents, taking their orders from the German General Staff and receiving their funds from the German Imperial Bank." Documents to sustain this charge were certainly turned up by Creel's overseas agents, but their authenticity was and remains a matter of doubt. Less dubious was the irritation caused Robert Lansing by the independent activities of C.P.I. representatives abroad. This Secretary of State at the time complained, and later publicly charged, that professional diplomatic work was dangerously hampered by their free-wheeling. It was the beginning of that amateur and dilettante interference with foreign policy which has continued to affect adversely both the morale and efficiency of the Department of State.

Creel was anything but a conservative. The "socialistic tendencies" which Lansing found in him had indeed been amply demonstrated in countless newspaper and magazine articles. He had a much-emphasized belief in the American form of government as "the best system ever devised by man," yet seemed profoundly mistrustful of American ability to make intelligent individual judgments. Of his attitude on taking office in Washington he wrote: "From the first, nothing stood more clear than the confusion and shapelessness of public opinion. The country as a whole accepted the war, but there was no complete understanding of it as a war of self-defense that had to be waged if free institutions were not to go down under the rushing tide of militarism."[1]

To me there seemed not only paradox but even serious danger in the consequent conclusion that public opinion in the United States should be molded by governmental agencies. It was, almost, a justification of the authoritarian system against which the country was arrayed. Painful results of this whipped-up patriotism were soon apparent in the draconian Espionage and Sedition Acts which threw hundreds into jail,

---

1. *Rebel At Large*, George Creel, G. P. Putnam's Sons, New York, 1947, p. 163.

105

ironically including old Eugene V. Debs, who had polled nearly a million votes as Socialist candidate for President in 1912. What I thought contemporaneously was put concisely by the historians Samuel E. Morison and Henry S. Commager years later, in discussing the Creel accomplishment. ". . . one of the most appalling revelations of the entire war," they wrote, "was the ease with which modern technique and mass-suggestion enables a government to make even a reasonably intelligent people, with an individualistic, democratic background, believe anything it likes."[2]

Many members of Congress privately deplored Creel's demagogy, but felt it would be politically impossible—"pro-German"—to oppose it publicly. A consequence, deserving more consideration than has ever been given, was to turn a number of Senators against President Wilson. His determined sponsorship of Creel's methods itself made the President's advocacy of the League of Nations suspect. And "Gorgeous George" did not hesitate to pile inflammable material on smouldering Republican embers. Asked what he thought of Congress, at a public meeting in New York, Creel replied: "Oh, it has been years since I went slumming."[3] He should not have been surprised when the election of 1918 gave the Republican opposition a majority of 40 in the House and two in the Senate, this small number sufficing to make implacable Henry Cabot Lodge chairman of the important Committee on Foreign Relations.

In the prior (65th) Congress I had established useful contacts, and many of the lawmakers intrigued me for their personalities as much as for their politics. I kept a roster of the membership on which I checked names "with whom I can consult," and on the Senate side it does not seem either geographically or ideologically slanted. On the House side the list is even more numerous and the name of Joseph Gurney Cannon, of Illinois, is underlined. That was the twentieth Congress in which the former Speaker had served, and he was still good for a couple more.

---

2. *The Growth of the American Republic*, Oxford University Press, 1956 edition, Vol. II, p. 477.
3. Creel, *op. cit.*, p. 186.

Amid the lights and shadows I was concentrating a lot of thought on Isabel. She, consciously or otherwise, was bringing matters to a head by insistence on proceeding to Columbia for academic study. I argued that living with me would of itself be education at the highest level, pointing out that with our joint earnings we could well afford to marry. When she went to New York I shortly followed to press my arguments more strongly, and they prevailed. Isabel returned to Washington, resumed her job at the Haskin Information Service and, on December 8, 1917, we were joined in a quiet marriage at her parents' apartment on Rhode Island Avenue. I had been Best Man at the wedding of Francis Davis, and he came over from Baltimore to reciprocate. Noting the street sign outside he said to my father, in his quiet way, that this made the ceremony "Providential." It was a snowy Saturday afternoon and that evening the newlyweds took the steamer to Old Point Comfort for a week-end honeymoon. On the following Monday we were both at work again, willing, if inadequately prepared, to face the trials and tribulations that are a normal part of every married life.

❰For Christmas, 1917, my wife and I went to Baltimore, giving my parents opportunity to become better acquainted with their new daughter-in-law. Though rather shy, and partly because of that, she got along well with both and in time became really close friends with "Belle-Mère" as, in the pleasing French phrase, Isabel came to call my mother. She also adjusted easily to brother Frank, who at the close of his sophomore year had transferred from Haverford to the Johns Hopkins, because his specialty of mathematics was better taught at the larger institution.

These brothers had seen little of each other for over a year and the younger, now verging on 19, had caught up mentally as well as physically. We were not wholly of one mind about the war in which Frank, before its end, would receive the lieutenancy denied to me. Nobody rubbed that raw nerve though Frank warned me, unnecessarily, that to oppose the government in a time of crisis was to risk being broken "like a butterfly on the wheel." I retorted that opposition to tyranny in another country made little sense if one accepted dictation obsequiously at home. The discussions were amicable and were followed through the years by many more, though neither of us ever strongly influenced the will of the other. We agreed, however, in admiring the literary skill of Kit, who had recently published *Parnassus on Wheels* and was then a successful columnist on the *Evening Ledger*, having brought wife and baby to Philadelphia just before I left there. This paternal status made the war a somewhat remote matter for him.

Early in 1918 conscription also became improbable for me. An acquaintance, Alexander D. Chiquoine, had been made Director of Information for the newly-launched U.S. Employment Service, a branch of the Department of Labor designed to systematize the placement of civilian war workers. The situation here was chaotic, with many mushrooming plants poaching workers from each other and with a heavy drain on agricultural manpower just as the need for increased food production became acute. To stabilize employment procedures a service publication was desired, to go to all State employment agencies, to farm organizations, personnel officers and labor unions. I was invited to become Managing Editor of this "U.S. Employment Service Bulletin," with draft exemption assured and at an initial salary of $2,500 per annum.

The figure was a trifle less than my wage from the *North American* and I did not want to be a draft dodger. But the offer was nonetheless decisively attractive. Unlike the propaganda output of the C.P.I., the nation-wide matching of job vacancies and seekers seemed to me a proper and desirable function for the Federal Government. And the opportunity to expand my newspaper training, by assuming directive duty for even a specialized publication of limited circulation, was indubitably attractive. Moreover, I wanted more first-hand knowledge of the organized labor movement, the rising importance of which was daily more evident. So I accepted the offer, after first persuading Angus McSween to replace me with Gene Pharo.

It proved a wise decision. In addition to the minor technical skills needed to prepare the *Bulletin* it was necessary for me to develop a close liaison with Department of Labor officials as well as with the Chamber of Commerce and American Federation of Labor. The full cooperation of both was essential for the success of the Community Labor Boards, of which some 1,600 were rushed into being to work voluntarily in assisting local war labor recruiting and distribution throughout the country. They illustrated most effectively the American genius for solving on the spot problems which are often only tangled and complicated by directives from Washington. The importance of this localization was impressed on me by three influential friends who took the time to reminisce on their broad experience.

First in this trio was Samuel Gompers, the initial and most far-sighted president of the A.F. of L., who was then daily demonstrating the vital importance of organized labor to any concerted national effort. The second was Louis F. Post, the Assistant Secretary of Labor, a stalwart single-taxer who had been a strong Wilsonian but was deeply disturbed by the wartime authoritarian trend. The third, and most romantic, was Terence V. Powderly, a veteran of the turbulent "Knights of Labor" period who had been three times mayor of Scranton and now, as an aging departmental officer, was especially charged with the problems of immigrant workers. All three of these veterans were in their late sixties. Each had a different background and outlook on social reform which together gave me perspective on the labor movement which I had heretofore lacked. Each impressed me by their respective fears that a ruthless peace would turn German trade unions from moderate to extremist leadership. All three helped to guide my work. It must have been conducted efficiently, since my annual salary was raised to $3,000 at a time when that of the Secretary of Labor was only $5,000. And I was selected to write the history of the wartime employment service for the 1919–20 edition of the American Labor Year Book.

The Federal Employment Service, today much developed and a fully accepted part of governmental machinery, was in 1918 ahead of its time. With the signing of the Armistice appropriations were sharply cut and the work of replacing veterans in civil employment could not be managed as anticipated. The *Bulletin* ceased publication in its existing form at the end of 1918, and on December 31, the resignation submitted by me at the end of the war was accepted.

109

I had learned a great deal from the experience, beyond adaptation to the operation of bureaucratic machinery. I had learned that, in the United States at least, government works best when it leaves responsibility to local leadership. I had learned that even a condition of national emergency will not materially lessen the mutual suspicions of management and labor and that those who govern must deal even-handedly with both types of organization. I had learned, finally, that jealousy between the Executive and Legislative branches is built into the American political system and can only be exacerbated by any effort of one to dictate to the other.

One reason for regretting American participation in the war was the difficulty found by Woodrow Wilson, despite his theoretical knowledge of the subject, in preserving the balance of power so carefully written into the original Constitution. Long before his ill-fated fight for the League of Nations this stubborn President was seriously at odds with Congress. In a small way, with an amusing outcome, I had sought to help my distant Chief. I had been requested to write a few paragraphs on the Employment Service needs, to be incorporated in a Presidential Message on wartime labor policies which Mr. Wilson had decided to deliver to Congress in person. Before doing this I consulted several Republican friends on the Hill to determine what would, and would not, be effective. Unanimously the advice was to emphasize immediate and visible necessity; avoid long-range and visionary plans. Heeding this in the writing, I decided to witness the climax of my effort. There was delay in transit to the Capitol, and hastily turning into the corridor leading to the House Press Gallery I was relieved to see an almost empty elevator just taking off. "Wait a moment," I shouted. Checking its upward start the car returned and its door opened. I rushed in, to confront a confused operator, two scowling Secret Service men and the President of the United States, for it was by this car that the latter had easiest access to the rostrum of the House. Though infrequently used, Woodrow Wilson had a charming smile. He flashed it on me, saying: "I wouldn't want to impede so energetic a reporter." I would have liked to reply that I was there to observe Presidential handling of recommendations that I had authored, but fortunately confined myself to a mumbled apology. It was consolation to find that, in this instance, my careful phraseology was utilized, practically verbatim.

There was a lesson in the little incident, on which I reflected the more because my failure at Fort Myer had been so clearly due to immoderate expression. And I concluded that discretion is particularly important in political speech. No matter how great their mobilized power there is a severe limit to what governments can accomplish, simply because they are human instruments and therefore subject to the limitations of human reason. That was why the flamboyant rhetoric about "a war to end war" and "to make the world safe for democracy" was destined to ring so hollow. The criticism was equally valid for the lyrical enthusiasm with which my radical acquaintances regarded the Russian Revolution. Once the Communists took over, Lenin had written, "the State will wither away" to be replaced by a free society of unexploited producers. This seemed nonsense to me and I was led, by revulsion from both extremes, to a closer study and deepening appreciation of the original American idea of limited and divided governmental power. Manifestly that political philosophy had, on the whole, worked well, whereas the Grand Designs now sparkling would end in shattering disillusion.

Here was ground for argument with my socialistic friends, whose skepticism about the war I shared but whose reasoning seemed to me doctrinaire. I could not agree that munition makers, international bankers or entrepreneurs in general had been factors of large import in the origin of the war. This seemed to me to root in easily inflamed concepts of nationalism, which could be more dangerous under a state-controlled than under a free economy. Indeed Germany, the most militaristic of the Great Powers, was also the most highly-developed in socialistic practise. Furthermore, I deeply feared the extension of centralized governmental power which socialism implies. The workers certainly would not gain by substituting public for private exploitation of labor. Their future lay in the general prosperity to be achieved by disarmament, elimination of trade barriers and other obstacles to international cooperation for which a pretentious nationalism, not capitalism, was fundamentally to blame.

With confirmed Marxists, of course, I was in total disagreement. They had no doubt as to the basic responsibility of capitalism for the war and were equally certain that universal communist revolution, on the Russian model, was on the way. I anticipated that free enterprise would probably in time succumb, even in this country, to state intervention. But the process would be slow and would be defined by a pleasant word like "Liberalism," since most Americans prefer to call a spade an agricultural implement. In any case I did not foresee a cheerful political picture when the United Press declared the Armistice prematurely. It would require humility, compassion and intelligence to bind the deep wounds in Western Civilization. And all these qualities were in short supply.

It should not be implied, however, that I was weighed down by anxieties during these interesting wartime months in Washington. I was deeply in love with my young bride and she reciprocated without any meek surrender of her often variant opinions. The outset of our married life, in the rooming house near what was then called Iowa Circle, could not be called luxurious. It was a Box and Cox menage, since Isabel went early to work while I returned late from mine. But as our pooled earnings mounted we moved to a more commodious apartment, where we could entertain modestly. When I went with the Employment Service our leisure hours coincided and expeditions became feasible. The Potomac, virtually unpolluted in 1918, was attractive both for swimming and Sunday canoe trips—down river to picturesque Alexandria and upstream to Great Falls or beyond, by way of the still functioning C & O canal. Horses could be hired cheaply for romantic rides through a beautiful countryside only later disfigured by sprawling suburbs. Washington was still a small town, but the patronage of the diplomatic corps encouraged the amenities of cosmopolitan restaurants, attractive museums and above average theaters and movies. Great boxes of steel and glass had not yet stereotyped the variety of the downtown streets, and the many parks were the more interesting because old and often historic residences surrounded most of them. It was a pleasant place to live and one could wander in any part of it with absolute safety.

We had many friends, Isabel in part because her parents

112

and two of her grandparents were native Washingtonians, I because my diverse work encouraged interesting contacts. For medical or other reasons both Jo Lalley and Sam Dashiell had escaped their military service so, when Pharo arrived, the old Philadelphia circle was largely restored. With the senior correspondents of this period, like courtly Dick Oulahan of the New York *Times*, brisk Fred Essary of the Baltimore *Sun* and amiable Charley Ross of the St. Louis *Post-Dispatch*, I was scarcely intimate, for a good deal of dignity then hedged the top echelon of Washington's Fourth Estate. But with the younger members of the Press Club I was very much at home. A. J. (Monty) Montgomery of the *Christian Science Monitor*, Paul Hanna of the Socialist New York *Call* and Richard M. Boeckel of the strongly capitalistic New York *Tribune*, were particular friends of this era. With the latter, soon after the war ended, I concocted the idea of the Boeckel-Morley Farm Letter, which aimed to supply rural papers with the governmental news important to agriculture that was largely ignored by the press corps. The idea had promise but a major development forced dissolution of the syndicate, significant because the colleagues separately built on the scheme in later years to start successful enterprises—Dick Boeckel in the form of *Editorial Research Reports* and I in *Human Events.*

At Haverford I had sought to follow the strides of brother Chris by applying for a Rhodes Scholarship from Maryland. But it was awarded, for the year 1915, to another, clearly better qualified, youth. For 1916 there was no appointment, since under the system at that time each state chose candidates two years out of three, so that each would always have two representatives at Oxford during the normal three-year term. For 1917, accordingly, there was another appointment coming up from Maryland and while on the ambulance train I decided to try again. This time, to my real surprise, I received the award, undoubtedly because of my volunteer service with the British Red Cross. Regretfully I wrote back that because of the unpredictable duration of the war it did not seem possible to accept the privilege. The Oxford Secretary of the Rhodes Trust, later knighted as Sir Francis Wylie, replied that all were in the same boat and that attendance could be deferred until the end of the

113

hostilities. So it rested until my marriage which I reported, without having said anything on the subject to my wife, because I knew that only bachelors were eligible. Again Mr. Wylie wrote, saying that this restriction had also been temporarily waived and that if I could bring my bride we would both be welcome. Others of my vintage, several also with wives, would arrive for the Michaelmas term of 1919, and that course was suggested for me.

The prospect could not be disregarded. I wanted to read much more deeply in economics, history and politics, drawing the correlations between the three disciplines without which any one of them can be misleading. Isabel said that some study at Oxford would be full compensation for her abruptly terminated attendance at Columbia. We would have opportunity to travel on the Continent and, if we managed carefully, there would be savings to supplement the scholarship money. Moreover, I might freelance from post-war Europe and thereby improve my journalistic standing. So far the interruptions had not been any lasting impediment.

Between this arrangement, at the end of 1918, and departure for England, in September, 1919, lay nearly nine months to be filled constructively. Late in the war Gene Pharo had enlisted, and was held in the Quartermaster Corps, so it was easy for me to return to the *North American*. Angus McSween now assigned me to report on the important stories developing in Washington as President Wilson sailed for the Paris Peace Conference and opposition to the League of Nations crystallized in the Senate. It was a tense and politically very significant period. While the off-year elections had placed the Republicans in control of both Houses, many G.O.P. Senators wished to avoid partisanship on both League and Treaty. But it is difficult to be politically neutral in a system where the President is also a party leader. This problem was not lessened by Wilson's intransigence and the accumulating evidence that savage terms would be dictated to the defeated Central Powers. The decision to make the League Covenant an integral part of a punitive peace also insured support for the initially small group of "irreconcilable" Senators.

German delegates were summoned to Paris to sign the

Treaty of Versailles on June 28, 1919. But well before then the intent to humiliate and discredit the Weimar Republic had become apparent. With apprehension I watched the vindictive terms emerge. First came the enforced self-incrimination, asserting Germany's sole and total responsibility for the war. On this dubious basis was then erected the sharply punitive structure of territorial annexation, property confiscation, seizure of merchant shipping and established commercial rights. To this was added all costs of Allied military occupation, plus an immediate cash indemnity of a billion dollars, with a reserved right to future reparations eventually marked up to more than 25 times that sum. This combination of calculated impoverishment and astronomical financial obligation was an absurdity which should have been obvious for even an economic neophyte. The enfeebled German government of course could, and soon did, print huge quantities of unsupported paper marks. But how could that quickly depreciating currency be transformed into money acceptable by the victors? It was a basic question which neither Lloyd George, nor Clemenceau, nor Woodrow Wilson attempted to answer.

Although many shared these doubts, the enthusiasm over military victory made it all but impossible to raise them in print. The pessimism which this caused was deepened for me by the reaction of my left-wing acquaintances. They saw a silver lining in the tyrannical treatment of the German people. It would force them into partnership with the Russian Communists, already showing ability to defeat the Allied-sponsored intervention in behalf of souped-up Czarist military leaders. With this anticipated Russo-German unity, it was argued, Marxism would triumph in Europe and, eventually, in the United States. Already, under Bela Kun, the Communists had seized power in Hungary, and there were signs that Bavaria also would soon be under a Red regime.

Both the subjection of Germany and the spread of Communism should have been equally alarming, since separately or together they foreshadowed further degradation for Western Civilization. Sadly, I compared the Congress of Vienna, after the Napoleonic wars, with that proceeding in Paris a century later. At the former, defeated France, with the brilliant leadership of

Talleyrand, had been treated as an equal. In 1919, both the German and the Russian governments were completely excluded from the peace-making process. Wilson's efforts to sustain his "Fourteen Points"—on the basis of which Germany had stopped fighting—were in the outcome only pathetic gestures. Pathos was heightened by general cynicism about the League of Nations. Fundamentally, it seemed to me, much of the blame must be attributed to the democratic system. Its leadership, after deliberately inflaming popular passion, could not oppose such weird solutions as that implied by the Lloyd George formula of "Squeezing Germany until the pips squeak." In time they would do so very nastily, through Hitler's raucous voice.

In this mood the opportunity to reflect, in timeless Oxford, seemed to fit nicely with Arnold Toynbee's doctrine of Withdrawal and Return. Throughout the hot summer of 1919 we continued at work, accumulating financial reserves and watching the grim drama unfold with all the inevitability of Greek tragedy. Because of shipping shortage, passage to England was not easy to secure, but finally reservations were made on an Anchor Line freighter, from Boston to Glasgow. The skipper of the cheerfully named *Elysia* was Captain David W. Bone, already a well-known writer and one of three prominent British brothers with whom the Morley trio would later have many associations. With the date set, and farewell parties concluded, we spent two days in The Hub, where Isabel had an eccentric aunt and where uneccentric Governor Coolidge was getting helpful publicity from his firm stand in face of the Boston police strike. On the eve of sailing, which was September 24, we had a memorable evening watching incomparable Mrs. Pat Campbell in "Pygmalion."

Then, with the lumbering little *Elysia* scarcely at sea, the radio brought word that Woodrow Wilson, campaigning for the League of Nations in the West, had been stricken by paralysis. With the President's collapse went any lingering hope that the United States would pave a road to an improved world order. The virus of nationalism had gained strength during the protracted wartime agony. That made it the more important to have a long and searching look at "Balkanized Europe."

116

❰I was well on the way to my 26th birthday when I matriculated at Oxford in early October, of 1919. Isabel was just 23 and we had been married nearly two years. There was nothing unusual in this situation. Because of the war a majority of students, English and foreign, were also in their middle twenties; several had wives in tow and there were even a few scholastic babies. Married Rhodes Scholars were sufficiently numerous for the girls to form a club—"The Better Halves."

Although I did not intend to slight my studies, in the "School of Modern History," I also had other objectives. I deeply wanted to savor the almost mystical beauty of the ancient institution. But, like Matthew Arnold's Scholar-Gipsy, I meant to "wander from the studious walls to learn strange arts and join a Gipsy tribe." Put more prosaically, I planned to capitalize on my newspaper experience, not so much for desirable revenue as to strengthen my standing in the field. I had also decided in advance to familiarize myself with all aspects of the labor movement, on the Continent as well as in Great Britain. The Russian Revolution had, of course, given great impetus to this line of inquiry. And I had a distinct advantage from my not unimportant wartime connection with the Department of Labor. I was interested in the policies of organized labor not only for their social and economic implications but also because of the potential power of unionization in the direction of a peaceful world. If that could be achieved it would to some extent justify the holocaust of the immediate past.

In reconciling these objectives I was exceptionally fortunate in the tutor to whom I was assigned after acceptance by New College, where Kit had also studied. Shortly after the latter's graduation Ernest Barker had succeeded H. A. L. Fisher as Fellow and Tutor in History at New College. There, during the war, he had introduced short cuts for students expecting to be called to the colors, which proved equally adaptable for those who after war service could not afford the time traditionally required. This contraction worked well primarily because Professor Barker was a natural administrator as well as a thorough scholar, who had taken highest university honors in classical studies before turning to history as his field of teaching. Nobody who was not himself firmly grounded could so ably have cut out academic fat without injuring the meat. Barker accomplished the operation by personally demanding concentrated and thorough research from his pupils. This was exactly what I wanted, feeling that with my maturity I should obtain the Oxford degree in two years, instead of the three then normally required of Rhodes Scholars. "Probably no difficulty," said my genial preceptor at our initial meeting.

This outstanding teacher was also a most refreshing personality. He was of humble origin, his father a Lancashire coal miner and his mother a cotton-mill "hand" when the parents met. How Ernest Barker, in the last quarter of the Nineteenth Century, rose from this obscure background to become an Oxford Don and gain a knighthood, is a saga which he himself charmingly compressed in a booklet called *Father of the Man.* The story immediately attracted me, and I correctly inferred that this tutor would be sympathetic to my plan of studying not only the background but also the current activities of European labor organizations. While Ernest Barker steered clear of politics he was a sponsor of the University Labour Club which he advised me to join, also giving me introductions to several prominent trade unionists.

Isabel and I were also fortunate in finding very satisfactory lodgings, in a modest two-story dwelling in South Oxford. This was just off the Abingdon Road, a mile from the town center, which was of little moment with the bicycles quickly acquired. Norreys Avenue was not a distinguished street and No. 25 certainly not luxurious, but Jane Surman, our landlady, made up for all deficiencies. She was a neat and lively little widow, with a teen-age daughter, Dorothy, who was a shop assistant, and a nephew, Percy, who when we arrived was still in school. There was mutual amusement about the language difficulty, for in this respect town as well as gown has its distinctive Oxford stamp. Early in our stay Isabel brought home a can of baked beans, telling Mrs. Surman that: "You just heat them up." The beans came on stone-cold and the landlady explained reproachfully that she had not been told "to hot them up." On another occasion she informed me that she planned to build "a little

118

harbor" in the garden and was perplexed when I replied that if the rain kept on she would have one automatically.

We rented the small front sitting room, and good-sized bedroom above it, for the going price of two guineas a week, to which was added a small sum for service. In addition to bed-making, cleaning and other household chores this included the purchase, preparation and serving of meals by Mrs. Surman, whose cheerful disposition was never ruffled by hard work. Coal for the living-room fire was a shilling a scuttle with the same extra for a hot bath, which required laborious carriage of big jugs upstairs from the boiler in the kitchen. This task usually fell to Percy and after a time was obviated by installation of something called a "geezer," presumably geyser, actually a small gas water-heater above the bathtub. While artificial gas was "laid on" in the kitchen, the house had no electricity nor central heating and of course no telephone. On winter mornings it would be so cold and damp that the star boarders would exercize in the street to get warm, while the coal fire was "hotting up." We had a kerosene lamp for the sitting room and candles in the bedroom. But the total bills, including meals and laundry, ran just under £5 a week, when the pound was exchanging for $3.70, and we were made as comfortable as Oxford's dismal climate permits. Appreciating this, we kept the Norreys Avenue rooms for the two academic years that I was a student there, paying a small retainer to reserve them during vacation absences.

These were frequent and varied, depending on journalistic opportunities or other work that offered. Without extensive traveling we might just have scraped through on the scholarship money supplemented by savings which had foolishly been converted into pounds just before that currency began to slip down in dollar value. But I had life insurance payments to meet in the States and anxiety to build a reputation as a good reporter was stronger than my desire to shine scholastically. During vacations, traditionally supposed to be devoted to serious reading, we were generally off to another country, or else exploring at first hand the intricacies of contemporary British problems.

At the outset, however, I applied myself seriously to academic work, even attending several of the university lecture courses which, under the free-wheeling English system, is a

119

wholly optional matter. Weekly sessions with my tutor were very rewarding and I particularly admired the skill with which the subjects were selected to clarify the great landmarks of English history—political, economic and social—since the Roman conquest. This was a much more thorough discipline than anything I had experienced at Haverford and surprisingly taught me more about the fundamentals of American government than I had ever learned at home. I enjoyed the challenge of essay writing and the stimulus of the seminars at which my group would discuss the subject under Ernest Barker's kindly but sometimes acidulous direction. I preserved a large sample of these typewritten themes, each running to some 2,000 words, and they are generally clear, cogent and well developed. From the marginal comments it is evident that my tutor had this impression. On an early one Mr. Barker wrote: "A first-class essay—in which every sentence counts and everything is clearly put." On another, discussing "The Basis and the Composition of the Anglo-Saxon Witan," the comment is: "Again first-class. You promise well for attaining the highest honors in the Schools."

That promise was not fulfilled. At the conclusion of the gruelling final examinations I received a good "Second," or B grade, in the four classes which entitle the student to a B.A. Oxon. That was as well as brother Chris had done, after three as against two years of preparation, but I was a mature 27 when I took my finals, and Kit an immature 23. Only about five per cent of the candidates get a First which, whatever the subject, demands a breadth and depth of knowledge to which I did not aspire in history or the adjunct subjects (as taught at Oxford) of philosophy, political science and economics. A First is very important for an Englishman seeking a choice Civil Service appointment or the best sort of teaching position. It was of no real value for one who sought to make his mark in American journalism. Ernest Barker thought highly of me because I responded quickly to his remarkable leadership. Unfortunately, I only had him for two terms as he then became Principal of King's College, London. But even if I had continued under his direction I would have eased on routine study in order to progress in journalism. I

120

was quite satisfied to show that my Rhodes Scholarship was not undeserved.

To prove this it was also important to make firm English friendships, which I found the easier because of my bi-national background. Hamish Miles, with whom I had worked on the Ambulance Train, was back at Baliol and introduced me to the literary coterie at that somewhat consciously esoteric college. David Blelloch, another F.A.U. veteran, was at St. John's, living picturesquely in a charming riverside cottage in nearby Marston. Reuben Cohen, a Wadham scholar destined to rise high in the Ministry of Fuel and Power, was a fellow-member of the Labour Club, as were several who would in time achieve political prominence. Indeed, before my first year was out I had friends in most of the 23 men's colleges which, loosely federated, then composed the University. Tutorials, of course, were held at my own New College and occasionally I would attend chapel or dine "in hall" there. But whether one used the college facilities or not, whether one attended any university lectures, whether one even resided in Oxford after acceptance—all seemed a matter of indifference to the authorities. Permissiveness then strange to an American was said to date back to medieval times, when students at the college prototypes were directed by Masters whom they themselves elected. And, in 1919, the always lax discipline was further eased in deference to the character of post-war students, many of whom had held positions of command. This maturity of outlook certainly discouraged dissipation. During two years at Oxford I never heard of any indulgence in drugs and saw only one helplessly drunken student—a fellow Rhodes Scholar. It was a resounding scandal when a girl at one of the women's colleges had to be withdrawn because of pregnancy.

All this was no mere spasm of Puritanism in the incongruous setting of a Cavalier tradition. In 1919 a gentle but obvious melancholy pervaded all the activity at Oxford. It was not only the youthful amputees and cripples in the college quadrangles. Sadness went beyond these individual victims to mourn the vanished flower of a nation's youth. At the home of Lost Causes the faltering cause of civilization itself was now gallantly, but

121

none too hopefully, defended. In the cloisters of New College had been erected a vast tablet, thirty feet long, bearing the names of all its students who had given their lives for the cause that each supported. Amid the scores thus listed, in alphabetical order, are the names of several Germans who died fighting in that country's service. This deeply impressed me as a magnificent tribute to the superiority of Christian values. And after the Second World War several other colleges followed this noble lead.

In this mood of "What Price Glory," athletics was played down, sharply so by contrast with American schools. Rowing was still the thing for many, but seemed to me too time-consuming and mechanical. So for exercize I turned back to boxing, a minor sport but one in which a maximum of workout absorbed a minimum of time. Here I did quite well, until the trials to select the team to oppose the sister university of Cambridge. The choice in the welterweight class lay between me and a grim New Zealander named Meldrum, who hammered our hero so severely that for two days he was laid up with a black eye and swollen jaw. "Boxing," wrote Isabel to her mother, "is a disgusting sport." After this debacle I fell back on tennis and more frequent utilization of the canoe we rented to explore the lovely little Oxford rivers. We were constantly on bicycles, sometimes for over-night expeditions, and from Norreys Avenue it was a short walk across the fields to Hinksey, where John Ruskin had applied his zeal for craftsmanship by leading a group—including Oscar Wilde—in paving the village road.

But great events were stirring, and after a term of academic concentration I knew it was time to develop my journalistic side. To do so I must first make London contacts. Therefore, after a brief round of visits to English relatives, we took lodgings for the Christmas vacation in the great capital where a 15 per cent rate of unemployment, heaviest among war veterans, was producing a nervous atmosphere of which only the overtones had penetrated university walls. The news was in the growing restlessness of the labor movement, and in anxiety over the economic consequences of the Treaty of Versailles, which went into effect on January 10. So I introduced myself to critical editors whose work I had been studying—H. J. Massingham of the *Nation and Athenaeum*; H. N. Brailsford of the *New Leader*; George

Lansbury of the *Daily Herald* and James Bone, London editor of the Manchester *Guardian*. John Maynard Keynes personally confirmed my worst forebodings about the effects of the Draconian peace treaty and Ramsay MacDonald gave me an off-the-record interview on Labour policy "when we come to power." At Eccleston Square, political headquarters of the Labour Party, I was welcomed by "Uncle Arthur" Henderson as "the first American journalist to show any curiosity about our organization."

Altogether, while Isabel explored the delights of London, I had a most stimulating vacation, cheerfully letting the Anglo-Saxon Witan slip back to the recesses of my mind. On January 30, 1920, after return to the university, I had my first article of substance in the *Daily Herald*, being an interview with Professor Frederick Soddy, an Oxford pioneer in nuclear physics. Soddy spoke of the promise and global threat of atomic energy, saying that: "In the next war life could be wiped off the planet by science as completely as wiping off a slate."

The enterprise shown in obtaining this interview clearly impressed the two young intellectuals, W. N. Ewer and George Slocombe, who were than running the *Daily Herald*. I told them that in March I would be going to Paris, for the Spring vacation, and suggested that I should proceed thence to the Ruhr, to investigate the tense situation that had arisen as the miners there were pushed ever harder to meet the coal deliveries demanded by France as part of the reparations bill. I was given the assignment but just before leaving Oxford received a wire from Ewer asking me first to investigate a "miracle" picture of Christ, alleged to bleed periodically in the little town of Mirebeau, in southwestern France. This intrigued me and I persuaded Stringfellow Barr, a Virginia Rhodes Scholar who later became president of St. John's College in Annapolis, to accompany me. It was an extraordinary adventure, with opportunity for graphic description, and while the Sacré Coeur did not bleed for us the medieval atmosphere of the old walled town, near Poitiers, made a lasting impression. Many times, in many places, I would note this lingering strength of superstition, as in the faith in astrology shown by such New Deal leaders as Henry Wallace during the F.D.R. regime.

123

Rejoining Isabel in Paris, we located in a comfortable apartment on the *rive gauche*—at 23, rue du Cherche-Midi. But I was chafing to get to the Ruhr, where there was an increasingly tense situation which the German "Spartacists" (Communists) were working to exploit. Efforts of the struggling Weimar Republic to meet the reparation demands were spreading misery through the great focus area of German industry. The French Government viewed this with equanimity, since it fitted into the admitted plan for a separate Rhineland Republic. The greater the distress in Germany, the easier it would be to detach the western part under permanent French control. If the Ruhr went Communist it too could be occupied by French troops, as indeed it was a couple of years later. On April 6 the *poilus* moved into Frankfort, with little of the restraint which Goethe describes in the occupation of 1759. This time over 100 civilians were shot down for protesting the billeting of Algerian soldiers. The French explanation was that since the Reichswehr was about to police the Ruhr, a demilitarized zone, Paris must take the military precautions authorized by the Versailles Treaty. To demonstrate an imaginary Allied solidarity a battalion of Belgian soldiers accompanied the French to Frankfurt and its environs.[4]

I was at this time in close touch with the U.S. Embassy in Paris, where there was much anxiety over the aggressive French tactics, also viewed dubiously in Britain. A fellow-Haverfordian, John V. Van Sickle of the class of 1913, was on the Embassy staff and responded quickly to the suggestion that if given official credentials I would gladly bring back a report from the Ruhr. I figured that if the Reichswehr were in control these would be very helpful, while if the Communists had the upper hand my letter on *Daily Herald* stationery would come in handy. Thus doubly armed, I traveled by train to Cologne, made a short stay to familiarize myself with the German mood, and then pushed on to Essen. The tracks had been torn up in the outskirts of this great industrial center and all passengers were turned out. I went to a nearby tavern, ordered a beer and listened attentively to the conversation. It revealed that after some

---

4. The sorry story is told in documented detail by Dr. Karl Wachendorf, in *Rheinische Schicksalsfragen*, Berlin, 1928, pp. 100 ff.

street fighting the ill-organized Red rising had collapsed and that Essen was now under martial law. In the seclusion of the toilet I tore up my *Daily Herald* letter, flushed the fragments down the drain and proceeded by tram to the city center.

The Embassy credentials, however, proved an Open Sesame and with their aid I soon found myself in the Krupp plant headquarters of the Reichswehr general. This stout old officer regretted that it was necessary to apply tight censorship. He was formally cordial, but bitter that duty had compelled him to repress a revolt of German workers. He used the argument that I was to hear continuously in Germany—that the Reich had been tricked into surrender by President Wilson's Fourteen Points, all of which were violated by the Treaty of Versailles. "Tell your Embassy," he said, "that no people with a spark of pride can be expected to obey this *Diktat* except as it is enforced at the point of the bayonet."

Somewhere in the State Department archives, presumably, is the report which I made on this visit to strife-torn Essen. More easily accessible are the articles I wrote from Paris on my return. One, in the London *Nation and Athenaeum*, attracted a good deal of attention, since fair-minded Englishmen were becoming seriously worried, as well they might, about the long-range results of French ruthlessness toward prostrate Germany. I even sold an article on the subject to a French paper, but neither the timorous caution of its editor, nor the compensation of 25 francs, $1.70 at the then current exchange, were encouraging.

This foray in foreign correspondence illustrates my interest in being more than a routine reporter. Paris was then crowded with American newspaper men, many of high professional quality, but their focus was on the ceaseless round of diplomatic conferences. I remember none who took the abortive Ruhr rising seriously enough to visit the scene. To me it was a portent of the German desperation that would eventually come to hideous flower under Hitler. I returned from Essen saying, and writing, that the seeds of further war were generating. And this melancholy foresight strengthened my desire to report, as the journalistic cliché goes, "in depth."

But it could not be said that my wife and I were obviously

depressed by the uncertain future. Paris in springtime is always lovely and in that boding April of 1920 still savored the intoxication of recent victory. The beautiful old city stretched itself languorously along the Seine and the graceful ostentation of the boulevards concealed the grim industrial faubourgs where unemployment and inflation were breeding bitterness. Several factors gave us that intimacy with foreign environment which the tourist seldom acquires. Isabel had a cousin, Leslie Cauldwell, who for years had been settled in Paris as a moderately successful artist, and was most helpful. Equally so was the interest of a wealthy Franco-American, Mme. Caroline Levy, whose son was a student at Oxford and who busied herself lodging Rhodes Scholars on vacation in French homes and playing guardian angel to their wives, if any. Finally that old friend from *Public Ledger* days, Samuel Dashiell, was now with the U.P. in Paris, maintaining a lively love nest with his current girl friend at nearby and romantic Barbizon. Speaking good French, he brought us into a cosmopolitan group of Sorbonne students and aspiring writers who met nightly at the Près Aux Clercs, a Latin quarter restaurant as simple in appointments as it was excellent in cuisine and company.

The time sped quickly until the return to Oxford near the end of April, with much learned even though very little of the scheduled university reading had been accomplished.

◀With taste for journalistic inquiry thus stimulated, I went on to other self-imposed assignments. The end of June, 1920, found me in Dublin, then in the thick of the troubles leading to establishment of the Irish Republic. Hamish Miles, with friends in the Sinn Fein movement, knew of the infra-governmental structure built by the Republicans, with taxation, judicial procedure, banking, insurance and other civil functions operating wholly independently of British law. This, I thought, merited investigation, and I arranged with Massingham to examine the subject for the *Nation and Athenaeum*.

What I witnessed in Dublin, a city of faded but appealing Georgian beauty, was actually prelude to the approaching dissolution of the British Empire. Armed with letters of introduction I met many of the proscribed Sinn Fein leaders and was impressed by the ability with which they were laying the foundations of independence. It must, I wrote, have been similar to the situation in the American Colonies just prior to 1776. In guerilla warfare the imperial power must destroy the roots of the organized nationalistic movement, or fail.

As had been the case in the relations of Tories and Rebels during the early stages of our Revolution, so there were amusing social overtones in the Irish political upheaval. While British tanks rumbled through the streets of Dublin, and while the isolated rural barracks of the constabulary were being stormed and burned, comradeship between individual Irish and Englishmen continued. This was evident at the salon of fabulous Maude Gonne, where after an Abbey Theatre play I was privileged to meet James Stephens and other native literati. Conversation quickly swung from the cultural life of Dublin to that of London. The same mutuality was apparent at The Sod of Turf, a literally underground restaurant frequented by Sinn Fein leaders "on the run." Here, after an exchange of greetings in formal Gaelic, this was dropped in favor of colloquial English. Frequently a British officer, from the hated "Castle," would join the group and argue amicably until his stereotyped farewell: "Sorry, lads, me time is up. I've got to get back and check on your whereabouts." As Sir Horace Plunkett, a valiant advocate of Dominion status, summarized: "The Saxon will never govern the Celt, nor be at his best without the latter's aid." Under his conciliatory plan Ireland would neither be divided nor partitioned, since Ulster could have as much autonomy in an Irish Dominion as Quebec had successfully maintained in Canada.

Others were making first-hand investigations of the Irish situation at this time. One such was Viscount Bryce, Britain's former and most famous Ambassador in Washington. As a close student of his *American Commonwealth*, I was pleased by my informal meeting with this outstanding diplomat. Returning from Dublin by the early morning steamer I had spotted two empty deck chairs nicely located on the upper deck and sank into one for the nap which seemed desirable sequel to a ringing farewell party the previous night. I was soon rudely awakened by a shaken shoulder and looked up into the stern face of a stalwart Anglican Bishop, attired in all the anachronistic regalia of gaiters, breeches and corded hat. "Do you realize, young man," said this grim apparition, "that you are occupying the chair of My Lord Bryce?"

I jumped up, noting a small figure behind the Bishop, and explained that I had not realized the chair was reserved for anybody. Whereupon the little man observed: "I take it you are American. Sit down again and tell me what you learned in Ireland. Bishop Blank will bring up yonder chair." And so, for a couple of hours, we conversed, though the Very Reverend was mostly morosely silent.

What I had noted in Ireland interested Lord Bryce, but did not receive universal acclaim. Through the good offices of brother Kit an article similar to one written for Massingham was printed in the New York *Evening Post*. Its emphasis on constructive aspects of the Republican movement offended my strongly Anglophile mother, for whom Sinn Fein were dirty words, signifying murderous anarchy. In a letter which she preserved I wrote back: "I must say a word in my own behalf. In the first place it is the duty of a good newspaper man, as I see it, to report accurately and fearlessly things he knows to be true, without regard for sentimentality. No single article can attempt to cover the whole field in anything, and what I tried to do for the *Post* was simply to show the very obvious but unfortunately unappreciated fact that Sinn Fein is not a group of either murderers or supermen, but a body which is working intelligently along certain constructive as well as destructive lines. You cannot settle a problem until you know both sides. . . . "

Isabel had not been idle during the ten days that I spent in Ireland. Through the interest of the London Quakers she had secured a summer job supervising the girls at a camp for Austrian war orphans established by the Society of Friends at Fawkham, in Kent. Fairby Grange, made available for the purpose by its owner, was a delightful, rambling old house with spacious grounds, in the heart of the picturesque countryside that Dickens loved and described in terms that still applied. It was arranged that, on my return from Dublin, I should also come there to direct the activities of the dozen boys. From our viewpoint this stopgap occupation was well worthwhile, even though uncompensated except for room and board. It gave me time to write and I changed pace with a whimsical article on the relations between the somewhat riotous boys and well-named Mr. Rose, the meticulous old gardener who sought to keep his cherished flowerbeds intact from incomprehensible young vandals. For us it also meant a great improvement in knowledge of German, since conversation with children is the most natural way to learn a foreign language. With one of the little girls, a delicate, brown-eyed beauty named Helena Kohlmann, we established a relationship which would eventually bring her to our home in Baltimore.

This pleasant interlude was brief. As the period of hospitality for the Austrian orphans drew to its end, I received a request to report on the annual convention of the British Trades Union Congress, held that year in Portsmouth. Isabel, who was ambitious to run a bookshop, answered an advertisement which secured her a job in London as secretarial assistant to Martin Secker, a publisher with a small but uniformly first-class list of authors. This meant that she must forsake both me and Oxford. But as I had been largely neglecting my college work I resignedly returned to the care of Mrs. Surman, after an energetic week in Portsmouth. There, among others, I became well-acquainted with Robert Smillie, the soft-spoken, iron-hearted leader of the Miners' Union. From Wales to Scotland the word of "Auld Bob" was law among the hewers of coal, whose workaday travail had recently been grippingly described by D. H. Lawrence in *Sons and Lovers*. The miners, Smillie told me, were prepared to strike for nationalization of their industry and also, if necessary, to halt the "preventive war" with Soviet Russia that was then being rather wildly discussed. The latter type of direct action, neglected by International Socialism in 1914, seemed to me the more justifiable of the two possibilities.

Industrial unrest, heading toward the great General Strike of 1926, was surging up in England, and soon after the Portsmouth Convention the miners downed tools experimentally, demanding continuation of governmental control and an end of the royalty system whereby big landowners, like the Duke of Northumberland, had priority on profits merely be-

129

cause their ancestors had gained control of the properties on which, centuries later, the mines were developed. There were nationwide demonstrations backing the miners' walkout and great parades of ill-clad unemployed with red flags and banners satirizing Lloyd George's unfortunate promise of an England "fit for heroes to live in." The excitement naturally permeated the Oxford student body and because of my contacts I found myself in demand at undergraduate discussions. The Labour Club started a monthly magazine—*The New Oxford*—of which I was made editor, and in November this group gave a well-attended dinner, with Ernest Barker as chairman and Arthur Henderson, the future Foreign Minister, as principal speaker. I wrote to Isabel that: "The evening began with a toast to the King and ended with one to me."

I was not unduly affected by these heady draughts. I felt that I was fulfilling an objective of the Rhodes Scholarships by merging in an important element of English life. The British Labour Movement gave promise of restoring the great liberal tradition which I had savored in the writings of men like Lord Acton, but which the Lloyd George leadership had demagogically undermined. Labour stood openly for that Anglo-German reconciliation which seemed to me fundamental for post-war recovery. And this activity, I rightly believed, would make journalistic advancement easier. Frequently I differed with my English friends, for my thinking was never socialistic, yet with several of them relationships endured through life. Also there was balance in the arrival at Oxford of brother Frank, chosen as a Rhodes Scholar of 1919 and accepted as a candidate for the difficult Ph.D. in mathematics. Frank had little interest in ephemeral politics but much in the more profound inquiries of the human mind, and did not hesitate to criticize conclusions by his older brother which he considered superficial.

It seemed to me that the long Christmas holidays of 1920–21 should be spent in Germany, where I felt sure that the future of European civilization would be decided, for better or worse. The prospect was agreeable to Isabel, for while she enjoyed the work with Martin Secker its meager compensation, measured against the expenses of London lodgings and week-end trips to Oxford, was not advantageous. The British Quakers, satisfied with our work at Fairby Grange, offered to send us to Berlin with all expenses paid, Isabel to assist in the secretarial work of the relief office there while I was assigned to the student part of the *Quäker Speisung*, or feeding program.

Two years after the Armistice, and by contrast with the Oxford scene, the situation of the German undergraduates was indeed deplorable. Many of them, as in England, were war veterans but in addition to the stigma of military defeat, they had far worse economic problems to confront, as inflation progressively wiped out family savings. Every evening, in the Berlin headquarters, the Quaker unit served cocoa and black bread to all its registered clientele. For some of the young people it was almost the only food they got. From one lad, Hans Lindau, we took conversational lessons, for which he always came punctually to our modest pension on Holtzgartenstrasse in what is now Communist East Berlin. December can be bitter there but Hans always arrived without an overcoat, in an old army tunic buttoned to the neck. The pension was well heated and on our first meeting I suggested that Hans remove his jacket, so that he wouldn't feel the cold on leaving. The youth declined, somewhat stiffly. Finally he admitted that he had nothing under his field-gray uniform, no shirt, no underwear, no socks—no clothing other than the tattered jacket, trousers and worn-out boots in which he stood.

It was my special responsibility to ascertain from the *Deutsche Studentenschaft*, or German Students Union, the minimum food and clothing needs of penniless undergraduates, which were then met by the Friends Service Committee, so far as its resources permitted. The work took me to various university towns, always traveling third-class for economy's sake. The first of these trips was to Göttingen, where my father had done post-graduate work, because this was the national headquarters of the student organization. With remarkable efficiency these youths, on their own initiative, had developed a network, covering some thirty widely scattered universities, from which the basic needs of about 100,000 men and women students were tabulated and kept current. This accomplishment, together with the high degree of independence allowed to Oxford undergraduates, impressed me the more by contrast with the pater-

nalistic attitude of American colleges. I realized that many of
the German students, as with the English at Oxford, had exercized wartime responsibility. Nevertheless, this greater latitude
was taken as normal throughout Europe. I remembered this
when, years later, demand for campus self-government in the
United States flamed up the more violently because so long
repressed.

For Christmas week the work slackened, so I combined a
scheduled visit to South Germany with taking Isabel to Vienna,
where a holiday party for the Fairby Grange children had been
arranged. Stops en route were made at Leipzig, Halle, Dresden
and Munich, conferring with student groups in each. In the
Saxon universities leadership was in Communist hands
whereas in Bavaria, which had experienced some months of Red
rule, a trend toward the National Socialism later developed by
Hitler was apparent. From Munich, by slow, dilapidated and
crowded train, we proceeded to Vienna, which I described in a
letter to my mother as "a depressing city now—its misery accentuated by all the architectural evidence of former grandeur."
Drawing on our savings we took a palatial room at the Hotel
Regina, where we ordered rare ice cream, the incomparable
Viennese *Torte* and other goodies for the group of orphans whom
we had come to know and love. At first the children in their
patchwork clothing were embarrassed by the spaciousness and
faded elegance of the apartment, with obsequious waiters but
only one dim electric light bulb for illumination as the winter
evening closed in. But the ebullience of childhood soon
triumphed and there was gay re-enactment of a self-concocted
play about "Sherly Holmes" which had first been staged in
distant Kent. I was reminded of the prevalent saying, that "In
Berlin the situation is serious but not desperate; in Vienna it is
desperate but not serious," an aphorism well reflecting the different temperaments of somber Prussia and light-hearted Austria.

The close of 1920 saw us again in Munich, where at the
famous old *Vierjahreszeiten*, we planned to see the New Year in.
But here illness that was fortunately rare for both laid me low.
An ulcerated tooth, requiring emergency extraction by a local
dentist, flared up painfully and New Year's Eve saw me re-

cuperating in bed, with Isabel reading a Tauchnitz edition of Edith Wharton aloud. Next morning the ailment was over and we returned in a comfortable sleeper to Berlin where, on January 6, I celebrated my 27th birthday with a *Bierabend* for Hans Lindau and other German student friends. A fortnight later, in a howling blizzard, we returned to England via a Dutch steamer from Flushing to Folkestone. It was a dreadful, sleepless, storm-tossed crossing. But "the one and only Mrs. Surman" had our Oxford rooms in readiness and it was virtually a homecoming to see the "dreaming spires" again.

This wintry dip into Central Europe had been informative in many ways. It made me realize, far more so than on my earlier visit to the Ruhr, that the embittered German people could easily turn to some form of revengeful authoritarian rule. A large proportion of the students with whom I associated were outspoken admirers of Karl Liebknecht and Rosa Luxembourg, who had been executed after promoting the abortive Spartacist revolt of 1919. Under the crushing terms of the Treaty of Versailles unpopularity for any submissive German government was certain. To many the only way out seemed a close and defiant relationship with Soviet Russia, which was to be attempted by the Treaty of Rapallo in 1922. Inflation was clearly threatening the shaken stability of the Middle Class and anxiety was not abated by the ability of a few shrewd industrialists, such as Hugo Stinnes, to build constructively during the downhill slide. There was a growing animus against successful Jews, especially immigrants from devastated Poland, who were accused of getting far more than their share of governmental and professional jobs and were being indiscriminately labeled *Schieber*, or profiteers. The theater clearly revealed the temper of the times, with the *Revoluzion Drama* of Max Reinhardt packing people in for inciting productions like the famous *Danton*. No happy future was predicted by Maximilian Harden's brilliant little magazine—*Die Zukunft*.

On the other hand, we were greatly impressed by both the variety and undiminished cultural wealth of the German cities. We revelled in the opera, where excellent seats for sparkling performances could be obtained for less than a dollar at the constantly depreciating exchange rate. Majestic art galleries were equally a novel and fascinating experience, and even in extreme poverty there was cleanliness and dignity in all the homes to which we were invited. There was a touch of Muscovy in Berlin, apparent on a snowy night if one drove down the stark grandeur of Unter den Linden in a horse-drawn sleigh with jingling bells. Doing much traveling, I was struck by the wide differences among those whom I had been accustomed to lump together as Germans. I had noted the sharp contrast, drawn by Goethe, between the atmosphere of Frankfurt and that of Leipzig. From the *Buddenbrooks* of Thomas Mann, I had learned that Munich, a century later, was still regarded as a foreign city by the residents of northern Lübeck. Now I savored for myself such contrasts as that between massive Berlin and delicate Dresden. With regret I heard young people argue that this *Kleinstädterei*—provincialism—was a source of weakness and must give way to a greater unity and sense of purpose.

In my work with the students I had become aware of the efficient German system of *Arbeitsnachweise*, or Employment Exchanges, which sought, *inter alia*, to find even part-time and irregular work for undergraduates. This placement system was more developed than its English counterpart, which I had also examined superficially because of the deep concern about the severe unemployment in Britain and because of my own wartime connection with the problem. So, back at Oxford, I considered the desirability of studying this subject more deeply during the third year of residence allowed under the Rhodes Scholarships. It was already arranged that I would take my degree at the close of the second year, in June of 1921. Why not remain to write a thesis, with American implications, on "Unemployment Relief," continuing the part-time journalism which was working out so well?

Isabel was wholly in accord, which sharpened the issue but did not solve it. The locale for the contemplated research was obviously the London School of Economics, but the Rhodes Scholarships did not then envisage a beneficiary spending his third year away from Oxford. Mr. Wylie, father confessor as Oxford Secretary of the Rhodes Trust, was not optimistic about establishing such a precedent. He would arrange, however, to have me appear before the trustees to plead my own cause. On

134

this basis I applied for a fellowship advertised by the London School and simultaneously was accepted for an interview in London with the august Rhodes trustees, of whom I clearly recall impressive Lord Milner and keen-minded Sir Otto Beit. My case must have been well presented since permission to take the third year away from Oxford, now common practise, was graciously granted. To ice the cake the London School came through with a research grant of £175, renewable for another year, in behalf of the proposed study on "Unemployment Relief in Great Britain." Together with the £350 of the Rhodes Scholarship this made the projected year in London feasible, but also emphasized the desirability of a good grade in my upcoming final examinations.

Before that acid test, however, the six weeks Spring vacation intervened. I was anxious to visit Paris again, not merely to get up my French but also to examine the promise in the rise to power of Aristide Briand, who was endeavoring to lead his country toward a more cooperative relationship with its prostrate neighbor across the Rhine. Then the London *Nation* asked me to investigate *Le Malaise Alsacien*, which was adding a disturbing footnote to Daudet's francophile story of *La Dernière Classe*. Hamish Miles had volunteered to join me on this sidetrip, arriving in Paris shortly after us. Through the management of Madame Levy we had been lodged in the home of Madame Cuisinier, near the Bois de Vincennes, a section happily unknown to tourists, where nobody spoke English and where Isabel learned to bid *sans-à-tout* in amusing neighborhood bridge.

She stayed there happily while I went off with Hamish, the two of us carrying only knapsacks and stout walking sticks. We took train to Belfort and then trudged over the famous Ballon d'Alsace. Spring flowers were blossoming in the deserted trenches and amid tangles of rusted barbed wire. Thence slowly, with overnight stops in war-damaged Mulhouse and Colmar, to lovely Strasbourg, where we stayed several days. Here the tricolor waved again over the former Rathaus and French was back as the language of school instruction. In Paris the pre-war mourning on the statue of Strasbourg, in the Place de la Concorde, had been replaced by perpetual garlands. But the ordinary Alsatians, apart from their new French officials, seemed none too happy about their "liberation" from German rule and wished they could be left alone by both Paris and Berlin. If there had been real statesmanship after the war, I suggested in my article, Alsace, Lorraine and the rest of the Rhineland might have been reconstituted as Charlemagne's old "Middle Kingdom," a demilitarized but wholly independent buffer state between France and Prussia.

We met a very charming old lady who told us that while she had always lived in the same Strasbourg house, her first child there was born French; the third German. "I could never be certain about the second," she said, "because he was French at conception but German at birth." She poured tea for her visitors and then looked thoughtfully out at the nearby cathedral, whose non-political beauty soared above the intervening housetops. "My oldest son," she continued, "was conscripted here to help keep Strasbourg French. His two sons were conscripted, and one was killed, to help keep Strassburg German. Whoever wins, here we are always on the losing side."

"Does it make any difference to you, which flag flies over the city?" inquired Hamish.

"Very little. The taxes are higher under the French, but then it's easier to evade them than it was under the Germans. The chief difference is that now we have to leave out an "s" and insert an "o" in the name of what we would like to call our city. But the ironic little folksong puts an 'o' in the German version, quite amusingly."

"I don't know that song," I said.

"Why should you? But it's very popular here. It's called 'The Pitiless Captain' and tells our people—in countless verses—that it's their job to enlist and not to ask the captain—he could be French or German—for whom or what they're aligned. I'll sing you the opening verses and you'll see."

She did, and we did. And if the sweet old voice quavered a little, that was not unnatural.

O Strassburg, o Strassburg, du wunderschöne Stadt,
Darinnen liegt begraben so mannicher Soldat!

So mancher und schöner, auch tapferer Soldat,
Der Vater und lieb Mutter böslich verlassen hat.

136

Verlassen, verlassen, es kann nicht anders sein;
Zu Strassburg, ja zu Strassburg Soldaten müssen sein.

There could be no further procrastination, concerning the approaching final examinations, when we returned to Oxford toward the end of April, 1921. "Schools" were scheduled for the latter part of June and in those two months it would be futile to "swat up" on all the neglected minutiae. The alternative was to dig deep in some field where I was both well-informed and sure to be questioned, hoping this would suffice.

Such an area was the development of representative government and the effect of democratic belief on its evolution. Here was a subject to which I had already given much thought and certainly some of the questions, both written and oral, would give me opportunity to show this familiarity. I would be quizzed, in the sensible European fashion, not by professors with whom I had studied, but by a panel drawn from other universities. So it was futile to polish the apple for unknown examiners. On the other hand, the panel would assuredly contain some who would demand that I defend a positive position on a controversial issue, involving not merely history but also economics, politics, ethics and basic theories of law.

The issue most strongly to the fore in England that summer was the demand of Labour for "nationalization" of the coal mines. I thought that, as an American, I could derive credit for having applied myself thoroughly to this lively subject. Bob Smillie and others called it disgraceful that large landowners, by mere right of inheritance, should draw royalties on every ton of coal extracted from their property. Did I agree, and if not, why not? Even if this question were not actually asked, I would surely have opportunity to work it in. So, in the quiet of Norreys Avenue, I began by jotting down the latent secondary questions.

As a starter, was the advantage of the landowner different in principle from that which I derived by accepting payments from the estate of Cecil Rhodes? Would there be justifiable infringement of property rights if Parliament should adopt a law nationalizing the mines? Would it be appropriate for the miners' representatives in Parliament, subsidized by their Union, to vote on such special-interest legislation? Why had the Union, though strong on denunciation of the existing system, failed to

137

specify how the industry should be operated after governmental takeover? More broadly speaking, what is the difference between underlying Law, to which men appeal for Justice, and laws which are made by legislative authority in a fumbling quest for that objective? Asking myself these questions I was by no means sure that the miners had more than an emotional case.

But I knew that the issue was one on which I would have to come clean. And it was the sort of issue which I must learn to confront convincingly if my aim was to become a responsible editor. I also knew the writers, from Plato, through Locke and Hume, Rousseau, Hegel and Marx to Maitland, whom I should be able to cite or refute in confirmation of my viewpoint. So for two months I really buried myself in source books. And I was lucky, in that the hypothetical question was actually asked when the gruelling week of ten morning and afternoon tests came around. My accomplishment, I was eventually told, was "spotty"—meaning that there were areas in which my research was clearly fragmentary—but also "distinguished" in that I had outranked all other American Rhodes Scholars who had that year taken the same examination.

It was a difficult period, more so because just before these "Schools" Professor and Mrs. Morley had arrived in Oxford to visit their two sons in residence. But Frank took most of the load here and after the exams the five of us traveled to Exeter to enjoy a family reunion in that old cathedral town. With my sexagenarian father I had a memorable walking trip across Dartmoor while Isabel went off on her own to explore the Hardy country by bicycle. Then it was time to make another, pre-arranged, trip to Germany. By the middle of July we reached Berlin for our second working stay in the capital of the deeply disturbed Reich.

Because of beautiful weather, Berlin seemed much more attractive, in the summer of 1921, than had been the case the preceding winter. The lake-dotted countryside, around Potsdam, was available for sailing and canoeing. Duties, this time under the International Y.M.C.A., were more varied than had been the case with the Quaker Relief. With my now reasonable fluency in German I was assigned to conduct American visitors to places and people of interest. Those who came ranged right across the political spectrum and habitually each sought

138

evidence to support a preconceived opinion. Thus a party of Congressmen, taken to hear Foreign Minister Walther Rathenau speak at the ostentatious *Flieger Klub*, were satisfied that Germany was much more prosperous than the official asserted. An amusing assignment was to take William Z. Foster and Sidney Hillman, on their way to Russia, for an evening at Berlin's famous Luna Park. From the general poverty these visitors concluded that capitalism was dying in Germany, and to me it seemed that F.D.R.'s later confidant ("Clear it with Sidney") was as confirmed a Marxist as the American Communist leader. An ambitious expedition to Prague, with a party of clerics headed by Sherwood Eddy, concluded that the new Czechoslovak nation was in good hands because President Masaryk neither smoked nor drank. "I could never divide myself from any man upon the difference of an opinion," I quoted the *Religio Medici*, in my diary.

Isabel and I were fortunate in our housing. Because of shortage all Berliners with spare rooms were compelled either to rent them privately or to accept compulsory billeting. Through friendship with Sanford Griffith, the energetic correspondent of the New York *Herald*, we were assigned to the spacious apartment of Dr. Karl von Lewinski, a former judge then employed by the Foreign Office to prepare defense against the mountainous American claims for war damages. Later our involuntary host became German Consul General to the United States and close friendship was long maintained with the quiet, scholarly Prussian and his American-born wife. Von Lewinski was a mine of information on the tangled reparations issue and told of the pathetic efforts of the Socialist government to meet the required payments, including the requisitioning of old family silver, then sold to visitors for dollars or other hard currencies in antique shops. To any who looked beneath the surface, indeed to any who noted the steady deterioration of the mark, it was sadly evident that before long the hard-pressed Weimar Republic must face a financial crash.

A disturbing portent was the generally hopeless feeling of German youth, with whom I was again closely associated by my work. In the *Studentenhilfe*, under Christian auspices, this had a religious direction and at formal conferences and informal bull

139

sessions alike there was much rather metaphysical groping for authentic answers to *Die Suche der Zeit*. But it was not all pacific. In spite of *Nie wieder Krieg* posters there were many who argued that Germany must prepare to overthrow the "Diktat" of Versailles. On this both the embryonic Nazi movement and the better organized Communists agreed. Both extremes were also increasingly anti-Semitic, the Right because the Eastern Jews were held injurious to German racial purity, the Left because so many Jews were influential capitalists. Behind these tensions there was much sex perversion and escapist immorality. Without warning, I took my wife to a smart café famed as a homosexual center. But she was disgusted by the perfumed, long-haired boys who postured and ogled there in women's clothing.

It was, on the whole, a depressing atmosphere and, as Autumn approached, we were not unhappy to leave Berlin, in leisurely travel via Nuremburg, Frankfurt, Mainz, the Rhine, Cologne, Brussels and lovely Bruges back to London. There we arrived October 2, just in time for the opening of the School of Economics but with the difficult question of where to live equally immediate. The burden of this fell on Isabel, since I had forthwith to arrange my research program with Sir William Beveridge, director of the School. Also I had to edit three articles written on the German system of unemployment relief for the *Nation and Athenaeum*, to which I was now an almost regular contributor. With this status came an invitation to attend some of the famous "Nation lunches," under the adroit direction of editor Massingham. Of these it has been justly written that "all who took part will remember for the rest of their lives."

By comparison with Berlin, living costs in London were high and to find a nicely furnished flat within our means was far from easy. Total scholarship income worked out at ten guineas a week and the rental of agreeable lodgings seemed to start at half that amount. Finally Isabel uncovered a pleasant "maisonette" in Chelsea which could be obtained for £20 a month and, with some misgivings, we took it. Extra income would have to be raised but in London that should not be too difficult. Even a neat little housemaid was engaged, to come for three hours every morning at the standard wage of eightpence (then about 12

140

cents) per hour, plus breakfast. The accumulation of two years, mostly books, was shipped up from Oxford under the direction of Mrs. Surman, who made her first visit to London to see us settled at Paulton's Square.

This was near the King's Road corner of a row of smallish three-story dwellings, many divided for rental purposes into two separate flats sharing a common entrance. The ground floor and basement at No. 6 were occupied by an Italian music critic named Calvocoressi and we had the two upper stories, each containing two rooms. The former "drawing room," across the entire front of the second floor was spacious and well-furnished, with a view over the park-like, fence-surrounded square— except when blotted out by winter smog. Back of this room was a smaller one, converted into a kitchen and pantry—no refrigerator but a tiny gas stove and passable sink. The floor above this had a big front bedroom and another behind, used by me as a study but available for overnight visitors, of whom there were many. As I was soon to write my mother: "We are almost a hostel for penurious Rhodes Scholars."

Accommodations at No. 6 were weirdly completed by a bathroom improvised on the roof, having no windows and reached by a precipitous stairway from the upper hall. It had an old-fashioned flush toilet; a gas water heater that generally worked, and a skylight right over the bathtub, where it was pleasant to lie and watch the moon sailing like Mary Poppins over London. The design, of course without any central heating or telephone, merits description because typical of the "make-do" way the old houses of English cities were then being adjusted for economic change. Paulton's Square, at a guess, was laid out around 1800, as a residential area for comfortably situated members of the lower middle class. By 1921 it had become a distinctly Bohemian quarter, where atmosphere was often achieved with extraordinary architectural adaptations.

The neighborhood was delightful, more so because several Oxford friends were now established there. Hamish Miles, working on his novel *Oxford Circus*, had rooms in Cheyne Walk, almost next door to the carefully restored residence of Thomas Carlyle. On Cheyne Row, looking across the river to Battersea Park, was the big house where George Eliot died, and other

Victorian shrines were all around. A couple of American correspondents lived on nearby Beaumont Street and nearly every evening a congenial group would gather at the Good Intent restaurant on busy King's Road for dinner, since few householders had kitchens which would rise to more than the simplest culinary demands. Only a few blocks away was Sloan Square, where a stock company at the Court Theatre gave weekly changes of dramatic fare at very modest rates. That winter we greatly enjoyed a cycle of Galsworthy plays, popular for their emphasis on current social problems as well as from the influence of *The Forsyte Saga*, the first parts of which were then newly published. Signor Calvocoressi gave us more concert tickets than we could utilize, and on weekends there were often overnight visits to more distant friends or relatives. Altogether, Chelsea was an excellent base and the pile of notes for the study on "Unemployment Relief in Great Britain" grew steadily larger. There was no progress in the alleviation of the ailment itself. For months on end the Ministry of Labour reported mean unemployment among trade union members at 15 per cent or a fraction over. London was not the hardest hit and the rumblings of bitter resentment and discontent reverberated from every industrial center.

I spent many hours at various Employment Exchanges, or in the offices of higher officials trying to cope with the problem. But I also attended conferences and lectures at the School of Economics, in Aldwych, which had a very sociable and stimulating faculty. Harold Laski was not less interesting because of his provocative Marxist slant. R. H. Tawney, famous for his study of *The Acquisitive Society*, spoke as beautifully as he wrote. Hugh Dalton, later to become Labour's Chancellor of the Exchequer, gave a good course on general economic theory. On the whole the faculty, headed by Beveridge, buttressed by Sidney and Beatrice Webb, had a strong socialist tinge, with exceptions such as Edwin Cannan, the monetary expert who was my supervisor and with whom I discussed almost every economic subject except unemployment relief. A particularly gracious lecturer was Graham Wallas, who never lacked an enthusiastic audience. At his opening presentation, that year, two American girls, equipped with handsome new notebooks, came early to get seats at the professor's feet and, as he developed his theme, labored as they had learned back home to get every point on record. Soon Graham Wallas paused and peered down at them over his spectacles. "My dear young ladies," he said, "may I ask what you are so busily writing in those books?"

"We're taking notes on your lecture, sir," murmured one of the disconcerted girls.

"I would much rather you didn't," chided the old gentleman. "I would like to think that if I say anything worthy of your attention you will remember it. And if I talk nonsense, which is by no means impossible, I would not like to have you in position to quote it against me."

The two put their notebooks away for good. They were Eleanor Dulles, younger sister of John Foster and Allen W. Dulles, and Emily Huntington, of that well-known California family. I enjoyed telling the story but in due course they had the last laugh. I took them to the famous Derby, on Epsom Downs, and went to place their one-pound bets with an agreeable bookie. Both Emily and "Dooles" had selected a rank outsider, called Corncrake, because they thought his name "so pathetic." It will be a pleasant surprise for them, I thought, if I throw away only ten shillings of each bet on Corncrake and put the other ten on the favorite, so that very possibly they'll lose nothing. This, in a masterful way, I did. Whereupon Corncrake romped home first, against odds of some 30 to 1. While the bookie paid up I had not the wherewithal to do so in full. It was a painful lesson on the deference due to feminine intuition, not less so because the girls firmly refused to accept my I.O.U.

Happily, Isabel had not been present to witness this humiliation. At the beginning of 1922 she had taken a job in the London office of the U.S. Shipping Board. Classified information had somehow been leaking to British competitors. So it was decided to replace all the English stenographers, who were paid three guineas a week, with American girls at something over thrice that amount. A friend brought word of this and Isabel, on the scene, secured one of the plums. The supplement put us on Easy Street for the remainder of our stay, relieving me from pressures of free-lance journalism.

Of one coup, however, I was proud. In Berlin, the previous

summer, I had made the acquaintance of Walther Rathenau, the Jewish Foreign Minister whom I have called "the most brilliant statesman I ever met." Rathenau was indeed an extraordinary man, whose book on *Von kommenden Dingen*, if heeded, might well have saved mankind much anguish. His engineer father had organized the great German electrical combine, A.E.G., of which Walther became president in 1915. Made wartime Economic Director for all German production, this industrial genius devised the arrangements whereby Germany so long withstood the Allied blockade. After the defeat he was made Minister of Reconstruction for the new Republic, an appointment changed to that of Foreign Minister when it became plain that Germany could not recover without some reasonable settlement of the reparations issue. As a step to this end Rathenau devised the Treaty of Rapallo by which, on April 18, 1922, Germany and Soviet Russia agreed to mutual renunciation of reparations and the resumption of even-handed diplomatic and economic relations. Presumably it was to inform the British Government of this project, certain to infuriate the French, that the Foreign Minister visited London in early December of 1921. I could guess that something big was in the wind and through a friend in the German Embassy a private talk with Rathenau was arranged. While of course guarded, he revealed enough to give me an excellent story. It was too hot to send to the United States by mail, so I sold it to the London bureau of the New York *World*, for ten pounds.

Acquaintance with this great German Jew meant far more to me than that acceptable check. From Rathenau's prescient book, translated as "In Days to Come," and from his conversation I received the inspiration of an extraordinarily lucid, objective and humanitarian mind. There was opportunity as well as tragedy in the international chaos left by the war, and the former should be emphasized. Rathenau feared State Socialism, in which militarism would become dominant and which would always deceive the public by specious promises of reforms which would never, in practise, be effectively achieved. He was equally critical of unbridled Free Enterprise, asserting that it would not only subordinate men to machines but would in time saturate cities with poisonous industrial waste. Capitalism, he thought, should be controlled not by venal politicians or dictatorial labor unions, but by better industrial organization in which workers and management would plan together with public representatives in a *Mitbestimmung* of mutual interest. Perhaps unrealistically, Rathenau hoped for an industrial aristocracy, with an elite leadership dedicated to the general welfare rather than to profits, restraining itself through cooperative organization of producers and consumers, without the incubus of bureaucratic prohibitions. After the Second War much of Rathenau's philosophy was adopted in Western Germany. But during his lifetime this brilliant man was anathema both to the Marxists and to the proto-Nazis who were already girding for their struggle to take over. In June of 1922, when Rathenau was assassinated in Berlin by anti-Semitic thugs, I could see the darkness closing in over stricken Europe. It was a factor of importance in my decision to come home.

There were attractive alternatives. The research fellowship at the London School of Economics ran for another year and the work there was going well. My thesis was far advanced and I was told that its inclusion as one of the School's respected "Monograph Series" was assured. A chapter had been accepted by John Maynard Keynes for publication in the *Economic Journal* on the strength of which, and other articles, I was later elected a member of the Royal Economic Society. I need only attend a couple more courses and pass an oral examination to secure the degree of D.Sc. (Econ.), and with Isabel's job and continued free-lancing, this looked feasible. My background in history and political science, my facility in German and French, would have helped to make me a better economist, and I seriously considered university teaching.

A good position was offered me by the International Labour Office, at Geneva. This was engineered by my Oxford friend, David Blelloch, who had joined the League of Nations Secretariat a year earlier and had there promoted me as a desirable recruit. The project was appealing, not only for good salary, pension and fringe benefits, but also because life in Switzerland, which we had missed because of adverse exchange rates, was

145

alluring to both Isabel and me. Another opening was a press association post in Berlin, but that did not seem to offer much security.

This was an important factor because of Isabel's newly-discovered pregnancy, with consequent loss of earning power which would have made another year in London financially precarious. Such would not be the case in Geneva, where seven years later Isabel would give birth to another baby. Sitting before our coal fire, we discussed the problem from all angles. But ever present in my mind was a deep disposition toward journalism. Neither teaching nor the international bureaucracy of the League of Nations, had an equivalent appeal.

At this juncture, destiny again stepped in to shape my ends. In John Haslup Adams the Baltimore *Sun* had an editor of great ability, a liberal crusader of the old school to whom the quest for justice was the primary function of a newspaper. He had been instrumental in bringing the Democratic Convention to Baltimore in 1912 and in securing Woodrow Wilson's nomination there. Though a modest and self-effacing man the name of Adams was therefore known to me. But I had not considered the *Sun* as an outlet because of its lack of interest in the international scene. Moreover, "Hass" Adams had earlier been overshadowed by Charles H. Grasty, publisher of the paper. Though the latter had retired at the time of the Versailles Treaty, the *Sun* had headlined his opinion of it as "a good treaty, a common-sense treaty." Such intellectual myopia seemed to me evidence of a setting and not a rising luminary.

But when President Harding convened the Naval Disarmament Conference in Washington, in December, 1921, editor Adams came into his own. "He felt that if the paper undertook to report it in a manner and on a scale hitherto never attempted by an American newspaper, it would make a marked gain in prestige and influence."[5] With this in mind Mr. Adams had the previous summer visited England with Paul Patterson, then the energetic publisher, to line up special correspondents and to arrange a hookup with the famous Manchester *Guardian*.

---

5. *The Sunpapers of Baltimore, 1837–1937*, Gerald W. Johnson et al., New York, Alfred A. Knopf, 1937, p. 407.

146

Several of those so approached—H. W. Massingham, H. W. Nevinson and H. N. Brailsford—were my personal friends. On a trip to Manchester, in connection with the unemployment study, I lunched with C. P. Scott, the renowned editor of the *Guardian*, who called the *Sun* "a good bet." So, in April, I wrote a letter of inquiry to Mr. Adams, suggesting my availability. The reply was cordial and asked me to confer with Frank R. Kent, a kingpin in the organization who with his wife Elizabeth was then in London. I telephoned and was invited to bring Isabel to their hotel for dinner. An enjoyable evening terminated with an offer to join the staff as an editorial writer "as soon as possible," at a starting salary of $3,600 per annum.

This financially was about the same as the Geneva opening. But Baltimore was home and close to Isabel's people in Washington. So in spite of poignant regret at leaving Europe, I accepted the offer toward the end of May. "As soon as possible," however, was not immediate. At the Shipping Board Isabel had recently been promoted and felt that she must give a full month's notice. I still had some gaps to fill in my research and also wanted to have another look at Germany, where the fiscal and monetary situation was daily worsening. I had selected Baden, an agricultural state hitherto unvisited, as objective and had already arranged a walking trip in the Black Forest with a close Oxford friend, Dan Brundrit.

Leaving Isabel comfortably located in Paris, in mid-July, we proceeded to Freiburg, where I had a letter of introduction to Professor G. von Schulze-Gaevernitz, a well-known political scientist who, as a member of the Reichstag, had courageously opposed the war. We found the Herr Doktor explaining to his doubtful wife that the oriental rug which had just been delivered was not an extravagance but a calculated hedge against inflation. This, after the assassination of Rathenau, was rapidly getting beyond control. Illustrations were all around. Before our climb over the Feldberg I priced Zeiss binoculars. An excellent pair was offered for 2,000 Marks, or $20.00. Penury made me delay the purchase until return from four days of outing, when the shopkeeper regretfully said that the falling exchange had forced a price increase to 3,000 Marks. In the meantime, however, the value of the dollar had jumped from 100 to 200 Marks, so that the 50% increase asked by the German seller nevertheless meant a 25% saving for the American customer. Here was an object lesson in the utter confusion caused by the currency debacle, destined to become intolerable in the months ahead.

It was time to be heading home, where at least one could talk—however vainly—of a "return to normalcy." There was a round of farewell visits and a great packing of accumulated treasures, over 300 books alone after discarding all that could be spared. Again kind-hearted Mrs. Surman came up from Oxford to assist. On August 10 we sailed from Tilbury, appropriately on the *President Adams*, with London friends on hand for a gala send-off. It would be six years before we would tread European soil again.

◀Chapter 4
By Professional Maturity

The Baltimore *Sun* was a newspaper with both character and promise when I joined its staff, as an editorial writer, in August, 1922. In John Haslup Adams, the editor, I had a chief with broad experience and, more to the point, a deeply humanitarian outlook with which I instinctively sympathized. "Mr. Adams," wrote an old associate at the time of his death, "saw a great modern newspaper as largely, if not mainly, an engine for rectifying injustice." Moreover, he "never made a visible compromise with his own matured convictions. . . . He could imagine getting beaten for an idea, and even getting beaten by it, but he was quite unable to imagine running away from it." Outwardly frail, inwardly of finely-tempered steel, this soft-spoken leader directed me skillfully, giving me freedom in my writing while teaching the flexibility necessary for a successful team operation.

It was a complicated organization since the two "Sunpapers," morning and evening, had no individual publisher, being properties of the A. S. Abell Company, some of its stock held by inactive descendants of the original founders. The Board of Directors was under the chairmanship of Van Lear Black, with other prominent Baltimoreans as his colleagues. Responsible to them was the president of the company, in 1922 Paul Patterson, who previously had been business manager. With notable abil-

149

ity Black and Patterson had together steered the enterprise out of financial difficulties, placing it in a position where the directors could adopt a somewhat pompous resolution authorizing "the improvement of all three editions of the *Sun* [morning, evening and Sunday] from the editorial standpoint."[1] An immediate result of this decision was the exclusive foreign correspondence launched under Mr. Adams' direction during the Naval Disarmament Conference, which had concluded its work in Washington early in February, 1922.

Mr. Adams, though his mind was luminous, was seriously crippled by degenerative arthritis, forcing him to use crutches and do much of his direction by telephone from home. So the handling of these contributed articles, displayed on the page opposite the editorials, soon devolved upon me. Here was a borderland between the areas of editorial comment and news presentation, helping the new recruit to familiarize himself with both aspects of the overall operation. Thus I escaped the departmentalization which has helped to make newspaper editorials timid and inconclusive, while simultaneously letting news accounts become opinionated and tendentious. From my intimate knowledge of the European scene I thought that some of this special correspondence was biased. I felt this particularly in the case of André Geraud who, under the pen name of Pertinax, faithfully supported the official French position at the expense of easily defamable Germany. When I complained to "Hass" Adams about this he gently observed that editors themselves are not immune from bias. "And in any case where you think a correspondent is unfair, you are at liberty to set him straight in an editorial, provided you can do so fairly and effectively."

Other members of the *Sun* staff were, in their several ways, equally impressive. Frank R. Kent, who had hired me in London, was now relieved of administrative duties to concentrate on his sparkling column entitled "The Great Game of Politics." In the *Evening Sun* Henry L. Mencken poured out the smoothly acidulous commentary which delighted and enraged his readers

---

1. Gerald W. Johnson et al, *op. cit.,* p. 406.

in about equal numbers. Hamilton Owens, the debonair and charming editor of the junior paper, had been with George Creel's organization during the war and now followed joyfully, if not always impressively, in the Mencken wake. Hendrik van Loon, who contributed a novel column of his own, and Edmund Duffy, the very talented cartoonist, made delightful luncheon companions. Old Folger McKinsey, "the Bentztown Bard," had been with the paper longer than Mencken and churned out "Bright Good Morning" verses as a polarized opposite to the caustic comment of that iconoclastic colleague. The crowded offices, at Baltimore and Charles Streets, were indeed a stable of original characters, perhaps too diverse and individualistic for permanent success in the face of increasing journalistic standardization. Unregimented myself, I found it a very pleasant milieu.

Much latitude was allowed. Nobody was pigeon-holed. Stanley Reynolds, the able managing editor of the morning paper, recognized me as a good reporter. So I was "borrowed" from Mr. Adams for assignments that seemed to fit my experience. With a serious coal strike looming, I was dispatched to Indianapolis to get the labor side of the dispute from John L. Lewis, then recently become president of the United Mine Workers. An evening with John L. proved to be the beginning of a lifelong friendship. Impressive to me was the plan whereby the miners' demands were made in the form of royalties on coal actually mined, so that increased remuneration was linked with increased productivity. Emphasis on labor-saving machinery, to increase output per man-hour, was also a healthy contrast to the "feather-bedding" indorsed by a large proportion of union leadership. I knew that among the A. S. Abell Company directors were some with personal interest in coal mining, from the side of ownership, and wondered whether my sympathetic report on U.M.W. strategy would appear as telegraphed. Not a word was changed. What I did not then anticipate was the rapid deterioration of this union when the powerful direction of John L. was withdrawn.

I was encouraged to write signed feature articles, such as a series on "How the British Choose Their Parliament," whenever these would be timely. And Hamilton Owens soon

151

enlisted me as a regular reviewer for the Book Page carried by the *Evening Sun*. One June day in 1923 a small volume entitled *Germany's Capacity to Pay* was placed on my desk, "As of possible interest." It was largely the work of Dr. Harold G. Moulton, a well-known economist who had left the University of Chicago to become director of an independent and prestigious institute of economics in Washington. This would soon be combined with its sister Institute for Government Research to form the Brookings Institution, which would later play a large role in my life. But this also I did not foresee as I scanned the little book, very newsworthy at a time when inflation had made German currency worthless and when French troops had occupied the Ruhr in a vain effort to coerce the stubborn German miners into digging coal for reparations.

As I read Dr. Moulton's study, at home that evening, I was deeply impressed. Here in wholly dispassionate language, backed by unquestionable statistics, was objective confirmation of everything on the subject told me by Rathenau and von Lewinski in Berlin; by Keynes and Laski in London; by many others including French economists who were not blinded by the vindictive policies of their government. Either the sadistically punitive terms of the Treaty of Versailles, or the fantastic reparations claims on Germany, must be severely modified. This book showed why. It was the complete answer to the popular fallacy that: "If the Germans would quit whining and get to work there'd be no trouble."

The Moulton book, as must be the case with anything written on international payments, concentrated on the transfer problem. It is no solution for the debtor nation to raise the money demanded in its own currency. Germany could, and perforce did, quickly print many times the 132 billion marks claimed by the Reparations Commission. But the Allied demand was for gold marks and Germany had virtually no gold with which to support its paper. How, then, convert German assets into something valuable to the creditors? To a small extent this could be accomplished by taking reparations "in kind"—coal, timber, machinery, rolling stock, ships and other tangible assets. But confiscation of this sort could only amount to a tiny fraction of the sums claimed and even so was injurious to German productive capacity. Exports, bought with foreign currencies, could theoretically produce acceptable cash, but Allied business interests quickly protested such German "dumping." Up to a point German dollar bonds might be issued to pay reparations, but in the event of default this would merely mean that the foreign purchasers would suffer.

I turned the argument here summarized into a book review and the next morning phoned Dr. Moulton to ask for an interview. It was important to emphasize the economist's belief that the runaway inflation in Germany had been forced by Allied pressures on its feeble government. I wanted development of Dr. Moulton's assertion that: "Paper-currency inflation once fully under way cannot be checked," since this would be as true for the United States as for any other country. Also, having sampled extremist sentiment in Germany, I wanted to convey the warning that with uncontrolled inflation a substantial proportion of the population affected "writhes in desperation and wishes to destroy in blind fury whatever is left of a government and a society that permits such conditions."[2] It was, of course, on that state of mind that Hitler came to power.

I got the interview, which was featured and played its small part in the turn toward a more reasonable reparations approach, first in the Dawes and then in the Young Plan. Dr. Moulton also outlined his coming publications schedule, showing that the problems of the British, French and Italian war debts to the U.S. were essentially similar to those of German reparations. He agreed, though not for quotation, that the sensible procedure would be to cancel them all, as Rathenau and Trotsky had arranged for the German and Russian claims against each other. At luncheon I met W. F. Willoughby, director of the sister Institute for Government Research, who congratulated me on being "an old-fashioned political economist," placing as much emphasis on the adjective as on the noun. As this was my objective I was pleased when, years later, I was invited to preside at a joint meeting of the wholly distinct American Economic and Political Science Associations. There was healthy deflation on

---

2. *Germany's Capacity To Pay*, Harold G. Moulton and Constantine E. Maguire, McGraw-Hill Book Co., New York, 1923, pp. 217–18.

learning that each had approved me on the assumption that my specialty was in the other field.

What was not deflating was a letter from Dr. Moulton, a few days after my visit, offering me appointment as Public Relations Counsellor for both Institutes, at a salary above what I was getting. This was a hard choice, for I liked the glamor of Washington, had many good friends there, admired what the Institutes were doing and could see that wider dissemination of their products would be a worthwhile undertaking. But I had been with the *Sun* less than a year, was enjoying my work and had no disposition to abandon the newspaper business. I could give Moulton quite a little publicity help, I wrote him, without going on his payroll.

Indeed Isabel and I had by this time fitted pleasantly into the Baltimore scene. We had rented and sparsely furnished a two bedroom apartment in the Windsor Hills section, with good streetcar connections and a balcony giving a view over the beautiful Gwynn's Falls valley. On February 8, 1923, our first child, a daughter, was born, before which event we had moved temporariiy to my parents on Park Avenue, only a few blocks from where the Women's Hospital then stood. We had wisely engaged my old schoolmate, Lawson Wilkins, then a practising pediatrician, to care for baby Lorna and I had renewed contact with Francis Davis, Gideon Stieff, "Ferdy" Turnbull and other boyhood friends. New ones had been made in the neighborhood, where there were several young mothers who remained intimates into grandmotherhood and beyond.

I was busy not only on the *Sun*, every day except my Thursday off, but also in completing my thesis on *Unemployment Relief in Great Britain*, which was unfinished when we left London. This necessitated correspondence with my English sources. When all was in order I submitted the manuscript for the annual Hart, Schaffner and Marx Economic Essay Prize and was agreeably surprised to be awarded second place for the year 1924. The book was published by Houghton Mifflin and simultaneously in London as one of the School of Economics series, establishing me as a recognized authority in its limited field, where the royalties received were far from overwhelming. From Dr. Moulton it brought high praise and a renewal of the job offer,

154

with assurance of opportunity for further economic research. But I stayed with Mr. Adams, for whom I was now a right-hand man. Brother Frank, entering the publishing business in London, had already appeared in cloth covers with his *Travels in East Anglia*, foreshadowing his unusual gift for gracefully combining geographical, historical and literary allusion. Brother Chris had meanwhile established himself in the upper fringe of personal journalism, with his "Bowling Green" column in the New York *Evening Post*. By this time he had authored a dozen volumes of pleasant verse, whimsical essays and agreeable novels. Compared with the work of either brother, *Unemployment Relief In Great Britain* was dry and uninspiring, yet not without admirers for its painstaking and, to some extent, original analysis. The roads of destiny, followed each to his own taste by the Morley brothers, had diverged to open very different landscapes.

Baltimore had a distinct appeal for me. The city has always maintained a fair share of highly individualistic characters who, for that very reason, prefer to remain outside the rather self-conscious circle of Baltimore "Society." Of such was Elisabeth Gilman, elderly maiden daughter of the first president of Johns Hopkins, who in the early twenties was perennial Socialist candidate for Mayor of Baltimore, on a platform of urban renewal and family welfare closely resembling that espoused by President Nixon half a century later. "Lizzie" Gilman lived in some state in the former residence of her father, at 513 Park Avenue, and there entertained all sorts of odd-balls. On Sundays, when the dreary downtown streets most sharply revealed their drabness, it was a memorable pleasure to attend the always stimulating, and delicious, lunches *chez* Miss Gilman.

Another older friend was Dr. John Jacob Abel, professor of Pharmacology at the Hopkins Medical School, who lived in an old farm house in what was then the open country just west of Windsor Hills. This brilliant scientist, who had much to do with the development of adrenalin and insulin, accomplished his research in an impoverished, rat-infested laboratory, with scorn and mistrust for all who favored governmental intervention in his or any other field. A venerable relic of a vanishing Americanism, Dr. Abel first introduced me to the short-lived

155

Freeman weekly and the lucid thinking of its editor, Albert J. Nock. Equally different from the individualistic professor, and from socialistic Lizzie Gilman, was suave Theodore Marburg, formerly our Minister to Belgium, a staunch Wilsonian and advocate of the League of Nations, who often invited me to his luxurious apartment on Mount Vernon Place.

Though Baltimore could not be called a literary center it then had many residents, aside from Mencken and F. Scott Fitzgerald, who were bibliophiles and modestly creative writers. Of such was the teacher–poet, Lizette Woodworth Reese. Another great woman teacher, Edith Hamilton, had just begun her literary career. Sidney Nyburg, an aristocratic Jewish lawyer, loved to uncover sentimental romances in what he called "the mist-enshrouded fields" of the city's early days. Pleasantly provocative was my Rhodes Scholar predecessor Emory H. Niles, always critical of the thesis that the future of Germany could be of any great concern to the United States. The talented architect Harry Scarff, who would later design homes for both, would listen with tolerant amusement to hot arguments on this issue. The Teutonic side was fortified when the psychiatrist Fredric Wertham, already an authority on the phenomenon of social violence, came from Munich to the Phipps Clinic, permitting acquaintance begun in Germany to ripen. About this time I obtained a position on the *Sun* for my cherished Philadelphia friend, Jo' Lalley, leading to companionable explorations of the inexhaustible Chesapeake. The scope of these widened when we bought our first automobile, in time to take Isabel to the Women's Hospital for the birth of our second daughter, Christina, October 3, 1924. An always enjoyable family trip was to visit Hulbert and Gladys Footner at their historic home "Charlesgift," on the Patuxent River near Solomon's Island.

Our many friends, not lack of alternative openings, held us to Baltimore. Overtures came from out-of-town newspapers and when Major Enoch B. Garey took over as the dynamic, if inexperienced, president of St. John's College, I was urged to join the faculty of that mellow but storm-ridden Annapolis institution. With my book finished, and wishing to try my hand at teaching, I agreed to conduct a seminar for seniors, on "Current Political

Problems," during the academic year 1924–25, sacrificing my day off to this purpose. My technique was to work back from the morning headlines, say some extravaganza of Mussolini's Fascists, to the formative era which, in this case, preceded the consolidations of Cavour and Garibaldi. The students, as ignorant of history as most American youth, responded actively. And the experience confirmed my conviction that some academic instruction could helpfully be more journalistic; some journalism reasonably more academic.

All this, and other amenities and friends, made life in Baltimore pleasant, wholly aside from the interest of work sufficiently remunerated for us to buy a small, and overpriced, bungalow in modest Windsor Hills. Yet I felt dissatisfied. Slice it how you would, Baltimore remained a provincial town, with babies, bridge and banalities an uninspiring trinity of adulation. Moreover, the miasma of the dissolute Harding Administration hung heavily over the country and the promise of the Naval Disarmament Conference faded with revelation of degrading scandals in and around the White House. The abomination of unenforceable prohibition was a clearly corrupting influence, with the fumes from bathtub gin obscuring the grievous situation in Europe. There, as I saw it, the seeds of another war were already sprouting. When President Harding died suddenly in San Francisco on August 2, 1923, the morbid hysteria surrounding his funeral train filled me with a deep disgust. I had been reading Gibbon and saw all too much resemblance to the shallow emotionalism of the plebs over the passing of an unworthy Caesar. I found myself longing for the less befogged intellectual atmosphere of England. Isabel, never a mere housewife, felt much the same.

A way out of this web seemed to be at hand. In November, 1924, after much preliminary consideration, the *Sun* opened a London Bureau. I had been told of this plan before joining the paper and had the impression, though there was no solid evidence, that I might look forward to this assignment, for which I seemed to myself to have superior qualifications. The first representative chosen, however, was John W. Owens, the paper's chief political reporter, who was ten years senior to me. Then, in

157

the Fall of 1925, I learned that Fred Essary, head of the Washington Bureau, would succeed Owens, and was aggrieved at being passed over a second time.

I went to Mr. Adams and asked him bluntly whether my hopes for getting the London assignment were vain, and if so why. I had earlier told him of refusing Dr. Moulton's offer of work in Washington but that opening, I said, was still available and if I were not making good on the *Sun* perhaps it should be reconsidered. Having two small children I should not be content with a dead-end job.

Mr. Adams was always gentle and took no umbrage at my plain speaking. He told me to sit down, then quietly filled and lit his pipe before saying anything more. In his experience, he then observed, most newspapermen achieve what they deserve, even though reward may come more slowly than desired. He would do nothing to dissuade me from the position in Washington, if that appealed to me. On the other hand he could assure me that my work on the *Sun* was appreciated and he sympathized with my wish to use my experience constructively. He did not see, however, why I thought correspondence from London more important than editorials written in Baltimore. If the former were good reporting it would not be opinionated and if the editorials were well done they would be convincing. This would be the more true as the influence of the paper gained from careful teamwork, the importance of which I had perhaps inadequately considered. I would admit that I had been given much latitude to express opinions on the editorial page and he was sorry if I felt dissatisfied. As a matter of fact the high command of the paper had recently made certain plans for me. If I would now see Mr. Patterson they would be disclosed.

Somewhat abashed I proceeded to the president's office. Paul Patterson was a very direct man and spoke without circumlocution. "We don't plan to send you to London," he said, "because we think it important for other members of the staff to get the experience there that you have already had. But we would like to send you to China. Can you go?"

"To China!" I gasped. "But I know next to nothing about China!"

"That's one reason why we're choosing you," he smiled.

158

"You'll have a fresh and unprejudiced approach, which wouldn't be the case in London. We want you to visit Japan and the Philippines also—perhaps six months away all told. Talk it over with your wife and then tell me your decision."

Before I got back to my desk I had decided not to miss this opportunity.

◀It was appropriate that the *Sun* should have decided to send a reporter to China toward the end of 1925. That year had seen developments there which no newspaper with an international reputation could neglect.

The first significant event, in the rapidly gathering storm, was the death of Dr. Sun Yat-sen on March 12, 1925. This remarkable man had been a leading figure in the overthrow of the Manchu Dynasty in 1911; had organized the Kuomintang, or "National People's Party," to replace the corrupt and incompetent monarchy, and had then served as provisional President of the new republic. As long as he lived there was some coherence and restraint in the forces working to modernize China. With Dr. Sun's death, the native resistance to foreign impositions grew more embittered, while simultaneously internal dissension made the orderly removal of these restrictions more difficult.

The "Shanghai shootings" of May 30 revealed the ugly tension that was shaping. On that day a big crowd of Chinese, under radical student leadership, had gathered in the International Settlement to protest the killing of a workman by a Japanese overseer during a strike in one of the many Japanese textile mills in that busy Treaty Port. The mob, getting out of hand, attempted to storm the police station in the heart of the foreign concession. The British officer in charge ordered his Sikh policemen to fire and seven demonstrators were killed. Immediately, a quarter million native workers of every variety went out on a spontaneous general strike, and sympathetic anti-foreign protests were staged all over China. In Hankow there were eight more Chinese deaths when naval forces were landed from gunboats to safeguard the British, American and

159

Japanese banks. In Canton, on June 23, came the most terrible of the many incidents. There the foreign concession occupied the river island of Shameen. It was protected by British and French marines who killed and wounded 169 Chinese when a mass attack on the island seemed to be developing. This "massacre" led to an immediate strangulating boycott of the nearby British colony of Hongkong.

These sorry episodes were exacerbated by inaction on the Nine Power Treaty, adopted by the Washington Naval Conference of 1921 to maintain "the sovereignty and territorial integrity of China," both of which continued to be glaringly infringed by several of the signatory powers. This Treaty, largely the achievement of Elihu Root, had been blocked by France, which refused ratification in order to bring pressure for American modification of the wholly irrelevant U.S. position on war debts. But conferences on curtailing the foreign extraterritorial rights in China, and on giving that country power to establish its own tariff policy, had been scheduled in Peking, and it was planned that I should report on these. There were startling consequences from the existing provision that China must not levy more than a five per cent ad valorem duty on any of its imports. For instance, I could buy a 15 cent package of American cigarettes in any treaty port for 11 cents, since the Chinese government was not allowed to place a duty on them even as large as the internal revenue tax imposed by my own government. The price of these same cigarettes in Japan, which had long since broken such foreign restrictions, was the equivalent of 30 cents.

There was, however, another side to the picture. In 1925, anarchic conditions prevailed in China and there was no central government competent to implement its side of any rectifying agreements with foreign powers. The huge land area was split up by rival "Tuchuns," or warlords. Each levied his own taxes and aspired to national supremacy, but none of them could effect the lasting combinations necessary for unification. Nor was there much likelihood that any would do so, since when the Japanese favored one aspirant the Russians would quickly find means to strengthen his chief rival and vice versa. On this kaleidoscopic scene I was also expected to report.

In spite of my protestation to Paul Patterson, I was not

wholly ignorant of the tangled situation. As far back as college days I had learned, from my Japanese and Chinese classmates, something of the sharply differing viewpoints of these two peoples. I knew that Japan had entered the European war primarily to seize the German properties in the Pacific and that China had also become a nominal belligerent, in alliance with the United States, in the hope that control of the strategic Shantung Peninsula would not be taken from Germany by Japan, but would instead revert to China. I had witnessed the failure of the Wilson Administration to check Japanese aggrandizement, culminating in the Lansing-Ishii Agreement of November, 1917, which announced that:

The governments of the United States and Japan recognize that territorial propinquity creates special relations between countries, and consequently the Government of the United States recognizes that Japan has special interests in China, particularly in the part [Manchuria] to which her possessions are contiguous.

This concession had made the Japanese friendly toward the United States, while they had become suspicious of Great Britain because of that nation's abrogation of the Anglo-Japanese Alliance. One result was that the Far Eastern policies of Britain and the United States were not aligned. In London I had noted the criticism that Americans took every advantage of extraterritorial rights in China, but disclaimed any responsibility for exacting these deeply resented privileges. On the *Sun* I had written editorials, reasonably well-informed, on the Asiatic upheavals which were increasingly getting front-page headlines. But this was far from making me an authority who could transmit the objective, accurate, comprehensive yet interesting correspondence that was desired.

Nor was there time to remedy deficiency in the fortnight allowed before deparure for the Orient. It was, in the first place, a very serious matter to leave Isabel and our two small daughters, aged three and one, for so long and potentially dangerous an absence. This was emphasized when I could find no major insurance company willing to write a term policy to add to my small coverage. But I knew this was an opportunity to be seized and was confident of my ability to research both quickly and thoroughly in political and economic subjects. Isabel

161

courageously made light of all my doubts and the *Sun* was generous about travel and monetary arrangements. So I took advice at the Department of State, got credentials and letters of introduction, and gathered a few especially recommended books and documents. Just before Thanksgiving, on the afternoon of Sunday, November 22, I left Baltimore on the first leg of this long journey.

It may sound ridiculous, but it took 17 days, by what was then the fastest transportation, to get from Baltimore to Tokyo in 1925. To spend even that many hours on the journey would now be considered wasteful. But I gained by the slow transit. All the country west of Chicago was new to me and I learned much as the train rolled slowly across the sparsely populated plains of Minnesota, North Dakota and Montana, thence to climb laboriously through range upon range of snow-covered mountains. My fellow passengers, I wrote, "are for the most part important farmers and ranchers, returning from business trips to Chicago or the Twin Cities." They are "taller, more square-shouldered, lean-jawed and clear-eyed" than Easterners. But Sinclair Lewis is justified in denying them a sense of humor. "Not far from Sauk Center, where the trainboy makes a gallant effort to dispose of copies of *Arrowsmith*, is a little place called Monticello, in a plain as flat as a tabletop."

As the short November days closed in, I turned from consideration of the American West to study my background books on China and Japan. For the latter, Lafcadio Hearn was one of the authors, but I did not expect to find much of the idyllic aspect emphasized by this romantic a generation earlier. A Japanese newspaper correspondent, Kyoshi K. Kawakami, had warned me in Washington that Japan now considered itself, and intended to be considered as, a Great Power and that I would find more machine guns than cherry blossoms in the penetration of China now actively under way. To the historical background of this process I addressed myself as seriously as any graduate student. I was no longer an ignoramus when, on Thanksgiving evening, I left the Oriental Limited at Everett, just north of Seattle. Thence I made connection to Vancouver, reached just three days after leaving Chicago. "I had no idea," I wrote, "that it could be done so comfortably and quickly."

162

In Vancouver, then a small but bustling city of mingled British and American characteristics—and therefore typically Canadian—there was a day of leisure before my steamer sailed. I wrote home and mailed back the books studied on the train. Equipped with only two suitcases, one of which carried my portable Corona, there was no superfluous space, less so because all had told me to take evening clothes and nobody had thought up drip-dry. Having some spare hours I decided it would make a good impression to send the *Sun* an article on the Vancouver system of liquor control, to obtain which I visited the offices of the *Daily Province*, chatted with a helmeted "Bobby" on his beat, drank a few beers in as many legalized "beer parlors" and checked other information against the waitresses there. It made an interesting story for prohibition-ridden Baltimore, but midnight struck before it was typed and mailed.

Next day, November 28, the *Empress of Canada* sailed at noon, myself in occupancy of a sumptuous private stateroom, served by an attentive Chinese steward. Indeed the entire crew of this beautiful ship were Asiatics except for the alert and well-groomed British officers. Most of the passengers, only 97 in the first class, were "Old China Hands" of the same nationality and I knew enough not to challenge their *froideur* prematurely. So, wishing that Isabel were along, I kept aloof as the *Empress* slipped out of the majestic harbor of Vancouver, stopped briefly at Victoria, then on through the strait of Juan de Fuca into the broad Pacific.

The crossing was smooth, for the time of year, and I enjoyed it hugely. My table companions included Mrs. Bruce Lockhart, attractive wife of a well-known British diplomat then stationed in Peking, and a snappy Mrs. Cassell whose mysterious husband I was to meet later in Hongkong. They were good dancing companions and helped to banish homesickness. But I found more substance in some of the men, especially three of my own age with whom I joined to form a companionable quartette, both for deck tennis and bridge. These were a Major Ridley, military attaché at the British Legation in Peking; a New York merchant named Sperling, who imported Japanese fabrics; and Carlisle McIvor, whose deceased father had long been U.S. Consul General in Yokohama. Ridley impressed me by saying that the

163

Chinese, for all their traditional contempt for the military, were building the basis of a first-class army out of the seemingly senseless civil wars. McIvor, who represented an American rubber company in Tokyo, spoke of the commercial shrewdness and industrial ingenuity of modernized Japan. He was accompanied by his mother, and after a short stay in Tokyo, they were going on to Peking to spend Christmas.

The fellow-passenger most helpful to me, however, was H. G. W. Woodhead, editor of the English-language *Peking and Tientsin Times* and compiler of the authoritative China Year Book. Woodhead was returning from lecturing at the University of Chicago and loaned me proofs of his then forthcoming book, *The Truth about the Chinese Republic*. From this I learned, *inter alia*, that the influence of Soviet Russia in China was far greater than I had realized. Like many Britishers, Woodhead was contemptuous of Chinese incapacities and sharply critical of the American willingness to abandon extraterritorial privileges. But this expert spoke impressively, from broad experience, while his fellow-countrymen for the most part were merely concerned with the adverse effects of upheaval on their own prestige and profits. I noted in my diary the bibulous observation of one treaty-port tycoon: "No longer any chance of getting a K [knighthood] just for sticking it out with those yellow swine."

From Mr. Woodhead I got my first thorough information on the clash of Russian and Japanese interests in Manchuria, which had led to the war between those countries in 1904–05, and where Japan deeply resented any American interference tending to limit the fruits of that hard-won victory. I was soon to learn, in thickly populated Japan, that economic control of Manchuria was regarded as essential for the development of Nippon as an important commercial power. In this, bankers and businessmen spoke in one voice with those whom we called militarists.

Manchuria was then, and still remains, an undeveloped, under-populated and enormous country of great potential wealth. Its area nearly equals that of all our states with an Atlantic coastline, from Maine to Florida inclusive. Its mineral resources, in iron, coal, sulphur, gold and silver, seem inexhaustible, while the forestry and agricultural potentials are limitless. Only the lack of oil there, I was told, could make Japan look enviously toward the East Indies. And the political picture favored the penetration which had been made feasible when Japan annexed adjacent Korea.

Like Korea, or Mongolia, Tibet, Indo-China, Siam and Burma, Manchuria had for centuries been a quasi-independent satellite of China. Then, in 1644, the Manchus had stormed south across the Great Wall, establishing in Peking the despotic alien dynasty which ruled China until the Revolution of 1911. By then the humiliation of foreign encroachments, the incompetence of the bureaucracy, the strength of local and family loyalties had all combined with dislike of the Manchus to create mistrust of any central authority. Their monarchy fell before any alternative system had been even roughly prepared to replace it, as Sun Yat-sen discovered during his brief provisional presidency of the nominal republic. His successor was an able general of the old regime, Marshal Yuan Shih-kai, who sought to build a centralized dictatorship without a royal household. In many ways he anticipated what Mao Tse-tung, building on the Communist Party, was able to accomplish a generation later. But the Japanese feared Yuan's ambitions and their intrigues did much to undermine him. When Yuan died, in June of 1916, virtual anarchy set in, with half-a-dozen of the old Marshal's leading generals each seeking vainly to take command by force.

One of the most astute of these warlords, and the one in whom Japan was naturally most interested, was Chang Tso-lin, under whom Manchuria was virtually independent but who nevertheless, through underlings, in 1925 was very influential in Peking. About this "Viceroy," as Chang styled himself, Japanese opinion was in a quandary. To support him would give Chang strength to block Japanese economic penetration. To oppose him would give the Soviet government opportunity to develop its already very considerable influence in Manchuria. Yet neutrality, in Japanese eyes, was impossible because their country, through the years, had built up a very substantial Manchurian investment.

Over the teacups, in the luxurious lounge of the *Empress of Canada*, Mr. Woodhead sketched the tangled situation for me,

165

always emphasizing the rapid, and to his mind dangerous, growth of Communist influence. While the Treaty of Versailles was being drafted, both Japanese and American troops had taken control of the Trans-Siberian railroad and it was hoped by many that Czarist generals would establish a successful anti-Communist regime. But Admiral Koltchak was captured and executed by the Reds at Irkutsk in February, 1920. A year later his associate, Baron von Sternberg, who had held Outer Mongolia, was defeated at Urga and also slain. The only lasting result of the White Russian occupation of this Chinese province was to turn it into the Red-dominated "People's Republic" which it has since remained and make it a base for the pro-Moscow warlord, Marshal Feng Yu-hsiang. Because this worthy called himself "the Christian general" he was favorably regarded by American missionaries. Even skeptical Mr. Woodhead admitted that Feng's Kuominchun, or People's National Army, was a well-disciplined and efficient outfit, though he writhed at its propaganda placards saying that: "People Subjected To Foreign Imperialism Are No Better Than Homeless Dogs."

While Feng did not at that time physically control Peking, his influence had been instrumental in bringing formal Chinese recognition of the Russian Soviet government, on May 31, 1924. The terms were such that none of the other warlords, nor any of the imperialistic powers, could openly oppose. Moscow agreed to abandon all extra-territorial jurisdiction and to return to China the former Russian concessions at Tientsin and Hankow. Peking accepted a restoration of major Russian control over the important Chinese Eastern Railway, which Russian engineers before the turn of the century had cut through Manchuria to shorten the circuitous line of the Trans-Siberian to Vladivostok. It was agreed that half of this vital railroad's 50,000 employes were to be handpicked Russian nationals, whereupon Leon Trotsky, in Moscow, exultantly referred to them as "the junior diplomats of the Soviet Union in the very heart of Manchuria."

So, as my ship moved slowly toward the shores of Japan, it was suggested that both the sun of that country, and of Great Britain, were setting over the Asiatic mainland, and that the red star of Soviet Russia was steadily rising through the prevalent shadows. This seemed to be the case not only in north but also in south China. In Canton, influential Sun Yat-sen had moved steadily toward Communism and before his death had welcomed the Soviet agent, Borodin, at the headquarters of his Kuomintang, or People's National Party. Between that and Marshal Feng's National Army there was an obviously developing, Russian-supported, collaboration. In Washington, the authorities for the most part pooh-poohed Communism as an unworkable system which must fall of its own weight. But earlier in Berlin, and soon in Peking, I found many who, with apprehension or adulation, saw this as the wave of the future. I was grateful for the leisurely crossing which gave me opportunity, denied by airplanes, to sort out dominant threads in what at first had seemed an incomprehensible Chinese tangle.

One day was lost, crossing the International Date Line, with the curious result that we skirted the remote Kurile Islands exactly sixteen years before the Japanese Grand Fleet would steam thence for the assault on Pearl Harbor. Then came the picturesque coastline of the main islands, with sunset gilding the perfectly proportioned cone of Fujiyama as we drew near to Tokyo Bay. The morning of December 10 we docked at Yokohama, still half in ruins from the devastating earthquake two years earlier. That afternoon, after the short trip to Tokyo and establishment in Frank Lloyd Wright's delightful Imperial Hotel, I presented myself at the office of the influential *Japan Advertiser*. There I was received with almost embarrassing hospitality by all from publisher Wilfrid Fleisher down. Mr. Fleisher, then the most influential American in Japan, insisted that I attend a welcoming dinner being offered that evening by the Japan–American Society to Charles MacVeigh, the recently-arrived and not too impressive U.S. Ambassador. It was an auspicious start, since many of the Japanese political leaders I wanted to meet were present, and were cordial to me.

◀At the dinner for Ambassador MacVeigh I found Hugh Schuck, correspondent of the New York *Times*, whom I had known as a fellow-student at the London School of Economics. He had an appointment scheduled with Baron Shidehara, the

Foreign Minister, on the following morning and offered to take me along. This was arranged with the easy informality that then characterized the dealings of Japanese officialdom with American journalists.

As realized later, I had arrived on the scene just as a historic change, leading slowly but surely to Pearl Harbor, was taking shape. The deterioration in Japan's relations with China, bringing a steady worsening of those with the United States, was actually triggered by a sudden alteration of the military situation in Manchuria. Of this there had been radio reports as the *Empress of Canada* drew in to Yokohama. A high officer subordinate to Chang Tso-lin, by name Kuo Sung-ling, had rebelled against the Manchurian warlord in the interest of the so-called Christian General, Feng Yu-hsiang. By this time I was familiar with the outlandish names and dispositions of these characters. I could understand the reasoning when Major Ridley, and others, surmised that this coup was further evidence of Russian influence operating to undermine the Japanese position in Manchuria.

This centered on the South Manchurian Railway, originally built by the Russians to link their fortress of Port Arthur with Harbin, on the Chinese Eastern mainline. After the Russo–Japanese war the long lease of this section, with control of all the towns it served, had been ceded to victorious Japan, although the nominal ownership still remained Chinese. In 1909, Secretary of State Knox had made a vain attempt to redeem all the Manchurian railroads by means of an international loan to impoverished China, but neither Japan nor Russia would accept this arrangement. With Czarist Russia preoccupied in the European war, the Japanese had strengthened and enlarged their grip on Manchuria, which they would eventually recognize as the separate, puppet nation of Manchukuo. In 1925, Soviet Russia was working deviously to regain the old Czarist influence. The Japanese military wanted to hit back but the government, under relatively liberal leadership, was at the time avoiding any provocative action.

Baron Shidehara had been Japan's Ambassador in Washington, from 1919 to 1922, and knew the United States intimately. He greeted me graciously, congratulating me on mak-

168

ing my first visit to Japan "at such an interesting time." Then, in answer to direct questions, he said in his excellent English that the government had "every intention of maintaining neutrality" between the warring factions in Manchuria, denying that it was in any way committed to the support of Chang Tso-lin. But if civil disorders should endanger the lives and property of Japanese in the leased territory of Liaotung, then the War Office would have to send additional troops "in protective reaction." It was a phrase later borrowed by the Pentagon for use in Vietnam.

There was no doubt of Baron Shidehara's sincerity. And his consistently friendly attitude toward the United States was emphasized when MacArthur sponsored him as Japan's first Prime Minister after World War II. But I had been warned that his power as Foreign Minister, like that of then Prime Minister Kato and other advocates of a temperate policy, was severely limited. Under the then Japanese Constitution the Supreme Council of War had direct access to the Emperor, whose authority was absolute. The generals and admirals could secure a decree overriding a policy carefully worked out by the Foreign Office and announced by the Prime Minister. Nor could the Imperial Diet impede such direct action. The hereditary House of Peers would never oppose the Emperor and in 1925 there was still only limited manhood suffrage in voting for members of the lower House. While I was in Tokyo the newly-organized Japanese Socialist Party was forcibly dissolved as contrary to the sweeping "peace and order" rulings of the Home Minister. So I reported that there might be a credibility gap between the assurances of the Foreign Minister and the military actions to be anticipated if anti-Japanese activities in Manchuria gave the necessary excuse for intervention.

A personal concern was my own immediate travel problem. The plan had been to go through Korea to Mukden, investigate the extent of Japan's Manchurian penetration, then down by the British-built railway from Mukden to Peking. This, Baron Shidehara informed me, would now be impossible. I could not get to Mukden because the lines were cut at the Korean border. And even if I got across the Yalu River, into territory now controlled by Kuo Sung-ling, there would be no transportation to Peking. "It would be better for you," said the Foreign Minister dryly, "if

Japan really exercised the control in Manchuria which your journalists sometimes attribute to us."

The one alternative, in those pre-airline days, was to take a Japanese ship to Tientsin, only 90 miles from Peking and connected by an "International Train" authorized by the unequal treaties to which the Chinese so objected. But it was by no means certain that this convenient route would be open. Tientsin was held by General Li Ching-lin, an adherent of Chang Tso-lin. With the discomfiture of the Manchurian warlord, the powerful "Christian general" was reported moving against this General Li. If Tientsin became a battlefield, the International Train would certainly stop running.

About all this, however, there was nothing that I could do, except hope that during my time in Tokyo the Chinese kaleidoscope would fall into some kind of shape, as indeed it temporarily did. Meanwhile there was plenty in the Japanese scene to occupy my attention, especially since my Haverford classmate, Yoshio Nitobé, had looked me up at the Imperial Hotel. We had been good friends at college so it was a double pleasure to be guided by "Tobe" on visits to many points of interest seldom seen by foreigners. Both of us had been favorite students of Rufus Jones and in recalling this Tobe emphasized that in Japan the political applications of philosophy had followed German lines, especially Hegel's mystical conception of the State as an embodiment of the Divine Will on earth. A Quaker training in the supremacy of individual conscience, he said, had not been good preparation for the complete subordination to political authority that was expected in Japan.

I was a good listener and learned a lot as this friend told of the difficulties of readjustment, after years of schooling in the United States. Yoshio was the adopted son of Dr. Inazo Nitobé, a member of the House of Peers and a famous scholar who was then serving in Geneva as Under Secretary-General of the League of Nations. Dr. Nitobé took pride in tracing his Samurai ancestry back for a thousand years, and it was Yoshio's duty to conform to family and social pressures for which he had lost the requisite reverence. Even his wife, Tobe confided, had been selected by his foster-father and was then in Switzerland with their two children because the head of the family thought that arrangement desirable. "In fact," said the poor fellow bitterly, after repeated drafts of saké had loosened his tongue, "my destiny is to be another ancestor and nothing much else."

Another side of the clan complex was shown by young Nitobé's connection with many of Japan's leading families. Through him I met a number of rising young businessmen who were supremely confident about their economic future. When the *Sun* correspondent observed that all the automobiles seen in Tokyo were imports it was truly predicted that he would live to dodge Japanese cars in the streets of American cities. When I commented on the crowding of flimsy little houses in the poorer districts I was asked if it were true in the United States, as in Japan in 1925, that there was not a home in the country unsupplied with electricity.

Notable among the contacts made for me by Yoshio was that with Viscount Goto, former president of the South Manchurian Railway and Governor-General of Formosa. Goto was, at that time, one of the few pro-Russian spokesmen among Japanese leaders, for which reason he feared attempted assassination sufficiently to keep a revolver close at hand. Through his son-in-law, Tsurumi, a close friend of Yoshio, he questioned me about American attitudes, saying frankly that Japan could not afford to be on bad terms with China, the United States and Russia simultaneously. His leaning toward accommodation with Communism gave the impression that the Viscount was not optimistic about the future of Japanese-American relations and I found these doubts frequent. They were emphasized in an interview given me by Viscount Eiichi Shibusawa, still active and alert at 86, who from his boyhood could recall the visit of Commodore Perry's "black ships" in 1853. This elder statesman was clearly outraged by the Asiatic Exclusion Clause in the then recent U.S. Immigration Act of 1924, saying for quotation that:

The sudden breaking of the Gentlemen's Agreement, in order to classify Japan with those people whom you discriminate against, has spoiled a splendid international relationship. The resentment aroused in my country has done much to wipe out the memory of past friendships, and it is well to remember that this resentment is as strong now as when the Immigration Act was passed. A proud and sensitive people are doubly offended if it is assumed that they can easily forget what seems a direct and personal affront.

Many observers have suggested that Japanese pride is stiffened by the belief that they are uniquely of divine origin—"children of the Sun God"—culminating in the thesis that the emperor is the deity incarnate; his palace in Tokyo a national sanctuary as the "Holy of Holies." Certainly religion and government are more closely entwined in Japan than in any other modern state, not excluding Israel. Shinto, "The Way of the Gods," will doubtless long remain the official religion. But deification of the emperor was first emphasized only a century ago, for the very practical purpose of subordinating the great feudal chieftains who were constantly at war with each other. Again, it was the need for centralized government which led the Japanese reformers to model their political thinking on that of Imperial Germany, where the Hohenzollerns had similarly acquired authority over all the other Germanic princes. I was assured by my Japanese friends that they were more disciplined by practical politics than by religious faith. When they called Japan "The Land of the Gods" it meant no more than the American claim to be "God's Country." Nevertheless, I could see that unification of religious and nationalistic loyalties gives rise to a stronger patriotism than is found in Christian countries, where faith may animate a "conscientious objection" to war which few Japanese would even pretend to possess.

I was less disposed to regard the Japanese as particularly "sensitive." Art, drama, literature, horticulture, manners, social customs, even religious practise—all seemed to me highly stylized, therefore inimical to that individuality from which personal sensitivity springs. There was no question about the collective appreciation of a basically unfriendly environment, this being one of the factors behind the national urge toward overseas expansion. Underlying the natural beauty of Japan lurks the hostile character of a barren and overcrowded country, constantly subject to shattering earthquakes, volcanic eruptions, disastrous floods and tidal waves. As it was put by Frank Hedges, perceptive managing editor of the Japan *Advertiser*:

"Fundamentally, these people are more to be pitied than feared."

This underlying factor was brought home when Yoshio took me to tea at the heavily westernized Nippon Club. As I raised my cup to drink, its contents suddenly sloshed over and I looked round to see what practical joker had rudely pushed me. Nobody was there but a picture on the wall was hanging out at a sharp angle, the entire building was swaying and a low rumbling sound came from every direction. Tobe was sitting tensely, face grim and pale, gripping the table with both hands. "Don't move," he whispered. "It'll be over in a minute; over in a minute!" Actually the quake was recorded as lasting only nine seconds and of "slight severity." For me, shortly moving on, it was merely a novel experience. For Yoshio, whose sister had been one of 150,000 casualties in the great disaster two years earlier, it was unnerving. "One can understand," I wrote in my diary, "why these people have a strong disposition both toward stable government and toward the annexation of stable territory."

Toward the Chinese victims of imperialistic ambition the Japanese were certainly insensitive, even the relative liberals then in power. Among these was Marquis Komura, chief of the Intelligence Service at the Foreign Office, who told me that Japan's interests in China were far more important, and far more difficult to handle equitably, than those of the United States in the same area. Equally outspoken on Chinese deficiencies was Baron Saito, then Governor-General of Korea and clearly proud of the progress made by that country under Japanese control. The pressure of Soviet Russia and the inimical nature of Communism were constantly cited as reasons why Japan could not abandon privileges secured on the Chinese mainland, especially in Manchuria. It was fear of American hostility, rather than any sympathy for China's problems, that was maintaining what was called "non-intervention." The uphill road for this policy was emphasized by the growing number of assassinations of liberal leaders by members of militaristic secret societies, as was the fate of Baron Saito himself a few years later.

Investigations were not limited to political and commercial

issues. I spent a delightful evening with Professor Raymond Bantock, a friend from Oxford days then holding the chair of English Literature, once graced by Lafcadio Hearn, at Waseda University. There was an equally informative afternoon at the modest headquarters of the Labor Federation. Here I found Bunji Suzuki, known as "the Samuel Gompers of Japan," equally disturbed by Communist infiltration and the extreme backwardness of existing social legislation. "The Public Safety and Order Regulations," for instance, proclaimed in one article that: "Those who, with the object of causing a strike, seduce or incite others shall be sentenced to major imprisonment of one to six months." The meaning of "major imprisonment," I learned, was solitary confinement "to give opportunity for the self-purgation of dangerous thoughts." Equally strange, to Western eyes, was the suppressed position of even highly-placed women, who seldom voiced any opinion at the meals to which I was courteously invited in several Japanese homes. Yet a reading of the Civil Code, as it was in 1925, seemed to give scope for something in the nature of a "liberation" movement. I sent home an excerpt: "Upon contracting a marriage a woman becomes incompetent. That is: It becomes necessary for her to obtain the permission of her husband in the conduct of important legal acts, as lending or borrowing of money, transfer of her own real estate or valuable pieces of movable property, bringing of an action in a court of law, etc."

So it was with a feeling that Japan was still a long way from either political or social democracy that, after an intensely crowded week, I left Tokyo to travel by comfortable sleeper through Kyoto and Osaka to Kobe. There I put up, together with the McIvors, at the famous old Oriental Hotel, memorialized by Kipling in *From Sea to Sea*. The day in Kobe was not a mere holiday, for one of my duties was to advise on the selection of a permanent part-time representative for the *Sun*; John Brailsford, brother of H. N., who was then working for the English-language Kobe *Chronicle*, was eager to be selected. There was also the obligation of an article brought unfinished from Tokyo. Indeed, on all my Far Eastern travels I found few spare moments for brooding, and at night was generally so exhausted that I slept like the proverbial log.

174

Two more passengers for Peking joined up for breakfast at
the hotel next morning. Blum and Freelander, recent graduates
of Harvard and Yale respectively, were making a globe-circling
trip together. Blum was a nephew of Mrs. Wilfrid Fleisher,
whose publisher husband had been so helpful in Tokyo that I
could not resent his request to "keep an eye on the boys in
China." Of what this might entail I had no idea and that morning's *Chronicle* already reported troops of the rival warlords
skirmishing around Tientsin. However, that was for the future
and, as always, I was delighted by the prospect of a sea voyage,
even though the little *Hokurai Maru*, just 2,500 tons, was a long
step down from the palatial *Empress of Canada*. The Japanese
vessel was a standard-size coastal freighter with six small passenger cabins, well-filled since four other Americans were already aboard, making a party of nine in all. Two of these strang-
ers, a rather grim lady missionary from Wisconsin and a young
New York fur dealer named Brinberg, would remain in
Tientsin. The other two, a nurse at the Peking Union Medical
College and the mother-in-law of an officer in the U.S. Legation
Marine Guard, were also heading to Peking for Christmas. How
the five men and four women divided the six two-berth cabins I
do not recall, except that I shared with Carlisle McIvor, conve-
niently next to the one toilet.

No body of water can be more beautiful than Japan's Inland
Sea, the more interesting because of the heavy traffic, steam and
sail, then utilizing its sheltered passages. The mountains of
Shikoku to the south, of Honshu to the north, make a majestic
frame for the maze of islets, some mere rocks but others, where
the slightest fertility offers, with fishing villages strung along
their rugged shoreline. This picturesque archipelago, the legend
says, was first fruit of the creator and creatress, Izanagi and
Izanami. And their divinity was in turn imparted to the first
Japanese who, seeking Paradise, came from the Asiatic mainland in prehistoric times. Unlike the comparable story of Adam
and Eve these progenitors did not fall victim to Original Sin,
providing another reason for the racial superiority of the
Japanese.

It was almost the shortest day of the year on which I meditated this and chilly nightfall drove me to the dining saloon, the

175

only public room on unpretentious *Hokurai*. Here Captain Oshii, the affable skipper, presided over early dinner for the strangely assorted company of Americans. He knew some German, from trading with that country's former concessions in Shantung, which Brinberg spoke as well as myself. The captain also had a smattering of Chinese, as did the missionary, Miss Wheeler, and the nurse, Miss Bird. And as both McIvors, *mère et fils*, were fluent in Japanese there was lively polyglot conversation, centering on conditions to be expected at Tientsin. No need for worry, the skipper assured us, since a Japanese warship would be there. Late that night I met Captain Oshii on deck and asked him the name of a city casting a glow in the northward sky. That, said the friendly seafarer, "ist mein Heimatstadt—Hiroshima."

Next morning, December 20, *Hokurai Maru* anchored off Moji, to refuel with cheap Kyushu coal. The price differential from Kobe, Oshii said, was partly because the low-grade local mines employed several thousand children under 15, about half of them girls. The product, however, was passed up a ladder from lighters to the ship's bunkers by an endless chain of adults, men and women alike. The loading took four hours, during which the male passengers went ashore by sampan, to enjoy a small and charming Japanese seaport then practically untouched by foreign influence. We were quickly joined by a volunteer guide who took us to a spotless hillside temple where a family which must have included many relatives was chanting prayers in memory of a deceased member. Then, at a wayside inn, using chopsticks as best each could, we were served lunch by a charming child who sank to her knees beside each guest to give service with the grace of a humming-bird lighting on a flower. The position of waitress, Lafcadio Hearn explains, was originally that of an adopted daughter, which the elderly proprietor confirmed by his paternal surveillance from the adjacent kitchen.

It was a farewell glimpse of Old Japan, so obviously losing much of its fragile beauty in gaining massive industrial power. Aboard *Hokurai* again Captain Oshii called attention to the storm signals flying from the flagstaff of the Naval Observatory. "Sehr windig," he said with his disarming smile. And indeed it was windy as the little ship steamed westward into the waters

176

where Admiral Togo had scattered the Russian fleet 20 years earlier, starting Japan on the course of expansion destined to play havoc with the ancient customs of a chivalrous and naturally friendly people.

Next morning, lumbering through the rocky Korean Archipelago, the storm was at gale force. Great waves broke over the bow, sweeping the limited deck space along with driving snow. Most of the passengers stayed in their narrow bunks, but I was happily immune from seasickness as was "Childe Harold" as we had nicknamed the young fur dealer. "I was born in Russia," he explained over the breakfast tea, "and therefore can stand anything."

Since all doors leading to the deck were locked, I had brought my typewriter to the dining saloon and worked there on what would be my final article on Japan. But the confinement was oppressive, the turbulence not conducive to composition, and it was pleasing to get a message from Captain Oshii inviting me to the bridge. In the shelter of the chartroom I admired the skill with which the Japanese sailor handled his laboring vessel. *Hokurai* shuddered whenever the aftermath of a pitch threw the single propeller out of water to race unhampered. Countering this the Captain continuously eased the engines down, which made progress very slow. I feared that our arrival would be delayed. "Macht nicht," said the affable skipper smilingly. "Wireless reports big battle around Tientsin. Ganz ruhig hier."

Actually it was five days out of Kobe, instead of the scheduled four, when *Hokurai* dropped anchor off Taku Bar. It was the morning of Christmas Eve. The weather, though cold, had moderated and the muddy water, colored by the huge volume of loess washed down by the great Hwang Ho, showed how the Yellow Sea gets its name. The reverberation of guns gave point to the order to remain at anchor, as transmitted by a Japanese destroyer maneuvering nearby. This was tiresome, but about lunchtime came word from Captain Oshii that the "Christian General" had captured Tientsin, that General Li's troops had withdrawn toward Shantung and that "except for stray bullets" the river passage up from Taku was now clear.

Next excitement was a conversation by fluttering signal flags between *Hokurai* and the Japanese warship. Sailors stood

177

at attention beside the uncovered guns as the latter moved slowly ahead toward Taku. With the symbol of the Rising Sun at her masthead *Hokurai* fell in behind. A quarter-mile farther back another Japanese freighter followed suit. The little convoy crossed the bar between the old Chinese forts, dismantled since the Boxer rebellion, and moved slowly upstream. Groups of Chinese soldiers were patrolling the river banks but there were no "stray bullets." The American travelers agreed that they were happy to have Japanese military escort, no matter how imperialistic.

Night was falling as we reached Tientsin, said farewell to Captain Oshii and were taken in rickshas to the deceptively named "Astor House Hotel," close by the railway station. Here all was confusion, since no train had run to Peking for a fortnight and aspiring voyagers of many nationalities jammed the meager accommodations. But the resourceful Chinese manager found cots for the newcomers in the crowded lounge and we were assured that there would be space on the International Train when it resumed service to the capital, under armed guard, next morning. I reflected that when I had spent Christmas of 1915 on an ambulance train in France, I had not anticipated the same experience a decade later on a military train in China.

The battlefield atmosphere, somewhat to my surprise, was equally pronounced, even including a grounded squadron of Marshal Feng's flimsy scouting planes. Fighting had been heavy and in several localities bodies dotted the snow-covered fields, lying in clusters where the attackers had been caught by fire from machine-gun nests along the railway line. These were now occupied by detachments of the Christian General's Kuominchun—big, strapping fellows in sheepskin coats who guarded the platforms at wayside stations and chattered amicably with the Chinese train crew. The rolling stock was pulled by a big American locomotive, gaily caparisoned with flags of the United States, Britain, Japan, France and Italy, whose well-armed soldiers composed the international guard. There was plenty of time to observe such details during the long halts to check the roadbed and allow consultations between the train director and Chinese officers.

So it took eight hours to cover the 90 miles from Tientsin to Peking. There we found a decrepit bus from the Grand Hotel de Pekin, where the McIvors, Blum, Freelander and I had reservations. At a crawl it carried us to our welcome destination.

◀"From the balcony of my big old-fashioned room on the fifth floor," I wrote, "I can fancy myself another Marco Polo and am probably as deeply impressed by Peking as was the Venetian traveler nearly seven centuries ago. Looking north the walls surrounding the roughly concentric Forbidden City, Imperial City and Tartar City are much as they were then, since growth has been mostly in the Chinese City to the south. I stand close to the 100-foot height that no building in Peking may quite reach. That is the level at which evil spirits fly and woe to those in a structure against which a demonic head is bumped. So, without offense from the horrid smells below, I can look down on the narrow *hutungs* and into the gardens and ponds around the almost countless temples and palaces. Up to my eyrie, at any hour of day or night, float the traditional calls of the itinerant street vendors, from the clashing steel of knife-grinders to the mellow gong of the sweet seller who can be expected to traffic in opium on the side.

"This orchestration is punctuated by the constant clamor of the streetcars which, to the distress of many, have recently been installed on broad Hatamen Street. While in transit the motorman never lifts his foot from the warning bell, for the Chinese love noise, even more so than the Italians, and happily drag around strings of exploding firecrackers if nothing better is available. Marco Polo was too early for the devil-wagons.[3] Even now there are only 3,000 of them in all Peking, say one to every 300 inhabitants of a metropolis where nobody even pretends to know the population accurately. But they seem to be numerous because every one in use is almost continuously blowing its horn. There is also a widespread tolerance of dirt, and ragged beggars display more extraordinary tumors and leprous sores

---

3. As was I, for the subway system which the Communists would later construct.

than I have ever before imagined. Jim Cash and Smetna, Hopkins doctors at the Peking Union Medical College, reverse Tennyson by saying that for the study of exotic diseases a year of Cathay is better than a cycle of the West. And they are emphatic in warning me never to drink any faucet water or eat any vegetable that has not been boiled immediately before serving.

"With these two young physicians I yesterday visited the beautiful Temple of Heaven, lying to the south, beyond the walled Legation Quarter, and therefore invisible from my balcony. I can, however, distinguish the altars of the Sun, the Earth and the Moon, beyond the outer walls to east, north and west respectively. And within the dull-red walls the forest of blue or green-tiled roofs is continuously interspersed by the usually golden outline of other temples and towers. There is a legend connected with all of them, especially popular that recounted by Lafcadio Hearn about the Bell Tower, whence a musical peal wells out above the street noises every evening as the sun sinks behind the distant Western Hills. Twice the famous metallurgist, Kuan Yu, failed in casting this great bell, 30 feet around its rim and 18 from top to bottom. A third failure, said the emperor Yung Loh, would cost Kuan his life, adding somberly that this was what the soothsayers predicted unless Kuan made a human sacrifice in propitiation. His lovely daughter, however, scoffed at this, encouraged her father and stood with him above the mold when it was time to run the metal for the critical test. Then, as the flames swirled up, the maiden hurled herself into the molten mass below, leaving a dainty slipper in the old man's hand as he clutched frantically at the plunging body. And true it is, after 500 years, that the rich tone of this bell tails away into a sibilant sounding like *hsieh*, the Chinese word for shoe, which is heard as the voice of Kuan Yu's pious daughter, calling for that article which she could not take with her to the after-world."

In short, I was fascinated by Peking. It was a unique metropolis to which I always wanted to return and might have done so, since Grover Clark, publisher of the struggling English-language *Peking Leader*, later sought to take me into partnership. And the winter of 1925–26 was an excellent time to visit this truly celestial city. Because of the civil wars there were no tourists, yet the Extraterritoriality Conference had brought

180

China experts from a dozen nations. A hundred miles away the authority of the allegedly national government was non-existent. Nevertheless, it kept perfect order not only on the few broad boulevards but through the predominating maze of narrow alleys which the Communists would eventually clear away. One might wander through these by-ways in perfect safety, at any hour of the day or night, and I did so.

But it was not on an ancient and alien culture that I had come to report. Work came before sight-seeing, though often the two happily overlapped. Thus it was when, after presenting my credentials at the Wai-Chaio-Pu, or Foreign Office, I attended the opening session of the big international gathering, held in one of the old palaces. The Chinese love ceremonial and put on a good show. It was certainly no accident that a crack regiment of the Kuominchun was always drilling in the great courtyard through which the foreign delegates were driven to the palace. But everything was handled suavely and decorously, with no premonition that eventually the Chinese would tire of argument and simply abrogate the restrictions on their sovereignty by unilateral act. That was certainly not anticipated by Silas H. Strawn, the hard-boiled Chicago lawyer who efficiently chaired the session and told me with irritation that copies of the *Tribune* were reaching him, if at all, a full five weeks after publication.

More sympathetic with Oriental deficiencies was Lev Mikhailovitch Karakhan, a clever Armenian serving as Russian Ambassador. With him I obtained an interview at which the *Tass* correspondent in Peking interpreted. This triangular conversation took place in the old Czarist offices, in the heart of the walled Legation Quarter, where the envoy lived and was the more disliked, because all his diplomatic colleagues were then merely Ministers. This lower status was not too cleverly designed to give China the rating of a second-class nation, since Washington then also assigned Ministers to Ethiopia, Liberia and the "banana republics" of Central America. When the early Bolsheviks decided to give their envoy to China the higher rank of Ambassador the effect went beyond making him automatically Dean of the Diplomatic Corps. It also gave Karakhan, and the nation he represented, an inside track with the Chinese, which advantage this half-Oriental Jew did not fail to exploit.

181

He fitted naturally into the Peking atmosphere, Karakhan said jokingly, since a remote ancestor, another Khan named Ghengis, had early made himself famous there.

The Communist spokesman laid stress on the gains in Chinese esteem made by a government that had voluntarily renounced extraterritorial privileges which others were surrendering very reluctantly. But he strongly denied that Soviet Russia was trying to steer chaotic China into adoption of Communism as a national creed. This I was inclined to believe, for one reason because the Chinese Communists were critical of Karakhan's "go-slow" attitude, asserting that Borodin, the Soviet agent in South China, was more effective in their cause. The Ambassador insisted that Russia's undisguised interest in Eastern Asia was nationalistic rather than ideological. The Franco-British policy in Europe, he argued, was to block the Slav off from the West, to deny him access to the Mediterranean and create what was openly called a *cordon sanitaire* isolating Russia behind French-dominated Poland and Romania. The inevitable result of this hostile compression was to increase the tempo of Russia's Asiatic activity and the evidence of this in China had nothing to do with Marxist philosophy. As for Japan, Moscow fully accepted that nation's need for expansion in Manchuria, and there was no good reason for a clash between Russian and Japanese interests there. When I said that Viscount Goto had told me the same in Tokyo, Karakhan was delighted.

From the Russian Embassy I went direct to the more modest Legation of the United States, for a luncheon engagement with John Van Antwerp MacMurray, an able career officer then serving as Minister. His wife, Lois, was the daughter of President Goodenow of the Johns Hopkins, himself well acquainted with China, and the couple were more than hospitable to the *Sun* correspondent, introducing me to all the Legation staff. With two Secretaries little older than myself, Ferdinand (Fred) L. Mayer and Clarence B. (Buzzy) Hewes, I contracted lifelong friendships. MacMurray, whom I would meet again at Geneva, had need of this competent assistance. None of the diplomatic representatives in China was under greater pressures. The British and French showed irritation whenever we failed to back them up. To support them was to bring thinly veiled and by no means idle threats of Chinese hostility. The Japanese and Russians complained that we failed to appreciate the often conflicting attitudes of both. "The only course for us in China," said MacMurray, "is to face forwards and walk backwards." Perhaps equally difficult was the task of the German Minister, likable and professorial Dr. Boyé. He spoke for a nation that had lost all its extraterritorial privileges but, unlike Karakhan, was under orders not to offend any of the victorious powers. I inquired about the experience of German nationals brought before Chinese courts. "Not too bad," he replied, then paused a moment before adding: "Not for quotation, under the Treaty of Versailles Germans consider Chinese justice rather better than that which we received at Allied hands."

Unlike my experience in Tokyo, I found the political leaders in Peking relatively indifferent to my quest for enlightenment. It was largely to Grover Clark, whose pro-Chinese line in the *Leader* was much criticized by the foreign colony, that I owed productive appointments. One of the most informative was with Wang Cheng-ting, better known as C. T. Wang, serving as Foreign Minister for the "Christian General." China will live up to the letter of her treaty engagements, said Dr. Wang grimly, "provided that they are quickly altered in our legitimate national interest." He then emphasized "the essential difference" between Feng Yu-hsiang and the other warlords. It was not merely that the Christian General's troops were well equipped and disciplined, as I had seen for myself. Their cause was nationalistic and not personal, asserted Dr. Wang. "Their loyalty is to China rather than to their general." Certain it is that this Kuominchun, or People's National Army, was the basis and prototype of the eventually famous Nineteenth Route Army, with which the Communists swept Chiang Kai-shek off the mainland and set up the dictatorship of Mao Tse-tung.

Interesting contacts were made at the Western Return Club, its membership limited to Chinese graduates of American and European universities. Without exception they were optimistic about the long-range future of their country, though in general agreement that the attempts to give it a representative form of government had been a bad mistake. For several reasons, it was argued, Western democracy would never take

183

root in China. Its people believe deeply in the sanctity of the family and clan but have no respect for the individual as such unless and until he proves himself worthy of consideration. "Human Rights" are a meaningless and undesirable abstraction. Contrary to wishful American thinking, this meant that the Chinese would welcome their own brand of political dictatorship, more so because the existing anarchy was undermining family life and clan integrity. China had more to learn from Russia than from any so-called democracy. But the coming Chinese dictatorship would be home-grown and tailored to the traditions of the Chinese people.

Active in the group was Dr. Geoffrey Chen, a Harvard Phi Beta Kappa then teaching American History at Peking's National University. He told me that he had long considered the original American system an ideal political model for Chinese reconstruction. "You," he said, "at first had an aristocratic central government with limited powers, controlling a few specified functions and leaving the rest to provincial and family direction. That was quite close to our old arrangements. But now you are undermining federalism to concentrate more and more power in Washington. So I give little attention to the half-forgotten government planned by your founding fathers. Indeed, I spend more time encouraging my students to demonstrate against your developing imperialism."

I enjoyed the comfortable Grand Hotel, operated to perfection by its French management. The spacious and beautifully furnished lounge, with obsequious "boys" at hand to answer every wish, was in effect Peking's International Club. Here leading Chinese and prominent foreigners assembled amicably for tea or cocktails, with tacit understanding that there should be no serious controversy. Thus I met youthful and delicate Henry Pu Yi, the quaint *soubriquet* of the last of the Manchu Emperors, deposed in childhood but cultivated by the Japanese as a potential puppet ruler. Another frequent visitor was Mei Lan-fang, the famous actor of female parts whose highly stylized stage performance somehow melded admirably with the ear-splitting discords of traditional Chinese music.

Among the small newspaper fraternity then in Peking was a young American correspondent—John Goette—who quickly interested me because he spoke Chinese and represented a Chinese news service which had developed the somewhat inflammatory idea of informing the native press, all over the country, on what the foreign devils were saying and doing. John lived with his foster-mother, a Mrs. Chase, in an elegant Chinese home deep in the native city. She was expert in the intricacies of Chinese art and made an obviously good living as a buyer for New York speciality stores. The disturbed conditions were a bonanza for this business. On the one hand they had brought abundant loot from the palaces and museums into the market, and on the other had made it difficult for foreign buyers to reach Peking and compete with established residents. Through John Goette this hospitable lady invited me for Sunday tiffin at her house on Ta Fo Ssu—the Street of the Great Buddha—and there had in a procession of the specialized "boys" with whom she dealt, exhibiting the exotic wares which could then be obtained at very modest prices. Recognizing the opportunity I decided to buy to the limit of my purse, whereupon Mrs. Chase invited me to stay at Ta Fo Ssu, making purchases with allowance for the lengthy bargaining appropriate to any commercial transaction in China. It seemed a good omen that the move was arranged for January 6, my thirty-second birthday, and for all the national upheaval I never lived more luxuriously than during my fortnight back of the gates with big "Sho" characters which certainly achieved their purpose of excluding evil spirits.

It was, of course, one of numerous dwellings constructed for members of the upper classes, very different from the dirt-floored hovels in which most Pekinese then dwelled. One passed from the street through heavy bright-red folding doors in the windowless front wall, immediately confronting a broad wooden screen around which the tiled passageway made right-angle turns. This baffles the evil spirits, even more than the defensive hieroglyphic, since when they descend from the 100-foot level the foul creatures are still happily condemned to travel along undeviating lines. With his attendant devils thus discouraged, and consequently purified himself, the visitor enters a charming courtyard, stone-paved but with open beds for trees and shrubs. This court is enclosed on all sides by one-storey dwellings, fac-

185

ing inward, that looking south being generally the owner's preserve. To east and west, also backed against the protective wall encircling the whole property, are the separate lodgings always held in readiness for family and friends, each with its private entry. Through an ornamental gateway in the lower interior wall is another courtyard, probably with vegetable and flower beds, around which are grouped storerooms and the sleeping quarters of the domestic staff, at least five in number for a household of any consequence. There may even be a third court, perhaps with a fountain and marble benches for quiet meditation, between the two, but 43 on Ta Fo Ssu lacked this. It had, however, a service complement of seven, with an extra ricksha man and subordinate "boy," in addition to the indispensable cook, coolie and always female amah, functioning as a resident sempstress as well as what the English call a "nannie." The No. 1 Boy, who in the present instance had fathered five children of his own, was in turn a less stereotyped replica of the traditional English butler. Wong waited at table, arranged all household purchases, kept the accounts and supervised execution of orders invariably transmitted through him. While I knew Mrs. Chase to be wealthy this plethora of servants was inconclusive evidence. The wages of the seven, I learned, was in sum less than double the compensation of faithful Martha, the "help" to Isabel in faraway Baltimore.

The *Sun* correspondent revelled in this luxurious hospitality. My scanty wardrobe was carefully restored by the amah. Wong served breakfast, at any stipulated hour, in my electrically heated room with bath attached. There I could write my articles in perfect tranquility, telephone at hand and with a ricksha available at any moment to take me to appointments. If I had an evening free there would be a delicious dinner, generally with interesting Chinese guests, in the beautifully furnished rooms of the main dwelling. I was not adept with chopsticks but quickly learned how to distinguish good jade and amber from that sold to tourists, how to interpret the stories told in Chinese embroidery, how to differentiate between the products of the Chien-lung, Ming, Sung and even earlier dynasties. Letters from home urged me to "take care" of myself. "That's what I'm doing," I wrote back.

186

At least superficially I had already explored every quarter of the fascinating city. With John Goette, who had a car, the field was extended. Together we traveled out, by the magnificent Summer Palace, to Wo Fo Ssu, the Temple of the Sleeping Buddha. His colossal bronze figure lies reclining at full length, and shelves around him are crowded with hundreds of pairs of shoes offered by the faithful in case the god decides to rise and cover his bare feet. That none of them could be pulled over those gigantic toes is one of the inconsistencies which do not bother the Chinese mind. A comparable incongruity was found at Pi Yun Ssu, the Temple of Green Jade Clouds, where the 500 original disciples of the Buddha are honored by a regiment of life-size statues. Here, on ordinary wooden trestles, in a plain oak coffin covered with dusty clusters of paper flowers, rested the body of Sun Yat-sen, inconspicuously awaiting removal to the impressive mausoleum then about to be built in the ancient capital of Nanking. This temple was deep in the Western Hills, not far from the caves where Roy Chapman Andrews would shortly discover the remains of primitive Peking Man, and here brooding antiquity seemed to press down on this timeless land. "Driving back," I wrote in my journal that night, "by crumbling village walls and tumbledown mud houses, through wintry fields dotted with countless graves, I sensed a national senility that does not seem to care what happens." But I concluded that the fiery spirit of Sun Yat-sen was breaking through this indifference, even as the revolutionist's body crumbled back into the prevalent dust of the countryside.

Another expedition with John Goette, equally memorable, was to the Great Wall. One train a day left Hsichihmen Station for Kalgan and on a frosty morning we were there at 7:40 for its scheduled departure. Punctuality gained you little in China then and it was another hour before the primitive cars, with wooden benches across their width, were assembled and hooked up. But there was lots of interest on the chilly station platform, crowded with fine-looking Mongols returning to their windswept uplands after sampling metropolitan delights. A purpose of these visits was shown by the metal teapots, pans, tools and even phonographs sticking from their bundles and strung around the odorous sheepskin tunics of the women, for

187

none of the tall and dignified men would thus burden themselves.

Most visitors to the Great Wall stop at Nankow Pass, where the spurs of the ancient barrier, climbing up and down the rugged mountain slopes, come closest to Peking. But Goette, who knew the terrain, said we would go farther, suggesting that we transfer to an empty coal truck at the very front of the train. After two hours of ceaseless spitting, opium smoking and casual urinating our over-crowded compartment had become worse than stuffy. So for another hour we stood in what was a chilly but splendid observation car, since the big locomotive pushed up the gradient from the rear. All the way, to a lonely station named Chinglung-chaio, the line climbs steadily with the Wall frowning down from the summits which it consistently straddles. I could well believe that, two centuries before the Christian era, 700,000 men had toiled to build this 1,400 mile monument to Chinese engineering skill. As often said, it had served better to keep the Chinese in than the Tartars out. That did not lessen the moral in the long tradition under which China has sought to protect its own customs, whether good or bad, from foreign incursion.

On the bitterly cold platform at Chinglung-chaio, or Green Dragon Bridge, the station master had a snug little shelter with a coal stove. Here was brewing the piping hot tea which makes a social occasion of even the most casual meetings in northern China. Thus refreshed, and side by side with a long camel train making its deliberate way to Mongolia, we walked a trail-like road. Soon this was left, to clamber up the mountain side to the surmounting barrier and a watchtower with stone steps giving access to the top. I had fulfilled a childhood ambition, standing on the Great Wall of China, its twenty-foot width paved evenly with flagstones, its twenty-foot height surmounted on the outer side by an additional brick parapet in almost miraculous state of preservation. But it was a chilly promenade, with the northwest wind bringing a stinging sandstorm down from the Gobi Desert. At the next watchtower, some half-mile up the mountain ridge, we made our circuitous way back to Green Dragon Bridge, in spite of its romantic name merely a cluster of mud huts around the bare railroad platform. The winter sun was setting behind the barren peaks and the station master, after providing more tea, agreed that the evening train from Kalgan was shortly due but was far less sure that it would run. Instead, he had been informed by telegraph, a military train was coming down the single track and by this we might conceivably get passage back. Otherwise it would be a bleak prospect and I was grateful for John Goette's fluent Chinese.

As night fell there came a long whistle from the mountain pass above, and soon the "military train" rolled in. It consisted of a big American locomotive pulling a single box car, at the door of which stood a couple of Kuominchun solders, half hiding a worried looking brakeman. Between him and the station master there was an extended conversation, following which one of the soldiers disappeared to consult some unseen personage. Then the marooned travelers were courteously invited aboard and their return tickets punctiliously collected by the brakeman. In the car a comfortable stove was burning, and from the roof a hanging oil lamp illuminated the cluttered interior—several crates of mildly indignant chickens and in every corner piles of untanned sheepskins, which in combination with unwashed Chinese emit a very penetrating odor. An elderly peasant, obviously far from well, lay with closed eyes on one of these piles, and behind a ragged curtain, drawn across the car, could be glimpsed a dapper Chinese officer, seated at a card table and going through piles of papers with another who was evidently his secretary. This commander, according to one of the orderlies, was a General Chang, bringing important orders to the Peking garrison from the Christian General's headquarters beyond Kalgan.

The abbreviated train lurched and rattled down the steep gradient, with the engineer blowing his whistle at what seemed like measured five-minute intervals. Soon the two orderlies produced a brazier, ignited its charcoal, and with food from a closet, began to prepare a savory supper. This was duly carried through the curtain and consumed by the general, who then called for a glass of brandy, the secretary bringing an unopened bottle of excellent French cognac to be decanted. Unfortunately there was no corkscrew until I remembered that my Boy Scout knife contained that instrument, which I ceremoniously

189

utilized. This happily placed the general under a sense of obligation, acknowledged when he emerged bottle in hand and passed it around all the company except the unconscious invalid. Now the ice was broken and seated on a hurdle the officer conversed familiarly with John, the two orderlies expressing their own opinions in polite but by no means obsequious terms. As Goette translated, it was this general's desire to emphasize that the chaos in China must be regarded as a transient phase in its long history, and that the nation would soon be unified under an army trained and equipped to eliminate any foreign aggression. "Even your Washington," he observed, "found it necessary to fight for years, with help from France, before the United States were stabilized."

Though I never knew it for a fact, evidence suggested that on this return from the Great Wall we had stumbled into the making of history. Immediately thereafter Feng Yu-hsiang announced the withdrawal of his army from Peking and his own departure to Moscow, for more study on the tactics and techniques of revolution. Into the trap thus created two other warlords, Wu Pei-fu from Central China and Chang Tso-lin, again dominant in Manchuria, would shortly pour their troops. This would open the way for the well-organized Cantonese to move north and, under the leadership of Chiang Kai-shek, begin the unification of China which Mao Tse-tung would conclude. I convinced myself that the orders which started this chain were carried by the officer whose brandy bottle I had opened.

In any case, and much as I hated to leave Peking, it seemed high time to move south. I so informed my young protégés at the Grand Hotel, whom I had promised to advise. I packed the "dunkshies" I had purchased into a small new steamer trunk. Then, after a farewell dinner at Ta Fo Ssu, I was seen off on the Kin-Han railroad by dignified and lovable Wong, the No. 1 Boy who had especially requested that privilege. The train pulled out, surprisingly on time, the night of January 19, 1926. It was almost the last one to get through to Hankow for several months.

❰❱

❰From Peking to Hankow is 755 miles, a little west of south, and the leisurely schedule allowed two nights and a day for the trip. Actually it took 48 hours since the roadbed was in ill repair and there was concern about the safety of several bridges, notably the well-worn structure across the Yellow River. There was some confusion at the outset since my Canadian roommate discovered that our berths had each been sold twice, a minor form of "squeeze" said to be commonplace on all the government-owned lines. This difficulty was solved by putting two upper berths into the compartment supposed to hold only two lowers, automatically changing the accommodation from first to second class. But the smiling attendant said any rebate must be obtained in Peking, where the "mistake" was made.

Even after doubling up with the courteous Chinese claimants there was no real discomfort, for one who had lived for months on an equally crowded ambulance train. I slept well and ate well in the European dining car. Here, between meals, I sought to do some typing, but was illogically annoyed when a group of missionaries swarmed in, seeking a warmth unobtainable in their unheated third-class carriage. "The Chinese," one told me, "must learn that they are sinners, unwashed by the blood of the lamb." Others were less evangelical and more informative.

There was interest in the landscape although, as I wrote in my diary: "If there were not still a novelty about it, the scenery would soon grow monotonous. The prevalent brown of the level fields is broken here and there by ice-covered irrigation ditches and patches of spring wheat, just beginning to sprout, giving an occasional tinge of green to the drab outlook. There are no fences, no isolated farms and very few trees. Only innumerable graves, around which the furrows curve, breaking the plane of the age-old plow land. Very similar one to another were the frequent villages and towns, all girt by walls mostly made of mud but sometimes stone ramparts with imposing arched gateways. Outside the larger settlements there is likely to be an enormous grave mound, perhaps 40 feet high, signifying the resting place of some man or family of importance. And here and there are burial groves of neatly planted fir trees, generally around a shrine or temple. The prospect is melancholy but not wholly funereal. There are flocks of sheep—hardly ever a cow—and always the active little black pigs in and around the villages. Smoke rises from the chimneys, and every frozen pond is thick with warmly dressed children, skating and sliding. It is well-watered country, and obviously well cultivated."

Across the Yellow River the traveler passes from Chihli into Honan Province, then under the nominal control of Wu Pei-fu but overrun with bandits who frequently were uniformed deserters from this general's ill-disciplined army. At every station now the doors to all the cars were locked. However, I would generally manage to get out, to stretch my legs and watch the loading and unloading of tenanted coffins, headed for the ancestral homes, which seemed to constitute a large proportion of the freight. As the long train slowly lumbered south the aspect of the country freshened. There were more orchards, fields in which cotton had evidently grown, groves of bamboo to color the dull brown scene. Steep hills closed in on the railroad, their summits generally guarded by military patrols clearly lacking the physique and élan of the northern Kuominchun. Some warlord will have to unify China forcefully, I thought, or else the poor country will be devoured by its swarms of military locusts. The former development was soon to come.

The night of January 21 had fallen when the train rolled into Hankow, largest of the three cities that cluster at the junction of the Han and Yangtze rivers and, even in 1926, the industrial heart of China. Across the Han was the pulsating glow from the Hanyang Iron and Steel Works, then Japanese controlled but destined for great expansion when the Communists took over. Wuchang, on the south side of the broad Yangtze, then unbridged, had much light industry. The handsome American, British and Japanese banks along the Bund, as well as the foreign gunboats moored in the river, emphasized the importance of the Wu-Han cities, as Hankow, Hanyang and Wuchang are collectively known. I found the U.S. Consul, Jay Huston, lyrical about the commercial potential of this complex, giving it his highest praise as the Chinese center most comparable to Chicago.

192

Because of its significance for foreign business many cases involving extraterritorial privilege arose in Hankow and the day after arrival I attended one. Because a rather commonplace affair it seemed the more worthy of report. The charge was against the captain of a junk who, with another junkmaster, had been distributing kerosene to nearby towns as agent for the Standard Oil Company of New York. According to custom each skipper reciprocally went bond for the other on safe delivery. In this instance both failed to report and eventually the two junks were discovered stranded on sandbars far up the river with about half of their cargo missing. Native detectives, said to be very efficient, had picked up one of the junkmasters who had been jailed for some weeks under the Chinese principle that a suspect is considered guilty until and unless he can prove his innocence. The unfortunate defendant, who had no lawyer to represent him, maintained to the Chinese magistrate that the wrecks were accidental, that he had stolen nothing and that only his fear of "American justice" had made him run away. But he could produce no witnesses in his favor and was returned to prison for another month on the understanding that he would be held responsible for the entire loss, valued at $1,250, unless he could by then produce the other junkmaster to share the blame.

The issue, as I considered it, was not whether the native defendant told the truth, which Mr. Huston thought highly improbable, but whether or not the scales of justice were weighted in the foreign interest. "Socony" was represented by a very alert Chinese lawyer, and the U.S. Consul, with his interpreter, sat as an "assessor" on the bench beside the magistrate, with whom he conferred privately before the trial. There was no jury and no real defense since, or so the accused pitifully complained, having stolen nothing he had no money for a lawyer and no opportunity as a prisoner to find witnesses in his favor. The cards were stacked against him and I reported, to the Consul's annoyance, that: "The objections to this system outweigh the advantages of continuation." This I felt the more strongly after investigating the notorious "Mixed Court" at Shanghai, where even the Chinese magistrates were then appointed by the foreign consular body.

Another self-assignment in Hankow, fulfilled with some

difficulty, was an interview with Marshal Wu Pei-fu, the prestigious Central China warlord whose headquarters were in a nearby village. I was received most courteously by the old general and departed with an autographed cabinet photo of this hope of Chinese conservatism. But I could see little promise in Wu's assertion that: "There can be no end to civil war in China until the military in touch with the Reds are overthrown." This confirmed the reports that Wu, in concert with Chang Tso-lin, would shortly move against Peking and therefore made a story worth cabling to the *Sun*, justified by the immediate outcome. But it was the last throw of the dice for these ambitious *Tuchuns*. The expedition left Wu's rear unprotected, open to an attack which was soon mounted from Canton by youthful General Chiang Kai-shek. The strongly nationalistic impetus of the Kuomintang swept everything before it and soon, much to Japanese distaste, this new "generalissimo" controlled all of China except Manchuria and the Mongolian area where outright Communist leadership was taking over from Feng Yuhsiang. The eventual triumph of Mao Tse-tung, driving Chiang to bitter exile on Formosa, was deep in the web of the future. But when this happened, in 1948, it was no surprise to any who had noted how cleverly the Communists had worked with outraged Chinese patriotism to gain the upper hand.

Forebodings from my interview with Wu Pei-fu were confirmed by a call on Bishop Logan H. Roots, who from his Hankow headquarters directed the Chinese undertakings of the Episcopal Church. In the opinion of this thoughtful man, events beneath the chaotic surface were moving swiftly toward the triumph of an anti-Western Chinese nationalism. The widespread failure to recognize this trend, he said, was of ill omen for American business as well as for missionary effort. I took this solemn warning seriously, as the unprejudiced opinion of a shrewd observer with thirty years' experience in China. But in Shanghai his reasoned viewpoint was furiously denounced. To make an unhappy diagnosis for the colonials there was to risk accusation of favoring the disease.

It was toward Shanghai that I was now headed, by Japanese steamer down 600 miles of the majestic Yangtze River. An attack of flu, with high fever, made my last hard-working hours in Hankow miserable. It was an effort to get my bags packed again. But when the coolies had carried them aboard the clean and comfortable *Yohyang Maru*, with her spotless blue decks and white trim, I felt better. Another lap of the long journey was completed; it meant nothing to me, pro or con, that a Communist Consul General had just moved with much fanfare from Moscow to Hankow.

All next day I slept in my comfortable stateroom, but rose for dinner to survey my fellow passengers. There were no other Americans on board and I was placed, by the smiling Japanese steward, at a table with three of the ubiquitous Russians. One, who spoke German, explained that they were buyers for the Soviet Textile Combine—"*Spezialist, nicht Kommunist,*" he emphasized. However, his enthusiasm for the Red regime in Outer Mongolia, whence he had come, aroused some doubt as to the distinction. Urga, or Ulan Bator as the alleged specialist called it, was now said to be in effect a Russian city. He smiled when I observed that in Peking Ambassador Karakhan had said that all Russian troops had been withdrawn from that area.

There was much further conversation, questioning on both sides, over this Russian's pocket chessboard, in sheltered sunshine on *Yohyang*'s promenade deck. Though only the end of January, there was a feeling of spring in the air and it was pleasant to watch the well-cultivated banks of the great river slip by. Often hills, generally crowned by shapely pagodas, came down to confine the stream, now low because of the dry season. Most of the busy waterborne traffic was in high-pooped cumbersome junks, carrying the produce of the endless fields to the riverside towns, at many of which the steamer stopped. Its arrival was as much an event as was contemporaneously the case with bay steamers on the Chesapeake. But there were differences. Pedlars hawked their wares; beggars implored alms; children stared wide-eyed; chattering adults jostled each other in the amiable and indolent confusion characteristic of China—in 1926. A long halt, with opportunity to explore, was made at Nanking, the ancient capital city, where industrialization was more advanced than I had expected.

On the morning of January 27, *Yohyang* drew in to metropolitan Shanghai, where merchant ships of many nations, and warships of the then dominant powers, cluttered the tributary Wangpu River. I was put up at the American Club and in its excellent library, at the very center of foreign authority, I furthered my studies of the unilateral arrangements which soon would be abruptly terminated. "These gardens," I read on a sign at entrance to the nearby waterfront park, "are reserved for the foreign community." I was told that formerly the prohibition had been more crisp—"Chinese and dogs not allowed"—but others vehemently denied this as a Communist *canard*, which it may well have been. Truth is an early casualty when tension is building between reactionary and revolutionary groupings, as was decidedly the case in Shangahi then.

I was not attracted by Shanghai, much greater than Peking in size but in no other respect. The hybrid architecture of the International Settlement was ineffectively ostentatious and not made more appealing by the constant emphasis that Chinese could live there only "on sufferance." This was particularly offensive to dignified Tang Shao-yi, who had been the first Prime Minister of the Republic and on whom I made a courtesy call soon after arrival. "It is the foreign plunderers who are here on sufferance," the old gentleman exploded in perfect English. "Without the service of my too patient people, the concessions would wither on the vine within a month. Already the Western imperialists live here in a virtual state of siege."

Such vehemence was surprising, for this former colleague of Sun Yat-sen had been described as a moderate, with conservative tendencies. But with my own eyes I could see that Shanghai was a powder-mine. It was apparent in the grim alertness of the bearded Sikh police, who under British command patrolled the settlement in pairs, viewed with sullen dislike by the Chinese, forbidden the loitering converse so congenial to them. Behind the Indian police stood the 2,000 well-trained men of the Shanghai Volunteer Corps, maintained by the taxpayers but under the command of a British army officer and with an armory of equipment "on loan" from the War Office in London. Patrols of this militia were posted, beside great rolls of barbed wire entanglements, wherever streets from the big foreign preserve passed into the enfilading Chinese city. Years later, going from West to East Berlin, I strongly felt that curious sense of *déjà vu*.

196

Although Shanghai was never technically a foreign colony, like Hongkong, the encroachment on Chinese sovereignty, under British leadership, had been proceeding methodically for three-quarters of a century. It was nowhere more pronounced than in the judicial arrangements, which I made it my business to study closely. I attended both a criminal and a civil case in the famous "Mixed Court," where foreign assessors dispensed justice for Chinese litigants, with no right of appeal allowed the latter. The general procedure seemed efficient, conscientious and fair. But the system was justified by no valid treaty right or diplomatic arrangement other than outright usurpation. It was abundantly clear that the "Shanghai Free State," as provocatively toasted in the International Settlement, would last only as long as the duration of China's civil wars. That was the strong opinion of J. B. Powell, a well-posted resident American journalist with whom I fraternized.

After a busy week, I was glad to leave a Western enclave which, though clean and sanitary, was as doomed as Herculaneum by eventual eruption. I would stop at Shanghai again, returning, and so left my trunk of "dunkshies" in storage there while I continued south. For the trip to Hongkong passage had been taken on the Dollar Liner *President Pierce*. Once aboard it was a surprise, both complete and delightful, to find that a fellow-passenger was Tang Man-hoi, my classmate at Haverford. Before leaving home I had tried vainly to obtain "Tango's" address. So it seemed close to a miracle to meet my one old Chinese friend by chance, among the hundreds of millions in their native land. Together we revived college days as the ship steamed down the rugged Chinese coast, glimpsing the distant mountains of Taiwan from the Formosa Strait. "Tobe's people will have to cede that island back to China some day," predicted Tang after I had told him of Nitobé's helpfulness in Tokyo. My Chinese chum was to prove equally considerate.

President Pierce steamed into Hongkong harbor in the early morning of February 4, with the rising sun silhouetting the beauty of this picturesque, semi-tropical outpost of British Empire. It was before the days of highrise and the tile-roofed dwellings, climbing 2,000 feet up the precipitous Peak of Victoria Island, peeped modestly from their screening of palms, banyans, bamboo and exotic shrubs. All nature was green and warm and pleasant—a welcome contrast to the bleakness of wintry northern China. I found myself reflecting on the continental immensity of this great country, only one-third of the provinces of which I had managed to visit. Now I would have a look at revolutionary Kwangtung where, in contrast to Shanghai, Chinese governed and white people, in their turn, were only allowed "on sufferance." As I brooded Tang joined me at the rail, describing points of interest. "The whole place," he said, "has been slowly carved by the English out of barren rock. So there is something absurd in the demand that it be 'returned' to China." It was an interesting example of a fairmindedness which seemed predominant among Chinese.

The same characteristic was uppermost in Sir Cecil Clementi, the recently appointed British Governor who consented to be interviewed. I wanted to ascertain the real purpose of the boycott of Hongkong applied by the Canton government after the "massacre" of June 25 in that city. Its leaders boasted that this pressure would force the British out of Hongkong and indeed the damaging effects were obvious in ways more serious than the painful withdrawal of domestic service. But Sir Cecil, a distinguished Sinologue and student of Chinese history, was not too worried about the future of the colony. Hongkong, he pointed out, was of great importance to all South China as a port and banking center. Because of orderly British control many Chinese had built up large investments there and would themselves resist any Communistic effort to take over. The main objectives of the blockade, he thought, were to develop effective labor organization and to teach his own people that the old high-handed days were over. Also there were some wholly legitimate Chinese demands, such as suppression of the opium traffic through Hongkong. And when the boycott was called off, as it was soon afterward, Sir Cecil proposed to deal directly with the Kwangtung government on all outstanding issues.

The fact that Hongkong is still British, I believe, is in no small part due to the enlightened attitude of this proconsul. And the interview stimulated my desire to visit Canton, the more so since from Peking I had brought a letter commending me to the leaders of the Kuomintang. It was a wholly feasible trip, ninety miles up the beautiful Pearl River, because the British were maintaining a bi-weekly steamer service to their Consulate, on Shameen Island in the middle of the river at Canton. Passengers were not allowed to land in the Chinese city but there were ways of getting there indirectly. Tang thought I would have no trouble, though he warily declined to go along himself, pleading his bad reputation as a prominent capitalist.

The six-hour trip was certainly interesting, on a little steamer with decks armored against sniper fire and under heavy guard of Sikh soldiers. But it proved uneventful, and I found a Chinese teacher, at Canton Christian College, who agreed to serve me as both interpreter and guide. Together we penetrated to the headquarters of the Kuomintang, where a rather startled member of the executive committee said that I was the first non-Russian newspaperman who had ever troubled to call there. This worthy affirmed the Nationalistic, rather than Communistic, policy of the Kuomintang, and predicted (as happened) that together with Feng Yu-hsiang "we shall eventually get rid of the treacherous warlords once and for all." Mao Tse-tung was then directing this bureau, and I believe I met him, but cannot be sure because I did not note the name. There was much talk of Chiang Kai-shek, the brilliant young commandant at nearby Whampoa Military Academy. Russian officers were giving instruction there, but it was denied that Michael Borodin, the Soviet envoy to the Kwangtung government, had more than ordinary diplomatic functions.

This I doubted, even before I talked with Borodin, whose original name was Gruzenberg and who had been an active Communist agent in the States before getting the South China assignment. In a strong New York accent, the Russian told me that "the basic concepts of Communism are deeply rooted in Chinese tradition and religious faith." He quoted Confucius: "We should not be distressed if the citizens are few, but only if each does not receive an equal share of what all produce." Borodin himself, however, was obviously receiving a great deal more than a fair share by modest Cantonese standards. He overplayed his hand and, with all his staff, was soon unceremoniously thrown out of Kwangtung by Chiang Kai-shek. Probably as a result of this failure Borodin was purged by Stalin and died in a concentration camp.

That, however, was in the future. I spent three crowded days in Canton and returned to Hongkong more than ever convinced of a pronounced leftward drift in China. In the north anti-foreign agitation had been largely directed by intellectuals—university students and younger faculty members. In the south the peasants and coolies were for the first time being organized to serve the same political end. Alike in north, center and south an unexpected capacity for disciplined mass action was being promoted by militarization. It had been the ideal of Hawaiian-born Sun Yat-sen that China might be modernized as a democratic federal republic, on American lines and with American guidance. With this in mind, Dr. Sun had founded the Kuomintang, as a national party committed to provincial self-government. But Japanese encroachment, Western arrogance and Communist encouragement had combined to make a strongly centralized dictatorship more probable. And this, I wrote to my paper, could tragically mean a substitution of Chinese hostility for traditional friendship with the United States.

I had a few more days in Hongkong, acquiring the tropical clothing necessary in the Philippines. With Tang I visited the neighboring languid colony of Macao, run by the Portuguese with full consciousness that their opium-supported rule was ending.

◄Established in the Manila Hotel, I undertook my customary study of the local press. This was always professionally interesting, for contrasts in make-up, objectivity of reporting and editorial assurance. Furthermore, it gave insight as to the psychology of an unfamiliar situation. In the issue of the American-owned Manila *Times* for February 17, 1926—the day of my arrival—an editorial entitled "Excess Baggage" gave me pause. I read:

It is a paradox that our [Philippine] legislature takes itself so seriously, when legislatures in most countries have been abolished. The

200

interparliamentary union of Europe now consists of Mussolini, Rivera, Hindenburg and whoever is on top at the moment in France. It works out well, with Latins at least. Just when Italy and Spain have been pigeonholed as decadent, they take on a new lease of life. Latins do better with a dictator than with parliaments. Filipinos do too.

At about the same time, half-way round the world, another embryonic dictator was reaching a similar conclusion. "By denying personal authority and substituting the number of the crowd in question," wrote Adolf Hitler, "the parliamentary principle of majority rule sins against the basic aristocratic idea of Nature. . . . There is no principle which, objectively considered, is so wrong as the parliamentary principle."[4]

I really believed in representative government. Never, until that moment, had I imagined that dictatorship could be seriously advocated by Americans as the most desirable political system for any people. But I would now discover that, by Governor-General Leonard Wood, it was deemed appropriate for the Philippines. The Jones Act, which then defined the political status of these islands, had promised "a more autonomous government" and established a bi-cameral legislature. But it also stipulated that: "All executive functions of the government must be directly under the Governor-General" and gave him a veto power which could be over-ridden only by the President of the United States. During the preceding session of the Legislature approximately one law out of every three enacted had been vetoed by the Governor-General. Several of these, such as one endeavoring to liberalize the Philippine regulations on divorce, could scarcely be called in any way hostile to American interests. The attitude of General Wood was the more resented because so sharply in contrast with that of his predecessor, Francis Burton Harrison, who from 1913 to 1921 had consistently favored Philippine autonomy.

It was not surprising, therefore, to find a Supreme National Council, under non-partisan native leadership, working actively and openly for independence. A measure of American military protection would be acceptable, said its spokesmen, but

---

4. *Mein Kampf*, Stackpole Edition, 1939, pp. 89 and 92.

not continued political domination. On Washington's Birthday, less than a week after I arrived in Manila, this Council declared a "National Prayer Day" throughout the islands, pointedly entreating God to "stay the hand that would smite our liberties." Unhappily this demonstration coincided with a formidable military parade, ordered to honor a departing American commander. Governor-General Wood thought it "damned impertinence" for the Filipinos to "advocate rebellion" on such a day. Senate President Quezon called it "the tactics of a bully" to overawe the protest gathering "with alien military might."

The conflict between American and Filipino attitudes, I soon realized, was deeply rooted. With the coming of the automobile the islands were visualized in the United States as an ideal source of rubber supply, for the production of which both climate and soil are admirable. But the Philippine Public Land Law, passed by the Legislature before the arrival of General Wood, made it extremely difficult for any American corporation to acquire an area sufficient for the profitable growth of rubber or sugar, or for the exploitation of undeveloped mineral wealth. While the Governor-General consistently blocked legislation promoting Filipino self-government, the native leaders were equally stubborn in refusing to assist the interests of American business. With this deadlock both sides were becoming embittered, the Filipinos insisting on real independence, the Americans on curtailing the autonomy achieved. As the *Journal* of the U.S. Chamber of Commerce in Manila phrased it then:

Let Congress. . .give us an actual unquestioned form of territorial government, with a Governor. . .preferably from the western part of the United States. . .who can look at a mountain and tear its guts out for the mineral it contains.

This he-man attitude was brought to my attention by the Dean of the University of the Philippines, who amused himself by collecting such samples of Americana. I quoted it to two Hopkins-trained Filipino physicians, to whom I had brought an introduction, when they took me for a picnic supper to beautiful Montalban, in the mountains north of Manila. The tropic night came down as we sat chatting beside a musical waterfall and the Southern Cross gleamed out above a still happily ungutted peak. For a moment Dr. Nañagas was silent, then spoke quietly in words that I never forgot. "We have seen," he said, "how the red Indians, the Hawaiians and the South Sea Islanders have successively succumbed to the pressure of your business, the iron march of your industrialism. For you the Philippine question is answerable in terms of more dollars and more national power. We are the weaker race. For us it is a matter of life or death. That is why every educated Filipino supports those leaders to whom Americans like to refer slightingly as 'politicians.' "

Among these Manuel L. Quezon, then president of the Philippine Senate, was unquestionably first. As a youth he had fought with Aguinaldo against American rule; from 1909 to 1916 he had been Resident Commissioner in Washington; later he would become the first President of the Philippine Commonwealth. In an interview accorded me, Senator Quezon evidently realized that I harbored no prejudice against the cause of independence. Consequently, he cordially invited me to accompany a group of leaders who were about to embark on a propaganda trip through the Philippine Archipelago. I welcomed the opportunity, especially on learning that Bill Kuhns, a friend who was Manila representative for the United Press, was also going. But it would be tactful first to consult with Governor-General Wood, who ruled in state from the old Spanish headquarters at Malacañang. The sexagenarian proconsul, who had come close to getting the Republican Presidential nomination at Chicago in 1920, was gracious. "By all means," he told me, "go along with the party. Eat with them; drink with them; sleep with them. You'll find them charming, delightful children. They're capable of any accomplishment—except self-government."

Thus primed I embarked on the coasting steamer *Cebu*, in company with all the outstanding political leaders, for a trip of a week's duration through the beautiful Philippine Archipelago. We visited the islands of Romblon, Sibuyan, Panay, Negros and Mindoro, received everywhere by enthusiastic local groups displaying the Philippine flag, that of the United States conspicuous by its absence. What impressed me most, once Americanized Manila was left behind, was the continuing strength of Spanish influence in the islands, the more striking because so few of that nationality had ever settled there. Spanish was not merely the

203

dominant language. Large and often handsome Catholic churches were everywhere the focus of provincial life, where tranquility and order joined hands with indolence and poverty. The local dignitaries usually claimed Spanish descent and in Ilo Ilo, the third city of the colony, I lunched well at the Spanish Club, proudly boasting a membership limited to those who could prove that ancestry. Commerce, however, was mostly in the hands of the Chinese, who then easily outnumbered the total of all other alien residents. Mate a Malay with a Chinese, the saying went, and get a businessman. Do the same with a Spaniard to make a politician. Permit a Malay-American mixture and the resultant Mestizo will be a bum. It was, inquiry revealed, an aphorism of English origin.

The ten members of the Supreme National Council, I learned aboard *Cebu*, were mostly part Spanish though a couple had Chinese forebears and Senator Sumulong, of the minority Demócrata, as opposed to Nacionalista Party, was said to be pure Malay. Illustrative of the emancipated status of Filipino women was the inclusion of Señora Rosa Sevilla de Alvero, principal of an exclusive female seminary in Manila, whose students in spotless white dresses came down en masse to see the flag-decked steamer leave. Indeed the whole trip was superficially gay, but with much to be learned from long shipboard conversations between the ports. The somewhat grandiose aim of the Supreme National Council and its local commissions, as I duly reported, was to establish a completely Filipino shadow government with a native counterpart for every American executive and judicial agency or official, all of which were then calmly ignored. Legislation desired in the field of, for example, health and public welfare would be drafted by that particular Commission and then passed by the Insular Legislature regardless of whether or not favored by the American Governor-General. Though often futile, and always irritating to General Wood and his predominantly military staff, it was a clever and wholly non-violent scheme, closely paralleling that used in southern Ireland against Great Britain. Unquestionably, the Supreme National Council laid the foundations of self-government for the Philippine Commonwealth, established by

Congress in 1934, and thereby for the independent Republic which followed World War II.

Aboard *Cebu*, which idled through languorous tropic seas to ten degrees north latitude, I learned much that would not have been assimilated in the island capital. So when the little ship returned to Manila, the morning of March 1, I felt justified in departing that very evening, on the Canadian Pacific's *Empress of Asia*, as the first leg of the long journey home. By diligent effort I had absorbed far more than I could put on paper.

In view of prevalent native antagonism to imperialism, this Canadian ship seemed provocatively named. But she was a well-ordered empress, with several ports scheduled en route to Yokohama. First came a two-night stop at Hongkong, with ample time to meet up with Tang Man-hoi and attend the annual races of the Jockey Club patronized with equal enthusiasm by British officials and upper-class Chinese. Then came Shanghai and a nerve-racking experience. The stop at this great city was only for a couple of hours, which I had thought ample time to retrieve my precious trunk of *dunkshies*. But at the American Club I was told that it had been sent to the Dollar Line "godown," since my expectation had been to return by one of its ships. This warehouse was some distance from the Canadian Pacific wharves and all taxi drivers were on strike. Promising unusual largesse I sent a ricksha boy ahead to collect the treasure chest, following as fast as Chinese legs could weave my own conveyance through the crowded streets. It was a close call, but the Peking acquisitions were safely hoisted aboard from the last tender even as the anchor was weighed.

Empress of Asia put into Nagasaki on March 9, and I disembarked. I had decided to spend another fortnight in the island kingdom, to absorb something more of its history, character and charm. Outward bound I had been primarily occupied with the tangled skein of current events. Now these did not need to be transcribed, since I would be in Baltimore almost as soon as any article sent by mail. Tokyo had been explored but the correspondent had seen little of other cities, or of the countryside. Nagasaki seemed an appropriate entry port, as it had been for Will Adams, that extraordinary English seaman who piloted a

Dutch ship there in 1598 and remained in Japan, not wholly by free will, until his death in 1620. Adams is recorded as being the first Westerner to marry a Japanese and have Eurasian children. He became a famous shipbuilder, under the Shogun Iyeyasu, and is said to have diverted the naval architecture of Japan from that of the clumsy Chinese junks to the sharper, swifter lines of Western shipping which were then developing. This mutual interest in ship design made Adams seem very real to me. Later, in the *Hakluyt Papers*, I would read the interesting letters occasionally sent back to England by Will Adams.

From Nagasaki I took train to Kyoto, the ancient capital of Japan where 28 successive emperors had reigned, including the sagacious Shirakawa who outdid King Canute by ordering his obsequious courtiers to imprison the rain when it one day interfered with a palace function. Many of such ancient legends were told me by Yoshio Nitobé, with whom I made several expeditions. Together we visited the old religious center of Nara, called by Ralph Adams Cram "the most precious architecture in all Asia." Spring was in the air, the plum trees in blossom and the sacred deer strolled gracefully up for biscuits on the long walk from the entrance Torii to the Temple of the Great Buddha. His size may be gauged from the four-foot length of an outstretched little finger. Toward the rear of this gigantic statue was a pillar with a sizable hole at its base, through which the faithful would try to squeeze because of the sign saying: "To pass this narrow passage will later help to enter paradise." The eye of the needle comes instantly to mind; by no means the only instance where the superstitions of different religions follow parallel lines.

Industrialized Osaka broke the romantic spell but it descended again when Tobe took me to remote Miyanoshita, at the base of Fujiyama, whence we climbed high on the sacred mountain and returned to spend the night at a spotless inn outside the foreign orbit. This was my first experience of mixed bathing in the nude, though the clouds of steam in the bathhouse were perhaps more veiling than the later beach costumes at home. Cleanliness, Tobe said, was not only next to godliness in Japan. It was also ranked far ahead of modesty.

Back in Tokyo, preparatory to sailing, I found in the accumulated mail a publisher's offer to produce my articles for the

Sun in book form. The idea appealed, though obviously some adaptation and enlargement would be necessary. But on the leisurely voyage, this time via Hawaii, the project could be shaped. As the cherry trees burst into blossom Tobe saw me off aboard the *President Wilson* at Yokohama. On April 1, I was at Honolulu and in a full day visited Pearl Harbor, Diamond Head, the famous Kali and went swimming at Waikiki. Then through the unbridged Golden Gate to San Francisco and so by rail to Baltimore, to be met by Isabel and our two little girls when the reliable Capitol Limited pulled into Mount Royal Station.

The older daughter, Lorna, had reached her third birthday while I was in Canton. Arriving at Willow Cottage she dashed in great excitement to beloved Martha, in the kitchen. "I've found my Daddy," she announced proudly, "and his name is Felix."

❰Five months of Asiatic assignment had made a profound impression on me. Never again would I succumb to the assumption, in which I had been reared, that civilization centered on the Atlantic and Mediterranean areas. China, for all its backwardness and humiliation at the hands of the West, seemed a latent force of incalculable potency. Japan, despite its aggressive modernization, appeared the weaker of the two in everything but military organization. The permeating Filipino antagonism to Governor-General Wood's regime had made me distinctly dubious as to the staying power of an imperialism which was obviously drawing to an involuntary close in China. If the British could not swing it, with such skillful administrators as Sir Cecil Clementi, what would be the chances for a bulldozing overlordship on star-spangled American lines? I brooded on the question as the long trans-continental train ride emphasized the enormous potential, for good or ill, of the United States. The route this time was via Salt Lake City, where I could savor the impress made by the Mormons on a society where diversity was yielding with reluctance to standardized thought.

Back on the *Sun* I was flattered by the attention my dispatches had aroused. Nelson T. Johnson, then Chief of the Far Eastern Division of the Department of State and shortly to become Minister to China, urged me to enter the Foreign Service. Dr. Moulton, at the Brookings Institution, renewed his job offer. Grover Clark, back from China to raise funds for the struggling Peking *Leader*, wanted me to join up and make that exotic city my permanent residence. The newly-formed Institute of Pacific Relations, through chairman Ray Lyman Wilbur, then president of Stanford University, invited me to organize the proposed headquarters office in Honolulu. There is no doubt that my ego was inflated by these many opportunities.

I recognized, however, that the *Sun* had treated me with great generosity, and I enjoyed the deference now paid me as the paper's leading authority on world events. Moreover, for several months, spare time was fully occupied in shaping my little book on *Our Far Eastern Assignment*. A shipmate on the voyage back from Japan had been Henry Morgenthau, formerly President Wilson's Ambassador to Turkey, and "Uncle Henry" had graciously agreed to write an introduction in which he helpfully referred to my "wonderful powers of penetration" and presciently predicted that China would "eventually. . .assert herself as one of the great world powers."

But expertise in foreign affairs was actually hedging me in, so far as advancement on the *Sun* was at issue. This was, after all, a provincial newspaper and to the great majority of its readers events within the narrow circumference of Baltimore were of paramount concern. I had little interest in most local matters and my long absences abroad had impaired familiarity with the intricacies of even national politics. Returning from Asia, with its premonitions of an eventually aggressive Japan, I believed that the weak machinery of peace was what above all else needed both understanding and strengthening. When Charles Lindbergh made his non-stop flight to Paris, in May of 1927, its implications for the conduct of another war stood out for me. Already fairly familiar with the work of the League of Nations, I felt that American participation therein should be the most important issue in the 1928 Presidential campaign. It would have been professionally advantageous if I had concentrated more on other national currents.

For some time I pushed aside all temptations to leave the *Sun*. The health of Mr. Adams, my admired chief, was failing and it was a pleasurable duty to take more of the load on my own young shoulders. I was happy to pick up the threads of domesticity and to foster both old and new friendships in Baltimore. Financial circumstance was less stringent now and after much discussion we bought a sizable wooded lot, in a northern suburb, with a view to building and permanent settlement. Negotiations were begun to bring Helena Kollmann, one of the Austrian girls whom Isabel had supervised in England, from Vienna to Baltimore as a mother's helper. Life was busy, but running smoothly.

An appreciated asset was the opportunity to see more of my parents. In 1926 Professor Morley, then 66, was curtailing his work at the Johns Hopkins and, except for summer trips and some lecturing at other universities, was in a position to enjoy his Baltimore grandchildren. The shy and self-contained mathematician, however, was anything but pressing in this relationship, where my mother showed more interest. She was unquestionably a great lady, fondly remembered as such in Baltimore for years after her death, in 1939. Isabel's mother had equal dignity and it was pleasant to be close to the relatives in Washington. Also I was glad to pick up the threads binding me to brothers Christopher and Frank, with both of whom I had lost touch during my Asiatic absence.

The literary success of the former was proving meteoric. A symbolic novel—*Thunder on the Left*—had found its way to the English bookstore in Peking, where I bought a copy as a farewell present to John Goette. Evidently Kit had the capacity to produce something more permanent than fragrant pot-pourri. He was now contributing editor, and indeed general sparkplug, for the then prestigious *Saturday Review of Literature*. Always generous, he took pains to see that *Our Far Eastern Assignment* was well reviewed there and in other ways contributed to its modest success. Visits to New York meant for me most hospitable and surprisingly deferential treatment by my more famous sibling.

It was more difficult to keep contact with Frank, who had married in England shortly before I went to the Orient and was now managing the London office of the Century Company. Though his personal writing was less extensive Frank had quickly gained a repute in London literary circles almost as

209

pronounced as that established by Chris in less critically competitive New York. In 1924, the youngest brother had published a compact but notable study of Dora Wordsworth's *Memory Book*, quickly recognized as a happy combination of careful research, original thought and finely chiselled writing. This book foreshadowed the synthesis of scholarship and imagination which would later stamp its author as a superior literary artist.

I was not without my own literary ambitions, though I sought to develop these in the furrows of current social problems. In China it had seemed to me that unlimited population promoted the prevalent anarchy. Excessive numbers encouraged indifference toward human misery and made an orderly individual life more difficult. Ahead of time I speculated on the implications of "the population bomb" and planned a novel to emphasize these. What would be the consequences, I pondered, if at a given moment all women became sterile? It was a provocative theme and I wrote several chapters before its mounting complications and pressure of immediate duties pushed the unfinished manuscript aside. I was honest enough not to attribute this incapacity to increasing family cares. If a writer really has it in him to do significant work, impediments will almost certainly be overcome.

Deficiency as a non-functional writer did not mean lack of literary appreciation. I was always an omniverous reader and evenings at home, in those pre-television days, gave opportunity. Isabel fully shared this taste and was naturally an acute critic. Together we read much aloud and subsequent discussion helped to knit the marital tie when frayed by household discords. I was also anxious not to lose my grasp of French and German. Often I would occupy myself with authors in these languages. French was easy, but for German I still need a dictionary.

An interesting writer discovered by us at Oxford had been Thomas Mann, whose story of the decline of a great merchant family in Lübeck *(Buddenbrooks)* had seemed to both as documentary as Galsworthy's similar *Forsyte Saga*. Interest in *Buddenbrooks* was promoted by meeting a German lawyer of my own age, Paul Leverkuehn, who had come to Washington as assistant to Dr. von Lewinski, assigned there to handle the

German side of the post-war Mixed Claims Commission work. Isabel and I had been grateful paying guests of von Lewinski and his American wife in Berlin, so renewal of the acquaintance was natural. There was an added fillip, in those prohibition days, by the German official's generous practise of pressing upon me a couple of bottles of carefully wrapped Rhine wine, to take home after every meeting.

Paul Leverkuehn, a tall, good-looking, humorous yet sensitive bachelor, appealed to me by his thoroughly cosmopolitan nature. The young German had studied at Edinburgh, spoke perfect English and was familiar with current Anglo-American literature. His father, as a judge in Lübeck, had held a custodial post for juvenile Thomas Mann. As friendship deepened, some of Paul's extraordinary adventures in the war were gradually disclosed. He had been with Max von Scheubner-Richter, later an early Nazi leader, when that Baltic baron was assigned to stir up Kurdish tribes and keep Britain from supplying Russia through the Persian Gulf. While the war had cost the life of Paul's only brother it had left him saddened rather than embittered, more so because he could see no prospect of an enduring peace. He was deeply involved in both the wars and in the second one lost all his material possessions. But his inexhaustible good humor and underlying Christian faith remained unshaken, never more so than after he knew that he was doomed by the weakness of an over-taxed heart.

As our two little girls grew more exacting, we pressed on with the idea of bringing Helena Kollmann from Vienna to Baltimore. I had friends in the Immigration Service who made the complicated arrangements easier, and on Decoration Day of 1927 I went to New York to meet the gentle Austrian girl who was to be with us through various shifts of circumstance. She was a poor disciplinarian but a lovable companion, an excellent sempstress and a willing helper in every household chore. Her presence also meant that we could enjoy a more active social life, although at first the advantage seemed anything but clear. Soon after arrival, Helena came down with an ailment at first diagnosed as tuberculosis, the more terrifying to me because I had of course assumed full responsibility. At the Hopkins Hospital, however, this proved to be only a transient summer pneumonia.

With Helena happily recovered, exploration of the beautiful Chesapeake Bay area became easier; by overnight steamer trip to towns on the various tributary rivers, by sail in Lawson Wilkins' amusing little skipjack and overland by car. Jesse Lee Bennett, an aesthetic Baltimorean, had what now might be called a "Commune" on the Magothy River, where Huntington Cairns and other intellectuals, among whom I was courteously included, would gather for informal *conversazioni*. The current rage was that off-beat philosopher Alfred H. Korzybski, whose system of "General Semantics" seemed to me largely highflown nonsense. However, I fully enjoyed the aquatic amenities and began to think of a bayside retreat of our own. Emory and Anne Niles were planning a summer cottage at nearby Gibson Island and urged us to follow suit. So we drove down, by what was then an unspoiled dirt road, to find the place over-pretentious and far beyond our modest means. Moreover, for the summer of 1927, a real vacation with change of climate, on seagirt Martha's Vineyard, had been arranged.

Early on a hotly humid July morning, reminding me of Manila, the family set forth, including Helena and with two adjacent cabins reserved on the steamer for New Bedford that evening. In New York we were met by jovial Uncle Kit, who stood lunch for the whole party and then escorted us to the cool Aquarium, in Battery Park. Here Lannie and Sistina, as the younger of the two small and active girls was then known, were particularly entranced by two penguins of approximately their respective sizes. Chris, with his ever alert eye for copy, saw, but did not divulge, an opportunity in this. Titled "The Escape of the Penguins," he later described how the pairs of children and quaint aquatic birds exchanged places, the former remaining in the aquarium while the latter were shepherded to the New Bedford boat by unquestioning Helena. The tale is found in Kit's charming juvenile, *I Know a Secret,* but it was a dilemma as to which penguin alternate should properly possess the copy inscribed to both "with apologies for taking a liberty, from Uncle Kit."

Meantime, there were changes on the *Sun*. In October, 1927, John Haslup Adams died and was succeeded as editor by John W. Owens. There is no doubt that Owens was the appropriate man for the position. He was sound, seasoned and well informed on local, state and national politics. But he lacked both the intellectual depth and the philosophic insight of his predecessor and I knew that, with the passing of my broad-gauge mentor, the paper would lose aspiration to be exceptional. Certainly it would not continue to make the idealistic fight for workable international order which, to me, had become a compelling objective. During the winter of 1927–28, I reviewed the various openings available but decided that none was what I wanted. This was to go to Geneva and there make a thorough study of the oft-derided League of Nations. Its patient uphill work impressed me strongly. My wife was wholly sympathetic and agreed that the adventure could prove a splendid family experience. She had recently come into a small inheritance which would help, but how to finance such a major undertaking was still a problem. The *Sun*, I could foresee, would accept some correspondence but could not be expected to pay me full salary for what would be considered a post of secondary importance, without the *réclame* of its London bureau. That assignment I might now have had, but my objectives had changed. After Asia I wanted a truly international listening post. The stimulating, if diaphanous, Kellogg-Briand Pact had been launched and Geneva seemed the ideal place to observe its hoped-for consummation.

The well-known Willoughby brothers[5] had both shown interest in my work. W. W. Willoughby had written a flattering review of *Our Far Eastern Assignment*, and W. F., as director of the Institute for Government Research, had warmly seconded Dr. Moulton's efforts to bring me to what would soon become the Brookings Institution. So I took the trio into confidence regarding my plan for writing a book on the constitutional development of the League of Nations, based on the first decade of its experience. All three were enthusiastic. Moulton offered to pub-

---

5. These identical twins had very similar careers, with W. W. (at the Johns Hopkins) leaning toward political science while W. F. concentrated more on economics. Both had been constitutional advisers to the Chinese Government. They took delight in pretending to me that each was the other. My reply was that I could happily learn from either.

213

lish the study, if it came up to expectations, and was even willing to help in financing, if the aspirant would join the Washington organization forthwith. However, I was not ready to separate from the *Sun*, which had agreed to pay me a small retainer while at Geneva. To be an accredited correspondent, I knew, would give an entrée there far better than that of any purely scholarly researcher.So, after much cogitation and maneuvering, I submitted a carefully planned project for one of the recently established Guggenheim Fellowships and to my delight received the award. The die was cast.

Naturally there were complications, more so as the 1928 Presidential election drew near. Political interest was running high in Baltimore, with Governor Albert C. Ritchie of Maryland considered by some a likely Democratic candidate. However, the Houston Convention nominated Al Smith on the first ballot. Largely because of "wetness" he was given ardent support by the *Sun* which annoyed me because, knowing Herbert Hoover personally, I strongly favored him. It seemed unpardonable when Mencken used the paper to describe Hoover as "a pious old woman, a fat Coolidge" and periodically in even less flattering terms. To leave so prejudiced an editorial sanctum was easier because, in this instance, I thought the policy of the paper both meretricious and ill-informed. To prefer Al Smith as a more likable personality was one thing; to assert that this narrow-visioned politician was the better choice for the Presidency was, in 1928, quite another. In the event, of course, the "Happy Warrior" failed to win even his own state, though his strength in the big cities suggested to many that henceforth the Democratic Party would work from urban bases, as F. D. R. soon proceeded to do.

Political excitements did not make actual departure less arduous, even with Helena to assist. I tried to sell Willow Cottage, in which we had spent four pleasant years, but there were no takers and finally I rented it to a colleague, at a pitifully modest figure. "Lester," the piano around which many pleasant evenings had centered, was loaned to Lucile and Lawson Wilkins, who used it as focus for a rousing farewell party. Another was held on the mosquito-plagued property of the Niles at Gibson Island. Isabel mildly rivalled Passepartout, in Jules Verne's

214

famous story, by purchasing some chocolate bars for the journey, then locking them in her desk for storage. A triumph of organization was to deliver the family car to its purchaser at the entrance of Mount Royal Station, after economically using it as a taxi to the train. It was a hot, steamy day, the morning of August 1, 1928, just short of six years after my return to Baltimore.

Through the kindly intervention of Dr. von Lewinski we had obtained excellent accommodations on the Norddeutscher Lloyd steamer *Dresden*, sailing from New York the following morning. Isabel and the children, with Helena, got off at Plainfield to spend the night with her brother George. I went on to do the same at Roslyn with Chris. Both families were well represented at the dock for the always romantic ship departure. It was difficult, Isabel wrote, "to realize that we are not just off on a vacation trip but are going into an entirely new situation into which we must fit and adapt ourselves."

Problems were not lessened by the somewhat unexpected resentment to uprooting on the part of the little girls, Lorna only five and a half, Christina not yet four. "We are going to spend ten days on this dirty, sloppy water," was the former's caustic comment as *Dresden*, its band playing familiar *Lieder*, backed out into the polluted Hudson. But *bon voyage* presents and the charming children's playroom were consoling. Helena, traveling Tourist, was allowed to spend the whole day caring for them. Thus relieved, the parents reveled in the clean and cool salt air. It would be good to savor Europe again.

◀Chapter 5
In Quest of Peace

Although I had never before visited Geneva I did not feel wholly a stranger to the lovely little city. A school classmate, Gilson G. Blake, was U.S. Consul there and we had been in touch. Gilson was the regular Consul, charged with all the normal duties of that office, but at Geneva then there was also a special political Consul, Elbridge D. Rand, whose assignment was to keep the Department of State informed on all League activities. Soon after arrival I was invited to lunch by Mr. Rand, whose obvious concern was to ascertain whether my assignment signified a developing pro-League attitude on the part of the *Sun.*

Three good friends from Oxford days were also resident in Geneva: David Blelloch at the International Labor Office; Raymond Kershaw, an Australian financial expert in the League's Administrative Section; and Francis P. Miller, a Virginia Rhodes Scholar who represented the World Christian Student Federation and was also correspondent for the *Christian Century*. Miller had been instrumental in promoting *Our Far Eastern Assignment* and showed much interest in the Morleys' advent. He had reserved accommodations for us at the Pension Diana, a pleasant boarding house standing in its own grounds in the northern part of town. There the little caravan established itself, after the long trip down from Bremen, via Basel.

I found the necessary adjustments easy. As an American newspaper correspondent I was welcomed at the League Secretariat, then modestly housed in a former hotel on the right bank of the beautiful lake. Pierre Comert, the French Director of the Information Section, furnished credentials and personally introduced me to the well-organized reference library. On my first day I lunched with Comert's principal lieutenants. H. R. Cummings of Great Britain and Arthur Sweetser, an experienced American journalist who, because of his nationality, enthusiasm, ability and financial resources, played a much larger role in League affairs than one might have expected from his official position.

What I was slow to realize was that my family would not adapt so readily. I spoke French fairly fluently, though with indifferent pronunciation, and enjoyed the constant opportunity for improvement. Isabel, however, had no schooling in languages and the little girls, psychologically disturbed by their uprooting, at first resented hearing anything but the English which they were only beginning to master. Helena's German was of little use in French-speaking Geneva. Consequently the idea of taking a furnished apartment, with all its housekeeping chores in a foreign tongue, was postponed. Instead, after a short stay at the Diana, we became privileged guests at the more intimate pension Les Laurelles, across the Rhone, near the picturesque Old Town and adjacent to the park-like grounds of the residential hotel Beau Séjour. From here little Lorna was entered at the bilingual International School, largely supported by Arthur Sweetser and his wealthy wife, Ruth.

I now had a room in which I could work without interruption, and also reflect on the magnitude of the task rather casually undertaken. Part-time correspondence for the *Sun* was easy. I quickly initiated "On the Quai du Mont Blanc" as a weekly column of international chit-chat. Opportunities for more significant reports from this ideal listening post were all around. The Guggenheim project, for a study of the constitutional development of the League, was another matter. It required not only close examination of the detailed operation of the organization, but also careful historical research into the complicated framing of the Covenant. Happily I soon made illuminating contact with Lord Robert Cecil and other veterans of this pre-natal period. Then there were helpful lectures at the new Institut de Hautes Etudes Internationales, of which that genial Swiss scholar, Dr. William Rappard, was Director. It was clear that I could not adequately complete my research project in a year. Furthermore, the financial pinch was going to be sharp. This could be eased by writing the extra articles which Sweetser enthusiastically encouraged, but only at the cost of putting serious research in arrears. Optimistically, I had visualized a Geneva year as another interesting foreign foray, which wife and children could also enjoy. It was not going to be that way and both young parents felt the unanticipated strains.

A visit from Frank emphasized the ubiquity of family problems. The Century Company was discontinuing its London office and my brother was uncertain as to whether he should return to the States or take a directive position with the small but admirable London publishing house of Geoffrey Faber. Professor Morley, then retiring from Johns Hopkins, had told his youngest son of several teaching posts which could be available to him as an Oxford D. Phil in Mathematics. The father's feelings in this were clearly mixed. He would have liked to see his only son with real scientific talent continue teaching, in an American university. On the other hand, our parents were considering retirement in England, in which case it would be pleasant to have a son anchored there. Moreover, father and son were collaborating on a very advanced mathematical study, in which frequent conferences were imperative. Frank came from London to Geneva, or so I concluded, as much as anything to discuss the matter. Lacking full knowledge of the younger brother's growing integration with London literary life, I strongly advised a return of the native. I doubted that over-populated Britain would ever really recover from the debilitating effects of the 1914–18 war. "The England that captivated Henry James is gone forever," I asserted. "The England that appeals to T. S. Eliot is very much alive," responded Frank. We argued the issue with point and counterpoint, over beers at the Brasserie de l'Univers, during excursions on Lac Leman, even while slithering on the *mer de glâce* high up the flanks of Mont Blanc. Isabel, as she wrote her mother, was sure that Frank, now nearly 30, would not make the break. Her premonition was correct.

There was prevalent, that autumn of 1928, a general op-

218

timism which did much to soften the small complexities of life in Geneva. The Locarno Pact of 1925, guaranteeing the Franco-German border as fixed at Versailles, had served to reduce tension between those countries. Further improvement could be expected as long as they were guided respectively by Aristide Briand and Gustav Stresemann. The Kellogg Pact was receiving universal approval for its "renunciation of war as an instrument of national policy." It was evident that Herbert Hoover would be elected President and closer American cooperation was expected from his thorough understanding of the international scene. With stabilization of the German mark there had been a measure of economic recovery in that country, now made a member in good standing of the League. I could report cheerfully when its Ninth Annual Assembly was held in Geneva during September, giving me opportunity not merely to meet many celebrities but, more importantly, to study at first hand the work of the technical committees on which the progress of the entire organization largely depended. Deep shadows, however, lurked in the background. Locarno had ignored the vexed question of Germany's eastern frontiers, so that France maintained treaties of mutual assistance with Poland and Czechoslovakia and found inexhaustible arguments against any but German disarmament. Skeptics, especially from observant Russia, pointed out that tanks could be driven through the self-defense reservation of the Kellogg Pact, as indeed they soon would be by both Italy in Ethiopia and Japan in Manchuria. Nevertheless, at the moment, the atmosphere was one of promise, to which the booming American stock market deceptively contributed. Arthur Sweetser, who was watching my work closely, gaily predicted eventual League membership by the United States. The *Sun* correspondent was at the right place at the right time, he emphasized.

The appeal of our new location strengthened after the Assembly adjourned and the little town settled back into the gentle tranquility of an Alpine autumn. Geneva's most advertised native son, Jean Jacques Rousseau, had written of it that "I have never found the equal in any country." Despite my love for London and faraway Peking, I was inclined to agree. The beauty of location, with the modulated Jura mountains to the north and the eternally snow-crowned Mont Blanc massif southwards, is sublimated by the deep blue lake from which the Rhone pours out tumultuously on its course to the Mediterranean. From the left bank the Old Town rises precipitously, up to the Cathedral of St. Pierre and the scarcely altered setting where Calvin and John Knox preached. All around are the walls that preserved this bastion of Protestantism, along one of them the great Monument of the Reformation with the heroic statues of its leaders. The narrow streets include many picturesque old dwellings, such as the one from which legendary Mère Royaume is said to have hurled her iron *marmite*, or cooking pot, onto the head of the invading Savoyard commander during the famous *Escalade* of 1602.[1] A banner *fête*, with everyone in costume, recalls this episode on its anniversary, December 12. Participation therein, wearing new ribbons, holding Helena's hands and well away from the trained bears, helped greatly to reconcile the little girls to Geneva. For days they paraded about, singing "*Escalade, Savoyard; Savoyard, Escalade; guerre, guerre, guerre!*" Prattle in an Anglo-French argot was intermediate to bilingualism. One day when Isabel was shopping at the nearby *épicerie*, a visitor asked Lorna where her mother had gone. "To the A. and Picerie" was the reply.

Nearing six, this young lady was enchanted with the many reminders of "The Olden Times." Indeed they were all around. Chillon, that *bijou* model of the perfect castle, was the length of the lake away, yet easily accessible by delightful steamer ride. Half way was Lausanne, the more attractive to me because there Gibbon had written *The Decline and Fall of the Roman Empire*, with all its premonitions for modern imperialists. Isabel was more interested in the historian's youthful love affair with Mlle. Curchod, who eventually married the famous French financier Jacques Necker and by him gave birth to the girl who became Mme de Staël. Of that illustrious and much portrayed lady Napoleon would say: "She carries a quiver full of arrows that would hit a man were he seated on a rainbow." Exiled by the imperious autocrat, Mme de Staël took refuge in the chateau at

---

1. This Catholic attack on heretical Geneva is the setting of Stanley Weymann's romantic novel, *The Long Night*.

Coppet, a charming lakeside village close to Geneva, and there established the salon which came to be called "the intellectual rendezvous of Europe." The term might also have been applied a little earlier to Voltaire's home at Ferney, distant only a few miles across the fertile countryside. Here and at the many less renowned shrines around the lake we would frequently visit, as interested in the history that had been made as in that then in the making.

The latter was never ignored for long. To get to know the League of Nations at that time was the easier because it was administered by a small and close-knit organization, on a total budget, in 1928, of approximately six million dollars. The entire Secretariat, excluding the smaller technical staff of the International Labor Office, numbered fewer than 200 men and women from 40 different nations. Consequently, it was feasible to become acquainted with every important member of this dedicated international civil service from the Secretary-General, Sir Eric Drummond, down. Attaining this objective I became increasingly impressed by the truly cosmopolitan viewpoint of the great majority, Mussolini's Italian spokesmen being the only notable exception. One of my early and most interesting friends was Ken Harada, a Japanese of my own age who served in the Political Section. Harada, discretely mistrustful of the growing power of the military in his own country, knew of the interest I had shown in Japanese foreign policy and discussed it at length in long and intimate luncheon sessions. To avoid gossip about such meetings we avoided hotels and patronized the simple little *estaminet* frequented by Lenin during his years of exile in Geneva. I had first been introduced there by Romm, the *Tass* correspondent. Years later, before Pearl Harbor but after the Second World War had begun in Europe, Harada visited our home in Washington. He warned that the two countries were on a collision course which, in his opinion, would be disastrous for both. In Rome, in June, 1945, Harada played a central role in a vain and as yet largely undisclosed effort to arrange a dignified Japanese surrender before the dropping of the Atomic Bomb.[2] He was one of

---

2. Part of the story has been made known by the Vatican and was referred to in an article in the New York *Times* of April 4, 1971.

several Japanese whom I was always happy to have known.

At Geneva, the annual Assembly and quarterly Council meetings were dramatic, attracting the political leaders of member-nations and with them an influx of big-name correspondents who generally took over from those permanently stationed there. In consequence, the latter for the most part were not professionally prominent. Two, however, appealed to me for their personal characteristics. One of these was Reginald Wright Kauffman, of the New York *Herald-Tribune*, who had authored some pleasant verse and several impermanent novels. The other was Hugh F. Spender of the *Christian Science Monitor*, a shy and sensitive Englishman with a far better-known journalistic brother. Hugh stuttered painfully, was temperamentally unfitted for the rough-and-tumble of newspaper work, and could not have survived with an organization less considerate than that of the *Monitor*. But he was a charming companion for a country walk or fireside conversation. The three of us had many rambles together, often to the wayside inn at Thoiry, just across the nearby French frontier, where Briand and Stresemann had hatched the Locarno Pact. Another close professional friend was Clarence K. Streit, who came to Geneva soon after me as resident correspondent for the New York *Times*. We had been fellow Rhodes Scholars at Oxford. Streit was a first-class reporter and soon showed his less ambitious colleagues how much good "copy" was tucked away around the League headquarters. He was already working on the idea of an Atlantic "Federal Union" among the victorious powers. Much more practical, it seemed to me, was the development of economic and eventually political union among the war-shattered nations of Western Europe, along lines already advocated by Premier Briand, Jean Monnet and Sir Arthur Salter. Here was a lively subject of discussion and argument among correspondents with interests deeper than the day's developments.

In December, 1928, the League Council decided to hold its scheduled quarterly meeting at Lugano, choosing that resort town in Italian Switzerland because the poor health of Gustav Stresemann, the German Foreign Minister, made wintry

Geneva physically hazardous for him. Although I had no travel-expense arrangements with the *Sun*, I decided to attend these sessions, which would also give opportunity to have a look at Fascist Italy. Also in mind was the desirability of an interview with Dr. Stresemann, whose placatory policy toward France was getting constructive results. This famous industrialist, turned statesman, did not like reporters but I pulled strings and was invited to take coffee with him after one of the Council sessions. The conversation was in German, and I asked to have an interpreter present as I wanted no risk of any misunderstanding. This was wise since Stresemann spoke very rapidly, in a curiously un-Germanic high-pitched voice. He was over-worked, nervously exhausted, yet stimulated by that burning sincerity sometimes found in those who know that their road is near its end. Though only 50, in a year Stresemann would be dead.

Nobody should be deceived, he said, by the superficial improvement that had followed the Locarno Agreements. Thanks to Briand, whom he praised highly, there was a breathing spell in which the perilous condition of Europe could be realistically considered, but that was all. The Kellogg Pact was self-defeating to the extent that people took its "renunciation of war" as actually accomplished. Among the victorious powers there was no tangible progress toward disarmament and Germany, ten years after the Armistice, was still ringed by hostile bayonets. This made his own pacific policy seem both unsuccessful and unpatriotic to the German electorate. American loans were making it possible for Germany to pay some reparations, but the distorted economy of the country was a house of cards that could all too easily collapse. Americans in particular, he argued, seemed unaware that runaway inflation had wiped out the once solid German middle class and that the vacuum was being filled by reckless adventurers calling themselves National Socialists. When I observed that not many seemed to take these Nazis seriously, the Foreign Minister laughed sardonically. A desperate people, he warned, would eventually adopt desperate remedies. Americans, he said, had largely failed to recognize the import of Mussolini. They would do well not to be indifferent to the rise of a similar *Fuehrer* for the much more competent Germans.

The beautifully gardened lakefront of Lugano seemed pitifully theatrical as I walked back to my modest hotel and typed this disturbing interview for cabling to the *Sun*. A couple of days later I was in Milan, getting from the helpful U.S. Consulate statistics on Italy's superficial gains under Fascist rule. It was with underlying anxiety for Europe's future that I returned to Geneva, to find a cable from my paper asking me to investigate the secret reparations discussions soon to be held at the American Embassy in Paris. This was my first intimation that the Dawes Plan would be revised downwards, because of President Hoover's anticipation that disaster threatened unless German solvency could be restored. Everything that Stresemann had said, I thought, was being underlined. While the United States received no reparations, as such, in Anglo-French thinking all war debt repayment was linked thereto. The indirect American interest was enormous and the forthcoming Young Plan[3] had to be clearly defined in advance so that The Hague Conference of the Allies, to be held in August, 1929, could accept it with a minimum of discord. When I journeyed to Paris only an inner circle knew what the Young Plan would be and this it was my mission to ascertain.

Largely because I had steeped myself in the reparations problem the effort was successful. Finding my inquiries well informed, the first secretary of the Embassy, Edwin C. Wilson, filled in the major gaps, including a preview of the foreshadowed Bank of International Settlements at Basel. Unquestionably the Young Plan was an improvement on its predecessor. Yet the terms laid down for Germany still seemed impossible. The plan reduced the annual payments to a realistic figure, but in so doing provided that these annuities should continue until 1988. Whatever the responsibility of the Germans for the war of 1914, I thought, it was fantastic to suppose that their great-grandchildren would 70 years later still be paying for the

---

3. So named after Owen D. Young, then Chairman of General Electric, its principal architect.

damage caused. Another war would be a greater probability.[4]

The handling of this assignment made a good impression in the home office, and I was informed that, on October 1, 1929, I would be placed in charge of the London Bureau of the *Sun*. Four years earlier nothing would have pleased me more. Now I was doubtful. It was not only that the necessary research for the Guggenheim study was far from completion. Arthur Sweetser, who through Raymond Fosdick had influence with the Rockefeller Foundation, had said to me several times that the American League of Nations Association should have a permanent office in Geneva, with increasing intimations that if so I would be the man to run it. I was impressed by Fosdick, who had been an important member of the League Secretariat in its early days and was now the dynamic guiding head of the non-partisan supporting organization in the United States. Not much attention was paid to these overtures, however, until Sweetser, shortly before leaving for a trip home, asked me what salary I would expect to run the proposed Geneva office. Observing that the job would demand much entertaining, I replied offhand that $10,000 per annum, plus all secretarial and office expenses, would seem requisite, the figure being considerably above what the *Sun* would pay me in London. "I think I can arrange that," said Arthur, "so hold everything until I return."

Although there was no commitment the prospects, one way or another, justified moving to a commodious four-bedroom furnished apartment available in the pleasant quarter of Champel. This gave desired *Lebensraum* and ushered in a generally excellent series of Swiss cooks. The family took time out for modest winter sports, at St. Cergue in the Jura. I played occasional golf at nearby Onex and even emulated Shelley to the extent of renting a small sailboat on the always alluring lake. Socially, that spring was agreeably crowded. Professor and Mrs. Morley came to Geneva, as did Isabel's sister Grace and her husband, John Herndon, who had received an appointment to the faculty

---

4. There is no doubt that German indignation over the Young Plan, combined with Stresemann's untimely death to forward Hitler's rise to power. Cf. J. W. Wheeler-Bennett: *The Wreck of Reparations* (N.Y., William Morrow, 1933), especially Chapters V and VII.

of Haverford College. Perhaps its correspondent neglected the *Sun* somewhat, but I pressed on with my book, and the Guggenheim Foundation renewed my fellowship for a second year. The children had minor illnesses but happily nothing very serious. The most momentous domestic happening was Isabel's pregnancy which, with this addition expected in mid-January of 1930, was helpful in pushing decisions.

Another precipitating factor of importance was the British General Election of May, 1929, which brought the Labour Party into power by a slim plurality—288 seats in the House of Commons as against 260 Conservatives and 59 Liberals. The customary support of the latter for the new Prime Minister, Ramsay MacDonald, made his leadership more secure, especially in foreign policy, and it was good news when "Uncle Arthur" Henderson was named Foreign Secretary. I had known him well in London, and the stout old trade unionist had visited our modest home in Baltimore. But again there were two sides to the coin of choice. Acquaintance with many of the new government's leaders would certainly facilitate the proffered correspondence from London. On the other hand, Arthur Henderson could be expected to promote European unity and therefore the promise of the League of Nations, making work in its behalf more satisfactory. As a historian of the period has written, Henderson ". . .became the first, perhaps the only British statesman between the wars who won the confidence of [both] France and Germany."[5]

In his straightforward way, moreover, Henderson saw that the ulcer of reparations was contributing greatly to the ten per cent unemployment in Britain which had helped the Labour victory. Confiscation of German merchant shipping had served to close Clyde shipyards. Deliveries of reparations coal on the Continent had deeply cut the once profitable British export trade in that commodity. British support for further reduction of German payments was therefore assured and, hopefully, German doubts about the Young Plan would be placated by withdrawing the Allied armies from the Rhine. All this would enhance the importance of Geneva and probably stimulate the

---

5. A. J. P. Taylor: *English History 1914–1945*, Oxford, The Clarendon Press, 1965, p. 272.

increasing, if cautious, cooperation of the Hoover Administration. I sought advice from Prentiss Gilbert, now the political Consul at Geneva, and from Hugh Wilson, the U.S. Minister at Berne. Both, of course unofficially, expressed the hope that I would take the position with the League of Nations Association, if it materialized.

The previous Assembly session had elected Spain to a nonpermanent seat on the League Council and dictator Primo de Rivera had successfully urged that its June meeting be held in Madrid. I planned to attend and Sweetser, who would return from America for the sessions, suggested that we should meet at Gibraltar, thence driving to the Spanish capital by hired car. It would give opportunity for thorough discussion of the presumable job offer, also, a glimpse of the Moorish influence which I had savored only through the pages of Washington Irving.

So, in due course, I travelled to Toulon, boarded an Orient liner and met Arthur and Ruth on the historic Rock. Thence we drove to Málaga and then on a nervously twisting narrow dirt road over the formidable Sierra Nevada to Granada, stopping a couple of days to imbibe something of the glories of the Alhambra and *Generalife*. Next was Córdoba, with its incredibly beautiful mosque, and then a cut-back to Sevilla. Here the well-planned Ibero-American Exposition was in progress, complete to replicas of the Columbus ships moored in the Guadalquivir. Agnes Repplier, the witty essayist known to all who knew anything of Philadelphia, was one of the United States Commissioners, and I stayed on to get an interview with her and write a feature article on the Exposition. "We Americans have no shadow of doubt," she told me, "that our good fortune is due to our good behavior." Then I took train alone to Madrid, noisy, tawdry and meretricious after the lovely Andalusian cities but largely redeemed by the majestic Prado, surely one of the world's most satisfying art galleries. Spanish hospitality was excessive and after the Council sessions I was glad to head back to Geneva, via lively Barcelona where I stopped long enough to write an article on the Catalonian Separatism which was to play so large a role in the coming Civil War. "No traveling salesman is a harder worker," I wrote to Isabel.

There had been opportunity, in Spain, to discuss every aspect of the Association opening for which Sweetser, with customary efficiency, had made all preliminary arrangements. But I still hesitated. I had been with the *Sun* for seven years, had throughout been treated with great consideration and did not want to break the connection summarily. John Owens was then visiting London, and early in August I journeyed there to confer with him and also get Frank's viewpoint. The latter, having himself decided to remain in England, could scarcely advise me against a continuation at Geneva. Owens was sympathetic, if somewhat unflattering in his assurance that the *Sun* would survive any shock of separation.

On August 20, Isabel's birthday, I cabled my regretful resignation. Our second year of residence in Geneva had already begun. As a part of the new arrangement the family would return to the U.S. briefly, my wife and children to visit her relatives and I to consult with the Association people in New York. Helena would go home to Vienna, promising to rejoin us later. In early September we left from England on the Anchor Line *Tuscania*, again with Captain David Bone. The return sailing, from New York on October 30, saw newspaper headlines blazing with the immediate effects of the disastrous stock market crash.

◀For me the woes of Wall Street had no immediately injurious effects. The resources of the League of Nations Association were well funded and there was never any doubt that I would receive my salary and office expenses regularly and in full. All of my savings were in life insurance or Baltimore real estate, only indirectly affected by the collapse of inflated securities. Though I was unable to sell Willow Cottage its rental was renewed and I thereupon purchased a new Chrysler to take back to Geneva. Most of that fateful October was spent in New York, working out plans with Philip C. Nash, formerly Dean of Antioch College and now newly-appointed director of the propaganda organization.

In the metropolis I saw much of Chris, paying three visits to the "Old Rialto" theater in Hoboken. There, on what he called "The Seacoast of Bohemia," he had been happily supervising a very popular revival of old melodramas. This amusing interlude in Kit's lively career was, however, soon to fold, not primarily by reason of the depression but more because coincidentally one of the light-hearted sponsoring group had put sticky fingers in the company till and made off with the financial reserves. It was a serious blow for Chris, in morale as much as monetary loss, and the effect on his trusting temperament can be traced in writings subsequent to this period. Isabel's family were also hit. So it was not without apprehensions that I shepherded my flock aboard the French liner *De Grasse* for the trip back to Europe. Isabel was now more than six months pregnant and what lay ahead seemed none too certain.

But the ship was charming, the quarters commodious and the crossing calm. There were few passengers to adulterate that perfect service at which the French are so adept. The staff nurse made it her responsibility to improve the Geneva accent of the Morley children and took full charge of them from breakfast to bedtime. Isabel could enjoy luxurious leisure and did so without anxiety over coming events. That mood was broken when on the night before reaching Le Havre little Teeny suddenly ran up a temperature of 104°, making the plan for an immediate drive across autumnal France seem perilous. The ship's doctor shrugged his shoulders: "How can one tell, with a child of five, whether it is serious or not?" The decision, *faute de mieux*, was to go ahead. Our route would start toward Paris and if Teeny continued ill she could be driven direct to the American Hospital at Neuilly. If the ailment proved trifling, we would maintain the plan of cutting south from Rouen, doing the 500 miles to Geneva by the leisurely schedule already mapped from the invaluable *Guide Michelin*.

It was a gloomy scene when we disembarked in pouring rain at Le Havre, the early morning of November 8, 1929. Teeny, still feverish, had been bundled in all available sweaters and coats for the wait on the chilly dock, while the car was unloaded and all the customs' formalities endured. At last we could drive off, finding the route to Rouen amid the maze of waterfront streets and traffic. Once out of the crowded port, the sun broke through and the Chrysler seemed cheerfully at home in the quiet Normandy countryside. There was a struggle on the back seat and

Teeny popped out of her nest of coverings. "Where are we?" she demanded, "And when do we eat?" Very soon now, at Rouen, she was told and there, at the hospitable Hôtel d'Angleterre, we found the child recovered from whatever the indisposition had been, filled her with savory *potage* and happily turned off the Paris road toward Evreux.

And so we proceeded, via Chartres, Orléans, Nevers, Autun and Bourge-en-Bresse, by easy stages to Geneva, spending four nights on the road at wholesome French inns where Madame's now obvious condition always aroused cordial solicitude. The little girls enjoyed it enormously, prattling French with a fluency that endeared them immediately to all around. At Autun they disappeared, but were discovered perched on stools in the hotel bar, shaking dice with the bartender according to some complicated local formula which he had taught them. Finally, to quote from a letter to my mother, "Once through the Gap de Bellegarde the snowy summit of Mont Blanc came in view, *couleur de rose* in the Alpine sunset glow, and thus down to what Lannie called 'dear old Geneva,' as night closed in." The next morning Isabel visited her obstetrician, excellent Dr. René Koenig, who found her condition normal but warned against any long automobile trips.

Before returning to the States I had arranged to place my office in the International Club, a strategic location where the Geneva Research-Information Committee was quickly organized. It was an informal, volunteer group, mostly members of the League Secretariat, who assisted in carrying out the functions which I felt able to initiate. These were, first, the reception of American visitors. If run-of-mine tourists they would be given a guided tour of the League and International Labor Offices with one or other of the volunteer workers always available from the semi-permanent American colony. When journalists, teachers or otherwise serious students of some League activity, I would confer with them individually and make arrangements for further reception by appropriate officials, nearly all of whom were now known to me.

A second function was the preparation of a monthly resumé of current League developments, running to eight or ten printed pages. This was supplemented by fairly lengthy "Special

230

Studies" on timely but ancillary subjects such as "The Palestine Mandate" or "European Union," for which qualified and objective authors were sought. Promotion of these publications, in the United States and at Geneva, was handled by the Secretary of the Research-Information Committee, J. McC. Sturgis, a dedicated and proper Bostonian who in spite of the depression soon pushed subscriptions to a respectable figure, especially in colleges, libraries and newspaper offices. Behind the scenes was an enthusiastic Chicago financier, James Forstall, who managed an investment trust—Victory Corporation—of which the capital gains were earmarked for our activities. Unfortunately, after the market crash, these were minute. Finally, there were contacts with the representatives of private associations working in various countries to promote the League, and also many social affairs.

There was a qualified optimism when the American colony in Geneva, nearly 400 strong, assembled for the annual Thanksgiving Dinner, held in 1929 at the recherché Hôtel des Bergues. While everyone had been shaken by the stock market debacle the worst effects of this seemed to be controlled, and under President Hoover's leadership a sure, if gradual, recovery was envisaged. On May 1, 1930, Mr. Hoover would feel able to tell the U.S. Chamber of Commerce, in Washington, that: "We are not through the difficulties of our situation" but "I am convinced we have passed the worst and with continued effort we shall rapidly recover."[6]

The President was referring only to the American scene, taken in isolation. I could not be confident, primarily because the European situation was so shaky. The push toward Franco-German reconciliation, given by the Locarno Pact, had petered out. Few realists in Geneva regarded the Kellogg Pact as more than a pious gesture. The effort to promote a general disarmament treaty was bogged down and Hitler was steadily gaining adherents in resentful Germany. As straws show the way the wind blows, so an early intimation of coming trouble was seen in timid Helena's decision not to rejoin us. While we were in the States the girl had obtained a job in a Vienna textile

6. Herbert Hoover, *The Great Depression*, Macmillan Co., New York, 1952, p. 58.

231

factory. If she should give this up, her brother wrote, she might never again find employment in stricken Austria. That was all too probable, for it was in moribund Vienna, of course, that the big bust would soon originate.

Now on the inside of League operations, I was in a good position to see how nationalistic jealousies vitiated its promise. A case in point was the effort for Euopean Federal Union, which had been publicly advocated by M. Briand at the Tenth Assembly, in September, 1929. "I think," said the great French statesman at that time, "that among the peoples constituting geographical groups, like the peoples of Europe, there should be some kind of federal bond . . . a bond of solidarity which will enable them, if need be, to meet any grave emergency that might arise. That is the link I wish to forge."

Of course the idea was not originated by the French Foreign Minister. But by suggesting that it be worked out under the aegis of the League, as a "regional agreement" of the sort expressly approved by the Covenant, Briand brought the vision into the realm of practical politics. I saw that any organized movement for a United States of Europe would appeal to Americans and secured an interview with Briand in order to explore his thinking. The brilliant old Socialist, so deceptively slouchy in appearance, argued that an economic union of France and Germany would be mutually beneficial and was now politically feasible. It was, indeed, the logical next step from the Locarno Pact which he had initiated with Dr. Stresemann. But this great German's diplomatic successors in Berlin were of inferior quality. Soon it was reported that Germany was planning a Customs Union (Zollverein) with Austria as a first step toward a European Common Market. The French nationalist press exploded angrily over what was called "this clumsy subterfuge" and Briand was forced to backtrack. The British also, then as later, were dubious about the merger of their empire in a federated Europe.

On the subject of disarmament, also, German diplomacy of this period was tactless, though the grim conditions in that country, and the growing threat of a Nazi takeover, explain why the Berlin government felt it must not seem pusillanimous. The argument here rooted in the ambiguous wording of the introduction to Part V of the Treaty of Versailles. This read: "In order to render possible the initiation of a general limitation of the armaments of all nations, Germany undertakes strictly to observe the land, naval and air clauses which follow."

Berlin's interpretation of this wording, equally equivocal in the French version, was that German disarmament was contingent on the "general limitation" which, more than a decade after the Armistice, had scarcely seen even an "initiation." The French maintained that there was no bilateral agreement— merely a hope that enforced German disarmament, as a condition precedent, would permit similar voluntary action by the victors. The querulous Germans should be satisfied by French magnanimity in withdrawing their troops from the Rhineland. Moreover, Paris argued that the Naval Limitation Treaty, concluded in Washington in 1922, must be applied to Italy before the security provided by land forces was jeopardized. When this was accomplished, by the London Naval Conference of 1928, the resourceful French found other excuses. The Communist threat made it impossible to envisage reduction of the defenses of their allies adjacent to Soviet Russia, meaning Czechoslovakia, Poland and Rumania. This negative attitude frustrated the work of the League's Preparatory Commission for Disarmament, on which that experienced American diplomat, Hugh Gibson, did his utmost to mediate constructively. With Europe's diminished resources wasted on armament, with no international monetary order, with trade barriers held high and unemployment everywhere acute, with Germany paying reparations only to the extent of American loans—prospects seemed grim. The League Secretariat could, and did, prepare ameliorative plans for consideration by the member-states. But this was futile when the major governments lacked both the will and wisdom to follow through.

As Geneva representative of the American League of Nations Association, I felt that I must report these difficulties realistically, When a Geneva "Conference with a View to Concerted Economic Action" bogged down, I quoted the dour summation of its outspoken Dutch chairman: "The most optimistic person could not regard the results obtained as remarkable." Such frank analysis was not appealing to Arthur Sweetser, an unswerving optimist on League activities who argued that its promise, rather than actual performance, should always be emphasized. The position taken and sustained by me was that nothing could be gained by trying to conceal the League's weakness. Better policy was to point out how these deficiencies would be minimized by the cooperation of the United States, which under President Hoover's direction was steadily tending to increase. I took counsel with Hugh Gibson, decidedly a League well-wisher, who heartily approved this stand. And I felt rewarded when the Hearst press labelled me editorially as "the most subtle League propagandist on the Geneva scene today."

The problems mentioned, and others like them, were for some months no more than clouds in a generally sunny sky. In the domestic area life was easy. Isabel's morale, understandably low before the birth of little Tony, recovered with his appealing presence. Only Teeny, who had wanted a younger sister, was negative when her mother returned to the apartment after the fortnight's hospitalization then normal for any birth. "We can change him for a girl, can't we?" Teeny inquired. But everyone else was pleased. Mlle. Doy, a professional nurse, came for another two weeks to show how "*un vrai citoyen de Genève*" should be diapered and otherwise acclimated. "Miss Mary," an excellent English housekeeper, joined us and soon a charming "Swiss Miss," named Liny, arrived to supervise the girls. We had not simplified the complications of living merely by moving to Geneva. But those pertaining to the household and those concerning my work each had interlocking interest.

I had scheduled a trip to Paris, Brussels and London, to confer with the unofficial League organizations in those capitals. At the first two I addressed the meetings in French, a courtesy that made a good impression. On return, Lannie, now seven, corrected me at the dinner table, both on points of pronunciation and of grammar. The little girls now spoke and read French as well as English and prattled gaily in the more melodious tongue. Even Isabel, somewhat reluctantly, began to speak it regularly, partly because neither her pediatrician, her dentist nor her cook knew any English. "On matters medical and culinary," she wrote, "I'm now bilingual." She took lessons and the quite good theater in Geneva helped, as did the cosmopolitan entertaining.

At the end of April we decided to take a short holiday in Italy. We had selected Florence but at the same time Hugh Spender, widowed some months earlier, was going there to honeymoon, after marrying a rather uningratiating Polish girl in the League Secretariat. Everyone thought this a deplorable mistake on the part of the shy and elderly English correspondent. "Just for his money" was the general verdict and since that was also our opinion we changed our plans so as to vacation at Stresa. It is a charming resort and, temporarily free from responsibilities, we explored Lake Maggiore and the Boromean Isles in all their springtime beauty. Thence on to Milan, where Leonardo's "Last Supper" could still be seen in unblemished glory on the walls of the *Chiesa della Grazie*. We lodged in a pleasant little hotel, in the shadow of the incomparable cathedral, where Isabel had an extraordinary experience. In the middle of the first night I was awakened by her sobbing and, on inquiry, was told that she was upset by a vivid and terrible dream—that Hugh Spender had just committed suicide in Florence. "Nonsense," I protested, "people don't do that on honeymoons, no matter how mistaken the marriage." However, the local papers, the next afternoon, brought almost incredible confirmation. At the very hour of Isabel's nightmare Hugh Spender had taken his life, a hundred miles away. I could lay no claim to extrasensory perception but fully believed it possible. Isabel, skeptical about anything savoring of the supernatural, called it pure coincidence.

The Chrysler, named Mercure by the little girls, greatly improved family mobility that spring and summer of 1930 and there were many week-end expeditions. Particularly memorable was one to the old walled village of Gruyère, famous for its cheese, which nestles in the mountains above Vevey. For the first time we made the complete shoreline circuit of Lac Leman. Close to one-third of this is in France, a part of that old Burgundian kingdom which flourished for some centuries after the fall of Rome, only to collapse in a manner which suggests how easily nations may disappear from all but unremembered history.

235

From Geneva, in the projecting southwest corner of Switzerland, all roads except the lakeside Route de Lausanne lead almost immediately into France. A favorite trip across the then almost open border was to Thoiry, famous for the unpretentious inn where Briand and Stresemann had found that fine food cements firm friendship. Here, at the end of May, was a gala christening party to celebrate the baptism of Anthony J. Morley at the American Church, a ceremony enlivened by Teeny's clearly audible suggestion that soap as well as water should be employed. Professor and Mrs. Morley were again in Geneva, for their second spring visit. Another welcome elderly incursion was that of Henry Morgenthau and his wife. While Isabel took her, and the little girls, for a *tour du lac*, I drove "Uncle Henry" to Chamonix, at the old gentleman's special request. He was full of sagely gloomy prognostications about the economic future, but soon dozed off to rest a venerable head on my shoulder. I was now accustomed to Alpine driving but was always puzzled by the frequent roadside signs warning: "*Attention aux chutes de pierre.*" What, I wondered, could one do to dodge a rockslide when it decided to fall?

In March I had moved my office to more spacious accommodations in an annex to the main League building, just across the rue des Pâquis from the Secretariat. To become a tenant of the organization emphasized the insider position achieved, and to be close to its officers and reference library was a great advantage. Circulation of the printed matter prepared under my direction was increasing rapidly, in amount and influence. Now it was easier to make use of guidance and assistance generously given by Fritz Schnabel, the German head of the League's efficient publications service. A further gain was to be closer to the building of the International Labor Office. In preparation for a busy summer, my bureau now had a staff of eight, three of them unpaid volunteers, and the work went smoothly.

When June arrived we turned our apartment over to our good friends Ben and Mary Gerig, proceeding with personal possessions to the rural mansion of the Sweetsers. It was a beautiful house, elegantly furnished and sybaritic beyond anything in our experience. On the ground floor was a magnificent *grand salon*, with *petit salon* adjacent for intimate gatherings;

236

also a book-lined library and a separate study, in addition to spacious dining room, kitchen and pantries. Above were six big bedrooms with three baths and on the third floor a warren of servants' rooms. The Sweetsers had left their gardener and Ruth's private maid to assist their tenants' housekeeping and we brought quite a retinue of our own: a cook, Miss Mary to oversee operations, Liny to care for the children, even Helena who had been able to take leave without pay from her job in Vienna to help out for two months as sempstress and general assistant. Nevertheless the place was understaffed by Sweetser standards as there was now no chauffeur, though an extra car which I took over, leaving Mercury to Isabel. For children the place was ideal, with an outdoor playhouse, a jungle gym and winding woodland paths adding a wilderness touch to the carefully tended cutting gardens. The baby slept peacefully and grew fat, in his pram under the whispering trees. Some consternation was caused when Lannie fell from the exercise bar and broke her right arm. But it was a clean fracture, chiefly memorable because her small sister insisted on wearing an identical sling, calculated to elicit equal commiseration from visitors.

Of these there were many. A part of the arrangement was that we should use the Sweetser pleasance for the lavish summer entertaining done by Arthur as senior American on the League Secretariat. This chore, though novel on the grand scale, was handled by Isabel with customary efficiency. A feature of the season was a big garden party for the Geneva Institute of International Relations, directed by scholarly Dr. Alfred Zimmern. Every summer he gave a course on League organization and undertakings for the more serious English-speaking visitors. As this Institute had over 200 members, in 1930, the soirée took a lot of arranging. Fortunately the weather was perfect and bushels of homemade delicacies disappeared amid light-hearted gaiety. Then there were innumerable lunches, teas and small dinners for handpicked celebrities and their ladies. In these we were careful not to overlook the Germans, being well aware that the future of Europe and the League hinged on the turn of events in that troubled country. One evening, as cocktails were served on the terrace, the majestic Graf Zeppelin came cruising down the lake, circled low over Geneva, then turned slowly back toward Friedrichshafen. The great dirigible was hailed by the guests as a symbol of German technological potency. But loosened tongues suggested that this applied to airplanes also.

Against a background of shrinking trade, rising unemployment and national humiliation, Hitler was rapidly coming to the fore. The general election of September, 1930, returned 107 Nazi deputies, making this the second-largest Reichstag Party, not counting the Nationalists, who looked benevolently on much of Hitler's program. I felt that I should make an exploratory trip to Munich, "*Hauptstadt der Bewegung*," and so wrote to my good friend Friedel Wertham, then engaged in psychiatric research in the Bavarian capital. Dr. Wertham wrote back that he and another mutual friend, Ted Hatfield of the St. John's faculty in Annapolis, were then planning a walking trip from Munich to Innsbruck and urged me to join them. This I was happy to do, but spent a few days in Munich first, finding opinion there much divided as to the magnitude of the Hitler threat. The editor of the respected *Münchener Neueste Nachrichten* assured me that the Nazis could not possibly gain power because their leadership was too unintellectual—"Few professors, fewer philosophers and no poets," he argued fatuously. I felt that precisely because it was a "Know-Nothing" movement, narrowly patriotic and responsive to demagoguery, a Nazi triumph under the existing conditions was all too probable. Wertham, who was returning to America, predicted that Germany would soon be unsafe for any Jew, himself included. In contrastingly beautiful autumn weather the trio took the little steamer down the Starnberger See and then tramped in leisurely fashion past Oberammergau and through the mountainous country to Innsbruck. At the Austrian border two ancient customs guards, one German and one Austrian, glanced at our passports and waved us on. "Unless you were French, no longer any frontier here," said the Austrian jocosely. Thus was the Versailles Treaty, specifically forbidding Austro-German union, collapsing of its own ill-considered dictates, months before Hitler actually came to power.

The summer at Merimont, delightful though it was, had convinced me that disaster was coming; that nothing the League could do would avert it. My laborious research was completed, and Moulton asked insistently how long the Brookings Institution must wait before I condescended to join its staff. I would arrive early in 1931, I replied. In retrospect those halcyon days preserve an almost dreamlike, end-of-an-era, quality. In their several ways the family enjoyed every aspect of life in Switzerland. They had many new friends, and old ones kept dropping by to enjoy the hospitality that was a part of the job. Rufus Jones was warmly welcomed. Emory and Anne Niles were with us for a week, predicting that the spoiled couple would never live in Baltimore again. Brother Frank and Christina came in August; together they visited Zermatt, climbed the Gornergrat, drank in the grandeur of the towering Matterhorn and exchanged views on the gathering shadows. The Sweetsers, always optimistic, returned for the Eleventh League Assembly, which showed a brave face to a collapsing civilization. "We think it time," I wrote to my mother, "to get our three small children out of Europe."

❰Domestic tragedy paradoxically made it less regretful for the Morleys to leave Geneva. At the end of November came a cable saying that Isabel's mother, while visiting her daughter Grace at Haverford, had been run down by a speeding truck and instantly killed. In character Isabel resembled her mother. Their relationship had always been intimate and the blow for the younger woman was the heavier because she was so far from home. Unable to participate personally in the family mourning she was naturally the more anxious to return to Washington and be of some help to her widowed father.

But there was then no trans-Atlantic air travel and steamer reservations, already made from Hamburg for February 12, 1931, could not easily be advanced. I needed all the intervening time to arrange the continuation of my office. It was also necessary to get a visa for Liny, who had agreed to accompany the family. This was difficult, with immigration regulations tightened because of unemployment, and I could thank my excellent relations with the Consulate that the approval came through in time. Then, after two and one-half years in Geneva, there was much dismantling, clearing and packing to be handled, which did something to overlay bereavement.

To break the prevailing melancholy, shortly before Christmas I suggested a trip *à deux* to Berne, the modest capital of Switzerland which we had not heretofore visited. Mercury took the snow-covered roads debonairly on what was its final distance drive for us, since I had arranged to sell the vehicle in Geneva for a little more than it had cost in Baltimore 14 months earlier. There is much of interest in Berne but most memorable was luncheon with J. Pierrepont Moffat, then the First Secretary at the U.S. Legation, and his charming wife Lilla. She was a daughter of Joseph C. Grew, also a career diplomat of Groton-Harvard background, who would soon become our much-tried Ambassador to Japan. Moffat was representing the U.S., either as member or observer, on several of the League committees with which Washington collaborated and I had always found him frank and forthright. On this occasion the young diplomat was far from cheerful, emphasizing the chaotic international monetary situation. Under the pressure of reparation payments, Germany was using all possible devices to stimulate exports and restrict imports. Even so the tortured country was borrowing two American dollars for one paid over to its creditor governments. General currency instability had spread so as to make all international trade a gamble and the stubborn French refusal to forward disarmament made both economic and political prospects even more grim. The future seemed no less wintry than the cold Swiss landscape as we drove back to Geneva, to a subdued Christmas and to the few weeks remaining before as a sextet, including Liny, we took nearly half a sleeping car to travel north to Hamburg.

Always somewhat forbidding, the great German seaport seemed doubly so under depression conditions. Through Paul Leverkuehn, then a practising attorney there, we had obtained comfortable quarters at old-fashioned Streit's Hotel. At Ehmke's famous seafood restaurant there was still perfect service, under engravings of Bismarck and von Moltke to memorialize the glories of the imperial era. But along the snow-covered streets, shrouded by cold gray skies, gangs of Communist and Nazi youths were meeting in frequent bloody clashes. One of every three men in the city was unemployed and crippled veterans begged at almost every corner. I made my wife promise not to stray from the well-policed Jungfernstieg before accepting Paul's invitation to visit Lübeck and stay for a night in the home of his elderly mother. It was a chance to see the Buddenbrooks setting under unreproducible circumstance and I was grateful for the opportunity. No place could have been more charming than the old Hanseatic town in its frozen winter setting; no hostess could have represented the *ancien régime* more hospitably than friendly Frau Leverkuehn. From Lübeck I returned with an early 18th century sea-captain's chest in time to take the little girls to Hagenbeck's famous zoo before we sailed. That was aboard the half-empty Hapag liner *St. Louis*, on Lincoln's birthday. The Elbe was choked with ice floes, its banks obscured by gusty whirls of snow, as the steamer moved slowly down river to the North Sea. For shipboard reading I had bought an early edition of *Mein Kampf*, then selling in every bookstore. It was a perceptive purchase.

By contrast with Hamburg, it was like spring in Washington and the city seemed undisturbed when we reached that destination, appropriately on February 22. Twelve years earlier we had been enjoying a carefree, unencumbered life in the capital. With three children and a nurse, re-establishment was not so easy. Fortunately I had kept my savings in solid Swiss francs and bought another Chrysler. Lannie and Teeny were entered at the French-speaking Maret School. After three weeks in the rambling Wardman Park Hotel we found and rented a sufficiently spacious yet unpretentious house at 2700 36th Street, N.W. Coincidentally, the first of a series of shocks reverberated through the newspaper headlines. On March 21, the Austrian and German governments announced that, in defiance of the peace treaties, they would establish the *Zollverein*, or Customs Union, which even prospectively had aroused such indignation in France. The response in Paris was to cut off the short-term credits which were providing oxygen for the shattered Austrian economy. "Apprehension," wrote President

Hoover of the crisis, "began to run like mercury through the financial world."[7] There were frantic flights of capital, moving in disruptive cross-currents from one unstable nation to another. Security and commodity markets in the U.S. slumped again. As prices fell there was a rising business outcry for curtailment of competitive imports. This almost instinctive protective reaction was of course promptly matched in other countries. In 1931 the European nations bought less—much less per capita—from the United States than they had in 1913. Protection for steel producers was quickly offset by loss of foreign markets for wheat growers, and so on.

In May the great Kreditanstalt, Austria's largest private bank, collapsed and Ambassador Sackett rushed back from Berlin to report that the Bruening government was at the end of its tether. Then came the unprecedented personal message from aged President von Hindenburg to President Hoover, emphasizing "the danger to Germany due to internal and external tension caused by distress and despair." On June 20, after long consultations with the Congressional leadership, Mr. Hoover announced the War Debts Moratorium, "conditioned on a like postponement for one year" of reparations payments. He added pointedly that it would help if this action led to some tangible progress on disarmament "inasmuch as the burden of competitive armaments has contributed to bring about this depression."[8]

Intimate knowledge of the European scene made me the more useful to the Brookings Institution during these dramatic weeks. Equally I profited from the economic and financial expertise of Dr. Moulton and his professional staff. My assigned job, however, was one of promotion. I had been employed to see that the research of the organization got more and better publicity, with a view to increasing its influence and reputation both in Washington and throughout the country. This was not dissimilar from the work I had been doing in Geneva. And again I would start from scratch, since Moulton had engaged no publicity director pending my long-delayed arrival.

Working conditions were admirable. The Institution, "De-

---

7. Herbert Hoover, *op. cit.*, p. 63.
8. *Ibid*, p. 71.

voted to Public Service through Research and Training in the Humanistic Sciences," occupied a brand-new building, now prematurely demolished, on Jackson Place, the west frontage of Lafayette Square, directly opposite the White House. Here the score or so staff members had their individual offices. I was assigned to one next to the big room occupied by Dr. Moulton, and was allotted a very competent secretary, Mrs. Evelyn L. Freer, a beautiful and talented young woman who was of great assistance. The building had its own dining room and kitchen, a charming central patio with fountain and miniature garden, a luxurious lounge, excellent reference library and even a squash court built in for the special benefit of Dr. Moulton, a champion player who utilized the facility to break the long hours which he devoted with equal energy to his executive duties. It was, in effect, an ideal university burdened with only a few graduate students, with deeply interested trustees but no troublesome alumni, nor, at first, any serious financial problems. Handsomely endowed by its founder, Robert Brookings, a wealthy St. Louis manufacturer, other foundation grants were zealously sought and often skillfully secured by Dr. Moulton. While wholly independent, the underlying plan was that the Institution should serve both federal and state governments, by research on pressing non-political problems, simultaneously doing a public service by clarification of these issues, whether economic, financial, social or all combined.

It was the latter phase of the work which I was expected to promote and I approached the task methodically. The Brookings' studies, though well screened for accuracy, were often appallingly professorial and dull. In consequence they received very little publicity, even though much of news value was buried in the heavy scholastic content. Therefore I first set myself to cultivate the corps of Washington correspondents, among whom were a number of old friends. As each study appeared, I would see that every bureau chief in Washington received a summarizing news release which I prepared, sometimes not without distressful outcries on the part of the book's author. This saved time for the correspondents, even then overwhelmed by the daily outpouring of publicity material. Soon the Brookings publications were receiving a much better share of newspaper notice and more book reviews in consequence. If desired, I would arrange interviews with the authors, with whom I conferred on the popularization of presentation. A somewhat similar technique was worked out with selected members of Congress, for the important lobbies, for the foreign embassies and for college and university libraries throughout the country, to many of which the major publications were sent, free and all too often stillborn. Purchase orders, which had been pitifully thin, began to flow in sizable quantity to the director of publications. This was John Anderson, a younger brother of the playwright Maxwell. He and I worked in close cooperation and enjoyed swapping anecdotes about our respectively famous literary siblings.

Other staff members soon became good friends. A number, besides Harold Moulton and W. F. Willoughby, are especially remembered. Edwin G. Nourse, the agricultural specialist, would become chairman, under President Truman, of the first Council of Economic Advisors. Leverett S. Lyon, a prolific writer on business problems, would eventually head the Chicago Association of Commerce. Isador Lubin, who like me had specialized on the problems of unemployment, went on to be Roosevelt's Commissioner of Labor Statistics. Russian-born Leo Pasvolsky later served the Department of State and participated in the drafting of the U.N. Charter. Lewis L. Lorwin, also of Russian origin, had worked closely with the International Labor Office. Charles O. Hardy, a financial expert, was especially informative as the shadows of the depression deepened. With all of these, in one way or another, I found myself highly compatible. Staff lunches in the Brookings dining room were always stimulating.

Difficulties had arisen to impede publication of *The Society of Nations*. I had brought the manuscript back from Geneva in nearly complete form, including a flattering introduction by the Secretary-General, Sir Eric Drummond, calling it "a valuable and permanent contribution." But there was still some scrubbing to do; the material had to be carefully reviewed and indexed. While it was understood that the Brookings would be the publisher, Dr. Moulton, as depression pressures mounted, was more anxious to get promotion into high gear. Having held this up so long, I could scarcely object. Consequently, the volume was only just ready for printing when, on the night of September 18–19, 1931, Japanese troops suddenly seized absolute control of the Manchurian city of Mukden, bringing immediate and outraged protest from Peking and confronting the League of Nations with an acid test of its efficiency for international order.

I did not for a moment regard this aggressive act as of secondary importance. From background acquired in the Far East, and at Geneva, I was sure that the Japanese militarists had set in motion their long-concocted plan of detaching all Manchuria from the nominal yet still firmly asserted control of Peking. The timing was occasioned both by the deepening depression in the United States and by the rising strength of Russia. With Washington absorbed by domestic problems and Moscow not yet in a position to protest effectively—that was the psychological moment for the Tokyo government to strike. The League would be no impediment, not merely because neither the U.S. nor the Soviet Union were members, but also because the Geneva organization was torn by Franco-German dissension and weakened by rampant economic nationalism. Nor was it ignored that at the moment the British Navy was riddled with unrest over pay cuts and that imminent devaluation of the pound was clearly foreshadowed.

For me the immediate issue from this explosion was its effect on my study of the League's political nature and constitutional development. I could either rush the book into print, ignoring the Japanese aggression as inconsequential, or I could delay publication until this had worked out in some form permitting conclusions. Reluctantly the latter course was chosen. It meant close attention to the tortuous windings as most of the League Council pressed, and Japan as a permanent member sought to evade, responsibility for the upheaval. It also meant deft editorial work to weld the current material with that already completed. What happened, however, served to strengthen the underlying thesis that the democratic Assembly, rather than the veto-ridden Council, was destined to become the major force in this or any subsequent organization of national governments.

That conclusion was confirmed by the special Assembly Resolution of March 11, 1932, after the Council had proved itself

245

unable to make headway against Japanese intransigence. This declared that: "It is incumbent upon the members of the League of Nations not to recognize any situation, treaty or agreement which may be brought about by means contrary to the Covenant of the League of Nations, or to the Pact of Paris." Secretary of State Stimson had already announced an American policy of non-recognition for any fruits of aggression, so that the greater force of the League when speaking with American support was now clearly demonstrated. Under this pressure Japan withdrew its troops from territory seized around Shanghai but continued quietly to tighten military grip on Manchuria. Indeed, on March 9, my Peking acquaintance of 1925, Henry Pu-Yi, last scion of the Manchu emperors, had been declared regent of an independent Manchuria in a Japanese-sponsored ceremony at Changchun. In spite of an adverse report, following most careful investigation by a League Commission of Inquiry,[9] this puppet state of Manchukuo continued under Japanese control until overthrown by the Russians at the close of World War II. Its independence from China, however, was never recognized either by the United States or by the great majority of League members. As I summarized the story in my book: "No society can be expected to give guarantees against occasional outbreaks of brute force. But any society deserving that name must insure that such outbreaks shall not be profitable to those who sponsor them." This was the principle of international law established by the Assembly, as sovereign organ of the League, by its Extraordinary Session of 1932.

The Society of Nations was published by the Brookings in June and, through the interest of brother Frank, simultaneously in London. Even with background knowledge I had found it difficult to trace the intricacies of the Sino-Japanese dispute both briefly and accurately, then mold them into the body of the writing. I knew that the banditry and disorder in China gave some excuse for Japanese aggressions. To maintain balance I had several conferences with my friend Kyoshi K. Kawakami, Washington correspondent of the Tokyo *Hochi*

---

9. Known as the Lytton Commission because chaired by Lord Lytton, of Great Britain. One of its five members, Maj. Gen. Frank R. McCoy, was American.

Shimbun. Kyoshi was a conscientous commentator and his contemporary book, *Japan Speaks*, carried an impressive introduction by Prime Minister Inukai. But this liberal statesman was brutally assassinated by Japanese army officers in May, 1932. Then the triumph of militarism was emphasized by Tokyo's resignation of membership in the League of Nations, an example followed with equal contempt by Germany as soon as Hitler came to power. Arthur Sweetser, to whom I gratefully dedicated my book, wrote with unconquerable faith from Geneva: "Half a League Onward!"

Though I knew it to be somewhat in the nature of a requiem, I was satisfied with *The Society of Nations*. It was a thorough study, reflecting the protracted effort of composition. Even after severe condensation the volume ran to 628 pages, not counting appendices and index, on which Evelyn Freer had labored long and valiantly. The work quickly gained a *succès d'estime*, was utilized (not always intelligently) in framing the Charter of the United Nations and still remains a standard reference book on international organization. Reviews were flattering. One especially appreciated by the author for its discernment of technique was by C. Delisle Burns, in the London *Spectator*: "His admirable method of combining exact description with appreciation of tendencies and principles, puts him at once in the front rank among students of international affairs." The academicians at the Brookings were so well pleased that they decided to award its Ph.D., hitherto given to only a few graduate students, in recognition of the research involved. I was happy to have earned the doctorate, which was to come in useful.

But there was not much optimism in Washington, that summer of 1932. Even in this favored non-industrial city, stabilized by governmental employment, grim effects of the depression were unconcealable. The most graphic illustration of simmering unrest was the Bonus Army, not wholly composed of actual veterans, who swarmed into the Capital to demand immediate cash payment of the soldiers' bonus which had been funded over a long period of years. President Hoover had persuaded the American Legion to refrain from actively sponsoring this demand, which would have taken some $3.4 billion. This could not reasonably be raised by taxes as already the Treasury was operating at a sizable deficit. Financial facts, however, did not quiet agitation in local Legion posts and a few Democratic leaders did not hesitate to exploit the issue. Yet there is some reason to believe the President's judgment that this demonstration "was in considerable part organized and promoted by the Communists and included a large number of hoodlums and ex-convicts determined to raise a public disturbance."[10]

Certainly men looking like "hoodlums" were much in evidence, pan-handling in threatening manner in Washington's downtown streets and stores. On July 28 there was a serious riot in which several policemen were stoned and clubbed while two "marchers" were shot and killed. The District Commissioners appealed to the President for "the assistance of Federal troops." General Douglas MacArthur was called upon to handle this unsavory task, accomplishing dispersion of the Bonus Army and demolition of its squalid camps with no further loss of life. Naturally the ugly episode got tremendous publicity. Many heard for the first time of Dwight D. Eisenhower when the Major of that name was mentioned as one of the General's aides. And adverse reaction practically guaranteed Mr. Hoover's defeat in the upcoming Presidential election.

Amid such excitements the Morley ménage was having its own difficulties. Another baby was to be expected, about the end of August. This was a factor in persuading Liny, the helpful "Swiss Miss," to seek an opportunity opened by her relations in New York. There was no serious financial strain, which had indeed been eased by sharply falling prices. But psychologically it was disturbing to face the responsibility of caring for four children, the oldest only eleven. "Every bairn brings his bannock wi' him," said a Scotch friend consolingly. Chris, who was having a tough time himself, wrote to call the dénouement reckless. He and his wife had recently spent a night at the White House, to be urged by the President to promote inspiring poetry, and presumably felt that the activities of his younger brother were not in keeping. I responded tartly that Chris had four children of his own and, as it turned out, Frank was also destined to sire a quartette. Badinage was not cheering to Isabel, who

---

10. Herbert Hoover, *op. cit.*, p. 225.

gave birth to her second son at Georgetown University Hospital on August 31. The event came during a solar eclipse, giving rise to prediction that something fateful must be in prospect for Felix Woodbridge Morley. Time was to prove this all too true.

It was not all worry and work. I kept fit with tennis and swimming and the new car was constantly out on family excursions in the Maryland and Virginia countrysides. The door was always open at Bill and Gladys Footner's historic home, "Charlesgift," on the lower Patuxent. An enterprising realtor sought to sell us land at lonely Point Lookout, where the broad Potomac joins with Chesapeake Bay, and the excellent fishing encouraged returns to the site of this Civil War prison camp. On one occasion the habitual quiet there was broken by a hurricane which inundated the ground floor of the decrepit old beachfront hotel, considerably dampening enthusiasm for the even more submerged lot we had been prospecting. Another adventure was on Stony Man mountain, where there is now a National Parks facility easily reached by the beautifully engineered Blue Ridge Parkway. Then there was only a modest private camp at Stony Man and a primitive dirt road winding up from Panorama to give access in fine weather. Torrential rains marooned us there, prolonging an outing taken shortly after Woody's birth. But we did not worry because in competent Annie Cooper we had found the perfect practical nurse who would "live in" to care for the children when needed. So, as the rains descended, I sat by an open fire in the cozy log cabin and pressed on with Oswald Spengler's work *Decline of the West*. It was topical reading in October, 1932.

❮It takes a very ill wind to blow nobody good. Both the art and business of broadcasting benefitted from the great depression. Few people had money to spend on costly entertainment and the air waves were increasingly tuned in to dispel ennui for stay-at-homes. Soon it was evident that what Al Smith in 1928 called "raddio" would play an even larger role in the Presidential Election of 1932. It was further apparent that a pleasing technique at the microphone, which Franklin D. Roosevelt early demonstrated, would give him a great advantage over Herbert Hoover. The latter's clipped staccato speech, monotonous delivery and penchant for dull statistics came in deadening fashion to the average listener. The President had called upon brother Chris to emphasize the national need for inspiring poetry. Inspiring broadcasts would have been of greater political advantage.

Soon after return to Washington we installed a good radio. I had filled a few air spots for the League of Nations Association and had picked up the elements of broadcasting. Now I listened often and attentively, with a view to utilizing this instrumentality in my work for the Brookings. On its staff was the talent, and possibly the technique, for a series on causes and consequences of the depression. I conferred with Dr. Moulton, who thought the prospect promising. The next step was to explore the possibility with Levering Tyson, who directed the university extension work at Columbia and had been named director of the National Advisory Council on Radio in Education, in which the Carnegie Corporation was taking a financial interest.

At luncheon in New York's impressive University Club I got along well with Dr. Tyson, who would later become president of Muhlenberg College and a close academic colleague. But discussion considerably modified the original idea. Tyson shrewdly observed that the Brookings Institution did not yet command the public attention which its representative admittedly wanted to promote. Therefore some big names from outside must be brought in to attract the requisite listeners. So in due course Tyson's Council established a Committee on Economics of which I was named chairman. In this capacity I cooperated with other agencies in arranging a program of 32 compact quarter-hour broadcasts, divided into three sections: Economic Aspects of the Depression; Roads to Economic Recovery; and New Social Responsibilities. Dr. Moulton was satisfied with the revision because the Brookings would have staff members among the chosen speakers; perhaps also because the Council agreed to pay one-half of my salary, plus expenses. It was rapidly becoming more difficult to meet the substantial overhead of the handsome establishment on Jackson Place. I, however, was not so pleased to have this management piled on top of other duties,

250

including the problems which had arisen in the completion of my book.

The program got under way, over the NBC network, on October 17, 1931, with an opening talk by prestigious Nicholas Murray Butler, recipient of 37 honorary degrees. Among those who followed at weekly intervals, speaking from New York and Chicago as well as from Washington, were Jane Addams, Harold Moulton, Edwin G. Nourse, Leo Wolman, Jacob H. Hollander, James Harvey Rogers, Rexford G. Tugwell, Lewis L. Lorwin, Stacy May, Sumner A. Slichter, Walton H. Hamilton, Frances Perkins, Paul H. Douglas and John R. Commons. With all of these I handled the arrangements and also gave the closing talk, on "The Depression and the World Community," on May 21, 1932. I was then called on to edit the collected papers, published by the University of Chicago Press under the title *Aspects of the Depression*.

The undertaking was successful. It started with a chain of 40 participating stations, which had grown to 55 when the series ended. It produced a large and interesting correspondence. The American Library Association, which cooperatively compiled reading lists available to auditors, reported an unexpectedly heavy demand for this source material. Most satisfactory, the experiment was continued, on a smaller scale, as a purely Brookings project, with the innovation of dialog among the speakers. I frequently sat in on these as interlocutor and believe that these radio colloquies were forerunners of the later unrehearsed discussions on TV.

The summer of 1932 found me not only weary but apprehensive. It was clear that Hoover would not be re-elected and his anti-depression measures, whether or not adequate for the emergency, were in large part being frustrated by a hostile Congress. In the Brookings library I studied the gloomy statistics. Agricultural and industrial production, capital investment, retail sales, foreign trade, prices of securities—all were steadily declining while unemployment and governmental debt mounted as rapidly. Treasury receipts for the fiscal year ending June 30 were under two billion dollars, less than half the pre-depression level. In spite of Mr. Hoover's alleged parsimony, federal expenditures during the same period exceeded $4.5 bil-

251

lion, highest since the World War I years. As nobody had then thought of "full employment" budgets, economies, both public and private, seemed a grim necessity. Salaries were cut at the Brookings and we were relieved when Liny left for New York. In her place as mother's helper came a reliable high school girl, Dale Fisher, who lived in and worked from school closing to children's bedtime for four dollars a week.

As the campaign developed, the sharp philosophic difference between Hoover and Roosevelt became apparent. The Republican in office would not indorse direct federal relief to individuals. New federal agencies, from the Reconstruction Finance Corporation to the widespread Intermediate Credit Banks, were uniformly designed to assist the hard-pressed through institutional improvement. Direct relief, in any form of handout with no repayment obligation, was left to the decision and direction of the several states, with very sparing aid from Washington. The Democratic nominee, on the other hand, was increasingly advocating direct assistance to individuals from the Federal Treasury, even while speciously maintaining that the budget must be balanced and all loose fiscal practise stopped. I was well versed in American political theory and it seemed to me both improper and dangerous to give the necessitous, no matter how deserving, control through the ballot over the dispensation of federal funds. That policy, once adopted, would make national elections a contest in demagogic and probably unfulfillable promises. To my Democratic friends I recalled John Stuart Mill's argument that every recipient of even "parish relief" should be excluded from the franchise: "He who cannot by his labor suffice for his own support has no claim to the privilege of helping himself to the money of others. . . . As a condition of the franchise, a term should be fixed . . . during which the applicant's name has not been on the parish rolls as a recipient of relief."[11]

With Charley Michelson[12] and other hatchet men at their

---

11. Mill, *On Representative Government*, Ch. VIII.
12. Chief of the Washington Bureau of the New York *World* until 1929, when he became the efficient and high-paid director of publicity for the Democratic National Committee. Of him Frank R. Kent, a staunch old-fashioned Democrat, would write: "It has been his pleasant task to minimize every Hoover asset. . .to obscure every Hoover virtue and achievement."

disposal it was easy for the Democratic strategists to inflame public opinion against the President. In the face of much real suffering, loyalty to Constitutional principles could be portrayed as callous and hard-hearted, even to the point of suggesting that Mr. Hoover was more interested in saving foreign rather than American children. The method of attack was by sweeping generalities and innuendo. Thus in Boston, on October 31, F.D.R. rhetorically asserted: "The present leadership in Washington stands convicted, not because it did not have the means to plan, but fundamentally because it did not have the will. . . . It is a leadership that is bankrupt, not only in ideals but in ideas. It sadly misconceives the good sense and the self-reliance of our people."

Damned both for action and inaction, President Hoover nevertheless fought gallantly for the inherited system of limited and divided governmental power. And his closing campaign speech at Madison Square Garden was prescient. "The proposals of our opponents," he said, "represent a profound change in American life. . . .Dominantly in their spirit they represent a radical departure from the foundations of 150 years which have made this the greatest nation in the world. This election is not a mere shift from the ins to the outs. It means deciding the direction our nation will take over a century to come." As to this Franklin D. Roosevelt readily agreed, once he had won the election. In his first inaugural the Democratic victor warned that if necessary he would seek "broad executive power to wage a war against the emergency, as great as the power that would be given me if we were in fact invaded by a foreign foe. . . . The people of the United States have asked for discipline and direction under leadership. They have made me the present instrument of their wishes."

At the same time, in curious coincidence, Adolf Hitler by constitutional process became Chancellor of the German Reich. He too was willing to be "the present instrument" of a people far closer to ruin than could with any accuracy be said of Americans.

As a resident of the District of Columbia, in November, 1932, I could not be numbered among the 39.6 percent of the active electorate that voted for Hoover for a second term. Nor, being then in Switzerland, had I been able to vote in 1928, when

Hoover obtained 58.2 percent of the popular vote. But I was cheered by the relatively small percentage change, considering the grinding effect of the depression and the unscrupulous character of the Democratic campaign. What was depicted as a landslide was, in fact, a shift on the part of only one voter in every five. So there was still a strong adherence to the principles of federalism, and I wondered in what way I could best exert my talents, such as they were, to the renaissance that seemed so important. The Brookings work was valuable, but perhaps I should be doing more.

Then, as seemed to happen frequently, fate took a hand. I was invited by Lyman Bryson, director of adult education for the Columbia Broadcasting System, to participate in the Adult Education Forums which were being organized in cooperation with the public schools of Des Moines. I cannot recall the sponsorship of this project but the scheme intrigued me. I was asked to lecture for an hour, six nights a week, on subjects of my own choosing, at the six public high schools of Des Moines, each rotating talk to be followed by an open discussion in which I would field questions and serve as moderator. The expectation was that the undertaking would stimulate citizen interest and assist understanding of the country's problems. The time to launch it was clearly just after the Presidential election, when politics would be at a minimum. And Des Moines was chosen for the pilot role partly for its central location, partly because of the excellence of its school system and partly because John W. Studebaker, the local superintendent of schools, had proved himself an imaginative and competent administrator. A year later Dr. Studebaker was named U.S. Commissioner of Education, in Washington. From his work there, following the Des Moines experiment, can be traced the evolution of the Community Colleges which, after the Second World War, proliferated so widely throughout the nation.

The engagement would be for six weeks, at $250 per week. This was more than the Brookings was paying me and, at the depth of the depression period, seemed a handsome wage. With four children Isabel could easily use the extra income. Dr. Moulton readily gave me leave without pay, suggesting that I would doubtless be willing to give assistance in a survey of Iowa State

Government which the Brookings had under way. I chose my six subjects, nicely balanced between domestic and international issues, wrote some preliminary outlines, and on February 24, 1933, took my favorite Capitol Limited to Chicago. It would be my longest trip away from the family since the Far Eastern adventure and my first opportunity to make more than a cursory acquaintance with the American Middle West.

In Chicago I was met by Jim Forstall, the maecenas of Geneva days, now financially busted but as full of optimistic enthusiasm as ever. Together we went out to Winnetka, where the still solvent mother of Ruth Sweetser and other League proponents were gathered for a luncheon with much praise for *The Society of Nations*. Then a bibulous literary party with brother Chris at his hotel, together with Frank Henry, sales manager of Doubleday Doran, Ben Abramson, proprietor of the famous Argus bookshop, and Phillip Guedalla, who at the moment was the English author cultivating the Chicago area. Chris was on his way to Honolulu, to lecture at the University of Hawaii on "Shakespeare as a Symbol." I had titled one of my forthcoming talks "War Debts as a Symbol." Building on this and some stronger physical resemblance, I suggested that we exchange destinations, subjects and identities. Chris did not bother to call this bluff but said in later years that it prompted him to grow a beard, so as to throttle any such mischief at birth.

His *Human Being* had just been published and was selling well. It was less biographical than *John Mistletoe*, which had appeared the previous year, and less interesting as a story than *Kitty Foyle*, which would follow. By reading the current novel carefully I learned more about my older brother. The title was well chosen since what deeply interested Chris, and what he was skillful to portray, was in his own phrase "the rich variation of human types." His characters, male and female, step from the pages uncartooned yet just as vividly as those of Dickens. And he mirrored a portion of the New York microcosm, for the period between the wars, as faithfully as the Victorian novelist had done for his slice of London a century earlier. Perhaps explaining his great popularity in the colleges, Chris was evocative as well as sentimental. "What, then, is a human being?" he asked himself. And in a long and lyrical definition concluded: "a mov-

255

ing eddy of self-consciousness seizing desperately upon cruel laughter . . . the chorus of a song whose verse everyone has forgotten." I made no such exuberant appraisals of my fellow-men. For me Human Events rather than Human Beings were of supreme interest.

As was to be expected, on arrival in Des Moines, I made immediate contact with its much-above-average newspaper, *The Register and Tribune*. This was then directed by the brothers John and Gardner Cowles, Jr., the latter of whom would go on to build an over-extended publication and broadcasting empire. He put me up at the comfortable Des Moines Club and introduced me to his able editor, W. W. Waymack, and lively managing editor, Basil (Stuffy) Walters. This was a most inappropriate soubriquet, for nobody carried a more refreshing atmosphere than "Stuffy" Walters. Through these executives I was quickly in touch with the Governor, the Mayor and local leaders. From John Studebaker I learned much about the problems of public education. Ruth Wallace, young sister of the new Secretary of Agriculture, and other attractive ladies were hospitable. I enjoyed the forthright and uninhibited attitude of the Mid-West and was interested in the efficient and generally honest operation of both the municipal and state governments. It was my first experience in a great agricultural state and Hoover's unpopularity with the run of its farmers was all to obvious.

Des Moines itself, as distinct from its people, was depressing. In population the town was then almost exactly even with Geneva; in every other respect a dreary contrast. "It has no natural advantages," I wrote, "and mighty few created by the *Einwohner*." On top of architectural banality Des Moines was then a singularly dirty city, due to the industrial consumption of poor-quality local coal. To have a clean shirt for each of my nightly forum appearances was no mean achievement. And the drill was more exacting than anticipated. At 7:30 every evening, except Sunday, I would appear at one of the local high schools to conduct my well-advertised meeting. For six nights, at six different locations, I was expected to give the same talk, but soon found that repetition was not feasible. In the alert west-end, one could count on easy receptivity from large audiences. In the poorer industrial districts, those who came were both less numerous and less informed. It was necessary to prepare two or three different presentations of a single topic. Then each week I must change my subject. Iowans seemed to love argument and often it would be after ten o'clock before I could escape for a belated supper. "There isn't much time for dalliance with the corn-fed maidens," I wrote home.

Complications caused by the bank closings were uppermost in the minds of Iowans, as the Roosevelt Administration took over. There was little interest and less faith in the League of Nations as a preventative of war, but a virtually unanimous opinion that the United States should keep clear of any hostilities that might occur. At a high school concert, to protracted applause, the band played: "I Didn't Raise My Boy To Be A Soldier." I noted that school equipment and facilities in the poorer sections of Des Moines were just as good as in the wealthier areas. The strong general interest in public education was seemingly largely due to the virtual absence of any independent secondary schools. Often discussion at the forums came around to educational policies, giving me welcome opportunity to ask instead of trying to answer questions. I visited Drake University, where Dr. George Gallup as professor of journalism had been developing the technique of his later public opinion polls. I was driven, through endless cultivated flatland, north to the big State University at Ames and east to small but excellent Grinnell College. Here provincial literature was encouraged, and I lunched with the editors of *The Tanager*, a valiant little magazine which sought to moisten the encompassing cultural aridity. In spite of diversions, as spring approached the traveler grew anxious to breathe again the less restricted atmosphere of the eastern seaboard.

This was in part because I knew that, at home, life was not being easy for my consort. There was a good deal of sickness in Washington that winter and Tony was down with tonsillitis and worrisome ear trouble for nearly all my absence. The medical bills piled up and the Bank Holiday was less than helpful. With the two girls, now at Friends School, Isabel had watched the Inaugural Parade, from the Brookings building, and wondered what the Roosevelt leadership, with its sharp emphasis on governmental intervention, would mean for all of us. "New Dealers" were flooding into Washington, she wrote, and the Old Guard, of the Harding-Coolidge-Hoover era, was everywhere in retreat. Living on credit at the Des Moines Club, I channeled all but small spending monies to my wife. As during the Far Eastern trip, she managed the finances and this time that arrangement stuck.

Returning to Washington, on April 8, I found an exciting letter from Professor Arthur N. Holcombe, Chairman of the Department of Government at Harvard. It asked whether I would take over the courses and tutorial work handled there by Professor Bruce Hopper, the specialist on international relations who was to have a year's leave of absence. A less formal communication, from my friend William Yandell Elliott of the Harvard faculty, assured me that the position could become a permanency. Calculated for the academic year, the remuneration would be approximately what the Brookings paid and I was the more pleased because job offers, except in government service which I did not want, were far from plentiful that spring of 1933. I did not realize that one of my pupils would have been Henry Kissinger but believed that I would be a good teacher and my respect for Harvard was high. Moreover, Isabel was quite enthusiastic about the proposition.

That, however, was not the attitude of Dr. Moulton. He bridled at granting another leave of absence, pointing out that various projects had been shelved by the Iowa interlude. If I went I would have to be replaced at Brookings and therefore the separation would be permanent, against which the older man advised. His counsel was always highly regarded, so the door to the Harvard Yard was reluctantly closed. Shortly thereafter a building lot was bought, just over the District Line in Montgomery County, Maryland, where a house better attuned to the needs of a family of six might be erected. There was little cash for this, but the developer of Westmoreland Hills was anxious to get his property moving and agreed to take Willow Cottage, in Baltimore, in trade. It was the removal of an incubus rather than loss of an asset.

Leaving Miss Cooper in charge, we drove to Charleston, S. C., for a delightful holiday over May Day. Then I set myself to developing contacts with the New Dealers who had swarmed to Washington in the churning wake of F.D.R. But a change was coming. In June of 1933, Eugene Meyer, President Hoover's appointee as Governor of the Federal Reserve Board, had anonymously bought the Washington *Post* at auction, with the intention of making it a paper of national significance, which it then certainly was not. In the early autumn he asked me to visit him and, quite surprisingly, soon afterward offered me the editorship. This was an opportunity which, as Moulton fully agreed, could not be overlooked. Frank Kent, as I learned later, had given me strong recommendation. On December 18, one week before a gay family Christmas, I moved my office to the old *Post* building, on E Street, overlooking Pennsylvania Avenue. On the eve of my 40th birthday I could enjoy the smell of printer's ink again.

◀Chapter 6
With Journalistic Success

Eugene Meyer, age 57 when he acquired the *Post*, had been a key figure in the Hoover Administration. As Governor of the Federal Reserve Board and first chairman of the Reconstruction Finance Corporation, he was intimately involved in the effort to get the stagnant economy moving. In anti-depression measures he was one of the most influential of the former President's advisors. Meyer and Hoover did not always agree, however, and the new editor soon learned that the financier considered his ex-chief deplorably bull-headed. In one of our first conversations, as publisher and subordinate, Mr. Meyer told me to avoid any editorial criticism of Hoover "partly because the man is down but more because we had our differences." It was a superfluous warning since, with some reservations, I was a longtime admirer of the repudiated President.

The new publisher's differences with Hoover were minimal compared with his distaste for most of President Roosevelt's nostrums. "He thinks that to be righteous is to be right," Mr. Meyer grumbled in a discussion of one of the early New Deal projects. I noted the aphorism in the confidential diary I started on assuming the editorship. But while the *Post*, from the outset, was critical of many aspects of the New Deal, this was never on narrow or partisan lines. Meyer liked to recall that his first governmental service had been under President Woodrow Wil-

260

son and he promptly squashed an attempt to make him chairman of the Republican National Committee, soon after his purchase of what was to become a very influential newspaper.

This was not immediate. At first Mr. Meyer's great abilities were largely submerged by his complete ignorance of journalistic practise. He was accustomed to personal direction and to undisputed acceptance of guidelines from the top. For months he failed to recognize the inevitably amorphous character of newspaper composition, where each day's product is selective and where largely autonomous individual judgments are therefore necessary. On the one hand this fluidity permits a lively and readable publication; on the other the speed and flexibility of operation encourages blunders, both in the valuation of "copy" and in its presentation. Mistakes were frequent and serious enough to irritate the perfectionist publisher, more so because he had chosen his executives carefully, though without understanding the conditions of their work. Newspapermen are, or in that pre-guild era were, highly individualized. Criticisms by "Butch," as Mr. Meyer was soon labeled, were often hotly and openly resented. So morale was not good, as I soon realized when I joined the staff in a key position.

The new editor was fortunate in two respects. Both in and out of newspaper work, I had learned how to merge my viewpoint in an overall program, in a persuasive rather than aggressive manner. Furthermore I could see that the editorial page gave the most latitude for Meyer's ambition to build a journal of real significance in the national capital. I soon established good personal relations with the publisher and was thereupon left largely to my own devices. Of course this emphasized my responsibility.

It was hard work, for there were only two regular editorial writers when I came to the old building on E Street. One was Merlo J. Pusey, a holdover from the McLean period who happily was a thorough, competent and wholly reliable wheelhorse. Offsetting his limited knowledge of world affairs, Pusey was expert on Washington's unique system of local government and on its many municipal problems. Obviously the *Post* had to be a good local paper before it could aspire to national significance and in this preliminary Pusey was quietly invaluable. The other writer placed under my immediate direction was Anna Youngman, whom Meyer had brought with him from the Federal Reserve Board. There was little in the financial field that Miss Youngman did not thoroughly understand but she had difficulty in reducing her expertise to the comprehension of the average reader. Nevertheless, this was an area, at the beginning of 1934, to which all responsible newspapers should have been giving major attention, despite its many and confusing complications. What was happening there was making resumption of war more probable.

The Hoover Moratorium, on the enormous international debt burden from the First World War, was not formally renewed. The unpopular President knew he could not get this approach to cancellation approved by a hostile Congress. But German reparations had virtually ceased and since this source of income had been drained dry, the debtors to the United States maintained that they also could not pay. A conference of the debtor governments at Lausanne, in July, 1932, showed that this attitude was uniform, with the exception of unimportant but much lauded Finland. The tangle was increasing the world-wide strangulation of trade and, in the hope of a constructive solution, the United States was asked to participate in a general exploration of the mounting monetary and economic problems. President Hoover had quickly agreed, but because of the approaching election it was thought best to postpone this crucial conference, even though delay could only add to the urgency of the situation.

Franklin D. Roosevelt was not well informed on this background and it was clearly imperative for him to consult closely with Hoover during the four-month interim between election and inauguration. This liaison was never achieved, even though events daily emphasized its need. A month after Hoover's defeat, the French Chamber of Deputies voted to default on the war debts payment then coming due, overthrowing Premier Edouard Herriot in the process. Thereupon the outgoing American President again sought, tactfully but unavailingly, to establish communication with his successor on problems that would brook no delay. When there was contact it was mutually suspicious and unproductive.

Part of the fault for this failure in communication can be

attributed to the absurd delay between change of Administrations. Ironically, the Constitutional Amendment (No. 20) advancing the date of Inauguration from March 4 to January 20 was then on the eve of ratification. That this reform was belated was doubly unfortunate because, while the government of the United States was practically paralyzed, those of Japan and Germany were moving swiftly toward aggressive positions. There were no "lame ducks" in Tokyo or Berlin during the period that outgoing President Hoover and incoming President Roosevelt were eyeing each other with ill-concealed distaste. Rancor as to how, and by whom, the banking structure should be saved was only the final touch in this deplorable failure of orderly transition.

Whatever its recuperative effect for the national economy, the grave international disorder was aggravated by executive activity during "The Hundred Days"—the first three months of the New Deal. Shattering confusion resulted from Roosevelt's arbitrary decision to devalue the dollar and loosen its tie with gold. This increased international currency fluctuations and consequent trade uncertainties, at a time when our representatives were telling the Europeans that the great need was monetary stabilization. Moreover, it became clear that F.D.R. was not unwilling to resort to printing-press money, in order to raise prices, even though this would undermine the monetary controls of the Federal Reserve System.[1]

Roosevelt's cavalier attitude, as it was regarded in other countries, led to a flood of special missions to Washington in the spring of 1933. All of them were disturbed by the calculated American inflation, certain to be disadvantageous to European exports. The German delegation, headed by Hjalmar Schacht, brilliant president of the Reichsbank, was (or soon became) the most acrimonious of all the visitors. Germany was back on the gold standard, after a runaway inflation that had completely wiped out the savings of its people. Above all, they now demanded the currency stability which the Roosevelt policies

---

1. Cf. Herbert Feis, *1933, Characters in Crisis,* Little, Brown & Co., Boston, 1966, pp. 128–31. Dr. Feis, at the time Economic Adviser for the Department of State, gives a graphic account in this important study.

seemed to threaten. Dr. Schacht warned that unless Germany could increase exports, dollar payments on its obligations to U.S. banks and bondholders would necessarily cease. He was perhaps arrogant in demanding that there be no American blockage of German exports to South America. The U.S. side was at least equally stiff-necked. With apparent pride in his extraordinary incivility, Dr. Herbert Feis later recalled: "Because of my deep resentment at the way in which the Germans had allowed Hitler to gain control of their destiny, I had refused the dinner which the German embassy gave in honor of the mission and also an invitation to lunch at the White House with Schacht."[2]

With so embittered a preamble it seemed probable that the international Monetary and Economic Conference, finally scheduled in London for June 12, would be a failure. This, in a big way, it proved to be, thus making the chances for another war perceptibly stronger. Nobody could say with any certainty what President Roosevelt wanted. In the words of Dr. Feis: "His ideas veered and waffled." So: "In any meaningful sense the conference never really got under way."[3] The *coup de grace* was Roosevelt's public statement—"the bomb" of July 3, asserting that independently managed currencies should be preferred to "old fetishes of international bankers." On July 23, after an extraordinary exhibition of bad manners, infighting and uncertainty, the conference adjourned. It had succeeded only in compounding the international monetary confusion and in persuading both Berlin and Tokyo that there was no viable alternative to policies of nationalistic self-sufficiency. In Washington the new alphabetical agencies—NRA, AAA, etc.—were also striking out on isolationist lines. Mandatory neutrality laws were pathetically regarded as reliable insurance against involvement in the hostilities which both German and Japanese policies seemed to envisage. Foreign trade naturally showed no sign of recovery and domestic anxiety increased as the American economy continued stagnant. The case for further monetary stimulants was pressed. After much tinkering, the President, on January 31, 1934, formally devalued the dollar to 59.6 percent of

---

2. *Ibid.*, p. 137.
3. *Ibid.*, pp. 144 and 172.

its former value in terms of gold. The enormous profits involved were simply confiscated by the Treasury.

Failure to cope with international monetary disorder, in 1933, had accentuated international economic collapse. This in turn worsened the political situation. In mid-October Germany withdrew its delegates from the futile Geneva Disarmament Conference, ending all hope of accomplishment in that field. At the same time the Japanese, with no American opposition, successfully imposed a truce on Chiang Kai-shek, emphasizing his weakness and stimulating the well-led Chinese Communist movement which he had been vainly endeavoring to subdue. The only off-setting American move, in mid-November, was the formal recognition of Soviet Russia, which thereupon joined the greatly weakened League of Nations. It was reasonable to suppose, said President Roosevelt hopefully, that future relations between the two giants would "forever remain normal and friendly."

Most of these kaleidoscopic events occurred before I came to the *Post*. But they were closely followed and professionally discussed at the Brookings Institution. I knew Feis well, as also his opposite number in the Treasury Department, Daniel W. Bell.[4] I saw much of Kenneth Bewley, the charming and much harassed financial adviser at the British Embassy. Eugene Havas, who filled the same function for the Hungarians, gave the viewpoint of those who feared a Nazi takeover. Especially informative were several long talks with Ambassador Hans Luther, former German Finance Minister, Chancellor and Reichsbank president. Dr. Luther, who had been a close friend and colleague of Gustav Stresemann, was no apologist for Hitler and did all he could to patch deteriorating relations between Berlin and Washington. His growing melancholy reflected the clouds that were gathering.

In the financial field the cosmopolitan background of the new editor combined nicely with the wisdom of the publisher and the technical expertise of Miss Youngman. Soon the *Post*'s editorials on this subject were being widely quoted and re-

---

4. Mr. Bell later became president of the American Security and Trust Company, where I served as a director for many years.

printed. I realized, however, that neither this insight nor Pusey's alertness to local problems would of themselves create a significant editorial page. It must have broader coverage, cultural as well as political authority, humor in addition to dignity. But the *Post* for some time lost money, at an alarming pace, and while there were plenty of candidates for jobs the budgetary provision was lacking. Soon, however, there was a vacancy. The editorial copy boy, whose job was to run errands for the department, resigned. In his place, with apologies, I hired Bett Hooper, a young applicant who had recently authored a clever book called *Virgins in Cellophane*—of the *Gentlemen Prefer Blondes* type of literature. Bett was eager to get into newspaper work and readily accepted the copy-boy entrance. Though her writing for a time needed modulation it immediately brought a freshness the more acceptable in a somber period. Mary Scaife, my new and always self-sacrificial secretary, made the work much easier. On June 18, 1934, I confided to my journal: "Six months ago today I started as editor of the *Post*. In that period we have developed an editorial page of national significance. . . . Above all I want this page to be both impartial and dynamic. It is a great relief to feel thoroughly assured, after various qualms in the early stages, that Meyer is thoroughly in accord."

Impartiality was perhaps not equally desired by Mr. Meyer's forthright wife, Agnes, who freely expressed her strong feelings on current events to me, but never intimated that I should be a mouthpiece for them. This freedom of action was amusingly illustrated when the publisher one morning brought Joseph P. Kennedy, then chairman of the Securities and Exchange Commission, into my office. "I never know what the policy of the paper is," said Meyer jocosely, "until I read the editorial page at breakfast." "It's none the worse for that," the visitor shot back quickly, thereby prejudicing me in favor of all his ultimately famous family.

There was more general encouragement from a questionnaire sent to a cross-section of 5,000 *Post* subscribers. This, surprisingly, showed the editorial page the most popular part of the paper, which stimulated me to extend my influence. Content of the "page opposite" the editorials is always debatable ground

266

and nowadays is frequently filled with syndicated articles, divided about equally between conservative and liberal commentators so that the publisher can say he presents all viewpoints. The net result, however, is to suggest that the paper has no firm position of its own, which always seemed pitiful to me. Remembering the excellent Page Opposite developed by Mr. Adams on the old Baltimore *Sun*, I persuaded Meyer to let me make the same use of special correspondence on the *Post*, building it around articles by the able writers—Raymond Clapper, Ralph Robey, Elliot Thurston and Franklyn Waltman—who had been hired by the publisher without any very clear idea of how their talents would be used. This was the easier because the paper lacked, and for some time continued to lack, the strong managing or executive editor who normally directs all parts of an American newspaper except the editorial page, and sometimes even that. By the same token this meant that eventually there would be internal discord over the apportionment of authority. But this was slow to develop because I felt my way carefully.

An early sign of success was the number of "letters to the editor," pro and con, which soon began to flood in. It is axiomatic that these are a popular feature, but the letter column requires careful supervision. Space considerations often necessitate cutting, which must be done without injury to the point the writer seeks to make. Libel suits lurk, as I would learn, in impugnments that are not carefully modified. It would be false economy to give this chore to either Pusey or Miss Youngman, so I obtained permission to hire Reggie Kauffman, who had returned jobless from Geneva, to assume this task. Reggie would also write light editorials, for which he was well qualified, and supervise an editorial page column, called the *Post-Impressionist*. Knowing how many able authors had made their start in newspaper contributions, I visualized something like the European *feuilleton*. And indeed some very good literary and descriptive writing can be found in the Post-Impressionist columns of the middle and late thirties. A further step was to bring the moribund Sunday Book Page under my control, getting a cross-ruff by emphasizing volumes that received editorial mention. This added to the staff a talented, sardonic but somewhat

267

erratic lieutenant with the fittingly journalistic name of Karl Schriftgiesser.[5] He was eventually replaced by John Clark, a recent Dartmouth graduate with extraordinary ability as a newspaperman.

Editorial policy was mapped out cooperatively at a mid-morning conference where everyone was supposed to have chosen the theme on which he or she would like to write. Approval was often subject to further research as I insisted that my staff should utilize the advantages of Washington by personally consulting with specialists—then seldom muzzled—in fields where the news made comment timely. I wanted no ivory tower operation and frequently the editorials contained more information than opinion. Applying this ruling to myself, I lunched nearly every day with some friend or acquaintance who was "in the know" regarding matters at issue. Occasionally this activism had important consequence, as in the case of U.S. membership in the International Labor Organization.

Because of my past association with the League Secretariat, it was almost routine for officials whom I had known in Geneva to look me up when visiting Washington. One of these visitors, soon after I became editor of the *Post*, was Edward J. Phelan, a brilliant Irishman who was an Assistant Director of the ILO. Under President Hoover there had been increasing American cooperation with this autonomous arm of the League and it was Phelan's thought that President Roosevelt could logically develop that into formal membership. He discussed the matter with Frances Perkins, the new Secretary of Labor who had previously been Industrial Commissioner for the State of New York. Miss Perkins suggested that Phelan get a line on probable newspaper reaction from me, whom she had earlier named to membership on an advisory committee for unemployment relief. This being a nominal duty, unremunerated and wholly nonpartisan, I had not resigned it on leaving the Brookings for the *Post*. But the desirability of becoming personally involved in the ILO issue was a more dubious matter. While that agency was actually separate from the League organization the relationship

---

5. The German name translates as "type pourer," or compositor.

was so close that League opponents, still strong, would certainly rally in opposition to U.S. membership.

However, I knew Meyer to be a League advocate and could see nothing improper in discussing the matter with Phelan. The latter wanted to bring Michael MacWhite, then Irish Ambassador to the United States, into the consideration and a private dinner *à trois* was arranged. Here the Irish skill in political maneuvering was amply displayed. Nevertheless, it was my suggestion that the best tactics would be to secure an enabling Congressional Resolution, merely authorizing (but thereby encouraging) the President to join the ILO by executive order at some unspecified time. This was the procedure successfully followed and on August 20, 1934, F.D.R. formally accepted the invitation for U.S. membership in the ILO. Unhappily, this success made the next desired step less probable. That was ratification of the carefully-drawn protocols for adherence to the World Court, which failed to secure the requisite two-thirds majority in the Senate. A demagogic campaign mounted by Huey Long, Father Coughlin (the "radio priest") and the Hearst press had made Roosevelt apprehensively cautious. Arthur Sweetser, always over-optimistic, showed in a letter from Geneva that he was crushed by the setback. In my journal, on January 31, 1935, I wrote: "I regard this as a turning point in post-war history and the turn is backward."

The quiet part played by me in accomplishing that membership was obviously appreciated. The development meant that an American Assistant Director would be appointed by the ILO, and in October, 1934, I was offered the position by Harold Butler, the experienced English civil servant then heading that organization. Financially it was an attractive proposal. The salary in gold francs was approximately what the *Post* paid me, but there were substantial annual increments plus diplomatic privileges and pension rights completely lacking in the editorship. The thought of returning to Geneva, in a position of real importance, was even more seductive. Possibly I might help to avert the threatened war! If the offer had come a year earlier I would have had no hesitation in transferring from the Brookings Institution. On the other hand, my opportunity on the *Post* had been given antecedent to this proposal and I knew that I had as yet barely scratched the surface of journalistic advantage. I thought that at this stage I should not merge my individuality in an international bureaucracy where both my writing and speaking talents would tend to be buried.

Both my father and Dr. Moulton, with whom I took counsel in the matter, agreed. But this was offset when Secretary Perkins and Pierrepont Moffat, then Chief of the Division of Western European Affairs in the Department of State, separately advised acceptance. To discuss the issue with Meyer would put him in an unpleasant bargaining position. Relations with Mrs. Meyer, however, were so good that I visited their home on Crescent Place to get her confidential advice. She assured me of the publisher's high regard and I repressed a smile when, with characteristic *élan*, Agnes said spaciously: "Right now I would rather trust Eugene than any international organization." The observation had bite. So, after severe mental struggle, I refused the offer. It was then accepted by John G. Winant, the ex-Governor of New Hampshire, who went on to be our not overly successful Ambassador in London.

An element in the difficult decision had been the new home which we were building on Westmoreland Circle, where Massachusetts Avenue then terminated in a country road which meandered its unpaved surface westward into rural Maryland. Construction of this house, with Harry Scarff as architect, had been started in May, five months after I joined the *Post*. Completion coincided with the ILO invitation. Other factors aside, it would have been grotesque to put this gracious residence on the market without ever living there.

"Millstone" we called this property, which restored us to full citizenship by standing just across the District Line in Montgomery County, Maryland. The name came partly because it anchored us; partly because Emory Niles had unearthed two old stone grinders and gave one to feature our walled terrace. All the family, even to little Woody as a curly-haired cherub of two, were enthusiastic about the new quarters, with its splendid sunset view over the Potomac Valley to the west and south. I had achieved my ambition of a study lined with built-in bookcases, storage closets and a fireplace of my own. My parents came over from Baltimore for Thanksgiving and, though the ménage was far from ordered, there was much, in 1934, for which to express gratitude.

Brother Frank had approved the site when he came from London in the spring, among other objectives seeking English publication rights for any successor to the President's anthology of crisis speeches—*On Our Way.* Through Steve Early, I arranged an appointment at the White House and was glad to go along and experience the unquestionable Roosevelt charm at first-hand. Chris did not get to Millstone until nearly a year later, when he came for an overnight stay. Now a very popular author, the older brother caused quite a flutter on visiting the *Post* and writing some overdue copy while his sibling attended to chores. I was envious of the junket the Christophalians had lined up for a Grace Line journey to Peru (*Hasta la Vista*) during the coming summer. I had taken no substantial vacation since our return from Geneva.

◀I assumed editorship of the Washington *Post* with a clear vision of what I would like to accomplish. My secret ambition, which I disclosed to none, was to make the paper something of an American version of the famous Manchester *Guardian.* That is to say: its outlook should be international; its philosophy independent and liberal in the classical sense of the word; its foreign correspondence informative and impartial; its editorials well reasoned, well written and forceful; its adherence to strictly Constitutional government unquestionable. This was a large order, but essentially similar to the objectives that John Haslup Adams had visualized for the Baltimore *Sun* years earlier. They had greatly appealed to me as a subordinate of this great editor. At 40, much more experienced and mature, I saw reasons why the *Post* could succeed where the *Sun* had fallen short.

In the first place, the Washington paper had sunk so low, under its previous ownership, that a wholly different policy was requisite. Then Eugene Meyer, for all his ignorance of newspaper management, was clearly eager to give distinction to his new property. There was no problem of divided ownership, which had made Mr. Adams' ambitions more difficult to achieve.

271

And Mr. Meyer, both scholarly and innovative, was always receptive to new and even unconventional ideas. Finally, the cosmopolitan atmosphere of Washington made it a better field for journalistic initiative and leadership than provincial Baltimore could ever be.

The first task, for which I had full responsibility, was to make the editorial page impressive. To accomplish this it had both to look and be arresting. Few outside the newspaper profession realize how much an effective cartoon improves the page which does most to express journalistic personality. In young Gene Elderman the *Post* had an able cartoonist, though one who was none too abstemious or dedicated. Usually the new editor had to suggest the ideas which Gene executed with clever and often humorous delineation. An immediate rule was that every drawing must carry its own message, with no "balloons" or labels to prop the thought. This took time, but it was well spent.

Under the cartoon is the traditional place for "Letters to the Editor," which were a meager and uninspiring assortment when I came to that position. I was well aware, however, of their potential. The London *Times* had a staff man assigned exclusively to the handling of these communications, in its case always literate and generally thoughtful. There was no hope that the *Post* would elicit high-grade commentary until it had earned public attention. But improvement could be hastened by adopting a procedure practised on the *Evening Sun*—getting staff members to write provocative letters in order to stimulate bona fide correspondence from outside. I enjoyed composing an occasional missive, under a *nom de plume*, outrageously criticizing points I had made anonymously in editorials. This could be doubly beneficial, bringing praise for receptivity to hostile opinion as well as affirmation of the editorial viewpoint.

Though there was soon no need for such tricks, the importance of having a bright and lively page continued. Here the *Post-Impressionist* was helpful. Under this standing head were printed 600-word articles of a variegated but always nonpolitical nature. There were critical essays on current cultural events; travelogs or reminiscences of Washington as it used to be; occasionally even a short, short story. Contributors responded eagerly to this literary opening, though acceptance brought only a $5 payment. Isabel, who had a nice touch, wrote quite a few under her maiden name. It was a popular feature but required careful editing, since most articles had to be trimmed, or occasionally padded, to fit the procrustean column.

The major concern, of course, was the editorial expression. The three left-hand columns of the page were filled by half-a-dozen of these daily commentaries, with a bit of carefully chosen reprint if necessary to fill out. Elderman's cartoon, with four truncated columns of letters beneath and to their right the *Post-Impressionist*, filled the space for which the editor was directly responsible. All this material had to be composed between 10 a.m., when the staff conference assembled, and 6 p.m., when the page was "put to bed." As distinct from the news columns the editorials would customarily run through all four editions—from "Bulldog" to Late City—without revision. But as a necessary precaution a member of the small staff would stay on until midnight to be sure that late dispatches, especially from abroad, did not invalidate anything written. Since I must determine this it meant that, like a physician, I would leave the phone number where I might be reached at any time. John McLane Clark, unable to marry on his miserable salary, was doubly exploited by assignment to the "dog watch," spending some 14 hours a day, six days a week, at the *Post*. When Clark in 1938 applied for one of the new Nieman Fellowships, for "working newspapermen," at Harvard, I reluctantly bore witness to his rare combination of ability, reliability and industry. John received the fellowship, went on to interesting war service and in 1948 became publisher of his own newspaper, in Claremont, New Hampshire. Here, less than three years later, his life was cut short in a tragic boating accident.[6]

The light touch, provided by Clark, Hooper and Kauffman, was the more important because, in 1934, much of the editorial comment was necessarily of a disturbing order. Monetary problems were to the fore, with Germany being steadily pushed toward Autarky and foreign trade failing to respond to the assumed stimulus of dollar devaluation. This was Miss

---

6. His biography has been charmingly written by David Bradley: *Journey of a Johnny-come-lately*, Dartmouth Publications, Hanover, N.H., 1957.

Youngman's field. But her highly technical comment often had to be carefully simplified in deference to the low level of public understanding in these matters. Pusey was always competent in his coverage, which came to include the important Supreme Court decisions of the period and much of Congressional activity. When this affected foreign policy I took over, as also in the Administration's major actions with an international bearing. I was not enamored of President Roosevelt, noting in my diary on March 5, 1934, that "the man appears to me almost excessively smug and undistinguished in his thought."

Fortunately 1934, compared with what was to come, was relatively tranquil. On March 1, Henry Pu-yi was enthroned as emperor of the puppet kingdom of Manchukuo and Japan eased its pressure on the rest of China in order to press on with the exploitation of Manchuria's rich resources. In Germany, Hitler was busy consolidating his power and, after the assassination of Chancellor Dollfuss of Austria, had publicly renounced any territorial ambitions at variance with that country's independence. Soviet Russia was also in pacific mood, pressing disarmament from its permanent seat on the Council of the League of Nations. In Italy, Mussolini was making threatening gestures at Ethiopia and kaleidoscopic French governments—three of them in 1934 alone—emphasized the underlying weakness of that country. But one would have to be very pessimistic to conclude then that another major war was inevitable. Indeed, there were some hopeful signs. At Geneva successful effort was under way to terminate the protracted hostilities in the Chaco, between Bolivia and Paraguay, with sanctions exercised against the latter when Bolivia accepted the League's peace plan. This recalled the reasoning of Alfred Nobel, Swedish sponsor of the peace award that bears his name, who at the turn of the century had written: "The only correct solution [for an act of aggression] would be a treaty in which all governments pledged themselves jointly to defend any country that was attacked."

The principle of collective action had been strongly supported by Henry L. Stimson, while Secretary of State in Mr. Hoover's Cabinet. But it was by no means in keeping with dominant American sentiment. This, in 1934–35, was deeply opposed to involvement in any foreign conflict, whether or not directed against a government definable as an aggressor. Such rigid neutrality meant nullification of American influence for the prevention of war. On this basis it was opposed by me in a series of strong editorials which simultaneously urged the orderly revision of unjust treaties, notably that of Versailles, in order to diminish excuse for nationalistic aggression. These much quoted observations were especially welcomed at the Department of State. I would often visit there, to test my ideas, and with an advance telephone call would be welcomed by Secretary Cordell Hull, whom I had first known as a Congressman.

The homespun Tennessean was intellectually sympathetic to collective action, but was more interested in his own remedy for mundane ills. This was the Reciprocal Trade Agreements program, permitting Presidential reductions of up to 50 percent on the then high American tariff rates. Congress had approved the measure, over sharp opposition, in the spring of 1934 and Hull, a staunch Free Trader, saw the program as a big step toward the recovery of international trade and the lessening of political tension. So, up to a point, it proved to be. In Latin America, however, it led to increased German and Japanese antagonism. Essentially Hull's concept meant that the U.S. should admit South American agricultural produce duty free, with the same concessions there for our manufactured goods. This conflicted with German, and to a lesser extent Japanese, desires to develop and supply Latin American industries, on a barter basis. The expansion of German commercial interest in South America was more pronounced after Dr. Schacht became Hitler's Minister of Economics, in August 1934, and was not less resented by the Roosevelt Administration because of Jewish influence there. "In the intellectual and emotional sense" summarized Dr. William Appleman Williams in retrospect, "an important number of American leaders began to go to war against the Axis in the Western Hemisphere."[7]

I got the German side of this argument from Ambassador Luther and checked the varying viewpoints from other diplomatic sources. Nearly all felt that the Open Door policy of the

---

7. *The Tragedy of American Diplomacy,* Delta Books, Dell Publishing Co., N.Y., 1962, p. 189.

U.S. would face increasing difficulties in confronting the state-directed foreign commerce of Germany, Italy, Japan and Russia. At the Soviet Embassy, where I now had good contacts, it was argued that a communist economy could cooperate with capitalist America more successfully than the Nazi dictatorship. Here was one of many signs that Moscow was holding an olive branch toward the West. The re-entry of Russia into Western European leadership was then greatly forwarded by the reintroduction of military conscription in Germany, despite the prohibitions of the Versailles Treaty.

Assuming Collective Action to be one side of the coin to be paid for peace, then Treaty Revision was clearly its obverse. There could be no international harmony if the concept of justice was ignored. This had been foreseen in the League of Nations Covenant. Its Article Ten promised preservation of "the territorial integrity and existing political independence" of all members of the League. But Article 19 authorized "reconsideration . . . of treaties which have become inapplicable and the consideration of international conditions whose continuance might endanger the peace of the world." During the drafting of the Covenant, Lord Robert Cecil had wanted these assurances combined, to make treaty guarantees contingent on occasional judicial review. But the French thought this would encourage German revisionists and President Wilson had weakly agreed to the separation and emasculation of what became Article 19. All this background I had documented in *The Society of Nations*, not excluding the ironic manner in which the naked guarantees of Article Ten became a chief target for American opposition to League membership.

Now I revived this largely forgotten background in a series of temperate editorials that captured widespread attention. Even after Germany's illegal rearmament, I argued, it would be wise to give formal approval to that nation's assertion of national sovereignty. Such equitable action, more than 17 years after the close of World War I, might well spill the wind from Hitler's sails. The Fuehrer's strength depended on the rankling sense of injustice among all elements of the German people. Let them see that they were no longer regarded as pariahs, give their diligence more chance to improve their economic condition, and the menace of the Nazi movement might well fade away. It was a national neurosis which the straitjacket would not cure. A distinction must be drawn between German military occupation of its own Rhineland on the one hand; Japanese invasion of China and Italian aggression against Ethiopia on the other.

This was a closely reasoned position, equally apart from blind isolationism; from dogmatic pacifism and from that emotional support of selected countries against which George Washington warned so thoughtfully in his Farewell Address. It was fully indorsed by Mr. Meyer, who told me: "Avoid labels of every kind; judge everything critically on its merits and be in fact the independent paper as which we define ourselves on the editorial masthead." But I could see that if persecution of Jews should continue in Germany it would be all but impossible to maintain so detached an attitude. No matter how fair-minded, the publisher could not afford to have his paper called "pro-German." Early in April, 1935, I reviewed the whole situation with my trusted friend Karl von Lewinski, then serving as German Consul-General in New York. Nobody could have been more hostile to Hitler but this scholarly ex-judge held little hope that the Fuehrer could be restrained. The stable German middle class had been almost wiped out by inflation; the calculated humiliation of the country had aroused too much resentment; the suffering had been too protracted; now the Nazi grip was too resolute and well organized. "I greatly fear it is too late," said von Lewinski sadly. A few days later the League Council acted in a manner which confirmed this melancholy appraisal. Under Russian leadership it adopted a resolution sanctimoniously condemning Germany, in absentia, for illegal rearmament but saying nothing about treaty revision. Why slap Hitler's face if unprepared to fight? I now felt thoroughly pessimistic about the outlook. Development of a valid and reliable neutrality policy seemed the essential next step for the United States.

Tension was increasing in Washington, that spring of 1935, and sometimes broke the surface in curious ways. One such sprung from a hard-fought law suit, won by the *Post* from the Washington *Times-Herald*. It was over the claim of this rival paper to utilize some comic strips—notably "The Gumps"—to

277

which the *Post* had rights prior to the Meyer purchase. This was not an issue that interested me, for I would have been happy to see the paper dispense with comics altogether. But in the tight competitive market, in which either the *Post* or *Herald* was likely to succumb, this material was important. It could make a difference, one way or the other, of several thousand subscribers. This, in turn, would determine advertising rates and thus profitability. So Meyer was very cheerful when, on April 12, the verdict came in his favor.

The next evening was the fiftieth anniversary dinner of the famous Gridiron Club, to which I was bid as Eliot Thurston's guest. I was clearing my desk that Saturday afternoon when Meyer, who would also attend the dinner, dropped by for one of the confidential chats his editor had come to relish. Soon Mrs. Meyer burst in, wearing a broad grin and holding a florist's box. She explained that this had just come to Crescent Place from "Cissie" Patterson, the unpredictable publisher of the *Times-Herald*. Eugene—and Felix—must share disclosure of this rival's graceful reaction to defeat. A small package, beautifully beribboned, rested on a bed of orchids and on it was Cissie's card reading: "So as not to disappoint you." Eugene smilingly tore the wrappings apart—and out fell a chunk of raw beef.

For a few moments none saw what it meant. Then I faltered: "It must be a pound of flesh!" Mrs. Meyer took it icily, as one to whom the affront was perhaps not altogether novel. "Of course," she said; "a dirty Jewish Shylock." But Eugene, as I wrote in my journal, "was too hurt to say anything. He looked half stunned—the only time I have seen him really taken aback. And it really was a foul and swinish gesture. Poor Meyer—a quarter-of-an-hour later he came in to ask me not to mention the incident to *anyone*—'as I wouldn't want her to get any satisfaction from it.' "

I of course agreed and kept my word. But Cissie must have spread the story herself for soon, in varying versions, it was all over Washington. This did not ease Meyer's difficult position, as Jewry closed its ranks against the growing threat from Germany. Though his grandfather had been Grand Rabbi of France, Eugene was neither a practising Jew nor Francophile. Yet as an apostate he was called upon to contribute double to Zionism. The

278

least that his editor could do was to keep that influential page free from any trace of anti-Semitism. It was tightrope walking to manage this while still giving a fair break to German claims for sovereign equality.

A hefty production of often nasty gossip compensates for Washington's lack of industrial output. Plenty of it circulated at the cocktail parties, diplomatic receptions and dinners to which we were now continuously bid. As the *Post* grew more influential, and national alignments more rigid, the rival Embassies were fully alive to the desirability of getting the ear of its editor. Fortunately I had the common sense to see that this was the motive behind my pronounced acceptability, and to guard my lips carefully. Isabel helped in puncturing inflated ego and responded nobly to the sharply increased demands on her social capacities. A friendly German girl, Johanna Bachmann, was now installed as mother's helper. Cooks, though transient, were generally competent. Of course diplomatic hospitality could not be repaid in full, but our new home quickly became the scene of small dinners at which carefully selected guests, often from the various embassies, explored the issues of the day. In the basement of "Millstone" was an attractive rumpus room ideal for a *Bierabend*. For these a score of *Post* colleagues were frequently invited, to talk shop and exchange ideas for the development of the paper. Other than the Meyers nobody else sponsored such gatherings and those held at the mansion on Crescent Place were inevitably stilted and inhibited by comparison. I could see that popularity with my colleagues was real and I was not above exploiting it to increase my influence.

As a logical step, already mentioned, I took over supervision of the Sunday Book Page, with the intention of calling upon my two literary brothers, in New York and London respectively, to make it really significant. But all this development took both energy and money, the limits of which were increasingly apparent. Late at night in my study I tabulated my net debt at $23,000, mostly in the 6% mortgage on the house but "still a painful figure." Tony had by now joined his sisters as a pupil at Friends School and the costs of private education for the whole quartette loomed alarmingly. Isabel had put a small legacy into much-needed furnishings and there was no prospect of further

279

windfalls. Life insurance would barely cover obligations and on short lecture trips, sometimes taken to supplement my over-taxed salary, I was inclined to avoid airplanes for fear of a crash. Meyer would not increase my remuneration, nor that of my underpaid subordinates, so long as the paper was operating at a heavy deficit. It was agreed, however, that I needed a lieutenant sufficiently well versed on the foreign scene to provide backing in that complicated field. So I opened negotiations with Herbert Elliston, whom I had met in Peking as the then correspondent for the Manchester *Guardian* and who, in 1935, was in Boston as financial editor of the *Christian Science Monitor*. It was a wise selection, for Elliston would eventually succeed me on the *Post*. But this tough Yorkshire journalist wanted too much money for the clearly subordinate position, and the same factors blocked other possibilities that were approached.

Meanwhile, I struggled on, getting most of my recreation from the exterior development of Millstone, and glumly follow-ing the steady deterioration of the international picture. The critical point, obviously, was the Italian pressure on Ethiopia, as both Japan and Germany were holding back to see whether collective action could be mobilized to frustrate Mussolini's ob-viously planned invasion of this primitive African kingdom. If *Il Duce* could be checked there would be less risk of aggression either by Hitler or the militarists in Tokyo. On this theme the *Post* hammered constantly, helped by evidence of firm British, French and Russian cooperation at Geneva. The defect was in our own mandatory neutrality policy. In the event of war this meant that the United States would treat both Ethiopia and Italy with majestic impartiality, denying to both the weapons that Haile Selassie lacked and Mussolini possessed in abun-dance. Such neutrality would make any sanctions by the League of Nations more difficult to apply, especially since Germany and Japan would certainly not participate. Confronting this gloomy picture I decided to visit Secretary Hull again, to urge a public reiteration of the Stimson Doctrine of non-recognition by the United States of any fruits of military aggression. Under Presi-dent Hoover this had been enunciated as definitive American policy, not merely a one-shot application to the Manchurian dispute.

Thus, on the morning of September 27, 1935, the editor was closeted with the Secretary of State for nearly an hour, finding him, as always, very friendly and sympathetic. Mr. Hull emphasized, however, that on so major a matter he would have to consult with President Roosevelt, who had left Washington the night before for a western swing and some fishing in the Pacific. Hull agreed that the curious alliance of ultra-pacifists and isolationists could indirectly strengthen an aggressor's hand and so bring the United States itself nearer to war. He said that he would on his own use every opportunity (except the one suggested) to improve cooperation with the League of Nations. But there was no time for this. On October 3, 1935, *Il Duce* ordered his legions into Ethiopia.

In retrospect it is evident that the unprovoked Italian attack on Ethiopia was prelude to the Second World War. In the 1914–18 conflict, Italy had been one of the victorious powers and had garnered a substantial share of the spoils. There were already large Italian colonies in Africa—Libya, Eritrea and Somaliland—all so poorly developed as to make Mussolini's claim for more *Lebensraum* absurd. His argument that Ethiopia was not an organized nation but an anarchic area requiring external policing was a clear invitation to Japan to say the same of China, and could be taken by Hitler as an excuse for invading Poland. It was an opportunity missed. If Secretary Hull had then shown the courage of Stimson, or if Roosevelt had possessed the insight of Hoover, it might, or so I have always thought, have been a very different and far happier future for all mankind.

Italy's most able general, Badoglio, proceeded expeditiously with the mop-up of Ethiopia. Under the neutrality laws, President Roosevelt had warned his fellow-Americans not to travel by the ships of either belligerent. Since Ethiopia had no seacoast, and no merchant marine, this was a scarcely perceptible slap at Mussolini. At Geneva the moribund League, without American, German or Japanese assistance, sought feebly to put restraints on *Il Duce*. The British Government, it became known, had offered to turn its part of Somaliland over to the

Italians if they would spare landlocked Ethiopia. But under such a deal there would have been none of the glory that Mussolini craved. When his troops occupied Adowa, where the Abyssinians (as they were then known) had destroyed an Italian army in 1896, it was thought that *Il Duce* might deem his shabby honor satisfied. But the Fascist tanks pressed on and early in May, 1936, rolled into Addis Ababa, the primitive capital whence Haile Selassie, courageous little "king of kings," had escaped to carry his story to the world. On May 9, Mussolini announced Italian annexation of ancient Abyssinia and on June 20, President Roosevelt solemnly removed the arms embargo against both Italy and Ethiopia, declaring that the state of war no longer existed. In effect that cancelled the Stimson Doctrine of nonrecognition for territorial gains achieved by force. From this action, friend Kawakami warned me, "the Japanese militarists will draw some sweeping conclusions."

The immediate result, however, came from an unexpected quarter—Spain. In mid-July a serious revolt, directed by General Francisco Franco, erupted in Spanish Morocco against the leftist, anti-clerical, Republican government at Madrid. This, after much political and social turmoil, had succeeded the dictatorship of Primo de Rivera. Franco was a strong admirer of Mussolini and there was little doubt that the latter's success in Ethiopia stimulated the well-planned rebellion. In any case, first Italy and then Germany proceeded to give help to Franco, which Russia countered by backing the Communist-indorsed "popular front" regime. Great Britain and France maintained neutrality, though sentiment in both was strongly anti-Fascist. With a Presidential election in the offing, Washington merely groaned. Existing neutrality legislation did not apply to civil war and there was no legal impediment to sales of munitions, to either side. Moreover, American sentiment was deeply divided. Jews feared the spread of Nazi anti-Semitism to Spain. Catholics were appalled by the atrocities of Anarchists and Marxists against the religious orders. Because of the legitimacy of the Madrid Government, the *Post* gave it restrained support. But even moderate editorial criticism of Franco brought calls for boycott from Roman Catholic pulpits. Publisher and editor traveled to Baltimore to confer with the Archbishop and learned that the hierarchy was dubious of its ability to restrain mounting political passion.

I could see that new ingredients were bringing the European cauldron to boiling point. Social and religious, as well as national, rivalries were now inflamed. And in these domestic convulsions the practise of representative government, loosely called democracy, was being undermined throughout continental Europe. Marching men, rather than the electoral process, were determining who would dominate the body politic. "Dictatorship of the Proletariat" had long been proclaimed by Marxists. Now there were rival, yet fundamentally related, schools of authoritarian rule—Fascism, Nazism and the Falange. The name of the latter was ominously derived from the Macedonian military unit responsible for the final destruction of democracy in ancient Greece. By the middle of 1936 it was apparent that one must think in terms remote from the presumably reasoned actions of national governments. Under this unstable cover earthquakes were weakening the infrastructure of parliamentary institutions. Across all of Eurasia, from the Pillars of Hercules to the Pacific, the whole achievement of Anglo-Saxon political development was under challenge.

I was perhaps ahead of my time in seeing the grim implications in this shift of popular faith to authoritarianism. A distinguished Spanish friend, Salvador de Madariaga, had urged me to read Unamuno, and I was influenced by his doubt that man can properly be called the most rational of animals. "More often have I watched a cat reason than seen it laugh or weep." Also I was impressed by the clear political thinking of a friend, Nehmann, who was then Press Attaché at the Soviet Embassy in Washington.[8] Often we lunched together and the brilliant young Russian would use the day's headlines as text for historical analysis. The essential prerequisite of Communism, he argued, was first the concentration and then the extension of executive power. That could rest provisionally in the hands of a Hitler, Mussolini or Franco. But these "primitive national socialisms" would prove stepping stones to the more refined

---

8. Though often quoted in my journal I never used Nehmann's first name and cannot now recall it. Sometimes the spelling is Neymann.

international socialism envisaged by Marx. With technological advance, national frontiers would in time become as anachronistic as walled cities and the chances were that another war would hasten this development. Private capitalism, Nehmann conceded, had proved marvelous in creating material wealth, but public education alone insured that henceforth distribution rather than accumulation would be emphasized. He sought to dismiss, as "anarchistic," the thesis that to very many Americans tyrannical government itself is the enemy and that from this viewpoint Fascism and Communism are equally distasteful. "You are a good example of liberal thought," he admitted after dinner at the Morleys one evening. "But you will learn that even in the United States classical liberalism is now a spent force."

I would not agree. But as the Spanish Civil War dragged on there came some change in my attitude. With the collapse of the League and the failure of Collective Action, a more isolationist attitude for the United States became not only plausible but desirable. Though Huey Long had been assassinated, demogoguery as a substitute for intelligent political analysis was gaining ground. My thinking is reflected in my long entry of July 27, 1936: "Under the circumstances it is hard to conclude that the United States can do more than constitute itself trustee for what remains of Western Civilization, perhaps emphasizing the organization of international relations in the New World, a course which is rendered more logical by the collapse in Spain. Such a policy would not be anti-League but would rather be carrying on the League tradition, now grievously menaced by the ascendancy of dictatorships and the general political retrogression of Europe."

Meantime, in the teacup sphere, the *Post* itself had been rocked by serious convulsions. In part these were the publisher's fault. Conscious of his own journalistic inexperience and anxious to end the paper's continuing deficit, Mr. Meyer sought managerial advice outside the organization. One result was an order that the Managing Editor must clear with the new Business Manager—Don Bernard—before making any promotions or salary increases. This was hotly resented by the then Managing Editor—Bill Haggard—who reasonably argued that within the limits of an established budget he should have full control over personnel under his command. I could sympathize with that viewpoint for I too resented having to plead with Mr. Meyer to secure an overdue five-dollar raise for a faithful subordinate. On the other hand, I was loyal to my chief and dubious of Haggard's executive ability.

The latter, however, had organized a *coup* with some dexterity. By a defiant attitude he virtually forced Meyer to accept a carefully phrased resignation, having simultaneously arranged that other key employes would leave with him. A score of reporters, telegraph and rewrite men agreed to walk out in what had aspects of a general strike, calculated to force the publisher to capitulate. It became clear that the paper might suddenly be forced to close down, a possibility of which its owner seemed wholly unaware. To avoid this disastrous humiliation I hastily conferred with Ray Clapper and Frank Waltman, who with me stood above the battle. We told Meyer, then at home with a touch of grippe, that he must come down and confront the disturbance personally. This he did, accompanied by Mrs. Meyer whose habitual self-assurance was clearly shaken by the episode. "Poor Eugene," she lamented to Frank and me as we explained the roots of the trouble to her while Ray Clapper acted as a sort of Ombudsman between Meyer and the dissidents. "Poor Eugene!" exploded Waltman, after many repetitions of the wifely commiseration. "How about poor Frank, poor Ray, poor Felix? We're all as concerned with the future of the *Post* as is Eugene."

This was at the end of October, 1935. The storm blew over and with the full approval of the mediating trio a new and highly competent Managing Editor—Alexander F. (Casey) Jones—of the Minneapolis *Journal* was appointed. Meyer learned from the episode, one result of which was establishment of a Newspaper Guild chapter on the *Post*. But he never found it easy to unbend with what Agnes called "petty minds." During this period the publisher called a mass meeting of employes to tell the entire staff of his impersonal ambitions for the paper. "We must all make sacrifices," he said. "You should realize that I have made no addition to my collection of French Impressionists since I bought the *Post*." It was an audience where all were more interested in money than Monet.

I got along well with Casey Jones and under his skillful direction the *Post* soon became a more professional paper. Much of the credit should go to Lowell LaVerne Leake, brought in from the Middle West as Assistant Managing Editor. Also helpful was Meyer's more complete realization that the less a newspaper publisher commands the better he will lead. But along with the confusion of the early days *élan* was also diminished. Of the original "four horsemen" Elliot Thurston had already left. At the end of 1935, Raymond Clapper went to the Scripps-Howard chain as political commentator. In a couple of years Franklyn Waltman would become publicity director for the Republican National Committee. I was one of the few original appointees left when Mr. Meyer, in 1938, asked me to let daughter Katharine join my staff as an apprentice. She was fresh from the University of Chicago, a well-poised and intelligent girl who evidently was to be groomed as the eventual owner-publisher. Such an attractive young lady was sure to marry and upon the character of that presumptive husband much would depend. Both at home and abroad I was forced to peer into a future of great obscurity.

At home, in the strict sense of the word, was also the area of deepest responsibility. Inside and out, "Millstone" was maturing nicely and I happily found time for friendship with my four children. On snowy Sundays there was much fun on the toboggan course worked out down the steep hill from Westmoreland Circle. In the valley below, Delecarlia Reservoir was still open for skating in winter; fishing for "blue gills" when spring decorated the woodland with dogwood, wild azalea and mountain laurel. The basement playroom was perfect for pingpong or fireside games. In the family circle, as well as on the Embassy circuit, the program was crowded with interest.

What I did not realize adequately was the strain on unremunerated success at home. After two years on the *Post* there had been no salary increase, though expenses were greatly augmented. In addition to an active social life, with much entertaining, Isabel had to chauffeur the children to school, supervise their homework, often transport her husband to and from his office, do the marketing, manage a series of indifferent cooks, keep the accounts, develop the garden, try to maintain her music and keep abreast of the international and domestic kaleidoscope which was the staple subject of Washington's luncheon, cocktail and dinner parties. Both her wardrobe and the house needed refinements but the tight budget meant that every outlay must be parsimoniously examined. I was a perfectionist who, in running my office smoothly, demanded household standards for which I could not provide the wherewithal. Isabel was an unostentatious woman who could not be coerced into a pretentious role. Needing recreation she took up horseback riding, for which she had natural talent, urging me to join her. I made the attempt but lacked both time and taste. I could get more exercise, more quickly, at tennis or squash, with more enjoyment to boot. Between us there was some malaise, not wholly glossed by the veneer of superficial success.

Of this unease, because of my more dramatic life, I was the less aware. As 1936 dawned I was concentrating on what this election year would mean for the *Post*, now stabilized internally and increasingly influential. On January 6 my diary rejoiced that: "The Supreme Court celebrated my forty-second birthday by throwing out the AAA [Agricultural Adjustment Administration] lock, stock and barrel." This six to three decision I saw as "a staggering blow to Roosevelt" because "based primarily on the thesis that the general welfare clause cannot be regarded as adding to the enumerated powers of the Federal Government at the expense of those reserved to the states." A fortnight later came the death of George V and, commenting on his successor, the diary doubts that: "the dignity and responsibility of the position will be congenial to him." Nevertheless, Edward VIII "would have to make a very bad mess of it to threaten stability. . . . This weary, satiated world cries for conservatism and clings now to tested institutions—our Court and the British Crown."

After a harsh winter, the sap was rising. On March 16, I recorded the appointment of Barnet Nover, of the Buffalo *Evening News*, as an editorial assistant. "Barney" was a good friend of ten years' standing, a student of history, well-read and well posted on the intricacies of international problems. He would strengthen the page in this field and thus ease pressures on the editor. But he was not my first choice. One doubt was how the new appointee would hit it off with Eugene Meyer. Barney, though not without personal charm, was the aggressively pushing type of Jew, with Eastern European background. In manners and mode of thought the publisher was western and distinctly aristocratic. Between these Jewish divisions, as I had first noted in my Baltimore boyhood, there was often latent hostility. This, however, was being obliterated by Hitler's sweepingly inclusive anti-Semitism. Meyer approved the appointment and immediately it lightened my load.

On the financial side, also, pressure was simultaneously lessened. Isabel unexpectedly received another helpful inheritance. While there was still no salary increase, I was told in confidence that the publisher would like to make me a personal non-interest loan of $15,000, sufficient to retire the Millstone mortgage as it then stood. This was primarily a psychological boost, since quarterly repayments of $450 to Mr. Meyer about equalled the interest and amortization I had been meeting. Still it showed that my services were valued and was coupled with assurance that an outright salary increase was delayed only by the "impossibility" of making these across the board as long as the paper was losing money. However, I was not happy with the paternalistic arrangement. From this time on I would listen more attentively to the alternative offers which came my way. With the Brookings doctorate I had become potential academic material and several colleges were showing an interest. Among these, in the spring of 1936, were Mills and Whittier, in California. I knew of the latter because of its Quaker background, and tentatively accepted an invitation to lecture there, wholly unaware that an ambitious youth named Richard Milhous Nixon was a recent alumnus.

But the trip to California, with a stopover in Kansas to visit Governor Landon, did not then materialize. In April, through the good offices of the British Embassy, I was invited to be one of a group of newspapermen to travel as guests of the Cunard Line on the maiden crossing of the *Queen Mary*, scheduled to leave from Southampton the end of May. The party would be taken to England on the *Georgic*, of the affiliated White Star Line, and have three days in London before returning. Aside from its intrinsic appeal this junket would permit some first-hand study of British foreign policy, thrown into the melting pot by Hitler's

288

denunciation of the Locarno Treaty and by the failure of League sanctions to prevent the Italian conquest of Ethiopia. The whole expedition would take less than three weeks and should be an ideal combination of recreation and investigation. Isabel strongly approved and Nover's arrival made arrangements easier. The trip would be a refreshing prelude to the strain of the coming Presidential campaign. From every angle it seemed a perfect plan.

Excitement was not lessened when, on May Day, Isabel phoned the office to relay a telegram from our good friend Robert Lincoln O'Brien, chairman of the Tariff Commission and an advisor to the Pulitzer School of Journalism at Columbia. The wire, from New York, said: "Please extend congratulations to your husband and keep secret until announced." Simple deduction suggested that I had been awarded the annual Pulitzer Prize for "distinguished editorial writing." This surmise, which proved correct, seemed valid enough to pass on to Mr. Meyer, then vacationing at White Sulphur Springs. The delighted publisher was not hesitant in promoting the honor for the *Post*, and soon congratulatory messages were flooding into the editorial office. One that especially appealed was from the Secretary of Commerce, Daniel C. Roper, saying: "Since your selection as editor of the Washington *Post* I have followed your editorials with an ever-increasing interest. Their stylistic clearness and simplicity and their notable lack of prejudice and bias have won for your editorials a well-merited place of esteem and appreciation." My diary recording of this tribute from a camp I often criticized was: "Such evidence that I have accomplished, at least in some degree, what I have sought so hard to do is about as welcome as anything could be."

Stimulated by this acclaim I brooded on how to use my brief stay in London to best advantage. Mussolini had just announced the annexation of Ethiopia. An interview with Anthony Eden, whom I had met at Geneva and who had recently become Foreign Minister, would be a bonus for the *Post*. To this end I sought the cooperation of Secretary Hull, the British Ambassador (Sir Ronald Lindsay) and "Bill" (Sir Wilmot) Lewis, genial Washington correspondent of the London *Times*. "If I can get this interview," I wrote in my journal, "it will be well worthwhile, even though all plans for purely personal recreation during my three days in London go a-glimmering." Yet such recreation was what I unconsciously craved. "I have rather outdone myself recently," I admitted in the same entry, made at home in the early morning hours of May 15.

That same morning Isabel saw me off to New York. Kit was not very well. Though only just past his forty-sixth birthday he had a prostate affliction which weighed on both mind and body. He was laboring with his first (1937) re-edition of Bartlett's *Familiar Quotations* but was also gestating the theme that would soon appear both as novel and play—*The Trojan Horse.* "What does the horse symbolize?" I inquired. "Ah, that will be for the reader to decide," was the reply. "Some form of man-made power, now built up beyond human control. The story is really a modern wave-length of Troilus and Cressida, if you remember your Chaucer."

But I didn't, at least not clearly. "The Georgics," I feebly japed, "are at the moment my favorite classics. And as I sail on one of them in just eight hours, I'm for bed." I always slept well at "Green Escape," amid its protecting trees and book-lined walls.

◀Aboard the *Georgic*, in addition to those of the newspaper contingent whom I already knew, was an English couple of whom I had seen a good deal in Washington. They were Major Frank Haywood and his attractive wife Rosalind, whom I had first met professionally but had come to know as close friends. The Major was Commercial Attaché at the British Embassy, where I frequently sought information on matters of international trade. Gradually, on the cocktail circuit, the Morleys got on first-name terms with this diplomatic pair and conversation progressed from interpretation of statistics to exchanges of a more intimate nature.

Rosalind Haywood was a remarkable woman with a deep, though guarded, interest in psychical research. Years later she would write a study of Extra-Sensory Perception—*The Sixth Sense*—which is a thorough and to me convincing examination of this phenomenon. But in 1936 she did not pretend to more than expertise in parlor pastimes like amateur fortune telling. How Mrs. Haywood had moved into this field was amusing. It was a part of her social duty to be hostess for delegations of British businessmen visiting Washington. These enforced gatherings were sometimes distinctly "sticky" so she developed the idea of reading the hands of selected guests as a pleasant change of pace. To give an authoritative impression she got some books on palmistry and learned the lingo of that art—or artifice.

To her surprise, there proved to be embarrassing accuracy in what some hands told her. She saw actual occurrences of which she had no prior knowledge. More than once abrupt termination of the "life line" suggested sudden deaths that soon took place. While Mrs. Haywood passed over such grim foresights with banalities she was nonetheless sufficiently impressed to take her studies seriously and to proceed from them to deeper consideration of psychic phenomena. Respecting this talent, I was receptive when on the third day out, after tea in a secluded corner of the comfortable lounge, she offered for the first time to read my palm, the Major having withdrawn to work on a report he had postponed for the ocean crossing.

Much of what Mrs. Haywood told me from this examination I had heard elsewhere. But a new point was given much emphasis by the shipboard oracle. I was, she asserted, at the moment in a state of psychological confusion, unaware of crises which would have to be resolutely resolved. If that could be read in my hand, I objected feebly, then it was Kismet and could not be averted, try as one might. There were indications other than those conveyed by palmistry, Mrs. Haywood retorted. As a friend she urged me not to be smug about my small accomplishments and to concentrate on preparedness for the trials that were coming to all.

While not disposed to exaggerate psychic problems it is my conviction that they can be as consequential as any physical ailment. For the latter one must rely on a medical practitioner. In mental or spiritual myopia there is more risk of quackery but the advice of a sincere and disinterested friend may well provide insight. So I took Rosalind Haywood's warning to heart and

291

believe that it helped to stabilize me during the difficult days ahead. This I had the pleasure of telling her, in London, after the emotional upheavals of the coming years had died away.

I chronicle this episode to show that I am not immune to superstition, but emphasize that it did not in any way interfere with either the gaiety or the professional aspects of my junket. Brother Frank met the *Georgic* at Southampton and through the soft spring night drove me to his charming old-world retreat, Pike's Farm, in Surrey. Everywhere the hawthorne was in blossom, nightingales were singing their hearts out in the darkness, and the narrow twisting streets of the little towns twined their way deep into half-submerged English memories. I could not believe that war would come again to shatter this contentment.

Next morning there was time for a survey of the bucolic exterior before proceeding by train from Oxted to London. At the Savoy was the anticipated message confirming my interview with the Foreign Secretary. I was to see the U.S. Ambassador at 4 p.m., then go with that envoy and remain at the Foreign Office for a private talk. Anthony Eden, soon to be knighted, was confidentially but frankly pessimistic about the future of Europe. Without firm opposition Hitler would not be stopped and the Fuehrer was now getting reciprocal encouragement from the Japanese warlords. With the failure of League sanctions against Italy, and with American mistrust of cooperative action, there was no longer any reliable check to Nazi ambitions. The only rational course for Britain now was large-scale rearmament and the introduction of peacetime conscription, unpopular though that would be. American understanding, as distinct from support, of Britain's hardening position was important.

Since I could not quote Eden's forthright observations directly, I felt it necessary, for a balanced report, to get the Opposition viewpoint. This was afforded by a dinner at the House of Commons that evening. My hosts, all known previously, were Hugh Dalton, late Chancellor of the Exchequer, Herbert Morrison, who would later become Foreign Secretary, and the two able M.P. sons—Will and Arthur—of "Uncle Arthur" Henderson, winner of the 1934 Nobel Peace Prize, then lately deceased. The quartette was critical of the Conservative Government for its failure to make resonable concessions to Germany before Hitler forced them. They saw no current need for conscription and emphasized that German objectives pointed east, not westward. Nevertheless, the mistrust of National Socialism was strong. Differences from the Tory viewpoint seemed of degree rather than kind. Reluctantly I concluded that German intransigence and British obduracy were on a collision course.

Early the following day I was again at the U.S. Embassy, to confer once more with Ambassador Bingham and to talk at length with Ray Atherton, an experienced career officer then serving as Counsellor. As matters stood, the latter favored a resolute American neutrality in the developing European antagonisms and hoped that the *Post*, which he credited with real influence in Britain, would uphold that course. Communism, he suggested, would be the only beneficiary from another war. There should be more clearheaded thinking as to whether it would be in America's long range advantage to line up with Russia. I listened appreciatively for this was very much my own opinion. But I felt sure that if Britain went to war with Germany it would be in expectation of American support.

Both on the Monday and Tuesday I lunched with my brother and some of his literary and journalistic friends. Most impressive was T. S. Eliot of whom, at that time, I had heard much but read relatively little. I was, however, familiar with *The Waste Land* and *The Hollow Men* and would have liked to question their author about "the Shadow" which inexorably falls between potential and accomplishment in the latter terrifying poem. But its author obstinately showed himself more concerned with what I thought of Anthony Eden, whom Eliot evidently admired. It is perhaps an occupational hazard that newspapermen are supposed to be interested only in what they can report. I was not that way but could not, or at least did not, convey to my readers the feeling of Doom which I sensed in London's springtime air. The evident misplacement of Edward VIII during his few months on the throne seemed somehow symbolic. Those royal misgivings could not be made into copy, any more than Eliot's veiled portents.

Time for brooding was sharply limited, since the *Queen Mary* sailed the following day. Frank, who had been most

293

cooperative throughout, drove me to romantic old Waterloo Station, in company with his unrelated but charming colleague Morley Kennerly. Others were there to say farewell. Like a dream London faded behind the comfortable boat train, where lunch was served. Then I was aboard the towering three-stack steamer, which cast off at Southampton promptly at 4:30 p.m. The long English twilight lingered until we had left the Isle of Wight astern, cutting diagonally across the Channel for Cherbourg and thence really home. It was 76 years since the maiden voyage of the *Great Eastern*, that prodigy of Victorian naval architecture most happily remembered as the ship that laid the first successful trans-Atlantic cables. There had been newspapermen along for that earlier nautical debut and the correspondent of the London *Times* reported his crossing as "dull," possibly because the maximum speed of the *Great Eastern* was less than half that maintained by the more stately and far more luxurious Queen. Both ended their days, however, as permanently laid-up "show boats."

For me, always interested in ship design, *Queen Mary* held much fascination. The journalists were given full run of the ship and very soon I had explored her thoroughly, from the captain's suite to the stewards' quarters, from the navigating bridge to the big turbines in the cavernous engine room. By good fortune the *Post* representative was placed at table with Sir Percy Bates, chairman of the Cunard Line, and from him gathered much history of this famous company, including sidelights on old Samuel Cunard, the Quaker Nova Scotian who started its regular trans-Atlantic service in 1840. From the original paddle-wheel quartette, of *Acadia, Britannia,*[9] *Caledonia* and *Columbia,* practically all its steamers had carried the "ia" termination to their names. That *Queen Mary* broke this tradition, I said to Sir Percy, was the only criticism I could make of the magnificent vessel on which we traveled. *Queen Maria* would have saved the day.

"Ah, there's a story behind that," replied the affable magnate, "which I'll tell you on condition you won't print it during

---

9. Charles Dickens made a grim winter crossing on *Britannia*, in January, 1842. His *American Notes* contain a graphic account of the 14-day voyage.

my lifetime. When we got in sight of launching Hull No. 39, as this ship was first known at Clydebank, I obtained an interview with George V to ask whether the Queen would graciously consent to christen our lusty infant. 'And what do you plan to name her?' the King inquired. 'Your Majesty,' I replied fatuously, 'the name selected is that of Britain's most illustrious Queen'—by which I meant Victoria. George smiled. 'Mary will be pleased,' he said. Thus was shattered the century of tradition which you so properly esteem. And rather than return to Victoria we now think we should go back to Queen Elizabeth for our upcoming leviathan. So you see why, if you tell this story, I shall promptly deny it as a canard."

"A Cunard canard," I observed, and was promptly debited for a round of drinks.

Because of fog the *Queen Mary*, on her maiden voyage, failed by 42 minutes to match the blue-ribbon crossing set by the French *Normandie* a year earlier. But the reception in New York was nonetheless enthusiastic. Few then realized that the sirens were sounding the swansong of the ocean liner; that the airplane would soon make even a four-day crossing seem impossibly slow. Isabel had come up for the occasion and that night we joined Kit and some of his cronies at the older brother's favorite restaurant and former speakeasy—Christ Cella's. The senior of our trio, I reflected, was as firmly wedged in New York as was the youngest in London. But there was a difference in the settings. Kit was stimulated by the admiration of lighter minds. Frank got more enjoyment from less frivolous intercourse with T. S. Eliot, Herbert Read and their circle. Was this a matter of age or temperament, I asked Isabel when we went on to the Rainbow Grill for an exchange of confidences. More the latter, she thought.

On June 2 the editor was back in his office, picking up the reins, completing a Sunday feature article on the *Queen Mary* and lunching with the publisher, managing editor and business manager. I learned that prospects for the paper were much improved—coincidentally with my absence, Meyer emphasized. But there was no time for relaxation between assignments. In a week the Republican Nominating Convention would meet in Cleveland. "It looks like Landon, very likely on the first ballot,"

295

I wrote in my diary. "I am not clear as to what line my 'analytical articles,' as advertised, will follow. But I expect I shall find something."

That was immediately at hand, traveling out in the same sleeper as Senator Borah, who was regarded as Landon's only serious rival for the nomination. Though deploring the Senator's hostility to cooperation with the League of Nations, I admired his forthright and independent spirit. In a long conversation the "Lion of Idaho" was doubtful about Roosevelt's will to stay out of war, should it come in Europe. Landon, if he could be elected, would be the better bet. "He is at least free from control by the Eastern Establishment," said Borah. "But that's a negative attribute."

◀▶

◀Nobody whom I knew, other than the pollsters of the *Literary Digest* and Agnes Meyer, believed that Governor Landon could be elected President in 1936. In international affairs he lacked both background and knowledge, at a time when foreign policy was becoming steadily more intricate and demanding. Outside of Kansas he was not especially popular in the agricultural states and his influence with Labor was minimal. Republican organization had not recovered from the collapse of 1932 and was further torn by bitter factionalism. Because Hearst backed Landon, the candidate received little or no support from Mr. Hoover. Western liberal leaders, like William Allen White, aroused no enthusiasm among the discredited but still financially important Old Guard. Caught in the G.O.P. crossfire, the Governor's leadership stumbled and the intellectual honesty that was his strongest asset blurred. The Baltimore *Sun*, which had indorsed him early, grew sardonic. It jibed that Republicans were "willing to exceed Mr. Roosevelt in public expenditures as a means of stopping Mr. Roosevelt's lavish expenditures."

Disarray in Republican ranks did not incline me toward the Democratic camp. The Convention of that party was held in Philadelphia, the end of June, closing with the acceptance in which F.D.R. virtually proclaimed himself a Man of Destiny. "I cannot see any hope for the country," I wrote, "in a party which so panders to ignorance and emotion, while relying on the twin evils of patronage and subsidies to hold its discordant elements together." Equally caustic was a review of *Whose Constitution?*, a polemic published by Secretary of Agriculture Wallace as a campaign contribution. It asked who "owns" the Constitution, if not the people of the United States? "The use of that word," said my signed review, "is revealing. How can anyone 'own' the organic law of the nation? . . . We should be very careful about easing the wise restrictions constitutionally placed on the working of democracy in this country."

My criticisms of both sides confirmed the decision that the *Post* should be above the battle in the Presidential contest. It should really be the "independent" newspaper proclaimed on the masthead. The advantageous position in the Capital should be emphasized not by any lack of critical comment but by complete impartiality in exercise thereof. This ideal was not easy to sustain, since both Mr. and Mrs. Meyer were bitterly anti-Roosevelt and I felt sure that during the former's absences in New York he was giving long-distance coaching to Landon and sound advice to John Hamilton as chairman of the Republican National Committee.[10] But on the paper's editorial independence the publisher never wavered. When Mrs. Meyer reproached me for criticizing Landon's deficiencies her husband said: "Pay no attention to her." At last the period of strain ended and on Election Eve I wrote a long and strongly cautionary editorial on the assumption of a sweeping Roosevelt victory. There was no point, I was sure, in having an alternative prepared for the eventuality of a Landon triumph. Nevertheless I had not anticipated the magnitude of the Republican debacle, in Congress as well as in the electoral vote of 8 to 523. By its scrupulous impartiality in this campaign, I confided to my journal, the *Post* has "laid a corner-stone on which we should be able to build great things."

In the upshot I reluctantly voted for Roosevelt's second term, assuaging my conscience by telling Isabel that I was supporting Cordell Hull. She, more perceptively, cast her ballot

10. Cf. Donald R. McCoy, *Landon of Kansas*, Univ. of Nebraska Press, Lincoln, 1966, pp. 229 and 267. In several of his campaign speeches Landon quoted almost verbatim from *Post* editorials.

for the Opposition. There was not long to wait before the President sought to capitalize on his power by striking hard at the chief obstacle in his path. On February 5, 1937, a fortnight after the new Congress assembled, F.D.R. unveiled his plan to pack the Supreme Court.

Unquestionably, the President's program for centralization of government was being thwarted by the judiciary. In his first term 30 cases involving constitutionality came before the Supreme Court and in 13 of these it was ruled that the Administration had exceeded its proper powers. Adulteration of the gold standard had been approved but vital New Deal Measures, such as the Guffey Coal Act, the AAA and NRA had been repudiated. With his smashing second-term victory Mr. Roosevelt evidently decided he could by-pass the stumbling block with some procedure quicker than Constitutional Amendment.

This had been foreshadowed during the campaign. F.D.R. then predicted that "over a period of five or ten years" it would be decided whether the national government should take over "control of social, economic and working conditions." These Fabian tactics seemed not unreasonable to me, among many others. The promised Presidential restraint was one reason I voted for him, believing that Governor Landon was too standpat on issues of Constitutional reform. Consequently, it was a double let-down when F.D.R. exploded his bomb. And it was unpleasant that Mrs. Meyer should be justified in saying: "I told you so."

Stripped of its camouflage the new Judiciary Bill was appallingly simple. For every judge on a Federal bench aged 70 or over, the President would be empowered to appoint an additional judge, up to a maximum total of 15 for the Supreme Court. That this tribunal was the real target was shown by the fact that two-thirds of its nine members had passed their seventieth birthday. With six new placemen, only two present judges would need to be sympathetic to the New Deal in order to give the President a sure eight to seven majority, instead of the seven to two repudiations which he had good reason to fear.

Urged on by Mr. Meyer I immediately prepared ammunition against this none-too-subtle attack on the principle of separate and divided powers. An almost daily editorial drumfire was

298

approved, with Pusey doing a large part of the firing. It was the latter's function to expose misrepresentation in the Roosevelt claims, such as the false assertion that the Supreme Court docket was overloaded because of the alleged senility of some members.[11] I commented on the vital importance of an independent judiciary, going back to Star Chamber and the historic position of the Democratic Party for effective argument. "Bind him down with the chains of the Constitution" had been Jefferson's prescription for the arrogant power seeker. In framing this instrument of government Madison had argued that: "The accumulation of all powers . . . in the same hands" is "the very definition of tyranny." Even Hamilton, the great centralizer, had agreed that "there is no liberty if the powers of judging be not separated from the legislative and executive powers."

For me there were two thought-provoking by-products of this acute issue, which fermented through the Spring and Summer of 1937. One was the character of the letters to the editor that poured in, mostly of a quality and cogency that made this column very interesting reading. Quite a number, however, asked why the paper did not "trust and support our great President." This tendency to follow the leader blindly bothered me, since its exploitation by authoritarian government would be all too easy. Fortunately it was countered by many Washington newspapermen, both aware of and loyal to the principles on which the Republic is based. At the annual dinner of the White House correspondents, which I attended, there were some bitter off-the-record gibes. The reporter impersonating F.D.R. proclaimed: "Whatever Hitler says, I'll double it!"

The second moralization sprang from my frequent visits to the Senate, to obtain advice on phases of the fight over the judiciary bill. The election had left the Republicans with only 16 Senate seats, so one might have predicted smooth sailing for the White House plan. Actually the opposition to it was nonpartisan, with Democrats like Burke of Nebraska, Tydings of Maryland and O'Mahoney of Wyoming outspoken in criticism. It

11. An excellent summary account of the whole struggle was authored by him while the conflict still raged: Merlo J. Pusey, *The Supreme Court Crisis*, The Macmillan Co., New York, 1936.

was a lesson, reminiscent of the fight against ratification of the Treaty of Versailles, on the Senate's potential value as a bulwark against executive arrogation of power. Bill Borah told me that while he had never filibustered he was "ready to keep the Senate sitting all summer" on the Court issue.

Such last-ditch tactics proved unnecessary. It was soon clear that the judiciary bill had no chance of passage, though the President continued to denounce the "horse and buggy" philosophy of the opposition. Here, as in his favorable estimate of Stalin, Roosevelt was slow to learn. In the 1938 elections he vindictively and vainly attempted to "purge" the Democratic legislators who had rebelled against his project. But on this *cause célèbre* the luck of F.D.R. was out. Fate threw three strikes. First the Court reversed the Georgia conviction of Angelo Herndon, a Negro Communist agitator, making it more difficult to argue that a renovated tribunal was needed to safeguard individual rights. Then Roosevelt's first appointee to the Court, when Justice Van Devanter resigned, was not considered happy. The choice was Hugo Black, the junior Senator from Alabama, who was not only lacking in judicial experience but also (as was quickly revealed) had been a member of the Ku Klux Klan. That Justice Black would in time become a highly respected member of the Court did not serve to make his original appointment more palatable. The final blow was the death of Senator Joe Robinson (Arkansas) who, as chairman of the Judiciary Committee, had been unable to get the controversial measure reported favorably.

The international scene was far from quiet, while this domestic issue was being played out to the President's discomfiture. Though European deterioration got the headlines there was evidence that serious trouble was boiling up again in Asia. For a time it was thought that Chiang Kai-shek, the Nationalist Generalissimo, would unify China, subdue the native Communists and come to terms, though probably unfavorable, with the Japanese. This last was for a time largely achieved and in the autumn of 1934 it had seemed probable that Chiang would be able to overrun Kiangsi Province, in Southeast China, where Mao Tse-tung, most able of the Communist leaders, was in command. But as the Nationalists closed in, Mao slipped westward through the cordon, with his ragged army, his civilian staff and many loyal peasant followers who had no use for Chiang's regime. For more than a year on this "Long March" the motley Communist caravan skirmished its way toward Tibet until all danger from Chiang's unenergetic forces was left behind. Then the anabasis turned north to Shensi Province in the shadow of the Great Wall, where indigenous Communism had been entrenched for years.[12] Almost unnoticed in the United States, except for the efforts of a few courageous correspondents like Edgar Snow, the success of the Long March had caused much concern in Japan. As emphasized to me by Kawakami it brought Chinese Communist leadership much closer to the puppet state of Manchukuo and was also final demonstration that Chiang Kai-shek, with whom the Japanese believed they could deal, was wholly unable to overcome the widespread Chinese opposition to his rule.

Both factors were incentives for the renewed Japanese aggression which was not slow in coming. It was further foreshadowed by the German-Japanese treaty, concluded shortly after Roosevelt's re-election, providing for joint defensive measures against the activities of the Communist International. This Berlin-Tokyo Axis seemed to me serious business and I signed up a special correspondent, Mark Ginsburg, for occasional articles from China. I had reason to think that Ginsburg, who wrote under the name of Mark Gayne, was not far from being a Communist himself. But if true, I reasoned, that could be an advantage. A decade earlier I had witnessed the rising tide of Chinese Communism and questioned the easy assumption that China would never go Red. Nevertheless, I checked Ginsburg's copy carefully for subtle propaganda. The most frequent instance at that time was reference to Chinese Communists as "agrarian reformers," which of course they were, but a great deal more besides.

Permission to purchase such special correspondence, even at a starvation price, was one indication that the *Post* was moving toward solvency. Another, more pleasing, was Mr. Meyer's decision, on February 13, 1937, to give his editor that

---

12. Cf. p. 190 supra.

long-deferred salary increase. The raise was only $20 a week, giving me the comparatively modest annual income of $13,500, and it came after more than three years of unremitting and undercompensated effort. But Meyer simultaneously emphasized that he wanted to make provision in other ways and very soon; in great secrecy, I was told that a brokerage account of a little over $100,000, in railroad and bank stocks, had been opened in my name. With this was a letter from the publisher "confirming in writing that I hold you harmless from any loss that may occur. But all, if any, profits that may accrue are to be yours." Actually no profits were ever distributed, though the potential beneficiary remained with the *Post* for three and one-half years after this "Meyer Account" was opened. All dividends were automatically ploughed back, no sales were made and the only result for me was troublesome inquiries from Internal Revenue. Nor was I happy with this further illustration of a paternalistic attitude on my employer's part.

I had, however, met my financial problems in other ways. My department was running smoothly. Pusey was steadily broadening his scope. Nover, though disappointingly careless, had the background necessary for insight on developments overseas. Reggie Kauffman, who proved a washout, had been replaced by Jo' Lalley, who managed book reviews and gave the editorial page that touch of literary distinction which I deeply desired. John Clark was also a graceful writer and completely reliable in every division of the work. Mary Scaife had proved herself an excellent, indefatigable and tactful secretary. In March of 1937, I felt able to put the editorial department on a five-day week, giving myself Saturday as well as Sunday off.

An advantage of this, financially, was that it enabled me to accept some of the speaking engagements which were offered with increasing frequency. In Washington I considered such service part of the job and seldom accepted remuneration. But elsewhere I saw no objection to taking fees and as I spoke pleasingly, never reading a paper and keeping my discourse short, the returns were often fairly substantial. An enterprising New York lecture agent, Clark Getts, conceived the idea of a series of debates between Kit and me, suggesting as subject: "Resolved, that Newspapers Do More Harm than Good." This brothers' act was appealing to both, since each believed in the side he took, and the show was put on with great brio, with juries to give a verdict, in New York, Boston, Philadelphia, Cleveland and Chicago. For the elder brother it was doubly profitable, since the booksellers had his titles attractively displayed at each performance. I could only counter by offering to take subscriptions for the *Post*, of which not a few materialized. The publisher was not pleased by his editor's lecture agency connection and said so. I replied that this was not an automatically binding commitment and that I always put duties to the paper first.

In other respects I was identifying myself with activities aside from daily work. The District Librarian, George F. Bowerman, persuaded me to fill a vacancy on the Board of Library trustees. George W. White asked me to join the Board of his National Metropolitan Bank and wishing to learn more of this esoteric business, I complied. Dick Cleveland, son of the former President, enlisted me for the Board of St. John's College, Annapolis, which two Rhodes Scholar friends, Stringfellow Barr and Scott Buchanan, were reorganizing to revive the fundamentals of classical education. But my most entertaining new membership was in the withdrawn, tranquil and very select Washington Literary Society.

This organization, once defined as *les élus des élus*, has been inaugurated in the home of John G. Nicolay, formerly Abraham Lincoln's private secretary, on January 6, 1874, which intrigued me because twenty years to the day before my own birth. Helen Nicolay, the daughter, clearly recalled the origin and still linked past to present when I was notified of my election, in 1937. The monthly meetings were dedicated to "literary exercises," meaning the reading of a well-prepared essay by a member, followed by wide-ranging discussion of its substance and finally a pleasant buffet supper. "The only topics excluded . . . are those which touch the realm of politics or the domain of religion." The first, at least, had been a wise exclusion in a capital still embittered by the strains of civil war. From its foundation the Society has done much to irrigate the literary aridity of Washington. Mrs. Frances Hodgson Burnett was an early member, followed by Edward Everett Hale, Richard Hovey, Percy Mackaye, Archibald MacLeish, Charles Nordhoff, Thomas Nelson Page, Mary Roberts

Rinehart, Margaret Landon and others scarcely less well-known. Jules Jusserand and Hu Shih were among the distinguished diplomats admitted. There have been several college presidents in the membership, numerous professional men, representatives from all three branches of the federal government but noticeably few from the marts of commerce and finance. Journalists were also eyed apprehensively and I noted that there were no others from the *Post*. Whether a Senator, General, Jurist or Doctor of any variety, everyone was democratically addressed as plain Mr. or Mrs., yet formal dress was *de rigueur* for all meetings, which until the Second World War were customarily held in private homes. Increasing membership—wives or husbands of those chosen habitually attended—and decreasing service ended that practise and the meetings now, though adhering to traditional pattern, are generally held at some club or institution. We found the gatherings charmingly redolent of decorous Victorian custom and a happy contrast to the chatter of the cocktail circuit. Problems of the day got little or no consideration and while older members often slumbered through the dissertation there was generally sparkle beneath the placid surface. If Armageddon were approaching, the Washington Literary Society would surely confront convulsion with the same quiet dignity that Kant displayed before Napoleon's army at Koenigsberg.

As I saw it, these various contacts made me a more valuable editor. But I was uneasily aware that the publisher was not wholly of that opinion. In Eugene Meyer's quite legitimate viewpoint he was the boss and even his top employes were subordinates. Toward his editor he was always *suaviter in modo* but sometimes the iron hand could be glimpsed through the velvet glove. When I joined the Metropolitan Bank board Mr. Meyer was not pleased, saying it would be better if the position were filled by Don Bernard, the Business Manager. Indeed "Butch" was at heart a ruler who would not tolerate over-mighty subjects. There were advantages for an editor under active individual ownership, but there were also disadvantages.

On a springtime lecturing visit to Richmond, I discussed the matter frankly with Douglas Southall Freeman, famous editor of the *News Leader*, who a decade earlier had sought to

304

lure me from Baltimore to the former Confederate capital. "Putting it too sharply," said Dr. Freeman in summation, "no man of character will be the Brisbane for a Hearst." The Virginian had then just completed his great four-volume biography of Robert E. Lee and explained how he had been able to write that while actively conducting his editorial page. A minimum of 14 hours a week was devoted exclusively to the outside writing and if this fell short by as much as an hour the deficit was doubled and entered in a diary which at each weekend would chronicle: "I owe D.S.F. *x* hours." Ideally, concluded Freeman, the publisher is himself the editor, like William Allen White. "But when the functions are divided a great editor should never sell his soul to the proprietor, for if he does he ceases to be great."

At this juncture, on May 5, 1937, Mr. Meyer unexpectedly suggested that I should accompany him on a trip to Europe. It would be a working journey, with the editor expected to send back reports on their observations, and I was not wholly delighted by the prospect. "I'll do the work and Meyer will have the fun," I told Isabel, to whom I had promised a vacation trip to Mexico. However, it was virtually a command performance, and for other reasons I felt that the opportunity must be seized. New neutrality legislation had just been enacted, and it would be informative to get the reaction of European leaders at first hand. I would have a look at Nazi Germany, even though Meyer himself refused to visit that country. Was the League of Nations as nearly moribund as reported? Was war coming or could it still be averted and if so, how? The editorial page could be safely left under Pusey's careful control. Millstone was running smoothly, finances were easier and the trip would cost me nothing. Isabel urged me to accept and I welcomed the opportunity to confer with Frank about our parents, who in spite of obviously failing health were again going to England, the day after the Meyers' scheduled departure on May 19. A fortnight was a short time to get everything in order but I was now accustomed to pressures of that sort.

◀I was not unaware that there would be travail in my travel

with Eugene Meyer. The plan was for the two to interview celebrities together, with the editor writing a series of informative articles on their findings for front-page display in the *Post*. The publisher had numerous European connections and rightly thought that his international financial know-how would serve to broaden the editor's outlook. On the other hand Mr. Meyer had little interest in average opinion and was wholly ignorant of the techniques of newspaper correspondence, in which I had learned my way through years of experience.

A good reporter does not argue with the person from whom he seeks information. He must, of course, question in a manner showing that he is both well-informed and alert to prejudice. But his basic function is to present a *tabula rasa* on which the selected interviewee is invited to express opinions, whether wise or otherwise. When the interviewer considers these deficient he does not directly contradict but seeks another source to present opposing viewpoints and thus obtain a balanced picture. Editorial opinion should be most sparingly used in writing a news story and never if the report is set forth as factual.

This was not Mr. Meyer's habit. In the triangular interviews throughout the trip he was never hesitant in presenting his own expert ideas. To these the statesmen interviewed would usually listen courteously, which did not justify the assumption of agreement. When the publisher heard a viewpoint in accord with his own he seldom thought it necessary to look further. In writing my articles, therefore, I was under intangible pressures which I had never before experienced. Nor was it easy to grind out the correspondence at the end of exhausting days, while my colleague relaxed.

Our social relationship was itself anomalous. In some respects I served as a courier, making many of the appointments as well as travel and hotel arrangements. This was important, since the publisher was not accustomed to handling details for himself. Taking a taxi to the station, after an overnight visit to Brussels, I noticed that Mr. Meyer was leaving without his suitcase and inquired. "I thought the valet would attend to that for me," he said ruefully. I could not refrain from observing that few newspapermen could rely on such service.

I also functioned as a traveling companion. Mr. Meyer liked

to talk and his wealth of experience, depth of knowledge and wide-ranging interests made him a very interesting conversationalist. But it was clear that my role was to listen rather than to dilate myself and as time went on the unilateral pattern became a little tiresome. Such annoyance, however, was offset by the publisher's unfailing generosity. He paid for everything, including tips. Federal Reserve notes fairly showered the decks of the *Normandie* as we disembarked.

The sumptuous setting of the journey was apparent immediately on boarding the great French liner, where Mr. and Mrs. Meyer, their daughter Florence and a maid were quartered in the palatial *Rouen* suite. Here a gala sailing party had been arranged, to which I was empowered to invite guests. Brother Chris was foremost among these, both because he got on well with the Meyers and because he had some messages for me to convey to the Third Garrideb[13] in London. I also brought my friend Roussy de Sales, from the French Embassy, a fellow-passenger, together with Herbert Elliston and David Wills, correspondent of the London *Economist*, with whom I had breakfasted in New York that morning. Both of these able British newspapermen, I knew, envied my job. I had as yet no intention of relinquishing it, but thought that Mr. Meyer should know them.

The Meyer ladies left the ship at Cherbourg, to establish a Paris base. Eugene and I went on to Southampton, passing through a big flotilla of the battle fleet still assembled in the Solent following the Coronation Review for George VI. That night in London Frank had us both to dinner at the Oxford and Cambridge Club, along with several of his journalistic friends, including Jim Bone of the *Guardian* and dear old Hamish Miles, now a member of the *Times'* editorial staff. The blow-out must have been a strain on the fraternal pocketbook, immediately following a vacation trip to Salzburg, but Frank stood to it as the perfect host. It was the last I would see Hamish, my cherished friend from Ambulance Unit days. In a few months the still

---

13. Among the Baker Street Irregulars, the Sherlock Holmes Admiration Society in which all three Morley brothers were active, the trio were known as "The Three Garridebs," after the Conanical story with that title.

youthful Scot would be stricken by an inoperable brain tumor. It seemed improbable that this delicate aesthete would get on well with so forceful a character as the aggressive Jewish publisher. But in social intercourse Eugene Meyer had an almost chameleon power of adaptation.

The Imperial Conference was sitting in London, considering bonds soon to be tested in the furnace of war, and I spent the next morning with Dominion contacts made for me by old friends on the League of Nations' Secretariat—Raymond Kershaw for Australia and Craig McGeachie for Canada. I lunched alone with my brother at Simpson's, afterwards meeting Meyer at the U.S. Embassy for a conference with Ray Atherton, now much more favorable to coordinated Anglo-American policies than had been the case a year earlier. Then publisher and editor caught a late afternoon train to Oxford where we were royally entertained overnight at Rhodes House, built since my last presence at this Alma Mater, fifteen years earlier. Little else, however, was changed in Oxford, and I had pleasure in acting as cicerone to my appreciative boss. By invitation we dined in Hall at New College (founded in 1386) where several old Dons of my day received us cordially. Then there was port, in the Senior Common Room, and a moonlight stroll through well-remembered quadrangles and streets. "What a glorious old place it is," I wrote in my diary, "how unrivaled; how redolent of the finest human aspirations." Next morning there was time for a visit to Blackwell's famous bookshop before returning to London and lunch with Geoffrey Dawson, editor of the *Times*, who had in, among others, Lord Lothian (the former Phillip Kerr), the newly appointed Ambassador to Washington. Dawson was moderately pro-German, to the extent of regarding that country's overthrow of the Treaty of Versailles as justified. But more outspoken in this regard was elderly James L. Garvin, famous editor of the *Observer*, who argued strongly against any British—or American—policy that could lead toward an alliance with Soviet Russia. Communism, for Garvin, was much more of a threat than Hitler to Western civilization.

There were many more talks, with labor leaders, economists, financiers and businessmen, during those nine days in England. I found it exhausting, having to produce articles, generally late at night, on the often conflicting impressions with which the daytime hours were crowded. This writing, featured in the *Post* as my copy streamed in, had to be objective, clear and convincing, also much more "in depth" than ordinary cable correspondence. I had the necessary background, and Meyer's comment, as we reviewed what we had heard, was often luminous and always helpful. But the publisher, for all his keen thinking, was congenitally unable to write simple newspaper English so that I had to compose to satisfy both. This was wearisome and when the weekend came I struck for time off, to leave London and visit quietly with my parents who were by then located in rural Woodbridge, the ancestral Morley home.

This had been arranged with Frank, who on the Friday took me down to Pike's Farm, to which I had been so pleasantly introduced a year previous. It was a perfect summer evening, fitting weather for Mr. Baldwin's surrender of his well-handled Premiership. After Munich the general verdict on his successor, Neville Chamberlain, would be otherwise. That was in the future, however, and my immediate interest was in understanding my younger brother's deep attachment to the English way of life. The influence of his literary friends was obvious. But much was *sui generis* in Frank's philosophy. "It is pretty metaphysical," records my journal under date of May 30, "but I honor him for the courage and intellectual integrity with which he upholds it."

Next morning the weather still smiled and with Christina, and two children, Frank was soon driving the long traverse of London, from south to north. Then through Hertfordshire to Royston where Aunt Florence, still cheerful and chipper at 82, welcomed us in the little house where Isabel and I had visited during Oxford days. From Royston to Cambridge, for lunch with another Bird sister—Margaret—and Uncle Hugh, bereaved of both their sons by World War I. From Cambridge by little-traveled byroads into Suffolk and to St. Joseph's Hostel, in Woodbridge.

I have always been grateful for this overnight stop in the placid, almost unchanging, East Anglian town. My father, now nearly 77, chatted happily of his boyhood days there, as we strolled along the river and through the familiar winding streets. We visited the abandoned Quaker Meeting House, then

309

up for sale, and he identified the simple family headstones in its little yard. The feverish panorama of this world's politics seemed far away. The old mathematician, back in his mid-Victorian childhood and never much concerned with current events, seemed to give little thought to the developing madness. In time, but not yet, I would assume the same protective armor. That night I was in London again, picking up threads with Eugene Meyer. More interviews had been scheduled before leaving, 24 hours later, by the comfortable train ferry to Dunkirk and Paris.

For the day of our arrival there an older sister of Mr. Meyer, wife of the Brazilian Ambassador there, had arranged a lunch with the then Premier of France, Leon Blum, as honor guest. My conversational French is adequate and I talked at length with the leader of the uneasy Popular Front government, finding him surprisingly temperate toward Germany. "Czechoslovakia," I wrote in my journal that night, "Blum finds in the position of Poland at the end of the Eighteenth Century, which would seem to carry a certain implication of an eventual partition." This pacific and gentle Socialist, who would oppose the Munich settlement, be interned by the Germans and surface briefly after World War II, was at the moment on the eve of overthrow by the Chamber of Deputies. Another Premier, Camille Chautemps, was in office a few days later. With him, as well as with former Premier Herriot, Georges Bonnet, René de Chambrun, Pierre Comert, Bertrand de Jouvenel, André Philip and other influential French friends I conferred at length. It was evident that France, far more than Britain, was both physically unprepared and psychologically unwilling to stand up to German demands, a fact of which the Fuehrer was certainly well aware.

The stay in Paris was broken by an overnight trip to Brussels, for a talk arranged with Prime Minister Paul Van Zeeland. The Belgian leader was about to visit Washington and welcomed the backstage advice which Mr. Meyer was both competent and glad to give. Van Zeeland, a forceful and able conservative, was more anxious to ask than to answer questions but asserted that Belgium could successfully maintain its newly-announced neutrality in the event of another war. He made plain his concern about French political weakness, with all the implications for a small adjacent country unable to resist alone. It made me the more anxious to get a slant on the Nazi attitude, when I took sleeper from Paris to Berlin the night of June 9. I would have a scant four days in the German capital, before rejoining Mr. Meyer in Prague the evening of June 13.

This dip into the Third Reich was my first visit to Germany since 1931 and I had not seen Berlin for 16 years. Thus I was in an excellent position to observe the changes brought by the Nazis, the more so because of familiarity with the language. In casual conversation it was easy for me to pose as a curious German-American, on a first visit to the *Vaterland* since childhood. The approach always brought an interested and seemingly frank response. Also I was fortunate in having good friends at the U.S. Embassy: Jimmy Riddleberger, well up the diplomatic ladder since our Geneva acquaintance; Loyd Steere, the agricultural attaché, whom I had known in Washington, and Douglas Miller, a Rhodes Scholar of my vintage, then serving as commercial attaché.[14] Foremost among German friends was Dr. Karl von Lewinski who described his country as a *sehr orderliches Gefängnis* (very orderly prison). Paul Leverkuehn, a reserve officer, was at the time away on military maneuvers. In Berlin, however, there was little evidence of armed force, some said because military preparedness was so unpopular. Persecution of Jews and Communists was still relatively restrained and I was disposed to think the police-state stories somewhat exaggerated. I had been told that my baggage would certainly be secretly examined and therefore, on reaching the Adlon Hotel, arranged papers in my unlocked suitcase so that I would know immediately if they were at all disturbed. Somewhat to my disappointment there was no evidence of this. On the other hand, von Lewinski told me of the police agents employed as doormen for every apartment house and anticipated questioning about my visit.

Germany seemed in more pacific mood than expected. Certainly the "man in the street"—taxi drivers, waiters,

14. In 1941 Miller published a strongly anti-Nazi book: *You Can't Do Business With Hitler*. A more balanced study of the period is found in *Failure Of A Mission*, by Sir Nevile Henderson, who in 1937 was the newly-installed British Ambassador to Germany.

shopkeepers—deplored the possibility of another war. Uninvited but welcomed I joined a random student group for a café *Bierabend*. The songs were all sentimental—nothing patriotic—and the boys and girls alike were unanimously critical of Hitler's saber-rattling. I went with von Lewinski to watch the Davis Cup tennis match with Belgium and noted how punctiliously the audience applauded points scored by the outplayed foreigners. Nor did the atmosphere seem exceptionally repressive. That evening the judge took his daughter and son-in-law, an Austrian architect named Wiedemann, along with me to dinner at the big outdoor restaurant in the Zoologischer Garten. Toward the end of a merry meal the young Austrian pulled a lock of his black hair down his forehead, held a small pocket comb so that it looked like a trim moustache, and began a high-pitched gabble obviously imitative of the Fuehrer. I was appalled, expecting immediate arrest by the Gestapo. But people at nearby tables only smiled. "For the moment one Austrian can make fun of another," said von Lewinski. Nevertheless Wiedemann, like everyone else, rose to his feet for mass singing of the *Horst Wessel Lied* and followed it with the Nazi salute from which I alone refrained. The architect was no Nazi but he viewed German-Austrian *Anschluss* as inevitable. "There was no work for me in Vienna," he said. "I had to come to Germany for employment. Either Germany takes over Austria or half my countrymen will migrate here, where jobs are plentiful."

It was extremely hot in Berlin—37 degrees Celcius *im Schatten* people complained—and the renowned energy of the inhabitants was somewhat subdued thereby. Having made no advance arrangements I could not get to talk with either Hitler or Goering, which was regrettable. However, with the help of the Embassy, I made appointments with several lesser Nazi functionaries. Notable among these was Dr. Walther Darré, Minister of Agriculture and Nutrition, a big man who received me in a baggy and unseasonable suit which he proudly explained had just been made from beechwood fibre. "The process will save us imports of wool," said the Minister. "And it is developing so well that we plan to plant thousands of beech trees in this area"—pointing to a big wall map—"where the beech flourishes." A few hours later, at the Air Ministry, I was told of plans for a new commercial airport north of Berlin, located for me on an identical map in the same area that Dr. Darré had designated for forestation. I asked whether this would eliminate precious farmland. "Practically none," replied the official. "It's very poor soil, growing nothing but beech trees useful only for firewood." Like big bureaucracies everywhere, the National Socialist planners were often working at cross-purposes. But this particular *contretemps* was doubtless straightened out by Goering, who was at the time director of both aviation and forestry.

Dr. Darré convinced me that "in case of need" Germany would prove more self-sufficient than had been the case in the first war. That this "need" was not imaginary I was forced to conclude from a significant interview, with Dr. Karl Haushofer, the geo-politician said to have been largely responsible for guiding Hitler's foreign policy. Though gracious, this scholarly old man would talk about his "Heartland" theory only under a pledge of no quotation or attribution "since Americans are so prone to misunderstand." With this reservation, Haushofer spoke eloquently. The "Heartland" of Europe, he explained, is the great prairie which extends without significant natural interruption from the Elbe River to the Ural Mountains. It is for the most part invulnerable to sea power and too huge for successful air attack. "Whoever dominates that plain will control the destiny of the Continent." Currently, he said, using a map and pointer in professorial manner, Prussia and Poland control the western part of this vital area, the great bulk of which is in Russian hands. Should Russia take over Poland and Eastern Germany, then Communism would be the master of all Europe and, working with a Red China, would control the Eurasian land mass and, in effect, the world. It was therefore in the interest of the West that Germany should conclude an arrangement with Poland, keeping a large part of the "Heartland" from Russian domination. This meant modification of the Polish Corridor, by which the Treaty of Versailles had inexcusably split East Prussia from the rest of Germany. To that end Nazi diplomacy was dedicated and he hoped his visitor would recognize that such a settlement was in the interest of all. There was no question of Haushofer's sincerity. His presentation was thoughtful and I

313

presented its essence, without mentioning the source, in one of my articles.

On the last afternoon of my stay in Berlin I was formally invited to the U.S. Embassy to have tea *à deux* with William E. Dodd, the much-tried Ambassador who was soon to give up his not-too-successful tenure of office there. In reply to questioning as to my findings I emphasized the contrast between the despairing German mood of 1921 and the completely self-confident, not to say arrogant, Nazi attitude in 1937. The Ambassador, a student of history, nodded his head sadly. "The wheel has turned too quickly," he said, confirming von Lewinski's gloomy prediction that Hitler henceforth would show little restraint. That night, after mailing a couple of articles to catch a German express steamer, I took train for Prague. There was a brief stopover in lovely Dresden; then across the contested frontier and through the seething Sudetenland to meet Mr. Meyer for breakfast at his hotel in the capital of Czechoslovakia.

◀Prague was no longer as picturesque a city as I remembered from my visit in 1921. During the intervening years Czech passion for modernization had swept away much of the medieval huddle around the Karluvmost, oldest and most decorative of the dozen bridges across the Vltava River. It had been called Karlsbrücke and the rigidly enforced change from German to Czech nomenclature was confusing. I could not accustom myself to speaking of the beautiful old Theinkirche as Týnskýkostel. The Christmas carol helped with the one named after St. Wenceslaus. But local pronunciation of the great Gothic Cathedral of St. Vitus was never absorbed. That seemed a particularly appropriate patron for a people as nervously energetic as the Czechs.

There was little time for sightseeing. Mr. Meyer had secured an appointment with President Eduard Beneš and by mid-morning we were at his office, in the great hilltop castle on Hradčany. It is said to contain 868 separate rooms and certainly many stately halls were traversed before we were ushered into the huge audience chamber where the President, a small and

314

sharp-looking man, seemed both physically and metaphorically lost. He sat at a royal desk with a magnificent view over the far-flung city, the winding river cutting through its middle. Through the tall windows of this room, onto the rocks far below, several unpopular governors of Bohemia had been unceremoniously ejected some centuries ago. This crude form of justice was euphemized in the official guidebook as "defenestration." I had no premonition that Jan Masaryk, foreign minister of the Republic and son of its first President, would be similarly "defenestrated" when the Communists took full control of Prague, early in 1948.

The interview was conducted in English, which Beneš spoke perfectly. It soon demonstrated that a prevalent British criticism of his policy—its extreme Czech nationalism—was fully justified. Czechoslovakia, a hybrid creation of the Paris Peace Conference, bore little resemblance to the ancient kingdom of Bohemia which was supposed to give it historical justification. The artificial boundaries included big blocs of discontented Germans, Magyars, Moravians, Poles and Ruthenians to whom the governing Czechs and Slovaks allowed little autonomy. Since there was also bad feeling between its two dominant elements Czechoslovakia reproduced, on a less stable basis, all the political weakness of the Austro-Hungarian dual monarchy from which it had been arbitrarily carved by the Paris peacemakers. And no minority president could hope to inspire the solidifying loyalty with which the Hapsburgs had cemented the old régime.

According to Dr. Beneš, his country had no problems that could not be solved with a little more time and a little less Hitler. Unquestionably the latter was working zealously to stir discontent in the heavily Germanic part of Czechoslovakia. But this only made the Czech leaders more adamant in refusing to Sudeten Germans the same right of self-determination with which Dr. Masaryk had so eloquently clouded Woodrow Wilson's political vision. Even in 1937, I thought, a really federalized republic, emphasizing home rule, might have solved the problem. Dr. Beneš could not see it that way so it was ironic that a decade later he would have to accept the Kremlin's solution, annexing the tail of Czechoslovakia and making the remainder a vassal

315

"people's democratic republic." Yet, as a predominantly Slavic country, this was a not unnatural fate for an area doomed by geography alone to a precarious independence. There was little apprehension among the merry group of Czech officials who took me to dinner that evening at a beautiful river-side restaurant. Since the United States had presided over Czechoslovakia's rise, they told me, Americans would surely prevent its fall. I was not so sure as I took the sleeper for Vienna, where Mr. Meyer had preceded me by plane. I was certain, from what I had learned in Germany, that the Nazi hammer would fall first on Austria.

Though no plebiscite on the issue was ever held it is probable that, in 1937, a large majority of Austrians looked favorably on union with Germany. The larger country was much more prosperous than the truncated remnant of Hapsburg grandeur and the Nazi movement had not by then wholly disgraced itself, except in Jewish eyes. The faded magnificence of Vienna only emphasized the poverty of the mountainous sliver to which the old dual monarchy had been reduced and in the disproportionately huge capital one worker in every three was unemployed. Scars from recent street fighting were apparent and the government of moderate Chancellor Schuschnigg wavered helplessly between the Nazi and Communist factions. Hope of stability had vanished with the assassination of Chancellor Dollfuss, three years earlier, and everyone seemed to agree that a German takeover, though feared by many, was inevitable. Again, the sorry consequences of the "peace-making" of 1919 were all too apparent.

My principal Vienna informant was the U.S. Minister, George S. Messersmith, a career diplomat who had previously been Consul General in Berlin and was familiar with the economic as well as political aspects of the situation. He confirmed the report, heard by me in Berlin, that Mussolini had withdrawn his earlier objections to *Anschluss*, thus making the Austro-German union virtually certain. The question was no longer whether but only when and how it would take place, a subject much debated at the Café Louvre where the foreign correspondents gathered to exchange reports and rumors. I felt so sure of the ground on *Anschluss* that I predicted it in one of my articles, following an interview with timid Foreign Minister

Schmidt. This was at the famous Ballhausplatz where the Congress of Vienna, by refusing to humiliate and crush Napoleonic France, had worked out a contrastingly durable peace. Meyer got virtual confirmation of the Hitler-Mussolini accord when he called upon Chancellor Schuschnigg the evening that I left for Munich, *"Hauptstadt der Bewegung"* (Chief City of the Movement), where I felt it important to look into the mechanics of Nazi organization.

Not the least illuminating meeting of my Vienna stay was one arranged with Helena Kollmann, the Austrian girl who had cared for our small daughters in Baltimore and then accompanied the family to Geneva. Helena had risen to the position of inspector in a textile factory and was engaged to an expert woodworker, Hans Mareda, who came with her to dinner. Hans was unable to find work, even as a plain carpenter, because of the cessation of almost all construction in Vienna. Consequently Helena could not marry, her own small wage being scarcely sufficient to support her widowed mother. Nobody was by temperament less of a Nazi than gentle Helena, but her comment on *Anschluss* was: "Most of my friends think that is our only hope." It would be nearly nine months before Hitler would actually incorporate Austria in the Third Reich. But certainly it should have been no surprise when he finally moved to do so.

At the British Embassy in Berlin, I had been advised to make contact with His Majesty's Consul General in Munich. This Mr. Gainor was said to be unusually well-informed on details of National Socialist organization. By pre-arrangement, therefore, I went direct from the railroad station to the British Consulate where this high-type civil servant described the "apparatus" built up by Hitler and his associates to control and direct the German people. It was a terrifying analysis of the manner in which principles of business management can be applied to keep an entire population in efficient subjection. Then I reported to the *Presse Abteilung* and was sent on with an escort to the famous "Braunhaus," national headquarters of the Nazi Party. Here, as everywhere, I was well received and shown in operation the complex organization which Gainor had already described. Great batteries of filing cabinets contained individual cards for every party member, cross-indexed both for

317

localities and skills. When a job of any magnitude was to be filled, either in industry or the professions, particulars had to be sent to the Braunhaus. If a registered Nazi met the requirements he or she would be "recommended" to the employer, whether that was a school board in Silesia or an insurance office in the Rhineland. In reply to a question, I was assured that there was no "legal" obligation to employ the referred *Partei Mitglieder* in preference to another applicant. "But we haven't set up this system just for the fun of it," the official added.

This careful melding of Nazi members and directive positions was curiously distorted in the highest echelons of government. There executive appointments were often given to obviously unqualified persons, merely because they had been cronies of Hitler in the early days of the movement. Ribbentrop, soon to become Foreign Minister, was one illustration of this bad staff work and a number of incompetent generals were equally disastrous. Goering was everywhere regarded as an able man; also Dr. Goebbels in his twisted way. But when war came many of those in the Fuehrer's intimate circle could not be called competent, still less distinguished. This was a point much emphasized by my Russian friend, Nehmann, whenever I argued that to me the Communist and Nazi dictatorships seemed essentially similar. "To be a Nazi," said Nehmann, "you need only goosestep and shout 'Heil Hitler.' To be a Communist you must first and foremost be well trained. Stumblebums do not last long in the Communist hierarchy."

A pleasant young official from the Press Bureau—Eric Gassner—was assigned as escort and on request took me to the "Temple of Honor" where Hitler's comrades killed in the premature Putsch of 1923 were buried. I had heard that this illustrated German sentimentality at its most maudlin. In a sunken shrine, reached by a ring of marble steps, a dozen great bronze sarcophagi were aligned, each bearing the name of the fallen under an elaborately carved eagle and wreath-encircled swastika. Below all this was the word HIER in large capitals, this being the presumed answer of the interred to the summons of the Fuehrer. This temple of *Ewige Wache*, or Eternal Watch, was continuously guarded by steel-helmeted, strapping S.S. troopers but did not seem to attract many visitors. I then asked whether I might visit Dachau, a concentration camp near Munich where many Jews were said to be confined. That would be impossible without a special pass and 24 hours delay, said Gassner, adding that only Communists, profiteers and other "criminals" were under detention there. "I expect you are going to have racial trouble with your Negroes," he added evasively.

Frau Gassner, blond, beautiful, petite and lively, joined us for lunch at the famous Hofbräuhaus, and surprised me by telling stories making subdued fun of Hitler. One stuck in memory, about a Muenchener who was arrested for causing a street disturbance. He was charged with repeatedly shouting: "First I come and then comes Hitler." The magistrate asked his name. "Heinrich Heil, your Honor, Heil, Hitler!" Many Bavarians would never use that sychophantic greeting, sticking to their traditional *Grüss Gott*. All told I was in Munich only 12 hours on this trip, but it gave opportunity to revisit several of the lovely old places which the bombings would irreparably damage. The Gassners saw me to my train, and I sought to balance my thoughts from the tidy and tended countryside, as I sped through the long summer evening toward the Alpine barrier and Geneva beyond.

At Zurich a *couchette* was available, but there were no covers and I spent an uncomfortable night, not much relieved by drafting my article on Nazi Munich. Then, as the train pulled into Cornavin in the gray dawn, there was a familiar voice and a broad, smiling face at the window. They belonged to my cheery Swabian friend Fritz Schnabel, the German chief of the League of Nation's Publications Division, with whom I had worked closely seven years earlier. Old Fritz had risen at 4 a.m. to meet me and take me to the Schnabel home for a hot bath and breakfast before the long day started. Respect for the many incorruptible German individualists whom I knew, like Schnabel and von Lewinski, kept me from ever falling into the conventional pattern of indiscriminate hatred. I would think of my friends across the Rhine when people denounced "the Huns."

It was a poignant experience to revisit Geneva, outwardly as unchanged as over-shadowing Mont Blanc since I had reluctantly left there early in 1931. "Except that Isabel was not with me," I wrote in my journal, it was all "unalloyed pleasure." Yet,

319

in the same entry, this was qualified. ". . . there is something tragic in the tranquility of the place, by contrast with the alarums and excursions for which solutions should be sought at the League H.Q., and are not."

For me the return had aspects of Homecoming Day. Many of my old friends were still, somewhat nervously, with the Secretariat and I was lodged at Merimont, the Sweetser residence which Isabel and I had occupied the summer of 1930. Joseph Avenol, who had succeeded Sir Eric Drummond as Secretary-General, gave a big luncheon for Meyer and me. Together we inspected the new and handsome Palais des Nations, with the many artistic gifts from various governments and the striking Sert murals in the imposing Council Chamber. In the fine library I was shown a shelf with several well-thumbed copies of my book on *The Society of Nations*—a "must" for every serious student of the League, it was said.

I could have stayed a month with pleasure but Meyer now was eager to get back. For those who had shown us attention at Geneva the publisher gave a big dinner at Eaux Vives, the modish lakeside restaurant which the Morleys had come to know well during their residence. Afterwards, at the more familiar Bavaria *Bierstube* there was time for a couple of steins with magnetic Robert Dell, roving correspondent of the *Guardian* and father of Sylvia Blelloch. During the first war he had been in trouble with the French authorities for alleged pro-Germanism but National Socialism he disliked intensely.

Then on to Paris, where the financial situation was desperate, the franc growing weaker daily. With Meyer doing the shrewd questioning an illuminating discussion with Prime Minister Chautemps was obtained. I cabled the essence of this to the *Post* and then hurried alone to London where a key Parliamentary debate on British policy in the worsening Spanish crisis was scheduled. A Labour Party resolution calling for aid to the collapsing Republican government was up for decision and Prime Minister Chamberlain's insistence on strict neutrality was roundly criticized. From a seat in the crowded press gallery of the House of Commons, I admired the perfect courtesy with which sharp acrimony was cloaked. When Chamberlain said it was "a time for cool heads," Lloyd George retorted that "any fish can have a cool head. What Britain needs now is a warm heart." But the Prime Minister had the majority solidly behind his pacific course, as later at Munich, and the move to intervene in Spain was defeated, nearly two to one. As I reported, confusion was dominant in France, caution in Britain, indifference in the United States and helplessness in the League of Nations. It was not a combination likely to deter a Nazi takeover in Austria, when Hitler got ready to strike.

This was my last report on a memorable circuit. The next day, June 26, I boarded the *Berengaria* at Southampton. At Cherbourg Mr. Meyer rejoined from Paris and we docked in New York July 2, just 44 days after departure. For me it had been a grueling six weeks. In addition to several cables I had written some 20 careful articles which the *Post* would soon republish in booklet form, titled *Europe Today*. On the whole, relations with my boss had been excellent but judgments were not always uniform. They could not be, in view of Mr. Meyer's very natural refusal to inspect the German scene. In a frank discussion on the return trip the publisher accused me of undue resistance to his viewpoint. To this I replied tartly that if a Yes-man had been wanted I was a poor selection as editor. The breeze blew over quickly and probably revealed, more than anything else, the anxieties which both men were bringing back.

It was obvious that the machinery of collective action had completely broken down. The League was moribund. War now seemed a probability. Hitler would force it because his growing megalomania would overstrain the breaking point of British toleration. There would be no resistance to German annexation of Austria, justifiable under the principle of self-determination. There would probably be no war if jerry-built Czechoslovakia were dismembered by German pressure. Britian had no treaty commitment there, aside from the general obligations of the disintegrating League Covenant, and France was in no condition to resist. But the following step in Hitler's program would be to recover Danzig and the territorial connection with East Prussia, at Polish expense. Here there would certainly be stern opposition, for different reasons, both from Britain and from Russia. Because of the significance of the Polish vote this would also shake American neutrality.

321

If war should come, what would be its effect on nations already half-ruined and morally debilitated by the degeneration of the last conflict? What Pandora's Box of lasting social evils would be opened by the vengeful emotionalism that renewed hostilities would inevitably produce? The idealized brutalities of Commando training, for instance, would surely have its heritage in a growth of organized gangsterism, most dangerous in American cities because of racial overtones. Belief in the sanctity of private property, dear to American hearts, would be weakened by countless requisitions, confiscations and indiscriminate destruction. Finally, what would be the effect of total war, with its enormous impetus for centralization, on the structure of a federal republic constitutionally dedicated to the dispersion, division and localization of power? There was more than a chance that such pressures would undermine the basic institutions of the United States, no matter who won or lost on fields of battle.

What then should be the policy of the United States, and what the editorial policy of the *Post*? The answer to the first question should also answer the second, but I was not too confident that this would be the case. It would be no gain for America if Communism should take over in Central Europe, which would be the probable result of a Russian defeat of Germany. The intolerable humiliation and impossible exactions of the Treaty of Versailles were fundamentally responsible for the mass neurosis that had swept Hitler to power. The movement was anathema to countless Germans and, unlike the deeply calculating Communist leadership, was unlikely to last if international stability could be restored. On the other hand, Americans were sure to become evermore anti-German if Nazi persecution of the Jews was stepped up, as seemed all too probable. And as a Jew could Eugene Meyer be expected to support the difficult policy of neutrality that pure reason suggested as the best American course, more so because the intervention of 1917 had been so barren of good results?

These questions deeply worried me on the voyage home. The sea was calm and the weather glorious. But dark clouds were gathering ahead.

◑

◀A review of that European survey was depressing. Prospects of war were even more serious than I had realized; defences against it much weaker. The League of Nations was powerless; the Kellogg Pact inoperative. Rigid American neutrality legislation was, if anything, encouraging aggression.

In a wholly logical manner Germany was proceeding to destroy the intolerable Treaty of Versailles. First, its disarmament clauses had been violated; then the Rhineland reoccupied; now Austria was about to be annexed; then would come dismemberment of Czechoslovakia and after that demand for the restoration of Danzig. It was idle to blame Hitler personally for these steps. They were justified by many Germans whom I knew to be anti-Nazi.

Italy and Japan, two victorious signatories of the peace treaty, were tacitly favoring its violation by Germany, while ignoring other international agreements that seemed to operate to their disadvantage. Much public opinion in Britain and France was opposed to fighting to uphold the discredited treaty, but in both these countries Nazi anti-Semitism was arousing deep indignation.

That Russia feared an eventual military defeat at German hands was obvious. It was at least equally clear that Stalin had less than no interest in supporting the liberal tradition of Britain and France. No faith could be placed in any provisional arrangement between Moscow on the one hand, London and Paris on the other. Some Marxists of my acquaintance even argued that war was in the Communist interest; that the resultant misery, impoverishment and proliferation of controls would strengthen the movement everywhere, no matter how the tide of battle flowed. This seemed to me the best argument for the American policy of absolute neutrality.

Certainly social antagonisms were becoming as important a factor as nationalistic hates. That was demonstrated by the bitterness of civil strife in Spain. The virus of class war was one from which America on the whole had been happily free, but given favorable conditions this divisiveness could also flourish

323

here. The whole American experiment, indeed, was affected and even jeopardized by the downhill slide in Europe. It was not easy to get the turmoil in true perspective. Yet I must do that, if I were to fulfill my duty as editor of an important newspaper.

It was, I concluded, fundamentally a problem of loyalty. To whom or what did an editor owe allegiance? Immediately, of course, to the publisher who had entrusted him with his position. Also to his wife and children, for whose well-being he had voluntarily assumed responsibility. But beyond those immediate obligations, what? By what guiding star should he compose his editorials when Mr. Meyer said: "Be sure you're right, then go ahead."

Supreme loyalty, of course, was to his God, and to the Christian tradition under which he had been reared. Next to that and generally in accordance came his country, meaning not the President nor any part of officialdom but the ideas and ideals that had been so clearly written into the Constitution. To get these principles more firmly in mind required some quiet reflection. So, soon after my return, we rented a cottage at Rehoboth Beach, where for a few days I could enjoy both healthy exercise and uninterrupted thought. The White House sent word that the President would like a verbal report from the returned travelers. Rightly or wrongly I felt that Mr. Meyer should go alone. My own conclusions might differ from those of my chief and, if so, I did not wish either to remain silent or to be contradictory. Gradually certainty returned. My country should do all it could to avert the catastrophe that threatened. But also, if humanly possible, it should avoid being sucked into a maelstrom which so clearly promised disaster.

There were more intimate anxieties. Letters from Frank, during the summer of 1937, were increasingly apprehensive about the health of both our parents. The elderly couple finally left England by the *Aquitania*, October 6, and communication with Chris from shipboard warned that our father must have a wheelchair on landing in New York. Terry McGrath, old friend of the Cunard Line, was very helpful in eliminating formalities. Forewarned by my older brother, I met the train in Baltimore at track level, driving the pitiful pair to their apartment where Dr. John Dorsey immediately took over. Professor Morley had suf-

324

fered a severe heart attack during the crossing and was an obviously stricken man. He died, as peacefully as he had lived, at home on October 17, with both older sons at his bedside. Immediately after the funeral, a Quaker service at which Kit spoke beautifully, our widowed mother entered the Johns Hopkins Hospital for lengthy examinations which revealed an inoperable cancer. Without foreknowledge, I learned from my father's will that I was named executor for the modest estate and from that time on had my mother's affairs in charge. There is no doubt that the passing of their deeply respected father affected all three sons.[15] Now the torch had been transferred, I realized much of what he had often tried to tell me, by example rather than by word. Kit, in his delicate elegy, quoted a passage which curiously he had earlier selected for that very date—October 19—in his own personal Book of Days. It was from Bertrand Russell: "Mathematics . . . builds a habitation eternally standing, where our ideals are fully satisfied and our best hopes are not thwarted."

But in the political world, where the editor had his habitation enforced, the hope for peace was being increasingly attenuated. Now it was in the Far East, quite as sharply as in Europe, that dismal "incidents" multiplied. The new series had started on the night of July 7, when Japanese troops from the Peking garrison clashed with Chinese soldiers at the Marco Polo Bridge, some 18 miles west of the city. Tokyo did not attempt to explain why its contingent was so far out of the permissible bounds. Instead, the Japanese forces in North China were immediately reinforced and the Nanking Government, of General Chiang Kai-shek, was urged by Japan "in the interest of peace" to withdraw its own troops from the area around Peking. When Chiang protested the Japanese found pretexts to put pressure on Shanghai, which after some resistance was forcibly seized at the end of October. The next aggressive step was to attack and capture Nanking, whence the Nationalists moved their capital up-river, first to Hankow and then to faraway Chungking. Japan's violation of willingly accepted treaty obligations seemed

---

15. The youngest wrote a charming sketch of Professor Morley's highly individualistic personality, in *My One Contribution To Chess*, B. W. Huebsch, New York, 1945.

more brazen than Nazi Germany's overthrow of the enforced Dictate of Versailles.

To this challenge, for many reasons, the Roosevelt Administration was slow to respond. Isolationist sentiment grew stronger as the war clouds thickened. Almost half of the Democratic Congressmen, and 61 per cent of the Republicans, were on record in favor of the Ludlow Constitutional Amendment, which would have required a nation-wide referendum on any declaration of war, unless American territory were physically invaded "or immediately threatened." In addition there were serious doubts about assisting Chiang Kai-shek, who seemed more interested in fighting the Chinese Communists than in resisting Japanese aggression. There was little general realization that a Berlin-Tokyo Axis was taking shape, although, as mentioned previously, Hitler had signed a five-year pact with Japan, providing for joint "defensive measures" against the activities of the Communist International. The Vatican was preparing to recognize the Franco regime in Spain and any suggestion that the United States should align itself with Soviet Russia was hotly resented. It was not an easy period for American diplomacy.

Editorial policy was equally full of pitfalls. Neutrality was not invoked, in the undeclared Sino-Japanese war, because the provisions of the law would have favored Japan, in full command of the sea and able to pay cash for desired munitions. On the other hand, pacifist sentiment was so strong that the Administration feared to urge collective action, which had been failing wherever tried. On August 24, Stanley Hornbeck, then Secretary Hull's chief advisor on Asiatic problems, came out to Millstone for dinner and confidential discussion. I had wanted to know why the Nine-Power Treaty, guaranteeing China's "territorial integrity," should not be invoked. Hornbeck thought that if this were done, Japan would find some excuse to repudiate the treaty, seeking a free hand for outright annexation which Tokyo's current "police action" did not as yet openly envisage. There was, said Hornbeck, a fair possibility that China would solve the problem herself, by making the Japanese invasion too costly for the latter country to endure.

I kept close touch with the leading embassies during this

critical period. Constantin Oumansky, the new Russian envoy, was a valuable source of information, though naturally always tinged with the Communist interest. Only joint Russian-American action could save China from Japanese subjection, Oumansky argued, expressing incredulity when I wondered aloud whether a Red China would be more acceptable to Americans than one dominated by Japan. Then, on October 5, President Roosevelt, at Chicago, called for "concerted effort" against aggressor nations, encouraging the League of Nations' Assembly, then in session, to condemn Japan as a treaty violator, as it did the following day. The *Post* gave strong editorial indorsement to both of these developments, though Mr. Meyer was doubtful about their effectiveness without more American rearmament. My hope was that strong expression of U.S. disapproval would of itself discourage Axis aggression, especially if coupled with a willingness to review outworn treaties. Lord Lothian, visiting Millstone on October 8, emphasized that the formula must not be merely a bluff. "In the event of sanctions against Japan," said the Ambassador-designate, "Britain must have advance assurances of what the United States is prepared to do if Japan takes reprisals against economic pressure." A subsequent editorial pointed out that neither Britain nor France could play a leading role in the Far East; that responsibility devolved on the United States.

Increasing Japanese pressure led to the accidental bombing of the American gunboat *Panay*, on the Yangtze near Nanking, January 12, 1938, killing two sailors and injuring a score. This and other irresponsible actions raised great difficulties for the Department of State, as Secretary Hull outlined to me in several confidential talks. Reports from the field were increasingly skeptical as to the good judgment of Chiang Kai-shek. The Generalissimo's overbearing and arrogant attitude, which later compounded his troubles with General Stilwell, made it the more difficult to meet the expectations of C. T. Wang, in Washington, for assistance of every kind. On the other hand, Ambassador Oumansky was plausibly arguing for help to Mao Tse-tung, rather than to Chiang, justifying suspicion that the Russian objective was a Communist rather than a Nationalist unification of China. On March 31, shortly after Hitler's annexation of Austria, I dined at the Chinese Embassy, finding Dr. Hu Shih and my other friends there very cheerful. C. T. Wang claimed there had been 300,000 Japanese casualties and that the tide was turning. The question was not well received when I asked what proportion of these losses had been inflicted by the Nationalists, and what by the Chinese Reds.

Between such cross-currents development of editorial policy was far from easy. The undiscriminating neutrality of the United States had merely encouraged the Axis powers to be increasingly aggressive. But national sentiment was overwhelmingly pacific and increasingly aware that collective action was now more likely to precipitate than to avert war. Moreover, any form of alliance with Russia would mean a great expansion of Communist influence, scarcely in the American interest. Mr. Meyer was clearly anxious not to have a policy which could be called narrowly pro-Jewish and left it largely to me to find the way. In the upshot I closely followed the State Department's line, helped by confidential advices to the extent that I became widely known as its reliable interpreter. The publisher, consistently anti-Roosevelt, was not too pleased with this but could suggest no better course.

Not only the editorial page, but the *Post* as a whole was receiving accolades. "Casey" Jones, as Managing Editor, had greatly improved the news and feature presentation. That advance tended to diminish the relative importance of editorial comment. During the early years of Meyer's ownership this, and the sports pages as ably conducted by Shirley Povich, had been the only parts of the paper with strong customer appeal. Now a well-knit whole received consideration, reflected in steadily increasing circulation. Though pleased with this progress it clearly made me a less essential cog.

Improvement did not mean that the *Post* was as yet in the black, though general economic prospects were turning up. In the twelve months following March, 1937, the Dow Jones Industrial average had declined 50 percent. In spite of all the New Deal experimentation, recession was almost as pronounced as that which doomed the Hoover Administration and there is ample evidence to support the thesis that it took the big armament program to save Roosevelt from political debacle. Faced with this grim picture, the *Post* was not raising salaries though, in early January, Mr. Meyer put $70,000 more, in bank stocks, into the intangible account maintained in my name. Having the utmost respect for my employer's financial acumen I thereupon began to build my own miniature portfolio. The fiscal situation was now indubitably better and in March, 1938, we purchased two adjoining lots at Gibson Island, with arrangement to build a cottage there by the ensuing summer. It seemed, and proved to be, the happiest way of handling the vacation problems for our quartette of children.

My mother's sad condition caused much anxiety and I felt relieved when Frank came over from England, in February, so that the trio of brothers could counsel together while I explained the handling of our father's small but comfortable estate. On February 24, the mathematician's ashes were interred at Haverford, in a secluded corner of the peaceful Meeting House yard, followed by a memorial service in which several old Friends spoke in their various ways of how a great teacher had come back to merge again with the institution to which he had given so much. The chore of sorting our father's scientific memoranda, for eventual presentation to the Johns Hopkins mathematics library, devolved on Frank as the only son competent for the task. From him also came the suggestion of persuading his former secretary—Margaret Evans—to come from London as a resident companion for Madame Doctors, as our mother had long since been affectionately named by Kit. That appointment was a happy idea though, like many such, there were awkward consequences.

A tiresome libel suit, filed in District Court against the *Post* and me as its editor, chose this difficult year of 1938 to surface. Its basis was a letter from Gilson Gardner, a courageous muckraking journalist, who had retired to Arlington County, Virginia. The letter referred to the local county commissioners as "the Courthouse gang" and had been published, unedited, on November 22, 1934, just as the Morleys moved into their new house. I had not actually seen the communication until, with justified foreboding, I read it in print. Nevertheless, I was legally responsible for printing this "scurrilous editorial," as the prosecution called the letter when two members of the alleged

329

"gang" brought delayed suit for defamation of character. This was not until after Gardner, author of the maligning document, had died, making justification by him impossible. I was certain that the suit had been brought for purposes of intimidation. Whether or not successful, it would tend to keep the *Post* from vigorously investigating the conduct of local government in the counties adjacent to Washington. Whatever its crusading interest no newspaper wishes to incur the nuisance and expense of libel suits, which are easy to file and expensive to combat. But in this case the presumed purpose failed. Counsel for the prosecution made great play with the word "gang," which he snarled out to make it sound thoroughly opprobrious. "Now, Mr. Morley," he demanded of the editor on the stand, "just what sort of people do you have in mind when you use that epithet Ganggg?" For once I was quick on the uptake. "Very good fellows," I replied, "when I sing 'Hail, Hail, the Gang's All Here!' " The jury roared with laughter, the judge repressed a smile as he gaveled for order and the case was won, not less so because the plaintiffs were awarded one cent damages.

Shortly thereafter we felt able to start construction on our summer cottage at Gibson Island, which with gentle satire Isabel christened "Compromise" as between her yen for a farm and mine for a place on the water. To finance the cottage Meyer generously volunteered another non-interest loan but firmly refused the further salary increase which I argued was my due. Though the *Post* was not yet profitable there were clear indications that it would become so. And I wanted my connection to be institutional, without personal bond to the publisher.

On April 5, Frank Waltman, the paper's star political writer, would become publicity director for the Republican National Committee. I had as yet no idea of severing my own connection though an offer from Carl Ackerman, to join the staff of the Columbia Graduate School of Journalism, was intriguing. Acceptance was warmly urged by Douglas Freeman, who said I would become Dean when Ackerman retired. But the latter was only four years my senior; I disliked New York and was furthermore skeptical about vocational education in journalism. "It's like teaching what they call 'creative writing,' " I said to Isabel. "If you have the gift, formal instruction is superfluous. If you lack the talent, no instruction can provide it." The tricks of the trade, I thought, could best be learned by the sort of apprenticeship I had myself served on the old *Public Ledger*, before the First World War.

The offer was modified to a weekly lecture but there were already too many speaking engagements. After the debates with brother Chris I had worked out a thoughtful paper on "The Public and the Press," envisaging some of the issues which later would be raised in regard to official suppression of the news. In 1938 I gave this as the Commencement Address both at Duke University and Haverford College. At the latter, members of the class of 1888, whose Senior year had been Professor Morley's first as a teacher there, were holding their fiftieth reunion. The fond memory in which my father was held by these old men impressed me and I altered my remarks to compare the value of personal loyalty to institutions as different as a college and a newspaper. This was the easier since I had recently completed a carefully researched history of the *Post*, distributed in its sixtieth anniversary issue. Also the fifth anniversary of Eugene Meyer's ownership was just coming up.

There cannot and should not be the same loyalty to a person as to an ideal, I concluded. To parrot "Heil Hitler" was certainly no evidence of loyalty to the best in Germany. One did not love America the less for being critical of President Roosevelt, then seeking to purge the Senators who had successfully opposed him on enlargement of the Supreme Court. The highest loyalty, as Quakers knew well, would always be to those ideals which institutions, better than individuals, could incorporate. Emerson was wrong in saying that an institution is but the lengthened shadow of a man. When that was true it was because the institution was either undeveloped, uncertain or undistinguished.

◐

◀In October of 1938 Christopher Morley produced a booklet—scarcely more than a brochure—entitled *History of an Autumn*. This was an outstanding piece of writing.

It was a highly personalized account of a sensitive reaction to the Munich crisis, deftly portrayed against the natural pageantry of the dying year. Written with artistic restraint it refused to cast blame, even at easy-target Hitler, for the partitioning of Czechoslovakia. Lamentation was reserved for the inability of mankind to confront its political problems without shocking emotional disturbance. "When a syndicated sibyl [Dorothy Thompson] announced: 'At a blow France has been reduced to a third-rate power,' a man in the suburbs meditated this without rancor. It occurred to him presently that French literature was still worth reading. . . . "

For all three brothers, the tragedy of Munich was intensified by their mother's sad condition. After the arrival and installation of Margaret Evans, accommodations for the two had been arranged at Blue Ridge Summit, cool in the hot weather and near enough to Washington for me to drive there in a couple of hours. I made the trip frequently that summer since "Madame Doctors" was failing steadily and suffering much. To bring cheer Chris made the journey from Long Island for our late father's birthday, September 9, remarking in his little history: "How far it seemed from Europe. . . . But . . . when he left the Summit, three days later, every radio on that inland hilltop was bringing the words of Adolf Hitler from Nuremberg."

Only three days after that it became necessary to bring mother back by ambulance to Baltimore, where she could have professional nursing and more specialized medical attendance. Isabel came over to help, while I kept in touch with my office by phone and completed duties as my father's executor. The sands were running out fast, both for my mother and for Czechoslovakia. "Between awaiting bad news about mother and from Hitler," I noted on September 28, "the last few days have been a perpetual nightmare." But the gallant old lady seemed to revive as the agreement maintaining peace was signed in Munich. When Frank came again from England, early in October, she was stronger and in less continuous pain. It was good to have the reunion of the three brothers extend to a colorful autumnal weekend at "Compromise."

New editorial policy had to be developed after the much-criticized Munich settlement. Prior to this "appeasement" it had been largely a matter of intelligently anticipating the course of

332

events. This had been done. Herbert Feis, economic advisor to the State Department, said mine were "the only current writings really to probe the issues." But after the dismemberment of Czechoslovakia, and with Japan becoming steadily more intransigent, more was required. Now it was a matter of presenting the desirable American course.

Like it or not, I thought, the prime necessity was to provide a stable basis for the Munich agreement. Lacking this it would be followed, presumably at the expense of Poland, by more peremptory Nazi demands. There was a better solution than abject compliance as the only alternative to war. This would be found if all the former belligerents would replace the liquidated Treaty of Versailles with some equitable and acceptable arrangement. The League of Nations, notably Article 19 of the Covenant, should be the mechanism for this new peace conference but League membership would not be a prerequisite for participation. In conjunction with the League Council the United States would take the lead in calling this vital conference, requesting only that acceptance be accompanied by pledges to refrain from any aggressive action during its deliberations.

There were, of course, substantial objections to the plan here outlined, but that would be true of anything that human ingenuity could devise. What was needed was a temperate approach, with no distinction between victors and vanquished, similar to that shown at the Congress of Vienna. There France had been treated as an equal in building the "Concert of Europe," despite Napoleon's ruthless aggressions and his attempted comeback from Elba. An urgent Congress of Geneva might similarly welcome even Nazi Germany on a basis of orderly international cooperation and if this worked it would isolate not only Mussolini but also the Japanese militarists. Since 1918, Justice, as a guide to international settlements, had been largely ignored. That was the basic trouble.

Much of this thinking had been done while in attendance on my stricken mother and, even before the Munich Conference, I had dictated a memorandum on the subject. This I polished and presented to Mr. Meyer, whose advance approval for any such drastic editorial move was of course essential. The publisher was

333

impressed but wanted to reflect on the implications. In any case, nothing could be said until the immediate crisis over Czechoslovakia was resolved, one way or another. Nevertheless, on September 21, I outlined my project in a long private talk with the Secretary of State. Cordell Hull was much interested but doubted that Hitler would be cooperative. He also thought the President would scarcely advance so controversial a proposal on the eve of the Congressional elections. However, the Secretary hoped that the *Post* would suggest the idea editorially, as a trial balloon to test public reaction. He further encouraged me to consult with the Ambassadors of the concerned nations, letting him know how they responded to the idea.

In the next few days I did this, a task made easier by the good relations I had gradually established at all the leading embassies. Sir Ronald Lindsay, for Great Britain, was sympathetic but questioned whether the United States was prepared to take the lead. There was more American disposition to criticize Prime Minister Chamberlain for trying to do this, he said bitterly. The Japanese Ambassador said that China, anarchic and disorderly, presented a problem wholly different from those of Europe; one in which intervention by the League of Nations had already failed. At the French Embassy M. Saint-Quentin thought the Deladier government would welcome the proposed *démarche* and said he would cable anything I wrote on the subject to the Quai d'Orsay. Constantine Oumansky, for the Russians, was approving, emphasizing that any peace plan attempting to ignore Moscow would be valueless. Dr. Dieckhoff, the able German representative, said he thought there was no immediate chance that his country would return to the League of Nations but added that Hitler would shortly make a disarmament proposal that should assist the desired stabilization. Signor Suvich, the unimpressive Italian envoy, emphasized Mussolini's desire for an orderly peace "if some issues with France could first be amicably adjusted."

Altogether the evidence favored a constructive American position, by contrast with the shrieks of "Munich Betrayal" with which rabid energumens were filling the airwaves. So, in consultation with Mr. Meyer, I prepared an editorial on the Munich Pact entitled *A Turning Point*. It argued that the debacle of

Czechoslovakia, though deplorable, could as well mean a turn for the better as for the worse. The disastrously punitive arrangements of 1919 had never been indorsed by the United States and were now discarded with the agreement of their principal sponsors—Britain, France and Italy. The ground was now clear for reconstruction. Here America had responsibility, not only for its national interest in peace, but also for the foresight shown in refusing to underwrite the Treaty of Versailles.

It was a controversial position, and there were brickbats as well as bouquets as a result of this and subsequent editorials in similar vein. But I have never regretted this last substantial effort to avert another war. My friends in the Department of State, from Cordell Hull down, were complimentary, as were many of the Embassies. It was psychologically helpful when the publisher chose this juncture to put through the much-desired salary increase, to $15,000. A further boost to morale came when my friend Jules Henry phoned from the French Foreign Office to ask for "sympathetic consideration" of the pending Franco-German treaty of amity, consultation and territorial guarantee. This treaty, reaffirming the cession of Alsace-Lorraine to France, was in line with the stabilization I thought essential. So I could appreciate Henry's argument that it would be wholly negative for the American press to condemn the accord as another concession to the Nazis by Deladier. Actually the concessions were on the German side. I was asked by Henry to confer immediately with Ambassador Saint-Quentin, who would show me the memorandum on the treaty prepared in Paris for the Department of State. Before doing so, I phoned Mr. Meyer in New York. He was pleased by this strong tribute to the *Post*'s influence and gave me carte blanche to proceed as I thought best. His only advice was: "Be realistic."

But Hitler was not ready for a stabilization of Germany's eastern border. Choosing a most unhappy moment, early in November, a young Polish Jew assassinated the innocuous Third Secretary of the German Embassy in Paris. Immediately a wave of clearly inspired pogroms swept the Reich, with synagogues burned, Jewish shops looted and families terrorized in their disrupted homes. Coincidentally, the controlled Italian

335

press began a campaign for the cession of Corsica, Nice and Tunisia by France. In the Far East, with Japanese troops occupying most of the cities, Tokyo announced a "new order" in China, meaning a protectorate terminating both the Nine-Power Treaty and the "Open Door" policy of the United States. Secretary Hull refused to recognize these unilateral declarations and, protesting Nazi anti-Semitism, the White House recalled Ambassador Hugh Wilson from Berlin. In response, conciliatory Dr. Dieckhoff was withdrawn, leaving the German Embassy in charge of Hans Thomsen, a slavish party member whose pretty wife was outspokenly and amusingly anti-Hitler. Amid this confusion we were visited by our old friend Paul Leverkuehn, now also a nominal Nazi, who said frankly that there was little likelihood of Hitler accepting any negotiated settlement in Eastern Europe. In Spain the civil war grew more bitter. Civilization was shaken by volcanic social tremors of ever-increasing intensity.

For all the Morley brothers 1939 dawned grimly. We knew that our mother was sinking under the ravages of her dread disease and suffering greatly in spite of the alleviation of drugs. She had round-the-clock nursing in her Baltimore apartment now. Margaret Evans was a sympathetic companion and Susie, the faithful cook, showed all the commiseration with which many Negroes meet the afflictions of those they love. On Madame Doctors' birthday, March 27, Susie presented her with a small glass bowl containing shells, a tiny celluloid duck and two goldfish. "It was a charming thought," I wrote "diverting and perfectly in keeping with mother's love for simple things." But, I added, "it is a hopeless battle we are waging. Somehow the spells of superficial recovery seem almost to emphasize the tragedy of the whole affair." After Easter, which fell on April 9 in 1939, she failed rapidly.

Professionally, that Easter was notable for me. On the Sunday afternoon Franklin D. Roosevelt had left Warm Springs by train, to return to Washington. To the group assembled at the little Georgia depot to bid him farewell, the President made a seemingly casual remark: "I'll be back in the fall," he said, "if we don't have a war." This was quoted in the papers the following morning.

I decided to take the observation seriously and to build a major editorial on it. Under the title "The Collective Pronoun" I asserted that by "we" Mr. Roosevelt meant the Western civilization of which the United States is an integral part. Thus the remark should be regarded as linking this country with the Anglo-French opposition to any further aggression. It had particular applicability because Mussolini had seized Albania only a few days before, intensifying anxiety in both Greece and Yugoslavia. By clear inference there was a warning to both Italy and Germany that American patience was wearing thin.

Undoubtedly the editorial went out on a limb. So I was delighted when the President, at his press conference on April 11, selected the argument for enthusiastic comment. It was, he said, "very good, very clear, very honest." When asked whether the writing had been inspired by the White House, F.D.R. said on the contrary he was so surprised, by the *Post's* vivid interpretation of his viewpoint, that he "almost fell out of bed." Then he ordered the editorial included in the minutes of the press conference "so that posterity might know what I meant" by the observation at Warm Springs. Of course this was all over the country in no time. Many papers immediately reprinted "The Collective Pronoun" and its full text was cabled to the British and French governments by their respective embassies. The radio networks carried large excerpts, and there were several days of lively comment, adverse as well as favorable, by columnists, other editors and in the Congress. Meyer was most complimentary but, I wrote in my journal, "I am a little fearful he may, as is his bent, over-promote this little coup."

"The Collective Pronoun," in any less powder-strewn situation, might well have been instrumental in a peaceful settlement. Three days after its publication, and by no mere coincidence, the President sent a personal message—half appeal and half warning—to Hitler and Mussolini. It asked for assurances that neither would in any way encourage the coercion of any neighboring government during a minimum period of ten years. In return for acceptance, Mr. Roosevelt offered not merely to obtain reciprocal guarantees but also to initiate disarmament and trade discussions designed to bring fundamental and permanent improvement in the Italo-German economic position.

There were intimations that restoration of Danzig to the Reich would not be regarded unfavorably, and that part of a general settlement would be formal recognition of the Axis gains to date. The initiative closely paralleled the procedure for stabilization which I had discussed earlier with Secretary Hull. It gave me some glimmering of hope.

Danzig had now become the key issue and Hitler obviously wanted that problem favorably resolved before making any commitment on Roosevelt's overture. The Old Hanseatic seaport, with its population of 400,000 over 90 percent German, had been separated from the Reich by the Treaty of Versailles. With immediately surrounding territory it had been made a "Free City," nominally governed by a High Commissioner responsible to the Council of the League of Nations, but affiliated with Poland for customs and railway control. The clumsy arrangement never worked well from any viewpoint and the Danzigers continuously demonstrated for return to Germany, more so as the League deteriorated and the peace treaty fell into desuetude. After Hitler's acquisitions in Austria and Bohemia he concentrated on the reunification of Danzig, but not in an unreasonable manner. Except for return of the Free City the only demand on Poland was for a corridor through the corridor by which the treaty had separated the two parts of divided Prussia. A width of two miles was suggested for this link and Germany would pay for an underlying Polish tunnel. But the Poles, now assured of Anglo-French backing, refused to make any concessions. Hitler's next move, kept tightly secret, was to make a deal with Russia for the overthrow and partitioning of Poland. I was one of the few who anticipated this, partly from the absence of any response to Roosevelt's pacific proposal, partly from a palpably changing attitude on the part of Ambassador Oumansky. "Today," says my journal for May 3, "Litvinoff was 'relieved' of his duties as Foreign Commissar, confirming my growing fear of a Russo-German rapprochement."

As the European crisis sharpened to climax, so did family anxieties. But a pleasing development was a cable from Frank saying he had accepted an executive position with the publishing house of Harcourt, Brace and would bring his family to New York from England in July. Chris and I were delighted by the

338

news, agreeing that this would surely be prior to a war which
Germany would not launch until the harvest was garnered.
We met at our mother's bedside on Chris's forty-ninth birthday
(May 5) knowing the end was near. Our mother's mind was
lucid, the pain had lessened and she was very happy about the
coming of her youngest son, though destined not to see him
again. The evening of May 24, when the doctor had summoned
me from Washington, she breathed her last.

So Mother never knew, in life, of the next memorable incident in the annals of the Morley family. This was the formal
presentation of Muskettian royalty to the British king and
queen, at their Washington Embassy on June 8. This regal visit,
following one to Canada, was of course primarily political, designed to impress Hitler with the solidarity of Anglo-American
relations. None of its festivity was lost because of this. Some
weeks earlier Isabel and I had received invitations to the big
garden party. But only the day before came word from Ambassador Lindsay that he wanted to have us earlier, in the much
smaller group who would be formally presented. This raised a
complication since the Meyers were courteously taking us to the
embassy garden party behind their chauffeur, but were not
listed for presentation. However, a call to Lady Chalkley, Sir
Ronald's admirable social secretary, swiftly rectified this contretemps. I was the more pleased because both Eugene and
Agnes had been very kind during mother's lingering illness and
Mrs. Meyer had driven over to Baltimore for the funeral service
at the Pro-Cathedral.

The introductions to Their Majesties was a real gala. Sir
Ronald presented Mr. Meyer as one "who after a distinguished
career in the government became a newspaper publisher," to
which George VI responded brightly: "Rather a dangerous
change of life." Next I was introduced as Mr. Meyer's editor.
"Then you're the one who does the real work," the king shot
back, with what in the case of a commoner would have been
called a grin. Everyone in earshot heard the little witticism and
it was widely picked up in print.

In Europe during the following weeks there was the lull
that precedes the storm, with some false prosperity induced by
feverish armament everywhere. By mid-June my family was

located at "Compromise," together with two of Frank's children when they arrived from England in late July. I got to Gibson Island most weekends, for some refreshing swimming, sailing and tennis. But for the most part I lived as a bachelor in Washington, writing what my philosopher friend Hu Shih generously called "the best editorials in the United States today." The strain intensified as it became clear that Hitler would not abandon the German claim to Danzig, and that the Polish government would make no concessions on the issue. Toward the end of August the terms of the Molotov-Ribbentrop treaty burst like a bombshell over those who had regarded Stalin as dependable. In effect, the *Post* commented, the Soviets had joined the anti-Communist axis. On August 24 I went to the British Embassy to pay a farewell call on kindly Sir Ronald Lindsay, about to be succeeded by Lord Lothian as Ambassador. It was dreadful, I argued, that the very existence of the British Empire should be jeopardized in order to restrain Germany from regaining an almost wholly Germanic city. This, said Sir Ronald judicially, was an over-simplification of the issue. "We may go under," he mused, "but I think we shall insure that the tradition will survive." On August 28, I wrote: "There is nothing to do now but wait and hope for the best." I packed my bag and drove to Gibson Island to get some sleep.

It was there that the dread news came. On September 1, German troops invaded Poland and the local government in Danzig announced the reincorporation of that city in the Reich. I was shaving when Isabel called up from beside the early radio. "The fat," she said, "is in the fire." I replied: "It will be fried out of all of us before this is finished."

◀It was on my forty-sixth birthday, January 6, 1940, at Hershey, Pa., that I first heard on good authority that I would probably be offered the presidency of Haverford College. I knew immediately that it would be a singularly difficult choice.

I had gone to Hershey to speak at the mid-winter meeting of the Pennsylvania Bar Association, of which a prominent Haverford alumnus, Gifford K. Wright, was then presiding officer. It disturbed me that lawyers as a class were doing far less to sustain the Republic than had been true in its early days. In Washington, at least, many lawyers seemed inclined to work around the law instead of working for it. There were cases in which the Administration clearly disregarded the legality of its actions and citing some I said that this boded ill for a country in which law is assumed to be above any special interest. The audience included my friend John Dickinson, the then Governor (James) and other impressive men who responded generously to the theme. As always in my native state I could sense its underlying strength, stability and sense of justice. When I mentioned this to the chairman he said he believed there would be opportunity to return there, to Haverford.

But I was too busy, that grim and chilling winter of 1939–40, to brood prematurely upon a prospective change of occupation. Too many attractive job offers had come over the horizon only to be dismissed. At the moment everything seemed in suspense. The hostilities, following the German and Russian conquests of Poland, had settled into the inconclusive sparring which Senator Borah called "the phony war." I had enjoyed a memorable talk with this great Constitutional lawyer only two weeks before his sudden death that January. The "Lion of Idaho" still stoutly maintained that the United States could and must preserve its neutral status. I was more doubtful, observing that the politically powerful Polish element was now added to Jewish and Anglo-French adherents in working for American intervention. Early in September I had written an objective and carefully balanced appraisal entitled "Is Neutrality Possible?" which was given front-page display in the *Post* and aroused much controversy, pro and con. "The country," I noted in my journal for September 9, 1939, "is generally appalled at the thought of being sucked in."

Soon afterwards, on the afternoon of November 19, I received an unexpected visit from Adam von Trott zu Solz, a former German Rhodes Scholar whom I had first met through Paul Leverkuehn a year or so before the outbreak of the war. This attractive young German, only just past his thirtieth birthday, was obviously nervous and asked me if we could have a confidential and uninterrupted talk. Fortunately the day's

341

schedule was in good order so I took him to the Child's Restaurant next door, this being a very secluded place at teatime. Soon the reason for secrecy was revealed. Von Trott, an official in the German Foreign Service, was simultaneously active in the anti-Nazi Resistance Movement. He wanted help from me in getting information about this organization, and its potential for a quick and reasonable peace, direct to President Roosevelt. The young nobleman's "cover" was an official assignment to report on a meeting of the Institute of Pacific Relations, at Virginia Beach, and he had come from Berlin, via Moscow and Siberia, shortly after the start of the war. He had, naturally, no credentials to prove his underground connections and feared that he was under surveillance, though whether by the F.B.I. or Gestapo he was uncertain. All this unfolded in a dim corner at the rear of the very humdrum restaurant, where any signs of espionage were wholly lacking. We sat there, consuming much tea, a full two hours.

The Resistance Movement, von Trott explained, was by no means confined to a fairly large number of sympathetic military leaders, though their help would be essential in the contemplated *coup d'état*. Prominent civilians were also engaged in the plotting, notably Dr. Karl Goerdeler, former Lord Mayor of Leipzig. Because of the risk involved the movement was divided into numerous units, each with a distinct function but very little contact with other groups. Von Trott's own association was the "Kreisau Circle," composed mostly of high civil servants and university professors, which concerned itself with the structure of a post-Hitler government and the problems it would have to confront immediately. His own present assignment, partly because of his Oxford background and perfect command of English, was to see that the British and American leaderships were informed on what was stirring beneath the surface in Germany. In England, early in 1939, he had worked with the Cliveden group, arguing that if the Danzig problem could be finessed the Resistance would be strong enough to prevent any further Nazi aggression. Now he was hopeful that at least a truce might be concluded before hostilities slid into unrestrained slaughter, admitting that overthrow of Hitler was an implied pre-requisite.

Certain principles had already been approved for the new

342

order that was to be established in Germany. The judiciary must
be wholly independent of the executive power. Freedom of faith
and conscience must be guaranteed. The right to an education,
to remunerated work and to ownership of property should be
established without regard to race, nationality or creed. The
new German state, federal in structure, should be willing to cede
sovereign authority to a projected Western European Federation with power to suppress aggression by any member. It was a
foreshadowing of the Common Market. "Eventually," predicted
the young German aristocrat, "the decisive development in
Europe—whether capitalistic or communistic—will be in the
social and political, not in the military, sphere."

All this, of course, did not surface in the discussion at
Child's. During the ensuing week von Trott came twice to
Millstone and I arranged a lunch *à trois* with Mr. Meyer. The
latter was suspicious that the visitor might be a Nazi agent, sent
to encourage American neutrality, a point which I was sure had
no validity. I arranged an interview for von Trott with Messersmith at the Department of State whence the German went
on to talk with Sumner Welles, then Under-Secretary and reput-
edly closer to the President than was Secretary Hull.[16] But
somewhere along the line channels to the White House were
blocked. It was von Trott's fear, made clear in the well-reasoned
memorandum which he left with the State Department, that a
war of extermination could only serve to consolidate behind
Hitler the hopeful elements that were seeking at the risk of life
to combine for his overthrow. In regard to the young man's
integrity, final proof came after the attempted assassination of
the Fuehrer and the abortive rising of July 20, 1944. As Hitler
said over the radio that evening: "This time we are going to
settle accounts as we National Socialists are used to doing it." A
month later, on August 26, Adam von Trott zu Solz, as one of

---

16. There is no evidence that Mr. Welles made contact with any Germans other than the
Nazi leaders when he went on his mission to that country in February, 1940. Nor is
there any mention of the Resistance Movement in his book: *The Time For Decision*,
Harper & Bros., 1944. This concludes that "partition is the only way of offsetting the
German menace in the future." Mr. Welles did not seem to envisage that this partitioning would place nearly half of pre-war Germany under permanent Communist
control.

some 5,000 summarily executed Germans, was garrotted for treason against the Nazi regime. I treasured his memory and years later was happy to be able to say so to his widow, then a physician in Hamburg.[17]

Another visitor from the Axis powers, shortly after von Trott's disappointed return to Germany, was Ken Harada, my close Japanese friend during the Geneva era. Ken, long since detached from the League of Nations' Secretariat, was on his way to Paris as newly-appointed Counsellor of Japan's Embassy there. He wanted to talk to me about the rapid deterioration in Japanese-American relations, recently emphasized by our termination of the commercial treaty between the two governments. If this were followed by the embargo then being advocated, said Ken during a long conversation at Millstone, the Japanese militarists would use it as argument for conquest of the East Indies and Southeast Asia. Japan was getting bogged down in China and there was a good chance that liberal leadership would regain control in Tokyo, if the United States did not now take a provocative attitude. This was much the same as the argument often advanced to me by Kyoshi Kawakami and there was no reason to doubt its sincerity. So I said I would pass it on to the Secretary of State, which was doubtless Harada's unspoken desire. On the probability of Japanese reformation, however, the tough old Tennessean was pardonably skeptical. "We have heard too much of unsubstantiated good intentions," he told me. Mr. Hull was also unimpressed by the von Trott disclosures, of which he had been sketchily informed. All this added up to a distinct hardening of the American position, making eventual participation in the war more probable. The President was already deviously angling for a third term nomination. If he gets it, and is re-elected, I thought, we'll soon be belligerents.

A direct consequence of the Russo-German agreement was the unprovoked Communist invasion of Finland, in early December, 1939. The Finnish Minister to Washington, Hjalmar Procopé, was also an old friend from Geneva days and confirmed

---

17. *Germans Against Hitler*, a well-documented and detailed study of the Resistance Movement, has been published by the West German Government and is available, in English, from its Press and Information Office in Bonn.

344

my fear that the future of all weak nations, creating an unstable buffer between Germany and Russia, was as insecure as that of Czechoslovakia and Poland had proved to be. All would necessarily become satellites of one or the other authoritarian powers and it could be assumed that this had been envisaged in the Molotov-Ribbentrop negotiations. I decided to investigate this assumption and as opportunity afforded raised the subject with the relevant diplomats. All unhappily agreed that the era of "Balkanized Europe," as set up by the peace treaties of 1919, was ending, to be replaced by the overlordship of either Berlin or Moscow. But there was disagreement as to where the line of demarcation between the two dominant powers would run, and as to whether the controls could be exerted amicably. Constantin Fotitch, the Yugoslav Minister and also an old Geneva friend, at that time feared Germany more than Russia. So did Pelyeni, the Hungarian envoy. But the Ministers of both Romania and Bulgaria, respectively Davila and Nauomoff, were more fearful of Russian expansion. Both Hitler and Stalin were naturally anathema to Jan Ciechanowski, the able Ambassador of the Polish government-in-exile, who did not reach Washington until after his country had been partitioned. After Russia came into the war, the fear of that empire gradually became dominant among all these border-state diplomats.[18]

The result of these discussions was to confirm my conviction that the United States could accomplish nothing constructive by entering the European war, regardless of what course might seem reasonable in the separate Far Eastern tangle. Whether under Nazi or Communist dominance, there was going to be a new Mittel-Europa, in which neither Britain nor France would any longer be influential and where Wilsonian theories of self-determination would play no part. If there were a split between Berlin and Moscow, then only one brand of dictatorship would eventually come to domination in Central Europe. In this case, by throwing its great power to the Russian side, the United States could doubtless tip the balance in favor of Communism.

---

18. Both Ciechanowski and Fotitch eventually put their disillusion into rather bitter books, the former in *Defeat In Victory*, Doubleday, 1947; the latter in *The War We Lost*, Viking Press, 1948.

But could anyone with liberal instincts regard such an outcome gladly? On February 22, 1940, I reread the Farewell Address and was again impressed by George Washington's isolationist admonitions.

It was at this psychological moment that the Haverford proposition came to a boil. A week earlier, while emphasizing no commitment, I had agreed to meet in Philadelphia with the nominating committee of the Board of Managers, two members of which had been my contemporaries as an undergraduate. I told the group that it would be a dreadful wrench to leave the *Post*, to abandon Millstone and tear up all our Washington roots. On the other hand, I was genuinely interested and could see that my answers to questions were favorably received. The problem at the college, I surmised, was not the perilous nature of the times but what was Haverford doing to justify itself in this period? After a long session I left early next morning, to fulfill a scheduled lecture engagement in Baltimore, expecting that the job would soon be formally offered and recognizing that I must clear my mind and talk it over with Mr. Meyer right away.

The choice was not less difficult because financially the equation practically balanced. Offsetting love for my work was the sentimental appeal of Haverford. There I had been born and as a student had seen horizons expand. There my parents' ashes were buried and there the war might even bring some advantage, by shaking stereotypes and deepening Quaker concerns. For the editorial page it would be quite the other way. With or without overt censorship, nothing sharply critical of governmental policy, no matter how short-sighted or deceptive, would be possible once hostilities were joined. It would be all too close to intellectual prostitution.

Other factors went into the wavering balance. The then dignified position of college president, or so I fondly thought, would give me leisure to do political writing more significant and enduring than anonymous editorials. It was suggested that I should also take the title of William Penn Professor of Government and it would be fun to do some teaching of upper classmen along the tutorial lines I had enjoyed so much at Oxford. For all the family the campus atmosphere would be healthier than that of war-time Washington, where excitement

346

was easily mistaken for enjoyment. And I felt some uncertainty as to my future at the *Post*. Mr. Meyer was now well into his sixty-fifth year. Daughter Katherine was clearly in line for the succession, but my relations with her prospective husband were wholly unpredictable.

Somewhat surprising, in view of my journalistic repute, was the advice I received in favor of the shift. Both my brothers were for it, though they shrewdly predicted that I would not remain more than a few years at Haverford. My old friend Francis Davis was of the same opinion. Dr. Moulton, of the Brookings, advised the change when I said I would not be expected to concentrate on fund-raising. President Cloyd Heck Marvin, of George Washington University, was enthusiastic, impressive both because he had already invited me to accept an honorary D.Litt. and because his only son was headed for Haverford in the Fall. Especially influential was an unannounced visit by my old and much respected philosophy professor, Rufus Jones. He urged me to return to Haverford "not because thee is a good Quaker but because some further exposure to Quakerism will do thee good." I was indeed already keenly aware that my life was deficient in spiritual values and that I had need of them.

The position was duly offered: some provisions which we thought necessary were accepted and then I had a final, rather sad, talk with Mr. Meyer who was already forewarned. He was, as always, courteous but said superfluously that he was not going "to bid" for his subordinate's services, something which had never been in question. "He shaped the issue," I wrote in my journal, "as to whether I am his man or my own master." On March 26, a grateful letter of resignation was delivered by hand which, the publisher generously said, left him "feeling groggy." He soon recovered, however, and later was not above showing resentment at the apostasy of this lieutenant. A certain patronizing insensitivity to underlings, I have always thought, was the characteristic which kept Eugene Meyer, for all his unusual abilities, from being a truly great man.

By curious coincidence this personal upheaval was followed, almost immediately, by a shattering termination of the stalemate in Western Europe. On April 9, the Germans invaded Denmark and Norway, placing the former under a "protectorate" and installing the Quisling government in Oslo. A month later came the invasion of the Low Countries and the Anglo-French debacle leading swiftly to the evacuation of Dunkirk. On June 10, "the Italian jackal" declared war on France and Britain. Many people seemed to anticipate that Germany would soon be shelling Atlantic City. But the measure of our response to Reynaud's last agonized appeal for help was symbolized by the State Department's *pro forma* dun for the uncollectable war debt installment, plus interest and arrears. On June 21, the day of the French surrender, I noted that: "the *Post* is not going to stand for intervention at least until after August 8," which was the day set for my departure.

After the hard winter, the spring and early summer were lovely in Washington, making regrets over departure more poignant. Lorna, the older daughter, headed for Bryn Mawr College, was graduated from the Madeira School on June 4, and soon after the family departed for Gibson Island. I stayed on the job, feeling it no hardship to live alone at Millstone where every tree and shrub now rooted on the once barren hilltop had come to seem a personal friend. At the end of June I went to Philadelphia for the Republican Convention, not wholly prepared for the nomination of Wendell Willkie over both Dewey and Taft, with the latter of whom I was increasingly *en rapport*. Through Alf Landon and others I had a finger in drafting the foreign affairs plank which I described as "a not unhappy compromise between non-intervention and narrow isolationism." But Roosevelt's mind was more decisive. He had decided to seek a third term by the clever device of holding himself in ostensibly unwilling reserve, thus making it impossible for any other Democrat to seek the nomination.

And so the clock ticked on. Hundreds of kindly letters of appreciation were answered. Bushels of accumulated papers were destroyed. Surplus books went to the public library and everything left at Millstone was packed for transportation to Haverford. The house was rented on a four-year lease, which I had said would be my minimum stay. There was a round of farewell parties and presentations, of which one from the Composing Room pleased me most. I brooded over Spengler's conclusion that "The Decline of the West" would sweep away the values which I, as a child of the nineteenth century, had always cherished. *Ducunt Fata voluntem, nolentem trahunt.* As to whether the Fates were leading, or dragging, me I was uncertain.

On my first night back at Haverford, September 10, 1940, I wandered around the quiet, moonlit campus, where my father had come to teach mathematics more than half a century earlier. Beyond the library the old mock orange tree still stretched its distorted length and I recalled the little lad who had climbed among its sturdy branches, long before. The wheel had come full cycle, but on a different and ominous plane.

◀Chapter 7

During Wartime Education

In the summer of 1940 it seemed improbable that the United States would again get involved in a European war.

Up to its new borders with Russia, the Third Reich was then in effective military control of most of the Continent. Great Britain, fighting with its back to the wall, had staved off the invasion threat and showed no disposition to respond to Hitler's overtures. Nevertheless, an eventual negotiated peace was indicated. So long as the Russo-German pact endured there was no possibility that the British would reverse Dunkirk and again establish a base on European soil. In spite of Churchill's peripheral movements, in North Africa and the Middle East, it was stalemate.

That was not the situation in the Far East, where Japanese policy became more aggressive after the German conquests in Western Europe. With the occupation of France and Holland the Tokyo warlords saw opportunity to increase their leverage by threatening the helpless French and Dutch colonial possessions in the Pacific. This quest for essential raw materials was intensified when, on July 2, 1940, President Roosevelt approved the "Act to Expedite the Strengthening of National Defense." It authorized the Executive to regulate by license, or to prohibit entirely, the export of any commodity deemed necessary for domestic military needs. This legislation permitted spot embargoes to be applied to one nation, not necessarily others, without the action having admittedly partisan intent. In his autobiography, *Present at the Creation,* Dean Acheson, then Assistant Secretary of State for Economic Policy, relates how this device was employed to bring pressure on the Japanese. He "constantly pressed for such action as lay immediately within our power to impede the axis, to aid its victims and to prepare ourselves for the inevitable hostilities which Colonel [Henry L.] Stimson predicted."[1]

Tokyo's reply to these unilateral impediments did not stop with formal protests. It proceeded to assume military supervision of the French colonial government in Indo-China, thus cutting off supplies that had been going to Chiang Kai-shek through Haiphong. And, on September 26, it was announced that by command of the Emperor the Japanese Ambassador in Berlin had been instructed to sign a treaty of defensive alliance with Germany and Italy. If the United States actively aided Great Britain in the Atlantic, in other words, Washington might anticipate a Japanese attack in the Pacific. Given the drift toward armed support of the British, this was a clear foreshadowing of Pearl Harbor.

So far as was possible in my new position I followed all this development closely. "Every prospect for 1941 is ominous," I wrote in my journal as the old year ended. But I was sure that President Roosevelt would move very cautiously until after the November election. There was considerable opposition to his third-term candidacy and public opinion, while resigned to a big defense program, was still strongly opposed to belligerency, as every Gallup Poll confirmed. It was politically necessary for the President to assure the country "again and again" that no American boys would be sent overseas by him. On October 19, at my formal inauguration, I was able to assert optimistically that Haverford had a role quite independent of the war clouds. This, in conformity with its traditions and established standards, I would endeavor to maintain. Amid the enveloping fear and hate there was the more need for faith and hope.

---

1. *Op. cit.* pp. 19–21, W. W. Norton Co., New York, 1969. Stinson was then Secretary of War.

Such continuity seemed the more plausible because Haverford, in 1940, differed little from the institution where I had graduated, in 1915. During that quarter-century the undergraduate enrollment had increased somewhat, to around 350, and the faculty in proportion. There were a couple of new dormitories, a new engineering laboratory and the library was being enlarged. Otherwise the campus seemed almost identical with that which I had known, first as a small child and then as a student. But while I felt no personal urge to make great changes, I could uneasily foresee that they would surely come during my third incarnation at the college. The hurricane into which the government was heading would make that certain.

The stereotype that persisted was in large measure due to the character and personality of my predecessor as president, William Wistar Comfort, who had graduated from Haverford the year that I was born there. President Comfort was a very conservative, austere and dedicated Quaker who, somewhat paradoxically, had specialized in the Romance languages. He had headed that department at Cornell, taking charge at Haverford in June, 1917, during the upheaval of the earlier war. That confusion, however, lasted little more than a single academic year and Dr. Comfort soon restored the school to "normalcy," though he would never have used that unhappy word. He did not agree with his successor's apprehension that coming events would turn the world upside down, along with Haverford as a part thereof. And as he continued to live on the campus, and sat on the Board of Managers, his freely-voiced convictions of ordained stability were sometimes a little irritating.

With the Board as a whole, however, the relations of the new president were excellent. They were a superior group of successful Quakers, most of them still living semi-patrician lives in the wealthy suburbs of Philadelphia but by no means unaware of the political and social turmoil that threatened. A major reason for choosing me, I was told confidentially, was belief that my cosmopolitan training and experience would bring Haverford out of the backwater in which Dr. Comfort had been content to have it moored. This was especially emphasized by Morris Leeds, formerly president and then still chairman of Leeds and Northrup, who was the universally respected head of

352

the college Managers. Morris was an engineer, an inventor and an industrial innovator of widespread fame and substantial wealth. He was frequently called to Washington, where he had served on the Business Advisory Council of the Department of Commerce. The plant which he directed was largely his personal creation and had won worldwide reputation for the manufacture of precision instruments and the development of process control systems. If hostilities came it would certainly be called into service. Morris Leeds nodded his head appreciatively when I promised to keep the atmosphere of the college pacific as long as possible, but said that if Congress declared war I thought Haverford must cooperate in what would undoubtedly be a totalitarian effort.

Other members of the Board were no less distinguished. Charles J. Rhoads, a prominent banker, was president of the Bryn Mawr College Board as well as a senior member of the Haverford body, and could be counted on to support all cooperative steps between the two adjacent institutions. He had been Commissioner of Indian Affairs under Herbert Hoover, when that office was still significant. J. Stogdell Stokes, a manufacturer of machinery, was president of the Philadelphia Museum of Art, a director of its equally famous orchestra, and with his charming wife a leader in the cultural life of the city. William B. Bell, a keen deep-water yachtsman, was president of the American Cyanamid Company and came to meetings from New York. The Scattergood brothers, Henry and Alfred, were successful businessmen and philanthropists who had done much to build the American Friends Service Committee. Fred Strawbridge, of that well-known merchant family, was equally proud of his Quakerism and his horsemanship. There were nearly a score of others, representative of the law, medicine and education as well as commerce and finance. All were graduates of Haverford and all, at this time, were members of the Society of Friends. Their general political outlook was Republican and mildly pacifist. It was a group with which I merged easily and I felt fortunate in the quality of my supervisors.

Of the faculty, three had been teaching when I was an undergraduate, illustrative of the permanence then characteristic of small colleges. Haverford had, on the whole, a distin-

353

guished group of professors but with a few weak spots. Since appointments were then primarily a presidential prerogative, a survey of the teaching staff was indirectly an indication of Dr. Comfort's administrative ability. He had clearly been uninterested in the field of civil government and it seemed a first responsibility to bolster this department. Even before coming to the campus I had arranged the appointment of my Geneva friend, Ben Gerig, to teach the traditional and attempted organization of international relations. And I had decided to offer a course myself in "The Development of Political Ideas." This would start with Plato and Aristotle, proceed through the Roman and medieval thinkers to the fruitful 17th and 18th centuries, terminate in a critical examination of Hegel and Marx and analysis of the contemporary struggle between representative and authoritarian government. A great deal of source reading was required and while at Oxford and since I had done most of it, I was hard pressed to refresh my memory and keep ahead of the dozen upper-classmen who were admitted to this elective. The course was made a seminar, meeting at the president's house one night a week and then habitually exceeding the scheduled two hours of discussion, followed by cokes, cocoa and crackers. It gave me opportunity to know this sample of the student body well and I was impressed both by their intelligence and work capacity.

That Haverford students were a superior breed was largely due to the insight and discrimination of Archibald MacIntosh, a virile graduate of Highland extraction, who was the Director of Admissions. I soon realized that "Mac" not only ran his key assignment supremely well, but was also a shrewd and well-posted observer on every aspect of campus life. On all major policy problems the new president consulted with this able lieutenant, whose wife Margaret, of impeccable Quaker background, was equally helpful to Isabel as we settled in. There was a very competent Superintendent of Buildings and Grounds. The remainder of the small administrative staff was less remarkable and before long some changes were needed to establish adequate financial controls. The president's own office, in Roberts Hall, was efficiently staffed. My faithful secretary on the *Post*, Mary Scaife, had come from Washington with

354

us, bringing her mother, and worked harmoniously with a second girl. In rush periods Isabel helped out. This backing was vital for it soon became evident that I had headed into feverish activity and equally hot controversy.

In offering me appointment the Board of Managers had made clear a desire that I bring the college into the limelight and, reciprocally, alert the campus dispassionately to the momentous events currently evolving. Under this formula the former editor had accepted an offer to write a weekly commentary for the Philadelphia *Bulletin*, which would also be published by the Washington *Star*. Preparation of these articles required occasional consultation with my sources in Washington. A plethora of speaking engagements, not all in the Philadelphia area, increased the travel load even when using airplanes. There were meetings with alumni groups in various cities; courtesy visits to schools which were regular feeders to the college; calls on foundations which were furnishing, or might be expected to furnish, grants of one kind or another. Equally important was the securing of objective but competent speakers for student assemblies and participation in the social life of the campus and community. All this would be overwhelming if not carefully organized and even so some activities had to give. By contrast with my predecessor I knew that I would be deficient in not taking leadership in the Haverford Friends Meeting, which was then compulsory every Thursday morning ("Fifth Day") for the entire student body. Not being assertively religious I felt that this would be hypocritical. Moreover, Dr. Comfort was still very active in the Meeting and I recognized that if I would succeed where my forerunner had fallen short, I must also to some extent fail where that one had been outstanding. In one of our numerous consultations I discussed this with Morris Leeds, who told me not to worry.

It was not easy to preserve an atmosphere of placidity while steering the college through the highly emotional welter of daily developments. I could easily have secured speakers from every belligerent embassy in Washington, but felt it improper to be selective here. After the French surrender, I invited my friend René de Chambrun, then visiting this country, to tell the student body of that catastrophe. This brought criticism because

355

the speaker was son-in-law of Pierre Laval, leader of the much-maligned Vichy Government. Clarence Streit, speaking on "Union Now," was condemned from the pacifist side as basically favoring American belligerency. Francis Davis came up from Baltimore to tell the boys about the problems of a family business in a socialistic era. Norman Thomas was called in to explain why socialism, in his opinion, would not be dictatorial. But such presentations, at once interesting and unprovocative, were hard to come by. Actually, public opinion was ceasing to be neutral, dividing bitterly on the now central issue of whether the United States should, or should not, get into shooting war. Pacifism was the more resented because most who favored fighting were fearful of saying so outright.

In the student body, happily, there was relatively little unrest. Undergraduates in good standing were still fairly well assured of draft deferment and the overhanging shadows encouraged concentration on academic studies. The college trustees were "dovish" almost to a man, though the ornithological distinction from "hawks" was not then popularized. But among the faculty, somewhat to my surprise, there was an active minority favoring American military intervention in Europe. This I attributed in part to the ardent pro-war attitude of the *New Republic* and the *Nation*, allegedly "liberal" weeklies with much influence in the academic world. The leader of this faction at Haverford was the Canadian-born professor of English Literature, Dr. Leslie Hotson, from whom I was destined to learn much about academic sensitivity.

Professor Hotson was a distinguished Shakespearian scholar who, during a decade on the Haverford campus, had established a privileged position. He was in the top salary bracket but nevertheless managed to be away from his college duties, doing research, for half the academic year, an anomaly which other full professors promptly drew to my attention. So, in constructing my first budget, I felt it necessary to tell Hotson that Haverford was primarily a teaching college and not a research institution. He must either give full time to the instruction of resident students or else take a salary cut for the period spent *in absentia*. The professor retorted that the president himself was spending a good deal of time away from the campus, and engaging in a form of outside research, if newspaper articles could be dignified by that name.

The confrontation was more difficult to compromise because of Dr. Hotson's self-imposed mission as a British agent on the college campus. Callers at his house were met with a request to contribute to "Bundles for Britain." I regarded this as a harmless idiosyncrasy until formal complaints about the practise were lodged by some of the undergraduates. Would collections for bombed-out German children also be tolerated?

This teapot tempest was brewing when, on a visit to Washington in January, 1941, I called on a Pennsylvania Senator, James J. Davis, as part of my effort to strengthen the repute of the college in potentially helpful political circles. "Pudler Jim," who had been an effective Secretary of Labor under Harding, Coolidge and Hoover, was by origin a two-fisted Welsh iron worker without a high regard for intellectuals. Nevertheless he had welcomed me as a constituent. On this occasion, however, his greeting was to hand over a telegram signed Leslie Hotson urging him, over the address of Haverford College, to press for prompt passage of the pending Lend-Lease legislation "without substantial modification." Jim Davis could handle a needle as deftly as a shovel. "Is this an illustration of Quaker pacifism?" he asked.

I suggested that the Senator put the question in a wire to me at Haverford. There I posted it on the bulletin board with a memorandum saying that while any professor, or any student, had the unquestioned right to express opinions on any subject, it must not be done in a way which might implicate the college as an institution. Hotson took this as an *ad hominem* attack and shortly made the tactical mistake of resigning, with a public statement that he was doing so because of the president's negative attitude toward "academic freedom and academic procedures." He was probably unprepared for the immediate student reaction. Overnight an enormous banner, made of bedsheets attached end to end, was strung across the facade of the biggest dormitory. "Bundle Leslie Back To Britain" it said in staring three-foot painted letters. This I had removed and dismembered, with charges to the Student Council, but not too quickly.

There was a final chapter to the Hotson episode. Presum-

357

ably he was stung by the failure of his resignation to flutter the dovecotes. Perhaps he had not expected it to be taken at face value, as was promptly done. Anyway, he requested and received a review before the Board of Managers in which he sought to show, with a sympathetic member of his department, that I had forced him out, contrary to the provisions of tenure for full professors, and that it had therefore become "a point of honor" to remain at his post, which he would never have relinquished voluntarily. Success in this maneuver would, of course, have been a body blow for the new administration. Moreover, I had already arranged to replace the controversial professor by Dr. Ralph Sargent, of Knox College, strongly recommended by brother Chris, and a magnetic and genial personality who soon established himself as a very successful teacher.

On the spot, I had an ace up my sleeve. During a visit to lecture at the University of Rochester its president, my good friend Alan Valentine, had given me a letter received from Hotson requesting a suitable appointment to the faculty of the New York institution. When the professor told the Haverford Board that he had never thought of locating elsewhere, I had only to produce this letter. With it the Hotson case crumbled and the acceptance of his resignation was confirmed, though sweetened by a year's leave of absence with pay. It was all really a symptom of the steadily increasing strain.

Indeed, the pressures were mounting daily, that last springtime of peace for the United States. During the Easter vacation I drove with Isabel and our two daughters to Montreal, a city at war, where I had been invited to speak to the local chapter of the Canadian Institute of International Relations and also give a radio broadcast. The International Labor Office, evacuated from Geneva, was then established on the grounds of McGill University and there was opportunity to meet with Phelan, the Blellochs and other old friends from Geneva days. Returning, there were visits to Vassar and West Point and at the Military Academy I visited several classes and discussed educational problems with the Superintendent, certainly the first Haverford President ever to do so.

In Montreal I had been disturbed by the casual question of a Canadian newsman, who had asked what I knew about

"Roosevelt's plan" to recruit pilots, from the Army and Navy airforces, for mercenary service with the Chinese Nationalists. They would, it was said, actually be paid by a dummy organization known as China Defense Supplies and would receive a bonus of $500 for every Japanese plane shot down.[2]

Journalistic instincts were aroused by this report of outright neutrality violation and, having an upcoming engagement with the Haverford alumni chapter in Washington, I also arranged an interview with Admiral Nomura, the Japanese Ambassador, with whom I was already well acquainted. I found this envoy in forthright mood. The United States, Nomura ssserted, was deliberately and increasingly provoking Japan, in a manner which looked to him like settled policy. While there was still time he hoped that five points could be brought home to the Roosevelt Administration. As I noted them down, in the handsome Embassy on Massachusetts Avenue, these were: (1) Neither Nationalist nor Communist China can any longer hope to defeat Japan. (2) To stabilize the "New Order" in the Far East Japan is endeavoring to improve its relations with Russia and expects no difficulties there. (3) Japan sees no reason why all matters in dispute with the United States cannot be peacefully reconciled. (4) Japan therefore seeks a settlement which will save face all around. (5) He [Nomura] considers this a great, if transient, opportunity for President Roosevelt to show constructive statesmanship.

While obviously one-sided, I felt it my duty to pass these five points on to the Secretary of State, together with my impression that the Japanese Ambassador was not bluffing. The latter's superior, Foreign Minister Matsuoka, had just completed exploratory conferences with Churchill, Hitler, Mussolini and Stalin. Japan was obviously coming to a decision on whether the hostilities, which the United States seemed ready to contemplate, could be averted. Cordell Hull had always been receptive to me and it was not the first time I had played the role of honest broker. Moreover, I suspected that visitors to the

---

2. This dubious practise was authorized by Executive Order in April, 1941. For its connection with Lend-Lease v. Barbara W. Tuchman: *Stillwell and the American Experience in China*, Macmillan Co., New York, 1971, Ch. 9.

Japanese Embassy were now being noted by the F.B.I. and it would be well to have a satisfactory explanation for that.

But I found the Secretary of State preoccupied by the rapid German conquest of the Balkans and seemingly indifferent to Japanese complaints, whether or not justified. Other friends in the department confirmed the impression that the old Tennessean was losing his grip. Sumner Welles, as Undersecretary, was now in much closer touch with the President and that able, if devious, Assistant Secretary, Dean Acheson, had moved up as a policy maker. It was the last time that I would talk with Cordell Hull, whom I had long respected and admired. It was the first time that war with Japan had seemed to me a probability.

Other contacts were refurbished on this trip, especially with Senator Taft whose anti-interventionist position seemed to me admirably well-reasoned and sustained. I told the Washington Alumni Association that the Hotson episode was the closest the war had yet come to the Haverford campus. But in the Capital it was clear that American involvement was drawing closer and it was pleasant to return to the currently more soluble problems of the college. Haverford in the spring is always lovely; the gardens and tennis courts were both in prime condition and there were many interesting visitors, including both my brothers.

Herbert Hoover had consented to give the Commencement Address, at the beginning of June, and the preparation for his nationwide evening broadcast, from Roberts Hall, was something of a strain. But it all went off very smoothly. Isabel arranged a big buffet supper on the semi-circular Morley porch. There was perfect weather for the twilight academic procession and clear transmission for the big audience which overflowed the auditorium and listened to loud speakers in the cooler outside atmosphere. Hoover's admirable theme was the additional importance, in a period of social disaster, of educational training like that given by Haverford. It was an honor to confer the degree of Ll.D. on the former chief executive, who graciously met and chatted with all the 83 young men who had also received diplomas from their president's hands. "A highly satisfactory finale to a successful, if not an easy, year," I noted.

A fortnight later, after much cleanup work, I went again to Canada, driving to Kingston, Ontario, as an invited guest at the annual Carnegie Conference on Canadian-American relations, at Queen's College. And it was on the trip there, the evening of June 21, 1941, at the little town of Cortland, New York, that I got the not unexpected news of Hitler's invasion of Soviet Russia. A month later, with the Communist giant so thoroughly occupied, Japan announced a formal protectorate over French Indo-China. By stroke and counterstroke, from Tokyo and from Washington, the road to Pearl Harbor was being bulldozed.

◀During my first year at Haverford I had learned a good deal about the administration of independent American colleges in general, aside from that of my own. I had monthly conferences with Marion Park of Bryn Mawr and John Nason of Swarthmore on cooperative measures which could be taken by these neighboring Quaker institutions, with similar backgrounds, standards and ideals. I met informally but fairly frequently with other presidents in the eastern Pennsylvania area. And I talked shop with the executives on more distant campuses whenever there was occasion to visit. Football games provided an exceptional opportunity to discuss mutual problems. The team was pleased when their prexy traveled to watch them play. Then I would generally stay overnight, to explore with my counterpart issues which the approach of war was making increasingly sinister.

There were several general weaknesses which would be sure to surface if, as and when the United States became more actively involved in the hostilities. War could be good business for a newspaper. Dramatic headlines bring readers and readers bring advertising. For a college it was the opposite. Conscription takes fees-paying students but leaves underemployed teachers to be compensated; increased taxation and patriotic demands tend to reduce bequests and gifts; and no institution is so subject to inflation as a private college, where it is very difficult to cut overhead, almost impossible to increase the economic productivity of instruction, and where higher charges may price the independent unit out of the market because of the subsidized rates at competing public universities.

To confront these challenges I felt that Haverford must become better integrated, in the old-fashioned general sense of the word. Its special application to racial and sexual mixture was not as yet in common use. As I saw the problem there were six distinct and disparate elements in the college organism: the trustees; administration; faculty; students; alumni and the community where the institution functioned. Among these groups there was at best partial coordination and sometimes no working relationship. This came home to me as I checked over the changes in the college catalog needed after my first year of incumbency. It was there stated that the consumption or possession of alcoholic beverages on the campus was strictly prohibited. Actually there was very little drinking but I had noted that several of the faculty enjoyed a social cocktail, as I did myself. For undergraduates the prohibition could not be enforced without an arbitrary and intolerable dormitory search. Nevertheless, suggestion that this archaic statute be eliminated was overruled by the managers, some of whom served vintage wines at their own tables. Because the college had been dry when they were students, it was pretended that it so remained.

Few of the faculty were really known to the trustees, and vice versa. On ceremonial occasions, such as commencement day, there was intermingling and the picturesque game of cricket, with many veteran players active in the Philadelphia area, was at Haverford a catalytic agent of more than traditional value. In the old days nearly all of the teachers had been Quakers, with the religious affiliation a valuable binding force. But by 1940 most of the younger teachers, and nearly 90 percent of the students, had no connection with the Society of Friends. There were no joint committees of faculty and board. Neither party had any but the most general knowledge of the other's problems. The Hotson episode helped to reveal this alienation and partly as a result the faculty, on its own initiative, was empowered to elect two non-voting members of the Board of Managers who, in person or by deputy, attended all its meetings. Simultaneously I established an advisory Academic Council, composed of two elected representatives from each of three divisions of the curriculum, which met with me or my administrative lieutenant, Archibald MacIntosh, both regularly and on call. This became, in effect, an executive committee for the unwieldy and inefficient faculty meetings, where hours were invariably wasted on trivialities, or consumed by professors anxious to dilate on personal rather than corporate concerns.

The student body was well organized and, in accordance with Quaker tradition, had for many years exercised a large measure of self-government under its own elected Student Council. In some respects I felt that this independence was carried rather far. There were, for instance, practically no regulations governing the presence of girls in dormitories, as President Park of Bryn Mawr drew sharply to my attention at the first three-college meeting. It was at least theoretically possible for a Haverford student to entertain a Bryn Mawr girl in his bedroom all night without violating any firm college regulation, regardless of what else might give. Meeting with the Student Council I endeavored to arrange a compromise, whereby that body would eliminate hard liquor in return for a liberal ruling on nocturnal females. The boys were hard bargainers, loath to give up any acquired privilege and insistent that the overall "Honor Pledge" taken by every student sufficed for all disciplinary problems. But eventually regulations satisfactory to neighboring Bryn Mawr were adopted and, as a part of the agreement, a representative of the Student Council was invited to attend all meetings of the president's advisory committee. I wanted to go further and have an elected student made a nonvoting member of the Board of Managers. This was rejected. It would be twenty years before that reform became a common college practice.

Relations of the general alumni body to the college were also unsatisfactory, although there were well-organized chapters in Boston, New York, Wilmington, Baltimore, Washington, Pittsburg and Chicago, that in Philadelphia being naturally the largest and most closely in touch. Visiting these groups, I found them eager to know more about the basic problems and policies of the college, on which they drew most of their information either from undergraduate sons or from the Haverford *News*. This very good weekly student newspaper was properly averse to serving as an administration mouthpiece. To provide this need, and to establish "annual giving" as a recognized alumni function, two coordinated steps were necessary. There should be a resident alumni secretary with an office on the campus, which was soon arranged, and there should be a college publication with a deeper outlook than that of the undergraduate newspaper, more interesting and forward-looking than the president's rather stereotyped annual report. Thus the Haverford *Review* was born, early in my second year of office, and has continued as the college alumni magazine, under one name or another, to the present day. I was fortunate in finding a very able student, Wayne Moseley, who took much of the burden of this. Indeed, a number of undergraduates had distinct journalistic proficiency and it was pleasant that many wanted to share the experiences of a veteran. There was even an undergraduate radio station, wholly managed by the students, which was building up an interested community following.

The relations of the college with its neighborhood seemed to require more cultivation than this. Adjacent Ardmore was on the fringe of Philadelphia's industrial development and I felt that Haverford should be less aloof from the circulation of modern commerce than it had been in my undergraduate days. Faculty wives were active in organizations ranging from the Needlework Guild to the League of Women Voters. A few of the professors belonged to civic associations and even dabbled in local politics. However, the Friends Meeting turned a rather austere face toward local problems. On the whole, the Quaker characteristic of withdrawal was dominant.

If war were coming, this isolation would soon become impossible. Without losing its Quaker identification, the college could be steered into the mainstream of American life, where it would in any case be swept if the totalitarian drift continued. Moreover, Haverford was no longer merely a Quaker institution. It derived no financial support from the Society of Friends as such. The lovely campus was primarily a private preserve for those privileged to teach and study there. The future of small independent colleges, I believed, would depend largely on their success in bringing cultural and intellectual leadership to their neighborhoods. They must be communal rather than parochial in the religious sense of the word. Haverford had drifted some distance from its original Quaker moorings, as had the new

364

president himself. But in so doing it had become Ivy League rather than democratic. There were no Negroes, few Jews or Romans and scarcely any proletarians in the enrollment. It was a WASP institution—White, Anglo-Saxon, Protestant—quite wealthy and somewhat smug. The way the social tide was running, this made it vulnerable.

Before coming to the campus I had thought of one way in which this situation might be modified. A longtime friend was John L. Lewis, the colorful and courageous leader of the then well organized United Mine Workers Union. Lunching with this labor boss, after accepting the Haverford appointment, I suggested that the U.M.W. might establish a couple of competitive scholarships open to ambitious sons of anthracite miners in the eastern Pennsylvania coal fields. John L., whose school-teacher wife had deeply interested him in education, was quite taken by the idea. It would probably have come to fruition except that Morris Leeds, when I discussed the plan with him, feared that it might be a too dramatic step for the incoming president to initiate immediately. So the idea was laid aside, to be lost with much else when the war clouds broke.

I pushed harder, however, when toward the close of my first year on campus an Engineering and Scientific Management Defense Training Program was initiated by the Federal Office of Education. There John W. Studebaker, with whom I had worked in Des Moines in 1933, was now Commissioner. In spite of its formidable title the program was actually little more than a vocational training course for young mechanics, geared to the many openings in the burgeoning defense plants. While designed primarily for engineering schools it was suitable for Haverford, which was reasonably well-equipped in this field. The teachers who would be involved were eager to cooperate. Morris Leeds also approved, though there was some Board opposition both to the defense aspects of the program and to the acceptance of any federal funds. In the fall of 1941 the venture got under way, with a number of neighborhood workmen attending evening classes. I was pleased to see the facilities of the college so utilized and the ice was broken for larger developments that were soon to come.

A good part of the summer of 1941 I had spent on the college campus, following with apprehension the accumulating signs of coming American belligerency. When possible I was with my family at Gibson Island and here, during the Fourth of July weekend, a long phone call from Herbert Hoover, in Palo Alto, led to a final effort to preserve the peace. The former President saw hostilities with Japan approaching and felt that this would end all hope of a negotiated settlement in Europe. He therefore suggested that I draft and join in signing a statement on America's potential role as peacemaker. This would be made public over the signatures of Mr. Hoover, Alf Landon, Charles G. Dawes, Frank O. Lowden, Robert M. Hutchins and a dozen other prominent Republicans who were not currently politically active, had not identified themselves with the America First movement and could not easily be attacked as "isolationists." The underlying idea was to show that much Republican leadership did not associate itself with the belligerent position taken by Henry L. Stimson and Frank Knox, who were both serving in Roosevelt's Cabinet and giving it the expression of a coalition government. Without great expectations I agreed to do the difficult drafting and arrange for release of the statement, which got national front-page publicity the morning of August 6.[3] A by-product was strengthening of my friendship with former Governor Landon.

As the Russians reeled back before the Nazi onslaught, Communist intrigue was added to the factors working for American intervention. Realization of this strengthened the last-ditch opposition to embroilment. I sought hard to keep my weekly articles unemotional and was pleased when the influential *Wall Street Journal* began to print them. The *Saturday Evening Post* gave editorial praise to these "scholarly essays" while, on the other hand, letters to the Philadelphia *Bulletin* increasingly denounced my questioning of Communist war aims. Would Russia be so popular if its armies were victorious? I inquired. "In that case, I expect, the consequences of a Soviet triumph for Western Europe would begin to dawn on us." To

---

3. It is referred to, as the work of "naysayers," by Morison and Commager in *The Growth of the American Republic*, Oxford University Press, New York, Fourth Edition, 1956, Vol. II, p. 660.

anticipate unemotionally, I concluded, "seems one of the most difficult operations for humanity to accomplish."

The deep fissures that were to stimulate bitterness in American thinking during the post-war years were already apparent, but I believed that the Quaker attitude, of relative detachment, could do much to bridge the growing chasm, if courageously and reasonably maintained. Denying that I was an "isolationist" I declined invitations to join America First. I accepted the Russian Embassy's continued invitation to attend the annual "Celebration of the Great October Socialist Revolution." The talk there was highly critical of Winston Churchill's "bombast" and of British "failure"—the better word would have been "inability"—to come to Russia's assistance. After the party I went off with Dmitri Naoumoff, the Bulgarian Minister and one of the most objectively thoughtful members of the diplomatic corps. A Russian victory, that envoy predicted sadly, would convert all the Balkan nations into Communist principalities. This opinion was reported to Senator Taft, whose oldest son I had appointed to an instructorship in the remodeled English department at Haverford. "But F.D.R. never thinks outside of or beyond the next election," said the Senator dryly.

A friend at the British Embassy, with whom I maintained close relations, was fiscal expert Kenneth Bewley, of the Supply Council. On a happily breezy Labor Day Bewley came down to Gibson Island to go sailing in the Morley Barnegat. "I wish our Treasury were as full as these sails," said the financial counsellor, explaining that British dollar reserves were now completely exhausted, so that all war material going to that country from the United States was necessarily "on tick." Even greater dependence applied to the "Free French" and other "governments-in-exile" endeavoring to function in London. The Nationalist Chinese were also being heavily financed by Washington. Secretary of the Treasury Morgenthau seemed to worry only about Congressional restrictions on the outpouring of dollars. All this outlay ballooned the deficit financing of the Defense Program and was reflected in mounting inflationary pressures. Because of rising costs, Haverford's new president ended his first year with an operating deficit of $16,000. It was a trifle, in a million dollar budget, but still a warning signal. Opposing any tuition increase, careful economies were necessary for the ensuing year. But I found the challenge stimulating.

After the customary winnowing MacIntosh had entered a Freshman class of 106—then the largest in Haverford history—and very few older students had as yet been taken by the draft, or succumbed to the lure of enlistment. At the opening "Collection" I emphasized that with conscription there was no patriotic obligation to volunteer but that everyone reaching the critical age must register. There was provision for anyone with conscientious objections to make his case before the draft board and I would personally support those who convincingly shared their scruples with me. One student, of good Quaker stock, nevertheless refused to register or accept alternative service and while I testified for him in court as a character witness, Arnold Satterthwaite was sentenced to a year and a day in federal penitentiary. "It is," I wrote, "a sad commentary on the times in which we live." Coincidentally a faculty member complained to me about the five percent "Defense Tax" then being levied. "Write 'paid under protest,' " I advised. This satisfied him for the moment, but soon the college would be required to withhold such taxation from salary at source. Only an obscurantist could fail to note the steady advance of totalitarian ideas. Increasingly it was argued that this was a temporary sacrifice which would be ended by a successful war "for freedom," in alliance with Communist Russia.

It was a happy circumstance that, in spite of my non-interventionist position, I could maintain the best of relations with both my brothers, who did not share this opinion. Christopher was particularly interested in Haverford and visited there frequently. He came down for resumption of the historic football game with Swarthmore, before a great outpouring of alumni which taxed entertainment facilities to the full. He brought with him, for presentation to the college library, a valuable first edition of Hobbes' *Leviathan*, one of the "seed" books discussed in my seminars and very timely as a seventeenth century treatise on executive privilege. Chris was then busy on his semi-autobiographical novel *Thorofare*, but consented to head a "Friends of the Library" organization destined to prove most helpful. Spearheaded by Mary Allinson it led,

368

eventually, to the Christopher Morley Alcove which is a showplace of the Magill Library at Haverford. Frank, whose older son was in school at nearby Westtown, was also a frequent and welcome guest. Earlier in the autumn, on what would have been our father's eighty-first birthday, the three of us gathered at Kit's secluded beach cabin—"Nostromo"—far out on Long Island Sound. Together we swam in the sparkling water, enjoyed a picnic lunch and talked of old times together. It was a delightful interlude, amid the gathering storm clouds.

These grew steadily more ominous. Announcement of the Atlantic Charter, on August 14, had been close to a declaration of Anglo-American alliance. Already Iceland had been placed in the "defense zone" of the United States. Now there were American destroyer clashes with German submarines patroling those waters. In November, the House of Representatives repealed the remnants of neutrality legislation, by the narrow margin of 212 to 194. The logistic difficulties in any invasion of *Festung Europa*, it seemed to me, were now the major preventative of war with Germany. The threat of hostilities in the Pacific, though much less publicized, were more imminent. Right after Labor Day there was a small dinner in Washington at the home of Kyoshi Kawakami. The Financial Commissioner at the Japanese Embassy was present, an elderly and impressive man who complained bitterly about the frozen credits and other measures which were intentionally strangling all Japanese-American trade. "Our relations with the United States," he said to me, "must either rapidly improve or else relapse into open war."

They certainly did not improve. On November 27, at Haverford, I speculated in my journal about stalemate in Europe. "Japan," I wrote, "to whose envoys we have presented undisclosed but seemingly unacceptable terms, looms as the enigma in the background. Japanese-American hostilities will prolong fighting indefinitely. If these can be avoided, the end of the war may not be so many months distant." Unknown to me, and to the vast majority of Americans, the issue was already joined. The preceding evening Secretary Hull, with President Roosevelt's approval, had presented a virtual ultimatum to Ambassadors Nomura and Kurusu. The third of its ten points demanded that

369

Japan "withdraw all military, naval, air and police forces from China and from Indo-China." The fourth point insisted that: "The government of the United States and the government of Japan will not support—militarily, politically, economically— any government or regime in China other than the national government of the Republic of China with capital temporarily at Chungking."[4] Nobody could have expected those then in power in Tokyo to accept these orders from Washington. And it is not the least of history's many ironies that the United States, a generation later, would itself begin to write off that same "national government" of Chiang Kai-shek which it had been willing to fight Japan to sustain.

But of the American provocation I, at the moment, had only an unconfirmed suspicion. I was becoming more and more engrossed in my college duties without, as I wrote, "feeling in a backwater on this quiet campus." On the night of December 5, I traveled to Boston to attend a meeting of the important New England Association of Colleges and Secondary Schools. From that President Remsen Ogilby, of Trinity College, took me to Hartford as his guest. There I was restless and confided to my journal: "I anticipate the Japanese will shortly strike and dare us to hit back. Then all hope of a reasonable settlement in the near future will be gone. I am sorry for Kyoshi."

The next afternoon came news of Pearl Harbor.

◀Hurrying back to Haverford, I summoned a special Assembly of students, faculty and all other college employes. The war on which the nation was embarked, I predicted, would be a long and arduous conflict, even though the overwhelming power of the United States insured an eventual victory of sorts. None could at the moment foresee the national requirements but, as these became clear, all would doubtless be called upon to participate. Hopefully this would include non-military openings for

---

4. The full text is in *Foreign Relations, Japan, 1931–41*, U.S. Govt. Printing Office, 1943, Vol. II, pp. 768–70.

those with pacifist convictions. In any case it could be a tragic mistake to desert the college prematurely and parents would probably give the same advice. I emphasized that the function of Haverford had always been to train for moral and civic leadership. Both would be essential in the period of upheaval likely to follow the fighting and I urged the students to project their lives against a long-range rather than a merely immediate future.

Although opposed to American entry, I had seen the war coming and well before Pearl Harbor was clear in my mind as to the course the college should pursue. No matter how strong the pacifist conviction, Haverford could not successfully oppose the authoritarian pressures which protracted hostilities foreshadowed. Nor, after the almost unanimous declaration of war by Congress, was it democratically justifiable for any tax-exempt institution to withdraw from the common effort. Haverford should participate and I must utilize my Washington contacts to make the contribution as constructive as possible. After Quaker Meeting on December 14, I was told by Lydia Sharpless, widow of my own undergraduate president, that: "Thee seems to have been specially trained for thy present task." But how to put this training into effect?

A minor opening came immediately in the form of a phone call from my esteemed Japanese friend, Kyoshi K. Kawakami, who on the day after Pearl Harbor had been arrested by the F.B.I., taken from his American wife and Nisei children, and interned at the Immigration Station of Gloucester Point, across the river from South Philadelphia. Could I visit him and provide the only two comforts the old journalist really wanted—a head of fresh lettuce and a copy of *Les Miserables*? This was a touching request and in it I saw an educational opportunity more profound than that of most classrooms. So I took with me two popular students, Dee Crabtree and Joe Jordan, knowing they would spread this illustration of the backwash of war among their fellows. In his not uncomfortable confinement Kyoshi received us with perfect Oriental courtesy, almost as though the trio were visiting him at home. The boys were charmed and when Jordan reached Okinawa with the Marines, some three years later, he wrote to remind me of the episode—shortly before his death in action there. As further opportunities to see the war

371

in perspective arose it was often possible to share them with the student body.

The immediate academic issue was the advisability of putting men's colleges on a three-year basis. If this were done there was some reason to believe the military would defer conscription of students until graduation, unless manpower needs became acute. The change would probably maintain enrollment, since additional pressures for matriculation might well balance the number of undergraduates leaving as volunteers. It would also quiet faculty restiveness, which could become serious if the draft age were lowered to 18 and professors saw their classes cut to such immaturity, plus a few physically unfit.

An accelerated program did not seem unduly revolutionary to me. There was obvious waste in the leisurely four-year course and good reasons for the long summer vacation had disappeared when farm families ceased to provide a significant number of students. To an economical mind it was shocking to contemplate the overhead in holding expensive plant idle for a quarter of the year. Many teachers, however, did not see it that way. They had come to regard the mid-June to mid-September holiday as a normal prerogative, reasoning that this freedom from campus responsibility was needed for recuperation and research. Why this abnormal leisure should be more essential for a teacher than for a doctor, lawyer or other professional worker was an evaded question. With more justification it was argued that teacher remuneration was geared to a nine-month working year.

Since conscripted youths would not get summer leave of absence, a hard-fought war was obviously the time to confront this curious educational anomaly. But I realized that I must proceed cautiously in the matter. So, at first, I merely requested my Academic Council to make a thorough study of the suitability of acceleration for Haverford, and then went off to attend the annual dinner for college presidents graciously provided by the University Club of New York, where the subject would be thoroughly discussed. Here Father Gannon, of Fordham, suggested that "boiled ivy" would be a suitable campus diet for the emergency. And here, at breakfast with my friend Gordon

Chalmers, president of Kenyon College, I received a suggestion which would become a landmark in Haverford history.

The Quaker college, of course, had no ROTC and I was as opposed as any doctrinaire sectarian to such infringement on a liberal arts curriculum. But it was evident that more professional military units would be quickly installed in all the larger educational institutions and the great majority of my fellow executives, seeing financial salvation in this, were already beating tracks to the Pentagon to get consideration. Chalmers, a former Rhodes Scholar, told me he had heard there might be a few pre-meteorology units established at small colleges with a high reputation for their instruction in mathematics and physics. Haverford filled that bill, and it would also seem an appropriate service since these would not be combat troops but trainees as weather officers, with later openings into commercial aviation and other civilian jobs. Would Haverford cooperate, Chalmers asked, in getting this undertaking on the road?

The question posed a quandary. A unit of this character would not only ease the financial problem but would also satisfy that majority of the Haverford faculty whose patriotism was already palpably inflamed. On the other hand it was doubtful that the Board of Managers would sanction such a break with Quaker tradition. I had a particular difficulty in the almost fanatical pacifism of my predecessor and knew that I must consult with Morris Leeds on the issue. So I told Chalmers I could at the moment cooperate only informally but would immediately write to my friend Colonel Herman Beukema, at West Point, who certainly would be on the inside of the development. An unexpected result of this approach was an invitation to serve as representative of the small independent colleges on the Civilian Advisory Board of the Army Specialized Training Program, which Beukema was soon to head. This appointment, leading to many interesting sessions at the Pentagon in ensuing months, I accepted on my own responsibility.

A great help in the prevalent confusion was the way the newly-organized Academic Council shaped up. I could talk with this small group confidentially, leaving it to the representatives to clear specific problems with the professors who had elected them. Archibald MacIntosh could chair these meetings competently and, at the end of January, 1942, I obtained permission from the Board to name him Vice-President, giving Mac control of all operations during my absences from the campus. These were becoming frequent as the Managers were anxious to have the college utilized more for what they vaguely called "civilian activities," little realizing how closely these would be merged with the military in the waging of total war. The imaginary separation was demonstrated at a meeting of the financial committee, when Dupont was sold because of its concentration on munitions while P.R.R., which transported what Dupont made, was held in the faith then extended to that railroad.

Nevertheless, in the weeks following Pearl Harbor, I made many visits to Washington to seek opportunities for peaceful service by the college. One idea was to have conscientious objectors man the rapidly enlarging Employment Service Offices, in which project Secretary of Labor Perkins encouraged me. On a limited basis this worked out but disclosed a rivalry between John Studebaker, Commissioner of Education, and Paul V. McNutt, heading the new War Manpower Commission, as to who should have the greater share of non-military campus control. I had to work with both and assisted solution by having both express their ideas at Haverford in commencement addresses, with the result that McNutt made me a consultant. In Washington I was also able, through Tom Woodward, to enlist the cooperation of the Maritime Commission, making it easy for undergraduates to enter the now hazardous merchant shipping service.

By then the accelerated academic program had been arranged. To the normal two-semester college year was added an intensive nine-week summer term, into which every course offered in the curriculum would be condensed. Provision for review work was made in the regular semesters, which were also lengthened by curtailment of the Christmas and Spring vacations. No student was forced to accelerate, but those who so wished could abbreviate the four-year course to two and two-thirds years under the new trimester system. It was hard on the faculty but they responded nobly, and about two-thirds of the student body, including a number of the incoming Freshmen,

374

chose the speed-up program. A difficulty was that the new arrangement, when fully under way, would mean three graduation exercises annually, one at the conclusion of every term. But this enabled me to bring to the campus more speakers of prominence, drawing them into cooperation in the various projects.

During the winter of 1941–42, as everyone knows, the war went very badly for the Allied cause. Hongkong fell to the Japanese on Christmas Day and soon that nation was in control of the huge Asiatic crescent stretching from Burma to Java and Sumatra. Rommel held the upper hand in North Africa and the Nazi steamroller pounded ever deeper into Russia. There were many, myself among them, who thought a separate Russo-German peace a probability and most of the Balkan diplomats in Washington, terrified at the thought of a Communist triumph, were in private conversation frankly hopeful for this outcome. At the end of January President Roosevelt promised the Poles "restoration of their democracy," leading Jan Ciechanowsky, their Ambassador in Washington, to inquire *sotto voce* whether Stalin had agreed. Some crystallization of Allied war aims seemed to me imperative, the more so after the British offer of Dominion status for India was curtly rebuffed by the native leaders as too little and too late. The British Empire east of Suez was visibly crumbling.

Wesley Winans Stout, then editor of the *Saturday Evening Post*, had asked me for an article analyzing the conditions necessary for a stable peace. This, I knew, would be difficult because of the deep ideological conflict between Russia and the United States. The former had never abandoned its hope for World Revolution in behalf of Communism. Americans, on the other hand, were for the most part implicit believers in the capitalist system and would resent any Soviet effort to undermine it. This fundamental difference could not be glossed over by a reconstituted League of Nations, less so because the British and French empires were dissolving, reducing those countries to inferior military status. The best hope for a lasting peace would seem to lie in regional organization with an overall international Council and Secretariat to coordinate this sub-structure. In the Americas the United States, with British goodwill, would be the most influential power. Japan, win, lose or draw, would doubtless remain an Asiatic leader because of the energy, ability and international outlook of its people. African republics, emerging from colonialism, would for a long time be relatively ineffective for good or ill. The big problem would be the future of Europe, where the United States would oppose both German and Russian domination while Russia would be equally hostile to either German or American control. The crushing defeat of Germany could only strip the wartime disguise from this latent Russo-American antagonism. A logical solution would be an independent federation of the small nations of Western Europe, with a strength in union which separately they all lacked, if they could forget their past mutually suicidal enmities. Such a federation, respected by both Russia and the United States, could in time rebuild that balance of power which had helped England to keep a European peace for most of the nineteenth century.

It was a wholly dispassionate, essentially intellectual, article which, when published on April 18, 1942, aroused an unexpected storm of controversy. I had titled it: "Peace through a Balance of Power" but editor Stout thought this too soporific and suggested change to "For What Are We Fighting?" which I accepted. Since very few in Washington ever addressed themselves clearly to this question, there was perhaps the more annoyance that it should be raised unofficially while the outcome of the war was unsure. In Quaker circles, however, the response was good, recalling the admonition of one spokesman that: "We . . . must give him [the Quaker] infinite credit for maintaining his sturdy common-sense during periods when all the rest of the world seemed to have taken leave of its senses."[5] Support in this key quarter was the more welcome because report that I wanted a military unit on the campus was spreading, to the distress of Bill Comfort and other intransigents. As long as condemned by both pacifists and militarists I felt myself on a constructive track.

Before writing this article I had conferred at length in New York with Herbert Hoover and former Ambassador Hugh Gibson, who right after Pearl Harbor had started collaboration on a

---

5. Amelia Mott Gummere, *Witchcraft and Quakerism*, The Biddle Press, Philadelphia, 1908, p. 68.

book discussing *The Problem of Lasting Peace*. Both of them were strong advocates of the idea of regional organization that I was suggesting. This arrangement, Mr. Hoover pointed out, would have the advantage of bringing localized pressures to solve relatively localized problems, thus relieving a reconstituted League of many peripheral controversies. Decentralization would lessen the argument for military alliances and "greatly relieve American anxiety lest we be constantly involved in secondary problems all over the earth."[6] Such development, however, would run counter to the theme of an "American Century," which grew stronger as the British Empire crumbled.

A consequence of the furor aroused by the *Post* article was discontinuation—by request—of the shorter contributions I had been writing weekly for the Philadelphia *Bulletin*. I rather welcomed termination of the controversy these had aroused. The college had wanted a president who would put it in the limelight, but sometimes now this seemed too lurid. Yet great changes, affecting *inter alia* the whole character of education, were obviously coming and it seemed a pity that an activist Quaker viewpoint should not be presented. I had the knack of simplifying difficult subjects and in my journal for May 2, 1942, toyed with the idea of an objective Haverford commentary which would periodically help "to achieve that synthesis of the college with the larger community life for which I have been working." There were too many other complications at the time but this was the seed that was to grow into *Human Events*.

With the draft reduced to age 18, attrition of the student body began to be serious and many of the faculty were also vulnerable under the upper limit of 45. Now there was much correspondence with local boards which were for the most part very cooperative when good reasons for deferment or alternative service could be advanced. Perhaps ten percent of those called raised conscientious objection and in each such case I examined the dissenter personally before underwriting his claim. I felt sure that the presence of a military unit on the campus would ease this collaboration with the draft authorities, but that was a

---

6. Notes made in talk with Mr. Hoover on December 18, 1941.

development which could not tactfully be hurried. Some of the faculty could have been spared but they were seldom the ones who yearned to shoulder arms. A resignation which I regretted was that of Ben Gerig, who left to accept a State Department post. As a replacement I was fortunate in enlisting the cooperation of Dr. Edmund H. Stinnes, eldest son of the famous German industrialist Hugo Stinnes, then living at Haverford as a refugee from Nazi rule. This required a lengthy F.B.I. clearance and of course aroused criticism. But it proved one of the happiest possible appointments since Edmund had both a knack with young people and unsurpassed knowledge of world economics and politics. I also engaged William Henry Chamberlain, a thoroughly seasoned journalist and a Haverford alumnus of my own era, to give a weekly lecture on the shifting international scene and myself offered a series of eight lectures on the development of American foreign policy. These were eventually developed into a short book on *The Foreign Policy of the United States*, published by Alfred A. Knopf in 1951.

So, before the country had been six months at war, Haverford's president was endeavoring to chart its course for the very troublesome postwar period which my dominant pessimism foresaw. All aspects of government, I knew, would be more important than ever before. Consequently there should be more direct training for governmental participation by the type of men that Haverford nurtured. My friend Samuel Harrell, of Indianapolis, headed a small Foundation for Education in American Citizenship and with its assistance a "Government House" was established in one of the fine old residences on College Lane. Here students interested in Civil Service appointment would be encouraged to live and mingle their ideas. Through my Washington contacts I built up here a specialized library of government reports and, as part of the remodeling, Isabel supervised the provision of a small guest suite for visiting functionaries, an important amenity which the college had heretofore lacked. The president's wife had more time for such activity as the day of Pearl Harbor had coincided with the installation of a competent Negro couple—Elizabeth, a talented cook, and Irving, a perfect houseman. This permitted some return of the hospitality extended by a number of Philadelphia

378

notables, which in turn led to an exaggerated rumor that I was planning to enter Pennsylvania politics. There was some basis for this, since overtures came from influential Republican circles. But my settled intent, if I could hold the helm steady, was to stick it out at Haverford for the duration.

On June 4 and 5, around Midway Atoll, the Japanese navy sustained its first serious setback at American hands. This gave a brighter tone to the Haverford commencement, held in pleasantly normal manner on June 6. Dr. Studebaker came up from Washington to give the address. He delighted me by saying that while some feared the government would take over the colleges, much of his time, as Commissioner of Education, was spent in fending off college presidents who hoped that he would do exactly that. Haverford, he said helpfully, was a notable exception to that rule and he pointed to two of the new graduates, who were going to Afghanistan to teach in a college at Kabul, as illustrations of what imaginative service could do privately in the general interest. This reference was made at my request, as I wanted some realization of the effort involved in getting these overseas appointments for two conscientious objectors. Far beyond their draft boards, the aid of the State Department had been enlisted as well as that of Munir Erteguin, the Turkish Ambassador to whom the Afghans then gave decision in all issues with even a remotely political bearing. But this was time well spent. From then until his untimely death Erteguin constantly advised me as to Russian plans and policies, a subject on which this brilliant Turk invariably proved well informed.

Right after the Haverford graduation the second Morley daughter, Christina, completed her work at nearby Baldwin School, whence she would proceed to Vassar. Brother Chris graciously gave the commencement talk for Teeny's class. Frank was about to start working in Washington, at least four days a week, as a public representative on War Labor Board panels mediating industrial disputes. He was still a high executive at Harcourt, Brace but more or less on leave from the publishing house for this wartime service. "The strain," he has written, "was to keep going in two intense, and completely separate worlds."

For me, the strain was rather the reverse. My intractable

379

problem was how to unite constructively the recessive values of a Quaker campus and the omnivorous demands of total war.

◀ The first full summer term in Haverford's history opened on June 25, 1942, less than three weeks after the preceding commencement.

In the interval I took a brief vacation at Gibson Island, albeit some very hot days in this interlude had to be spent in Washington, happily only 55 miles distant. Gasoline rationing was beginning to be a problem, though with proper credentials enough could be obtained right through the war. On the island a major distress seemed to be inability to obtain new tennis balls. But at the college food rationing threatened serious difficulties and there was evidence of mismanagement, to say the least, in the steward's department. Fortunately, Bob Johnson amply justified his elevation to the direction of all non-academic and non-athletic services. The loyalty of its minor functionaries to the college was outstanding and together with the Treasurer I set to work on the establishment of a regular pension plan, heretofore lacking, for all employes.

Despite wage increases the close of the fiscal year (August 31) showed a surplus of $5,000, by contrast with $50,000 of deficits accumulated in the three preceding years. No faculty member had been dropped and all participating in the summer term were receiving additional remuneration, approved by the Academic Council. In the coming months, however, serious attrition of the student body could be expected. The war was going badly and Roosevelt's efforts to purge dissenters did not take hold. In the November elections the Republicans gained more than 40 seats in the House and nine in the Senate. Of 137 House members pilloried as "isolationist," 110 were returned, 32 did not compete and only five were defeated. In Quaker circles this was cause for quiet gratification. "In stalemate," I confided to my diary, "lies the best hope of a really constructive peace."

Attempts to develop the civilian activities of the college were only partially successful, although the Board of Managers urged this incessantly. Both at the Pentagon and the War Man-

380

power Commission I soon learned that the campuses were regarded primarily as a source of officer material, with other functions strictly subordinated to this need. A few minor successes, other than those already noted, were achieved. The American Friends Service Committee had organized a unit for relief work in India but could not arrange transportation because of the shipping shortage. I could help in disentangling this through the good offices of Tom Woodward, of the Maritime Commission. In general, however, Quaker concerns were rudely trampled by militaristic pressures. So, without advertisement, I also worked sedulously to get a pre-meteorology army unit assigned to the college. In this I took Morris Leeds into full confidence and was greatly encouraged by getting his cautious approbation, as also that of the College Treasurer, Henry Scattergood.

Again within three weeks of summer-term closing the college began the academic year of 1942–43. As usual, a majority of applicants had been turned down, to insure that the traditional standards should remain high. Even so the total enrollment was far better than I had anticipated, only 15 fewer than the preceding year. But almost every day now the draft called some student and Mac reported that morale was below par.

To improve this he suggested special attention to the football team, which had done well the preceding season and for which prospects were excellent. I agreed the more readily because I admired the game and could see it as a unifying campus force. The junior coach, "Big Bill" Docherty, had enlisted in the Navy but older Roy Randall, a former Brown University star, an "All-American" and a natural leader, was very much on the job. Mac, himself an old gridiron warhorse, helped to advise. Whenever possible I made a point of watching the strenuous practise, continued until the autumnal evenings shrouded the picturesque setting of Walton Field, and of attending the games, enlivened by the somewhat haphazard college band. Cheerleaders, in gay short skirts of scarlet and black, came down from cooperative Bryn Mawr and the alumni responded with great goodwill to the ebullition of college spirit. The result was an unprecedented series of unbroken victories, over larger schools like Hamilton, Hopkins and Wesleyan which usually defeated

381

Haverford. It all culminated in the game with Swarthmore, held there on November 22 and won by Haverford in a cliff-hanging contest, 14 to 13. The winning point was kicked by popular Dee Crabtree, following a touchdown which had tied the score in the final quarter. "Crabtree's Educated Toe Brings Victory" said the newspaper headline that evening. So I could assure the post-game celebration that Haverford neglected no part of the whole man. Actually I believed, and often asserted, that the teamwork emphasized in football was the more important at the Quaker school because of the highly individualistic nature of most of its training. But from that climax on the game languished at the college and eventually was dropped as a competitive sport.

The termination of this season, with its football team unde-feated and untied, was the swansong of the civilian college. On November 11, American troops had landed in force in North Africa. From bases in Australia they were beginning to counter-attack against the Japanese. The training camps were now ready to absorb an unlimited flow of recruits and coinciden-tally the draft age was lowered to call up any who had reached their eighteenth birthday. Pressures were now bearing down. With considerable effort I secured deferment for two remarkable students who were unquestionably prodigies, one in music the other in mathematics. To attempt this on any general scale was both improper and impossible.

So it was time to go to bat for acceptance of the pre-meteorology unit for which I had already made informal appli-cation. The first step was to poll the faculty which, on November 19, voted 29 to three in favor of accepting this military incursion. Half-a-dozen more, on leave for government service, expressed themselves affirmatively by mail. Thus indorsed I formally pre-sented the plan to the Board of Managers, the day before the Swarthmore game, with my considered opinion that under the circumstances acceptance of a non-combatant military unit was a reasonable compromise with tradition, and one necessary to insure continuation of the college as a constructive force. I was careful not to pose the issue as a vote of confidence but knew that the outcome would do much to determine my tenure at the college. If favorable I would be committed to see the plan through; if unfavorable the inevitable contraction would soon divert me to more promising employment.

There was a full discussion, with former president Comfort speaking strongly in opposition while others helpfully stressed the lasting damage done to Quakerism when its representatives withdrew from the colonial legislature rather than have any participation in the French and Indian wars. Morris Leeds presided with complete impartiality and deferred decision for a week, during which members were requested to consult both conscience and intelligence. During the interval two pertinent reports came into circulation. One was that Swarthmore, though in a stronger position than Haverford because coeducational, was nevertheless planning to accept a unit of Navy trainees. The other was that the Pentagon had under consideration acquisition of the neighboring Baldwin School as a military hospital. If so, one might well ask, why not the better-equipped residential college?

On November 27, the Friday after the Swarthmore game, the Board met again, with all its 24 members present and myself, having fully presented the administrative case, a silent but fascinated observer. Customarily, in the Quaker fashion, decisions were unanimous, once the "sense of the meeting" had been obtained. But this time the cleavage ran too deep. After six hours of rather repetitive debate a vote was taken, with 16 favoring acceptance of the army unit, eight opposed. I felt satisfied that the minority would for the most part accept the decision with good grace. But I had mixed feelings, knowing that to operate the college now would be in some respects even more difficult. It indicated that Haverford would survive the war, no matter how protracted, as a solvent and fully functioning institution. But the victory was also a surrender, symbolic of the steady advance of governmental encroachment on independent education. In favoring this I felt that I had, in a sense, betrayed my trust.

December 7, the anniversary of Pearl Harbor, also marked 25 years of wedded life for Isabel and me. There was a quiet family celebration at "Transition," as we called our residence, including Isabel's old father, now past 80 and beyond any serious worries about the state of this world. A few faculty members also attended, notably Brinton H. Stone, son of a well-known Baltimore surgeon, whom I had appointed as my special liaison with the incoming military unit. Daily operation of the normal college could safely be placed under Mac's supervision but in melding this with the army, I needed special assistance, which Brint provided. A primary task was to line up additional teachers, in Math and Physics, which was begun as soon as the essential "Letter of Intent" arrived from the Pentagon. A "War Emergency Council," somewhat larger and more specialized than the superseded Academic Council, was established to clear these appointments and other preparations such as the scheduling, housing and feeding of the recruits. For the first time a non-academic employe, the Superintendent of Services, obtained a commanding voice in faculty discussions. Particularly pleasing to me was the offer of my old undergraduate Math teacher, Professor Albert H. Wilson, to come from retirement to help in any desired way. Dr. Wilson was a leader in Haverford Meeting, a modest, charming and universally respected gentleman. He did a superb job with the recruits and, even more important, popularized the decision to cooperate among those Quakers who harbored some resentment on the subject.

It was not difficult to enlist the additional teachers needed. Those small colleges without any government support were now in financial plight and only too anxious to release their faculty for the duration. At the same time industry as a whole was experiencing difficulties because of the magnitude of the draft. Casualties in the Pacific and North Africa were heavy. The hard-pressed Russians were demanding that European second front which Britain could not initiate without massive American aid. Fear of a separate Russo-German peace was real and under Pentagon pressures Selective Service was drafting men wholesale. The net result was growing dislocation which threatened both the war effort and essential civilian production.

The situation was unexpectedly favorable for me. For months I had been urging various Washington agencies to utilize the small colleges for specialized civilian training. While of little military significance they could be collectively valuable in maintaining a balanced production. I had sharpened the point

384

by a memorandum for the Secretary of Labor showing how Haverford students, with a little coaching, could service the overburdened Employment Exchanges in the important industrial area of Philadelphia. And by accepting a military unit for the college I had demonstrated that my thesis was not merely a dodge to keep Haverford out of any active participation in the war effort.

This had made an impression on Paul V. McNutt, a former Governor of Indiana, High Commissioner to the Philippines and rising Democratic politician who was now War Manpower Commissioner. In early December he asked me to prepare a working paper on my proposal that quotas for civil service training be assigned to selected Liberal Arts colleges excluded from the military program. As McNutt wanted the plan to be quickly effective it would involve temporary residence in Washington, to obtain approval of suggestions from the heads of various agencies that would be involved. It was all rather ironic. If I had been able to put this plan across earlier, Haverford could probably have survived without a military unit. On the other hand, having one gave me much more consideration at the Pentagon, where I was serving as representative of the small colleges on the Advisory Committee for the Army Specialized Training Program. This enabled me to get a modicum of Liberal Arts instruction, especially languages, into the curriculum arranged for the pre-meteorology units. An unexpected development was a request from the American Council on Education to clear any report through that organization, to which I was glad to agree as it would generalize my recommendations. The more synthesis the better, I thought.

The official assignment did not require leave of absence from Haverford, since I would keep my time in Washington at a minimum, return to the campus at least every weekend and be in constant touch with Mac and my secretary, competent Mary Scaife, by telephone. Decentralization of college operations, in marked contrast to the rigid centralization under President Comfort, had been carried far. The War Emergency Council was evoking notable administrative talent from the faculty and Bob Johnson, as Superintendent of Services, had physical preparation for the P-M unit well in hand. MacIntosh was amply capable

385

of keeping the various strings untangled. At the Capital I was assigned quarters, with secretarial help, at the Office of Education, then in the Interior Department. Instead of staying with friends, as had been my wont, I took a room at the Raleigh Hotel where the manager, Curt Schiffeler, was an old acquaintance who gave me preferential treatment. It illustrates the intensity of the period that during this stay in Washington I saw nothing of brother Frank, in his War Labor Board work.

This plunge into the bureaucratic maze of wartime Washington was also confirmation of preconceived skepticism. In the new, burgeoning emergency agencies, like the War Manpower Commission, there was much confusion. Often quite contradictory policies would be set in motion, leading to deadlock at operating levels. In the old-established bureaus, like the Office of Education, there was unimaginative adherence to established protocol and obvious resentment toward the introduction of new procedures. Between the tangle of hypertrophy and the quicksand of inertia, progress was slow. Frustration was not helped by the willingness of prestigious educators, like Conant, Day and Dykstra[7] to have all students of draft age remaining on campus enrolled in a para-military College Reserve Corps. This, it was said, was "desirable for psychological reasons." It certainly was not psychologically desirable at Haverford, the president of which expended much effort in countering the swing toward academic militarization. Returning weary to my hotel room I would turn on the radio and hear a forgotten commentator, named Edwin Hill, denounce the Japanese as "primordial beasts. . .one step removed from lower animals." In my diary for January 12, 1943, I wrote sadly that: "The prospects of a constructive peace grow, to my mind, fainter every day."

By this time my report on "Constructive Utilization of Small College Manpower" was complete. Equally important I had secured Governor McNutt's agreement to give the first accelerated commencement address at Haverford, scheduled for January 30. Some sixty Seniors who would normally have graduated in June, but had attended through the summer to get

7. James B. Conant was then president of Harvard; Edmund E. Day of Cornell; Clarence A. Dykstra of Wisconsin.

386

the necessary credits, would then receive their diplomas. More to the point, I had arranged to ghost the Commissioner's speech and by working over this tactfully could do much to pin him to an unmilitaristic position. This would be a critical occasion since some Board members were obviously baffled by their president's mysterious activities in Washington and the big dinner at "Transition," prior to the evening ceremonies, had to be most carefully planned. There were 16 at table, including members of the Board and senior faculty representatives with their wives. McNutt, a gracious, handsome and intelligent guest, made a great hit with all. The only contretemps was a sudden snowstorm which did not cut the big attendance materially, nor hamper the reception in the college gymnasium afterwards. Politically, McNutt was then a rising star, viewed by many as the next Democratic Presidential nominee, if F.D.R. decided against a fourth term. Undoubtedly more politicians than ever before found their way to the Haverford campus that snowy evening. "It was quaint," I wrote, "to introduce him and then listen to the speech I had so carefully prepared."

The war news improved, with some gains in the South Pacific and the great Russian triumph in capturing most of the German army which for months had been vainly attacking Stalingrad. But I was bothered by the apprehension over this turn of the tide in Russia, as expressed to me confidentially by the Turkish Ambassador, Munir Erteguin. Doubts were not lessened when the Soviet Embassy in Washington provocatively announced that the Baltic States, Esthonia, Latvia and Lithuania, recognized as independent republics by the United States, "are as Russian as California or Alaska are American." Anxieties for the future, however, were displaced by the arrival of Haverford's first army unit, after a slight delay occasioned by the required erection of fire escapes on ancient Barclay Hall, where the entire contingent of 200 was installed. This was not the only overdue physical improvement brought to the college by Uncle Sam. The rather antique kitchens were also thoroughly overhauled and modernized at government expense.

All of the boys in the P-M unit were at least high school graduates and 80 percent had been drafted from various colleges. They included two Haverfordians who were very useful in

387

acclimatizing their fellows, following an assembly in which I welcomed them all as authentic members of the student body. A chief problem, I could see, would be amalgamation of the unit with the civilian students, now reduced by draft inroads to about the same number as the incoming military. To smooth this possible irritant I had endeavored to have a well-known Haverford alumnus who had become an engineer officer, Major Samuel J. Gummere, assigned as Commandant. But this failed and an agreeable but unimpressive warrior, professionally an accountant, arrived in charge. He was soon replaced by Captain William Frey, an Air Force regular who had risen from the ranks and proved an admirable selection. His father had served in the German army in the 1914 war and Bill Frey was of that unemotional professional soldier type with which all but fanatical pacifists can associate to mutual benefit. He was an excellent organizer and soon set up from the unit personnel a first-class little band which played Haverford songs with as much brio as the popular Air Force anthem.

Intercollegiate athletics were now out, but the college coaches organized intra-mural games between the soldiers and civilians, helping to bring a semblance of normal life back to the campus. It was no longer necessary to consider salary curtailments, still less dropping any member of the faculty, and morale improved perceptibly. Mac also got along well with Captain Frey and if I was away consulted with him regularly on all the small difficulties which inevitably arose. An end to the war could be dimly foreseen when, in June, 1943, the Administration proposed the creation of an international relief organization. Now something could be done to press the reconstruction activities which everyone wanted to see established at Haverford. UNRRA—the United Nations Relief and Rehabilitation Administration—was not formally established until November. But with that in anticipation a way was found to utilize the college facilities for purely humanitarian ends.

◀Clarence E. Pickett, executive secretary of the American Friends Service Committee during the Roosevelt years, was a very able man. The efficiently organized humanitarian work of this organization—in city slums, in Appalachia, among Southern sharecroppers and elsewhere—had attracted the attention of Eleanor Roosevelt. It was possible that, through this White House connection, more might be done than I had been able to accomplish in developing wartime civilian public service at Haverford College.

I was doubtful. With F.D.R. breathing fire and brimstone, with Unconditional Surrender continuously emphasized as policy toward all the Axis Powers, it seemed unlikely that Mrs. Roosevelt's goodwill would be effective in the war zones.

Nevertheless, with solvency temporarily assured by the P-M unit, it was doubly appropriate that Haverford should exercise its pacifist persuasion more actively. It had the facilities to house a group enrolled for Relief and Reconstruction and the A.F.S.C. could furnish instruction for volunteers willing to go overseas and confront what would clearly be terrible needs. Some of the college faculty, especially in the so-called social studies, were now underemployed and eager to assist. Rufus Jones was anxious to see this synthesis and Douglas Steere, successor to Rufus as professor of philosophy and religion, was a potential administrator with great energy and ability. Here there was no trouble in getting a green light from the Board of Managers.

So I had several long meetings with Clarence and Douglas to find some formula whereby a volunteer relief organization could be coordinated with the rather vague governmental pronouncements about UNRRA. Theoretically easiest, we agreed, would be organization of a unit for service in China, where the suffering was appalling, the dislocation extreme and the chance of official approval substantial. Clarence would endeavor to enlist White House cooperation while I would do what I could with my State Department friends.

For some time the effort got nowhere. The catch was that the proposed unit obviously had to be in prime physical condition and all such youths were being snapped up by the draft boards. Also, as casualty lists lengthened, growing emotionalism made it increasingly unlikely that those agencies would direct conscientious objectors to any but distinctly unromantic forms of alternative service. "I have long realized," said my journal on July 4, 1943, "that participation in this war would turn us toward totalitarianism and make the volunteer service of the A.F.S.C. and kindred organizations much more difficult than in the last war." I was weary of chasing will-of-the-wisps.

The solution eventually found was to confine the proposal to what had been originally planned as its Women's Auxiliary, limiting it to girls who were willing to travel to devastated areas as they became accessible, lending their skills to whatever could there be accomplished. With few exceptions only college graduates were enrolled and a stiff training program was arranged, not devoid of religious motivation but concentrating on social and economic problems with some historical and linguistic background. The Board of Managers agreed that qualified and successful trainees should receive the Haverford M.A. and in September the new unit got under way, with a score of girls housed in what had been the Language House under the supervision of Señora Asensio, wife of the professor of Spanish. It was the first step toward co-education at the college.

Throughout 1943, the tempo of the fighting had steadily intensified. The German invaders were slowly pushed back in Russia and, following their expulsion from North Africa, in early July came the Allied attack on Sicily. A fortnight later Mussolini resigned in favor of Marshal Badoglio and coincidentally the formation of a "Free Germany Committee" of captured Germans was announced in Moscow. That this was the first formal step toward formation of a Communist Germany was asserted by the Turkish Ambassador, Munir Erteguin, whom I visited while in Washington to attend a specially summoned session of the Advisory Committee for the Army Specialized Training Program. Victory in Europe now began to seem probable and the issue was how the campus units should be revised in the light of this prospect. It was decided to launch Italian and German "Language and Area Study" units, to be intensively trained for the control of liberated districts. Termination of the Pre-Meteorology units was also discussed, although they had run only about half their scheduled course. "They really have very little military significance," said one of the officers, which I was happy to quote later to my Board of Managers.

The R & R project had not yet jelled and if the P-M unit were dissolved, Haverford would be cut back to about one hundred students, nearly all physically unfit or newcomers under 18. Faculty would have to be furloughed *en masse* and the whole humming campus structure largely liquidated. So, as representative of the small colleges, I immediately spoke up vigorously for the Language and Area Study project, emphasizing that with Edmund Stinnes as a faculty member Haverford was unusually well equipped on the German side. While this appointment had been criticized by some of the more fervently patriotic alumni, it was immediately seen at the Pentagon as a significant advantage. For Italy, too, the college was favorably situated since Howard Comfort, professor of classics, had studied, traveled widely and married in that country. I was not unaware that my predecessor, Bill Comfort, would find it difficult to oppose an undertaking in which that uncompromising pacifist's son would play a leading role. And actually there was no open opposition to LAS from the Board. The training would obviously be constructive rather than destructive and would also fit closely with that being designed for the R & R girls.

The Army was moving swiftly now. Even ahead of scheduled time, September 1, the first draftees for LAS began to report to Bill Frey, now promoted to Major, and were quartered by Bob Johnson in the college gymnasium until dormitory accommodations could be arranged. This was just as the third Commencement of the year was being held, with Judge Emory H. Niles, my old friend from Baltimore, speaking with an admirably light touch on "What a World!" At the June Commencement, William Henry Chamberlin, whose first-hand knowledge of Russia made him a great asset, had also spoken well and received an honorary D.Litt. from me. The many uncertainties, that summer of 1943, had been exhausting. So I felt somewhat overwhelmed when informed that the P-M unit would not be terminated prematurely, though comforted by assurance that Major Frey would remain in command of all the military at Haverford, as he had particularly requested.

With so many autonomous units the college more and more assumed the shape and presented the problems of a university in miniature. But difficulties tended to a large extent to resolve themselves as they were squarely confronted. Snatching a few days vacation at Gibson Island, during the summer term, I drafted a reorganization to handle the anticipated load. Howard Teaf, a hard-headed professor of economics with background of practical business experience, should serve as Dean of military students and curriculum coordinator for specialized units. Carl Allendoerfer, a very able mathematician, would be academic director of the P-M unit, charged with justifying the Pentagon decision to keep it in operation. Howard Comfort would direct the Italian and Harry Pfund the German side of the LAS units, with Edmund Stinnes backing them both. Douglas Steere would have charge of the R & R training, again with the active support of Stinnes. The curriculum and activities of the remaining civilian nucleus would be managed by Vice-President MacIntosh and a civilian Dean of his selection. Cooperating closely with Mac and Major Frey and with Brint Stone for general liaison, I would try to hold the diffuse organization together, under the general supervision of the Board of Managers. While unhappy over the obvious militarization of the college, there was partial consolation in the rosy financial picture. The fiscal year, ending August 31, showed a surplus of almost $44,000 in the operating budget, the biggest in Haverford history. With the $5,000 surplus achieved the preceding year this practically wiped out the $50,000 deficit accumulated during the three years before that. At least capital was being safeguarded for the uncertain future. To frugal Quaker business leadership this was important.

Moreover, it had been accomplished without the dismissal of a single teacher and with salary increases at least commensurate with mounting living costs. In consequence, morale was high and the faculty generously adopted a resolution thanking the president for his efforts in their behalf. I, in turn, was greatly encouraged by the ability shown by most of the staff in coping with unprecedented problems. This spirit of cooperation extended to the student body, until they were drawn away into various forms of service. Johnny Whitehead, the first student

392

representative to sit on the president's War Emergency Council, had there shown the tact and insight which a generation later made him chairman of the college Board of Managers. Dick Norton, a bilingual student from Texas, served simultaneously as Instructor in Spanish, filling a vacancy in that department. Others were equally helpful. Roy Randall, as director of athletics, maintained a lively program of organized sports, in which the military students were included. At the other end of the social spectrum the musicologist, Alfred Swan, arranged a delightful series of evening concerts, popular alike with students, faculty and college neighbors. Trying to show my own appreciation, I broadened the membership of my seminar course on "The Development of Political Ideas." It was a sad evening session when news came that Cy Simmons, one of the early members of this lively group, was lost in action in the South Pacific. Casualties were mounting rapidly as 1943 drew to its gloomy close.

What worried me most was the accumulating evidence that a Russian victory, now foreshadowed, would lead immediately to serious friction with the United States. On my frequent trips to Washington I had generally stayed with my friend Clarence B. Hewes, whom I had first met when this retired career diplomat was a Secretary at our Peking Legation. "Buzzy" Hewes was himself a close student of Communist techniques and, as a generous and wealthy host, gathered various Cassandras, such as Alice Longworth, to discuss the problem at his residence on Massachusetts Avenue. Among those generally present was Frank C. Hanighen, an able free-lance journalist[8] with excellent contacts including one high up in G-2, the Military Intelligence branch of the War Department. I soon met this officer, whose identity even now had better not be revealed, and was impressed by the massive evidence of Soviet ambitions, for the domination of both Europe and Asia, which he confidentially "leaked." It corresponded all too closely with what the Turkish Ambassador and all the Balkan diplomats were saying off the record.

Another pessimistic informant was Leopold Wellicz, the Polish Consul-General in New York, who came to Haverford to

---

8. He had also authored *Merchants of Death*, a trenchant indictment of private munitions makers.

tell me that Stalin unquestionably intended to turn Poland into a satellite Communist state. Dr. Wellicz was especially distraught about the Katyn Forest massacres, in which some 15,000 captured Polish officers had been mysteriously butchered. When the mass graves were discovered, Moscow alleged German responsibility but Berlin's retort, believed by Wellicz, was that the Russians had committed the outrage to lessen bourgeois resistance to an eventual Communist takeover. The Polish official wanted me to write up the terrible affair, offering to provide convincing evidence, but at this time, other factors aside, no reputable American publication would have touched such an indictment of our "gallant ally." Nor does truth, once crushed to earth, invariably rise again. The Katyn atrocities were curiously omitted from the Nuremberg indictments and have never received the impartial examination which the pre-Communist Polish government vainly sought.[9]

All of these informants, and others, strongly urged me to "come out of the cloisters" and be more active in preparing public opinion for the future shock which was so evidently accumulating. But the way to do this was not at all clear and I did not think that, at Haverford, I was leading a cloistered life. As Italian resistance crumbled, the Quaker leadership was eager to press for a negotiated peace and Communism would have been much less successful if that could have been achieved. I suggested as much in a broadcast series I was then doing over radio station WCAU in Philadelphia. The policy of Unconditional Surrender, however, was firmly entrenched and was hammering the Germans into an ever more embittered resistance. Any public expression savoring of pacifism had to be restrained. "In such a period," says my journal for September 21, 1943, "it is something real to be able to maintain the constructive contribution of Haverford."

Nevertheless, with the college seemingly secure in every aspect, I was beginning to feel that my duty to it would close with

---

9. In the fourth volume of his "panoramic history of the Second World War" Sir Winston Churchill was carefully non-commital about the Katyn tragedy. "I had heard a lot about it from various sources," he wrote, "but I did not attempt to discuss the facts. 'We have to beat Hitler,' I said, 'and this is no time for quarrels and charges.' " *The Hinge of Fate*, Houghton Mifflin, Boston, 1950, pp. 760–61.

the ending of the war. That would certainly open a new chapter for the institution and could well do the same for me. But it was doubtful that the two would harmonize. "It is not my ambition, nor would it help Haverford," I soliloquized, "for me to sink into old age here." I then recapitulated five possibilities which were currently open:

(1) The Pentagon had offered me a commission, probably as Lieutenant-Colonel, in Military Government. This temporary assignment, which would have sent me first to Italy and then Germany in the Army of Occupation, I had no difficulty in declining. The glamor of the uniform held no appeal. As a volunteer in the First World War I had sought a combat commission and had been rejected. In the second conflict, which I had strongly opposed, high military rank in a desk job was thrust at me. "I doubt whether I could give as much service in any army position as I am giving now," my diary concluded.

(2) Simultaneously I had been suggested as "Chief of Staff" for a Senate Post-War Planning Committee and had been called in by Senator George, the majority leader, to discuss this interesting possibility. It would require at least a six-months leave of absence from the college, at a critical time, and otherwise did not seem an economical arrangement. The Brookings Institution would be the ideal planning agency. But when this choice was made its head, Dr. Harold G. Moulton, asked me to renew my old connection there. This was amusing, since Moulton had been one of those who had advised me to leave the Washington *Post* for Haverford. "The Senate may propose but F.D.R. will dispose," I wrote back. Nevertheless the idea could be tied up with:

(3) An offer from the *Wall Street Journal* to serve as its "diplomatic correspondent" in Washington, writing a couple of signed articles a week and an occasional editorial. The remuneration would not be lavish but could be supplemented by any activity other than competitive journalism. It could be combined, for instance, with writing for the *Saturday Evening Post*, for which I had just completed a careful article on "The Future of Our Colleges." So far as income went, and with four children that was a real factor, there was no doubt that I could make a better living in Washington than at Haverford. My government

compensation there never fully covered even the expenses involved.

(4) Joseph N. Pew, Jr., Vice-President of the Sun Oil Company and a prominent back-stage figure in Republican politics, was also making unmistakable, if imprecise, overtures to me. During the summer of 1943, I was several times invited out to "Rocky Crest," Joe's palatial estate back of the Merion Cricket Club. There we had long discussions on American history and government, in which the oil magnate was very knowledgeable. It was obvious that he was feeling me out with some ulterior end in view, and I responded by working successfully to get Joe interested in the college, which in the past had strangely made no overtures to any of the powerful Pew family.

(5) Meantime Frank Hanighen was urging partnership in launching an outspoken weekly news letter, with special appeal for advocates of a reasonable, non-punitive and lasting peace. He would do the reporting for this if I would direct the critical comment. The idea was attractive. Quakers should be interested in such a publication and it might have a beneficial connection with Haverford. It would permit continuation, without external editing, of the analytical articles which I enjoyed writing but had ceased to produce. A good eighteenth century title for the undertaking, I told Hanighen, would be *Human Events*, after the resounding opening of the Declaration of Independence: "When, in the course of human events, it becomes necessary. . . ."

In none of these directions had I taken any initiative. But inevitably they made me aware that openings were available, if at any time separation from the college should become mutually advantageous. Perhaps paradoxically this strengthened determination to see the institution through its time of troubles. We have been far more successful than most in keeping up a good show of undergraduate normality," I wrote in my journal for October 6, after a reception for the incoming Freshmen. They included the first American Negro ever admitted at Haverford,[10] a few more Jews than had been customary, a couple of

---

10. There had earlier been two Blacks from Jamaica, but as both played cricket, and spoke with a broad English accent, they seemed distinctive.

Chinese lads, a Nisei Japanese and an Argentinian, Roberto Peyro, who was entered with the sponsorship of that country's distinguished Ambassador in Washington, Dr. Espil. With greater heterogeneity the proportion of Quakers still held up.

During the autumn months the war grew ever more brutal, and with it the need for sounding a humanitarian note. At Thanksgiving, Joe Pew unexpectedly volunteered to back *Human Events* for an experimental period of three months and I cleared my editorial cooperation with Morris Leeds, who was much interested in the venture. Hanighen took all the responsibility of management; the most I could do for the time being was to contribute some articles. As it was, in December overwork laid me low with flu, though I was up for Christmas with all four children home. We felt ourselves extraordinarily lucky, at a time when 3,800,000 American boys were overseas.

◀On January 6, 1944, I celebrated my fiftieth birthday. That night I sat long in my quiet study, seeking to discern the future of the college and my relationship thereto.

There were plenty of thought-provoking portents. Victorious Russian troops had just crossed the old Polish frontier and that country's government-in-exile was asking plaintively whether they came "as liberators or as conquerors." Dr. Wellicz, the anti-Communist Polish Consul, had no doubts in the matter and was continuously urging me to write up "the realities" of the situation. President Roosevelt, it was known, had been urged by the Pentagon to obtain a permanent "universal draft law," because of anticipated trouble with Russia if, as and when Germany and Japan succumbed. That was suggested to Congress in the Annual Message a few days later, but in tentative form, as part of a parcel containing more rigorous economic and industrial controls. For the first time it appeared likely that even the physically infirm—the 4F's—would be taken from their studies for such forms of National Service as the draft boards might designate.

More disturbing, because more immediate, was the prospect that Haverford would shortly lose both its military units. After a year of training, the Pre-Meteorology students would graduate in February while the Language and Area Study assignees, I had been informed, would be shipped to Italy in March, following six months of rigorous work on the college campus. There was some assurance, in no way guaranteed, that Haverford might get a small Pre-Medical unit. Here we could not compete with the big universities having regular medical schools and requisite technical equipment. So the chances were that by Spring the college would be reduced to fewer than 100 civilian students, for the most part not yet 18, plus the R & R unit, now increased to 50 girls, which while a stimulating undertaking was scarcely paying its way.

I had tried hard to find a way around the financial problem. I had made an arrangement, with the Immigration and Naturalization Service, for the campus training of newly recruited inspectors, who were being prepared for the rush of immigrants expected after the war. Here the college provided little more than board and lodging but at least it helped to meet overhead. I had also visited the Provost Marshal, with a scheme for accommodating prisoners-of-war, with regular classes in English and other subjects. This idea was taken under advisement at the Pentagon but in its tortuous way through channels was regarded as likely to arouse neighborhood antagonism, which I argued vainly would not be true at Haverford. Nevertheless I had already been criticized locally for adding Dr. Stinnes and a Nisei Japanese physics instructor to the faculty.

A century earlier, after several years of deficit financing, the Board of Managers had closed the college and kept its then one building—Founders' Hall—shuttered until solvency was restored. Rather than run deeply into the red that course could again be recommended. I was strongly opposed to such defeatist action. The endowment was healthy and even if the war should last two years more, as was predicted in the case of Japan, the drain would not be fatal. It would be necessary, however, to cut superfluous staff and otherwise institute stern economies.

One substantial saving, which would lessen the sting for others, would be to take uncompensated leave of absence myself. MacIntosh would be wholly competent to run a holding operation. I knew there would be no difficulty in earning my own living. Coincidentally with removing myself, I could hopefully chop some deadwood out of the faculty. Moreover, *Human Events* was getting under way and it would be pleasurable to devote more time to that promising undertaking. I was convinced of the necessity for realistic reporting on the ominous shaping of the post-war world. And it was not impossible to visualize a connection between the college and this newsletter as I visualized it.

Yet there were flaws to undermine any advantages in an unpaid leave of absence. Worthwhile employment probably would not leave me free to return when the war concluded. And there were several matters which I should personally direct at Haverford during the ensuing months. One was the firm establishment of annual alumni giving, which meant close and continuous personal contact with the various local chapters. Another was preparation of the post-war curriculum, which meant cooperation with my Bryn Mawr and Swarthmore colleagues as well as tactful supervision of the faculty committee already at work in this field. A third necessary development was reform of the honor system, recognizing the maturity of students returning to the campus from overseas.

The picture clarified as the embers died in the fireplace. I should stay at the college, and do my best to maintain its stability, until the war was over. Then a younger man should take the helm, for the assuredly different post-war navigation. After this period of withdrawal I would return to Washington and participate more actively in the coming readjustments. I could not subdue my inclination to write, which was frustrated by current responsibilities. An affirmation by that persuasive Elizabethan divine, Richard Hooker, was in my mind: "Though for no other cause, yet for this: That posterity may know we have not loosely through silence permitted things to pass away as in a dream."

On the heels of introspection came a burst of activity. It was prompted by acceptance, from Major General Joseph Dalton, of an invitation to give the Commencement Address to the nearly 200 members of the Pre-Meteorology unit who, after a year of residence at Haverford, were now about to leave for active service. Each would get an individual parchment certificate for his scholastic work and I made the affair as civilian as possible, with

399

the faculty in robes on the platform and myself bestowing the diplomas as Major Frey presented the candidates. I had also carefully written the speech for General Dalton, a jolly soldier in charge of all college military programs in the Third Service Area and therefore an important friend at court. He was undoubtedly the first officer of such high rank ever to spend a night on the Haverford campus and Isabel had arranged a gala dinner at the house, with selected trustee and alumni representation. Unfortunately the tense atmosphere was too much for Hannah, then the Morleys' pretty but intellectually feeble Irish maid. In the late afternoon she sought the solace of restoratives in her room and by dinner-time was palpably unfit for service at a military, let alone a Quaker, repast. Two students were hastily drafted from the college as replacement and played up manfully.

This cultivation of the General paid off. A few days later, on my next visit to the Pentagon, I learned that the Language and Area Study unit at Haverford might be maintained until June and that, whenever its dissolution, a small Pre-Medical unit would then probably be assigned to us. I attributed the favorable turn to a meeting arranged between General Dalton and Bill Meldrum, the impressive professor of chemistry who for years had steered successive groups of students into the medical profession. The Board of Managers was pleased with this prospect and again the survival of the college, on a strong financial basis, seemed assured. But it had become a cat and mouse procedure, with wartime strain playing the feline role and the president akin to the frantically dodging rodent.

Optimism was further discounted by informal dinner, *en famille*, in Washington that night with Munir Erteguin. Afterwards that scholarly envoy talked to me, alone and confidentially, until past midnight in the study of the Turkish Embassy on Sheridan Circle. Approaching death, I thought afterwards, gave a prophetic quality to the Ambassador's observations, and in my journal I sought to catch their essence: "His attitude has significantly changed. He now regards the collapse of Western Civilization not as something which intelligence could still avert but as a *fait accompli*. In the Moslem world, from Morocco to Mindanao, he finds mistrust and dislike of the Christian nations growing. All these people, he thinks, will accept the

400

westward surge of the Russian Asiatics—the biggest thing of its kind in history since the days of Goths and Vandals."

It seemed deplorable that long-range thought of this character, so vital to the future of the American Republic, could find no reflection in the country's hysterical wartime press. But by the same token this deficiency held promise for the success of *Human Events*, which had made its initial bow with an article on Stalin and Churchill, by William Henry Chamberlin, on February 2. The British Empire would have to pay, that writer concluded, for various earlier observations by Churchill, such as: "Everyone can see how Communism rots the soul of a nation. . . . " I had previously prepared a leaflet saying that the policy of *Human Events* "involves the reporting of facts which newspapers overlook." To this there had been a very encouraging response. After three trial issues there were 502 paid subscriptions with the number increasing at the rate of a hundred a week. All that I could then do for the publication was editorial supervision, leaving the entire production, circulation and promotion in the hands of Hanighen, who at first handled the task almost alone from his small apartment in Washington.

During the first year of *Human Events*, however, I produced one-third of the analytical weekly essays, dropping all other writing to concentrate on these. William Henry Chamberlin wrote nearly as many, with the balance made up either by Frank Hanighen or outside contributors. Herbert Hoover was one of these, Norman Thomas another and Oswald G. Villard, former editor of the *Nation*, a third. In its early years the publication was by no means aggressively conservative. Originally the major objective was to clear the ground for a durable peace, as well illustrated by an article on "The Unification of Europe," by Edmund H. Stinnes, published in the issue of May 31, 1944. This was almost a year before the German military collapse and advanced ideas later developed in both the Marshall Plan and the European Common Market. Other articles of the period continue to stand up in retrospect. Worthy of mention was one I wrote on "The Proposed Security Organization," published October 18, 1944. This pointed out that the State Department draft for the United Nations proposed "a permanent Four-Power military alliance between Great Britain, Russia, the United

401

States and [Nationalist] China," which was not merely a highly improbable outcome but also "makes no provision for checking possible aggression on the part of the four permanent Council members."

In this analysis I argued that it was "a political duty, as well as a political opportunity," for Republican leadership to scrutinize the United Nations plan more closely before the upcoming Presidential election. F.D.R. had decided that, "like a good soldier," he must let himself be drafted for a fourth term and there seemed a good chance that Governor Dewey might defeat him, on a platform promising a non-vindictive peace. In March, having to give a lecture at the University of Kansas, I decided to sample mid-Western sentiment, visiting friends in Chicago and Indianapolis as well as at Lawrence and Topeka. In the Kansas capital I stayed with Alf Landon, but that disillusioned leader, with 1936 fresh in memory, emphasized Roosevelt's enormous advantage as head of an ever-expanding war machine. Former isolationism was tending to swing into imperialistic thinking. Roy Roberts, the well-informed political expert of the Kansas City *Star*, thought that Roosevelt's failing health, if duly reported, might prove a decisive factor in the voting. Nobody anticipated that Wendell Willkie would die before the election but it was surmised that Dewey, as also against Truman in 1948, would lack the force necessary for an uphill fight. I was interested to find both Deane Malott, Chancellor of K.U., and Milton Eisenhower, then president of Kansas State University, as alert as myself to political winds, though Milton did not then suggest that eight years later brother Dwight would reach the White House.

Back at Haverford came the news that the Area and Language Study unit would be transferred to Italy immediately. Coincidentally, however, and as promised, a carefully selected Pre-Medical unit of 50 draftees would arrive for training under Professor Meldrum. This meant that following graduation of the Pre-Meteorology unit, in mid-February, and departure of the ALS boys, in mid-March, a student load of nearly 600 would be reduced by two-thirds. Consequently a first draft of the operating budget, for the fiscal year beginning September 1, showed a deficit of approximately $80,000. About half of this, I figured,

402

would be made up by the Alumni Fund, now at last set up on an "annual giving" basis. The other half must come from small economies by no means easy to accomplish. One that turned out happily was the transfer to Washington of Howard Comfort, who had few students left in classics, to give temporary assistance to Frank Hanighen in running *Human Events*, now able to pay modest remunerations. By such devices a paper balance was achieved, helped by the carryover of an eventual surplus of $1,500 from the then current fiscal year. Gordon Chalmers of Kenyon, and other small-college presidents who had secured only the Pre-Meteorology units, were deeply envious and were not reticent about invoking assistance from me as their nominal representative with the ASTP. I was probably open to criticism for using an inside position for the advantage of my own college. Such "conflict of interest" is always likely when an outsider is temporarily placed on a team organized by monopolistic government.

The relative quiet on the largely demobilized campus was welcome. There was opportunity to work deliberately with the faculty committee planning the post-war curriculum, of which Professor Ralph Sargent was chairman. It could be said of Haverford, prior to the war, that so far as studies went, Asia, Africa and even South America scarcely existed. No courses directly considered the history, the cultures, the politics or the economic problems of these populous areas and the library was deficient in material appropriate to them. Similar deficiencies were apparent at Bryn Mawr and Swarthmore. The presidents of these colleges, at our regular monthly meetings, discussed how freely admitted shortcomings could be cooperatively and economically met. Faculty opinions on the methods used in military training were reviewed.

In general, I argued conservatively—*festine lente*. Existing courses should be carefully reviewed before new ones were added. A large part of the problem, of course, was teaching competence. But underlying that was the identification of permanent values as opposed to mere educational experimentation. Nobody knew what sort of civilization would emerge from the war and, science aside, it seemed more important to glean from the past than to guess at an unpredictable future. Haverford had never

403

practiced vocational education and should be critical of specious arguments about "Life Adjustment." It was not the specialist who adjusted best but rather the generalist who was well grounded in the broad lines of human development.

This approach naturally led me to a re-examination of the purpose of Haverford, which I sought to review in intimate conversations with board and faculty members and with the scattered alumni groups. Basic purpose, I argued with general approval, must not be obscured by the contortions through which the college was passing in the struggle to remain solvent. Like all small colleges, Haverford was a product of the American tradition of local self-government. It could not rival a great university, private or public, in a multiplicity of offerings but could teach a few chosen subjects supremely well. It should be a teaching rather than a research institution, with a superior faculty interested in the students as individuals. They, however, should learn research methods.

To facilitate this there should be less emphasis on textbooks and stereotyped lectures; more on seminar and laboratory instruction. Enrollment should be limited to a number permitting every student to know all his fellows, furthering the comradeship and mutual self-education impossible in the factory environment of the universities. On the other hand, the student body should be sufficiently large and varied to bring each member in contact with types he would confront in later life. These objectives were difficult enough without introducing the complications of co-education, especially because of the developing cooperation with Bryn Mawr, only a mile away. The college should never expect a highly-publicized football team, nor a polished symphony orchestra, but could give both athletes and aesthetes opportunity for distinction in activities where all students, not just a highly proficient few, participated. And to these general characteristics of the better independent schools must be added, in the case of Haverford, its devotion to Quakerism. The separatist spirit of this sturdy sect, and its conviction of the validity of "The Inner Light," must be nurtured if Haverford's peculiar identity, and therefore its basic value to the country as a whole, was to be maintained.

Here problems arose, aside from the effect of that active war

404

participation for which I had been primarily responsible. One was the presumable effect on the Quaker tradition of admitting Negroes and removing the unacknowledged quota on Jewish students. Both seemed desirable reforms. I had already, in connection with the military units, appointed what I believe was Haverford's first Jewish professor. Abe Pepinski was a reliable psychologist, delightful gentleman and adept violinist who immediately added greatly to the informal musical life of the college. And I had agreed with Mac to admit the first American Negro undergraduate, who also adapted well. But I was uneasy because, in a wide experience, I had never met a Jew or Negro convert to Quakerism. I could not visualize groups of black students sitting appreciatively through the essentially introverted and semi-mystical experience of compulsory Meeting. Becoming more cosmopolitan, would not the college also become less Friendly, as had already happened at Bryn Mawr and Swarthmore?

A more immediate problem was the deficiency of instruction in those principles of government on which Quakerism, and all other phenomena of independent thinking, depend for their survival. In my seminar on "The Development of Political Ideas," I could see how little background in this field had been absorbed. The chairman of the history department, an excellent teacher, was an acknowledged authority on the medieval papacy. The associate professor of government had been a successful tax consultant. But few students working under him had realized that American institutions, including their college, were rooted in the division, separation and balance of governmental powers and that the war was steadily forcing an ever greater concentration of these powers in Washington. In such a conflict of diametrically opposing political tendencies, either the institutions or the developing imperialism would eventually have to give way. Meantime, I told my seminar, a form of national schizophrenia was to be expected. It was a lively subject of discussion, pointed up by the drilling on the college campus. But most of the faculty had implicit trust in President Roosevelt and refused to take alarm. Tenure hampered the dropping of an incompetent teacher, and the looming deficit prevented overlapping appointments. To bring the department of government

405

abreast of the times, I wrote pessimistically in my journal, "will take ten years. By then it will be too late for me."

The spring of 1944 was particularly lovely at Haverford. "The most beautiful that I can remember," said Rufus Jones out of his long store of memories. But over it all hung the shadow of impending doom, with the cross-channel invasion of Europe shaping up though the exact date, of course, was shrouded in secrecy. Frank Hanighen reported that very heavy losses were expected, and many more when the time came for attacking the Japanese home islands. This explained a new and disconcerting move to establish an "A-12" corps of reservists for all college boys under 18. They would be put in uniform and given basic training yet not actually drafted or sent overseas before reaching that age. The project was linked to the ASTP on the assumption that the lads could be immediately placed in the specialized training units as they were formally conscripted, thus saving valuable time. It was an outgrowth of the College Reserve Corps earlier favored by several important university presidents, and it seemed to me a subtle way of lowering the draft age without Congressional approval. I fought it, but not too hopefully, at my Pentagon meetings.

Indeed, the pressures of war were now really biting into American traditions. On Easter Sunday, April 9, Secretary of State Hull had broadcast an indictment of those nations— Sweden was particularly in mind—which continued trading with the enemy. This denial of the right to neutrality, which the United States itself had defended so vigorously in the past, seemed to me inadmissible under accepted legal concepts. At the end of April I was scheduled to speak in Washington at the annual dinner of the American Society of International Law and I decided to cross swords with the Secretary of State, knowing that neither of the other speakers—Lord Halifax (the British Ambassador) and Senator Tom Connally—would do so. For my text I chose the famous incident recorded by Thucydides, when the people of Melos resisted efforts by the Athenians to align them as an ally against Sparta. It was the sixteenth year of the Peloponnesian War and the Athenians were letting morality slide in their long frustrated passion for victory. "We see," said the Melians in response to Athenian pressure, "that you are come to be judges in your own cause." For such plain speaking they were promptly liquidated, which was the beginning of the end for the glory that was Greece. "Neither an Athenian, a German, nor an American Century," I concluded, "could be sustained by a nation that judged its own cause, sustaining the verdict by military power alone."

The talk won much commendation and was helpful to *Human Events* when substantially printed there. In spite of war propaganda, many people recognized that the Administration was going far and fast in compromising the destiny of the United States. This was curiously apparent even in Canada, which had defeated conscription for overseas service, when we took our two boys northward for a vacation trip the middle of that September. With brother Chris, his wife and Bill and Marjorie Hall, we had booked for the lovely Saguenay cruise from Montreal, stopping some days in Quebec returning. There the former reporter wanted to be in on the Roosevelt-Churchill-Mackenzie-King discussions. I had prepared myself with credentials and at the closing press conference sat close to the great men, in company with that same sardonic Canadian who years earlier had asked me what I knew about Washington's violations of its own neutrality legislation. Churchill was easily master of the conference. Roosevelt looked worn and vacant, concentrating with obvious difficulty when he tried to answer questions. It was pathetic when the session closed and two stalwart marines plucked F.D.R. from his chair to carry him to the waiting car.

"Why don't you write the real news about this conference?" said my Canadian friend as we walked back along the majestic battlements.

"What is it then?" I asked.

"That you are choosing a dying man to reshape a shattered civilization."

◀June 6, 1944—"D-Day"—had unknowingly been selected for the Bryn Mawr Commencement, with the older Morley daughter one of the graduates. Former president Marion Edwards Park gave the girls a wise and friendly talk, the inheri-

407

tance from Jonathan Edwards well flavored by her personal rich vein of humor. The president of Haverford, in full academic regalia, had tears in his eyes as he watched the girls, slim and pretty and all in spotless white, receive their diplomas. On Normandy beaches their brothers and lovers were at that moment dying in droves, to the presumable end of Communist control over much of Europe. Many other young lives would be thwarted and distorted by the ghastly upheaval. To say that the elimination of Hitler, the elevation of Stalin, would compensate for all this holocaust was just too simple a soporific.

The June Commencement at Haverford had preceded that at Bryn Mawr by three days. Of 104 boys who had entered the college as Freshmen, three months before Pearl Harbor, only eleven remained to graduate. All of these had accelerated to compress the course within three years. In spite of the small number of degree recipients Hugh Gibson, a former career Ambassador, gave a really distinguished speech. Pointing to the inadequacies of the State Department and "the fact that some Presidents have a weakness for personal, private diplomacy," he advocated a permanent Council of National Defense "made up of full-time representatives of all branches of the government [including Congress] having to do with foreign affairs." It was always a satisfaction to me that this suggestion, which found partial fruition in formation of the National Security Council, was first made at Haverford and on July 12 was further promoted in a *Human Events* article by Mr. Gibson. This was followed, a week later, by an analysis entitled "Only Two Great Powers" which asserted that "Russia . . . must be made a subject of close and impartial study in our educational institutions. . . . Communism as a political and economic system must be studied realistically, both in theory and practice, without the animus of prejudice either pro or con."

This recommendation was already being followed in the R & R unit at Haverford, under the leadership of Edmund Stinnes and William Henry Chamberlin. The former especially was becoming a most valuable teacher as the war moved slowly toward German downfall. He was personally acquainted with many anti-Nazi émigrés and brought some of the more distinguished, such as former Chancellor Bruening, to lecture at the

408

college on the latent strength of liberal thought in Germany. To enlarge the audiences the "Main Line Forum" was organized, with the cooperation of Bryn Mawr and nearby Rosemont College. The success of these public meetings, with American as well as foreign speakers all surveying the problems of reconstruction, was largely due to the initiative of Dr. Stinnes. It greatly forwarded my ambition to give the college active community leadership.

Equally helpful in this regard was the assistance of Harry Drinker, of that famous Philadelphia family, in the promotion of matters musical. As a leading lawyer this alumnus was helpful in clearing for the music department rooms heretofore reserved for an uninspiring autograph collection. The renovated quarters served admirably for string quartets, chamber music and other intimate performances. In Professor Swan the college had a musicologist of outstanding talent; in psychologist Abe Pepinsky an amateur of rare proficiency and enthusiasm; in Julius Katchen an undergraduate pianist of concert status; among the army trainees several who were eager and competent to cooperate. Under the dark skies of war, Harry Drinker led in bringing these refreshing elements together. He reminded me that he owed much to the encouragement of my musical mother, who half a century earlier had struggled to promote this field at Haverford.

With the Presidential election coming up, Roosevelt's bid for a fourth term was also a lively campus concern. I made no secret of my own Republican sympathies. Indeed I had written an article, in connection with the Tercentenary of William Penn, demonstrating to my own satisfaction that Penn, if still alive, would be most vigorously opposing Roosevelt. Not all the community liked this, nor approved when I took the chairmanship of an "Independent Citizens' Committee for Dewey and Bricker." It was charged that I was using Haverford as a base for political preferment, as Woodrow Wilson was said to have used Princeton. Yet none could say that I showed other than scrupulous impartiality in sponsoring meetings on the campus. A straw vote showed a strong student majority for Dewey; the faculty two to one for Roosevelt, and the R & R unit favoring F.D.R. very slightly over Norman Thomas, the Socialist candidate.

Desire to do some significant political writing had been growing. It was stimulated not only by the gravity of the times but also by the discovery that even in a college as superior as Haverford so little attention was paid, beyond the Quaker contribution, to the philosophic thought underlying the American political system. Curiously, it was as a Rhodes Scholar at Oxford, not in my own country, that this deeper meaning had come home to me. There I had closely studied the Puritan Revolution and realized how its motivation had shaped American colonial governments. There I had for the first time seen the connection between Cromwell's Instrument of Government and the later Constitution of the United States. I had traced the sequence between Milton's *Areopagitica* and the First Amendment. And I had been impressed by the tremendous audacity of William Penn's assertion, made just a century before the Declaration of Independence, that " . . . we lay a foundation for after ages to understand their liberty as men and Christians, that they may not be brought into bondage but by their own consent; for we put the power in the people."

"The Power in the People!" There was the title of the book I would like to write, stressing the Christian basis of the idea, its revolutionary character, the difficulties in making it operative, and the constant danger that such a fragile and complicated political scheme would collapse under the weight of human failings. In England the "Holy Experiment" had not been sustained. The Stuart Restoration had swept it away. But in America the people had retained the power, as citizens, not subjects. They had used it to build a dominant middle class and to accomplish a material advance unmatched in history. Now that very affluence had made them heedless and forgetful of their heritage. More and more power was being usurped by the Executive, and what was taken for war purposes would be difficult to regain in an uncertain peace. I could think of nothing more important than effort to show how much was hanging precariously in the balance.

I knew that I could write such a book. The gratifying response to *Human Events* was of itself demonstrating a widespread desire to probe the historical significance of current American policies. I could continue this enterprise, giving

410

Frank Hanighen the additional help he needed, and still have ample time for a more fundamental product. But to do this it would be necessary to give up Haverford. Ironically, I had myself argued against the "Publish or Perish" syndrome. The college should concentrate on first-class teaching rather than disconnected research. Moreover, I was exhausted by the constant maneuvering which had been needed to avoid disruption by the war. I could foresee that the post-war period would be filled with new but equally intractable problems. The desk of a college president, no matter how skillfully he might decentralize, would always be crowded with irritating and often inconsequential detail. Unless I could escape that, *The Power in the People* would remain unwritten.

With no concern for these reflections, the election campaign of 1944 drew to a close. Dewey had waged it with dignity and decency, winning 12 States, but the odds against him were too strong. The effective aphorism was not to change horses in mid-stream, forgetting that the worn-out steed might itself succumb to the torrent. In a sense Dewey was running against Truman, as he actually did four years later, but few cared to comment publicly on Roosevelt's obviously failing health. For me a sharper blow than the election was the death, on November 11, of my great and good friend Mahomet Munir Erteguin, the Turkish Ambassador in Washington. Not of our Western civilization, but apart from and above it, he had clearly discerned, and often in our long tête-à-têtes over rich Turkish coffee had warned me, of the symptoms of approaching dissolution. It was a further push to get back into the arena myself.

On December 2, the small Pre-Medical group was graduated, after nine months residence. It was the last of the military units with no prospect, now, of getting any more. Colonel Fitts of ASTP and his petite French wife came up from Washington for the occasion, and there was a very pleasant dinner, with the appropriate faculty present, in the big dining hall. This informal setting was now chosen for most of the graduation exercises closing each semester, since the number of civilians receiving diplomas at any one time had now become so small. As a part of the exercises, at the close of the preceding summer term, I had requested the Student Council to select two undergraduates to discuss the post-war policies of the college. It was my feeling that this viewpoint had not been adequately explored. Interestingly enough, the two elected were a Chinese, David Hsia, who later became a widely-known physician, and a Nisei Japanese named Masamori Kojima. Both spoke excellently, making valuable points.

Among these were the restrictions on student self-government at Haverford. Great care was taken to admit only boys who had given evidence of maturity, yet at the college they were in some respects treated as immature. Student judgment should be given more weight in listing attendance at faculty lectures and at "Collection"—a form of morning chapel. To drink a bottle of beer in a bull session with your buddies was technically prohibited, and immoral purpose seemed to be assumed if an unchaperoned girl visited the dormitories. The college prided itself on inculcating high ethical standards, yet was loath to trust those whom it had in charge. The student spokesmen wondered how this would set with the returning soldiers.

I had also been thinking along these lines. My first effort to enlarge the Honor System, soon after taking office, had been turned down by the Board of Managers. Now I felt that it was time for another try, though it also failed, and together with MacIntosh held discussions with the Student Council to that end. If there was substance in Penn's doctrine of "The Power in the People," I thought, it should begin to be applicable at college age. I believed in the principle that boys, as well as men, should be regarded as innocent of wrong-doing unless and until proved otherwise. I knew that the Student Council was always carefully chosen and therefore proposed that it should supervise liberalized regulations, reporting any violations to the Dean's office with appropriate disciplinary recommendations.

Given the opportunity to talk, the student representatives also criticized both the "memory test" examinations given in some courses and the meticulous grading, down to three percentage points, on the comparative basis of which many of the scholarships were awarded. They argued that there was no uniformity in the faculty marking and that the character of tests in social studies sometimes promoted a tendency to play to professorial prejudice. But I did not see how I could change this system other than by following a quite different testing procedure in my own course on "The Development of Political Ideas." Here I gave the final examination the form of a research paper. On this each student had not only a broad choice of topics but also a month of preparation, with free use of the library facilities and the one proviso a pledge that he would work on his own.

Possibly I made a mistake in listening so attentively to the student leaders. I could have called more faculty meetings for general discussion of all these questions, aside from my close cooperation with the post-war curriculum committee. There was no criticism as long as the teaching staff was fully employed with the military units. But as these folded, with consequent apprehension about salary cuts, irritation loomed. It was not lessened by permission to the college newspaper to compile and distribute student estimates of various courses for the guidance of incoming Freshmen. These were by no means always favorable and precipitated a three-point indictment signed by several teachers. (1) The President had been spending too much time away from the campus. (2) He further made himself inaccessible to faculty consultation. (3) He was using the college as base for the promotion of a personal enterprise, to wit *Human Events*.

To all of these charges there was some substance, but also a reply. (1) It had required long and tedious conferences with civil and military authorities in Washington to keep the college fully operative and solvent. (2) No professor or instructor had ever been refused an interview on any academic matter. Only when the subject was of household concern—domestic roof repairs, a new kitchen stove or a more commodious office—was there insistence that the Superintendent of Services be consulted first. (3) *Human Events* had been promoted from the campus by my secretary but always at my own expense, with the knowledge of the Board and in the belief that its editorial position was in the interest of the college tradition.

Behind this petty argument, I reflected, lay a general problem of considerable significance, which would probably come to a head in the post-war era. In the American college there is no clear-cut chain of command. The faculty is not responsible to its president in the way that he is responsible to his board. While there can be too much executive privilege, there can also be too

413

little. In the latter case the administrator will be buffeted by contradictory criticisms which he is really powerless to resolve. While he will soon spot an incompetent teacher, tenure will likely tie his hands in dealing with the problem. To raise funds it is necessary to cultivate off-campus contacts and risk the charge of absenteeism. If student demands are dismissed it is, to their thinking, dictation; if met it is, to some trustees, encouragement of anarchy. And, in the case of Haverford, there were special cross-currents. Some felt that its president should never have cooperated in the war effort; others resented his Republican leanings and his anticipation that trouble with our Russian ally was to be expected. Some of the faculty wanted a more liberal and cosmopolitan student body; one asked for an interview to say that if he were asked to teach Negroes he would resign. Unfortunately he failed to do so.

This flurry confirmed my developing decision not to remain at Haverford after the close of the war. My job had been to see the college through that storm and this was virtually accomplished. In the changed world that was coming it would be extremely difficult for any college president to reconcile all the discordant elements around him. What was most important for my successor would be a solid financial base, a tightened organization and a renovated physical plant. These could be my memorial.

So, in a long and intimate talk with Morris Leeds and Henry Scattergood, I told these strong supporters that the time for my resignation had come. Both sought to dissuade me and, agreeing that I had been overburdened, urged a year's leave of absence to write the book I had in mind. It was a generous suggestion, discussed at length in subsequent meetings, but I did not believe it would work out. Aside from the book, I wanted to employ my powers more actively in the critical period that would follow the ending of hostilities. *Human Events* was becoming significant and could be made much more so. At the end of a year, I would probably be deep in some project from which I would not want to break. It was not only that I felt blocked at Haverford. As matters were evolving, the role of the small sectarian college would probably become anachronistic. Some such institutions, Haverford among them, would survive because of built-in strength. But it would be a constantly uphill struggle involving changes that many would dislike. I had been asked to bring the college into the mainstream of American thinking and had certainly done so. It was now the turn of somebody else, probably with more dedication, more patience and fewer outside interests, to take over. What I sought was a country of my own.

The older men were sympathetic and understanding. For Morris Leeds especially—as for "Hass" Adams years earlier on the Baltimore *Sun*—I had an almost filial affection. Finally it was decided that nothing would be said about the resignation immediately, so that it would not seem in any way connected with current criticisms. I would remain in active charge until the summer term of 1945, by which time the war, in Europe at least, would almost certainly be over. Instead of a Sabbatical the college would keep me on its payroll throughout the year and on my departure MacIntosh would become acting president. Morris was solicitous about my financial situation, but I believed this would be a problem only if I stayed on at Haverford. During my tenure I had been unable to add appreciably to my meager savings. The money picked up from articles and lecturing had never more than covered uncompensated expenses. I would expect within a year to be earning well above what the college paid me, and so it happened.

The months that followed were among the happiest spent at Haverford, even though shadowed by the closing stages of the war. Except for one final session, the time-consuming meetings at the Pentagon were finished. In the early spring I went down to express appreciation for my appointment with the Army Specialized Training Program, then being terminated. Lunching with two affable generals I was told that the small colleges would again be called upon, if peacetime conscription were adopted because of the Russian threat. The Defense Department had a perfect case with Congress, one of them explained. If the United Nations plan went through, the U.S. would need the draft to make its peace-keeping activity effective. If the project failed, the draft would be necessary because of the absence of peace-keeping machinery. Both generals thought conscription should be at age 18, "when the youngsters can still be molded."

Quakers, as many others, were horrified by the prospect of peacetime conscription and it could materially affect the future of Haverford. To me this seemed not so much an isolated evil as a natural result of the Great Power complex which the war had so rapidly and effectively promoted. That was the hydra which must be fought as a centralized organism, rather than by attacking the various heads which circumstance pushed out. On the campus, however, there were socialistic thinkers who did not reason that way, especially some connected with the American Friends Service Committee. If that agency could do so much good with privately contributed funds, it was argued, then vastly greater benefits could surely be accomplished through the unlimited taxing power of the central government. Few seemed to realize that the end result would be a mutual advancement for both the welfare and the warfare state, like some gigantic Siamese twin. While I felt that I could do something toward making this clear, the *point d'appui* was not Haverford. There I was too bogged down to be philosophically effective. I must have elbow room. Meanwhile I would enjoy the campus quiet, with only about 100 regular students and the remnants of the R & R unit, whose members were now being drawn off for service with UNRRA and other agencies.

President Roosevelt died on April 12. Just a few hours earlier, in New York, Herbert Hoover had told me that he hoped F.D.R. would live long enough to reap where he had sown. I did not feel such understandable personal bitterness but wrote in my journal that: "I shall not be so hypocritical as to pretend that I am surprised, shocked or in any way devastated by the news." But "out of the upheaval should come a restoration of faith in principles, as opposed to faith in a seductive but hollow personality." The problem was what to say at the Memorial Meeting which was obviously requisite. I spoke carefully and I think well, stressing the courage, the personality and the political intuition of Mr. Roosevelt, asking thought and prayer for Truman, emphasizing that the institution is greater than the man and that our loyalties are to it, whether campus, national or religious.

There were many visitors that spring. Former Chancellor Bruening was dreadfully depressed about the future of shattered Germany, fearing the whole country would go Communist unless indefinitely policed and fed by a large American army of occupation. Albert Jay Nock, a great admirer of *Human Events*, came down to visit informally with the students and urged me to develop the news letter into "another *Freeman*," to which he said he would be glad to contribute. The same idea was advanced by Henry Regnery, the lively son of a Chicago sponsor whose support had been enlisted by Frank Hanighen. Young Henry also had a Quaker connection, his wife Eleanor being daughter of Alfred Scattergood, one of Haverford's more active trustees. This interest further promoted the prospects of *Human Events*, which now had a paid circulation of over 2,500, with income sufficient to maintain a small office, pay Hanighen a modest salary and employ Evelyn Freer, who had been my secretary at the Brookings Institution, as a very competent manager. I recalled that when Henry Adams first associated himself with the *North American Review*, that influential publication had only about 300 subscribers. Quality could still be more important than quantity.

In early May Russian tanks broke the last Nazi defenses in Berlin and Hitler committed suicide amid the shambles of that crumbling capital. Coincident with the German surrender, American war casualties to date were announced at 972,654, a grim background for the student assembly at which their president asked the boys for maturity in the chaotic period ahead, reminding them that fighting with Japan still raged. Already I had heard the rumor of an appalling weapon of destruction—the Atomic bomb—which, if used, would end the war both speedily and horribly. The Japanese warlords would be broken. Roosevelt and Hitler were already dead. Churchill was about to be repudiated at the polls. "The power to shape the future would be denied me," the British Premier wrote, with an apparent feeling of affront. The complaint was not wholly true. Powerful leaders had shaped a grim future for their countries, though usually not as they intended or desired. Of the company, Stalin alone had really been successful. Only Soviet Russia had really won the war.

As speaker for what I knew would be my last Commencement at Haverford, I had chosen Norman Thomas, whom I admired for that unflinching moral courage and independence which the college sought to inculcate. I sought to make the

417

ceremony as normal and traditional as possible. In addition to the little group of male graduates, ten girls in the dissolving R & R unit received degrees and there was an honorary D.Sc. for Henry S. Conard, the well-known botanist who had graduated in 1894, the year of my birth. Haverford would never again be the uncomplicated and withdrawn institution of those days, but the values for which it stood could be enduring. This I emphasized in reading the roll of the 22 Haverford men who had been killed in action or died in service. One was my undergraduate roommate, Eugene M. Pharo, who had been stricken en route to Germany with a commission in military government. Three on the list, to whom Joe Jordan on Okinawa would soon be added, should have graduated that very morning. In addition, several who had been on campus with the military units were dead. In no respect had the war left Haverford unscathed.

There was one more official function to fulfill. The Maritime Commission was naming a series of its wartime freighters after famous colleges, and Commissioner Tom Woodward, whose son had entered under me, included Haverford. On June 20 the *Haverford Victory* would be launched in Baltimore and I was invited to choose the sponsor and attend. My selection was daughter Lorna, then a "government girl" in Washington and on the appointed day a merry party assembled for a sumptuous private lunch before the christening ceremony. Several local alumni and personal friends attended, as well as Commissioner and Mrs. Woodward and representatives of the shipyard as free-spending host. Then came the launching, with the young Bryn Mawr graduate poised and dignified in the stellar role. Her father, pressing the button that actually released the ship, prayed that peaceful voyaging would be the lot of *Haverford Victory*. The war was over when she took her first cargo to shattered Europe.

The last summer term of the accelerated program opened the following week, but for this I would be largely a supernumerary. After much discussion the Board had agreed to accept my resignation, "with great regret," as of September 1, no announcement to be made prior to that date. It was understood, however, that the departing president would leave the campus, in charge of MacIntosh, at his volition and I had cancelled our tenant's lease in Washington as of July first. The hectic period of *déménagement* ensued and on July 11 I drove south with Isabel, the younger children being happily if somewhat riotously installed on their own at Gibson Island. "Transition" we had called the ill-designed house at Haverford, for neither of us had expected to grow old there. And transitory, because of the war, it had proved to be. In my journal, on the eve of departure, I wrote: "I think I shall be favorably remembered at Haverford and I believe my contribution here will grow as seen in perspective."

That would be for the future to decide.

◀ Chapter 8

. . . *So the Tree's Inclined*

On the evening of August 14, 1945, I sat with my wife on the familiar terrace at "Millstone," watching the rockets burst over Washington and listening to the confused murmur of jubilation that emanated from the city below. With the blasting of Hiroshima and Nagasaki, Japan had surrendered. The war was over.

That brought relief but no feeling of elation to our minds. The enormous power, technical ability and scientific skill concentrated under the national government had been most convincingly demonstrated. It was reported that in Hiroshima alone 33 schools, and all the children in them, had been incinerated. The blood lust of even the most vindictive was satisfied. The newspapers said cheerfully that Soviet Russia would henceforth be more careful about offending our susceptibilities. But what was apparent in many minds was now "the consciousness of being hopelessly adrift, of having lost contact with those standards by which men really live."

This estimate was published in *Human Events* of August 29, in an article entitled "The Return to Nothingness" which attracted considerable attention. I had been making a study of Thomas Aquinas, that great prophet who in an earlier age had worked for the universal synthesis which the atom bomb fragmented. Especially impressive was the passage in the *Summa*

Theologica concluding: " . . . that which is stable, since it is created from nothing, would return to nothingness were it not sustained by a Governing Hand." The use of that Governing Hand, in human affairs, was now seemingly in abeyance. In place of God fallible men, in the White House and the Kremlin, had assumed direction of mankind's destiny. "We have won the war," I concluded in this article. "Now what is our purpose for the Power we control?"

This was the question which *Human Events* was to ask insistently, in many forms, in the immediate future. Having no other responsibilities, except to my family, I was able to concentrate on development of the venture with the only serious impediment the problem of making an assured living as a free lance. This clearly would require far more than *Human Events* could pay me, even adding compensation for occasional newspaper correspondence. The dilemma was partly resolved when Lawrence Hurley, then editor of *Nation's Business*, unexpectedly asked me to write a column for that monthly magazine, "turning your collar backwards without becoming too clerical for a business audience." This was an attractive challenge and, starting in February, 1946, I continued this contribution without a break for almost a quarter-century. A free rein in my choice of subjects was agreeable and I devoted many of my editorials to the developing problems of postwar public schooling. Often these could be written in the peaceful environment of Gibson Island.

I was now not merely free from direction by others but was also soon to be in receipt of a larger income, discounting inflation, than I had ever received before. This enabled me to build up *Human Events*, which was made into an incorporated enterprise with Henry Regnery, in Chicago, serving as business manager. Henry, who was feeling his way toward independent publishing, arranged the production in book form of an important collection of official Communist documents—*Blueprint for World Conquest*—with explanatory preface by William Henry Chamberlin. Regnery also sponsored an impressive series of *Human Events* pamphlets, starting with an analytical study of the UN Charter—"Humanity Tries Again." This I had first written, in more condensed form, for the American Enterprise Association. As president of Human Events, Inc., I directed these undertakings while Henry managed the marketing role. It should probably have occurred to me that Hanighen, who had carried by far the major burden of the enterprise for its first eighteen months, would resent reduction to secondary status.

Joe Pew, as well as young Regnery and others, had made the development of *Human Events* much easier. The former's instincts were for mass propaganda, directed at the pocketbook nerve, a heritage of the old Republican "full dinner pail" technique. But the magnate, a thoughtful man, had listened sympathetically to my argument that it was more important to impress intellectuals. Get the journalists, the professors, the clergy and the women's leadership on your side, I argued, and the masses will in time follow automatically. Pew, dedicated to free enterprise, feared the centralization of power in the Presidency. To combat this, those who formulated public opinion must first be shown that it was contrary to their personal interests. In direct appeal to the Common Man the White House, with all the glamor and prestige of the highest office, would generally have the inside track. Regardless of economic theory Big Business would be drawn to the support of Big Government by Big Contracts, especially from the now dominant military establishment. Therefore the contrary appeal, as old as that of Cicero, should be clearly and unemotionally made to Reason, on the perhaps optimistic assumption that this would in time trickle down to lower levels. In matters political the average person had no clear-cut opinion but merely adapted those dominant in his environment. The target, therefore, should be the molders of opinion, to whom *Human Events* was directed. It followed Tolstoy's argument (in *War and Peace*) that events and not individuals determine the course of history.

Joe Pew, who was familiar with the great Russian novel, agreed that there might be value in this approach. With others he had already put up seed money to start the little venture. When I returned to Washington he inquired how additional help could best be given. I did not want cash, feeling strongly that *Human Events* could and should make its own way in the competitive market. But there was an agreeable alternative. The Pews already owned the profitable *Farm Journal*, of which Wheeler McMillen was the able editor. Now they were acquiring

422

the moribund *Pathfinder* magazine, with a view to making it over into a sort of small-town *Time*, under Wheeler's general direction. It was Pew's suggestion that I should take over the handling of the foreign news, in which connection Wheeler showed me the offices installed in a big converted residence on M Street, just off Thomas Circle. Since the top floor was not allocated, my counter-suggestion was that *Human Events* should move in there, in return for which both Hanighen and I would serve as consultants. The arrangement was approved and immediately got under way.

Our broadsheet was now well housed and staffed. Both Frank and I had a comfortable operating base and, since *Pathfinder* took the phone bills, it seemed of less moment that publication and promotion were centered in Chicago, under Henry Regnery. A friend of the latter, Alexander Boeker, a former German Rhodes Scholar and anti-Nazi émigré, was installed as a very competent researcher.[1] He also wrote an occasional interpretive article on portents in Germany. Kyoshi Kawakami, who had been released from internment to prepare psychological warfare material, gave well informed comment on conditions in post-war Japan. Constantin Fotitch, now deposed by the Communists as Yugoslav Ambassador, wrote on the critical situation in the Balkans. Carleton Beals, then one of the few available authorities on Latin America, discussed developments on that continent. Henry Beston and Norman Thomas made more philosophical contributions which stand up well. Seeking quality of reasoning rather than propagandist skill, I set myself to obtaining regular correspondence from abroad. Jo' Lalley was brought in to review significant books. In time, I thought mistakenly, *Pathfinder* might justify its name as the thoughtful intellectual weekly demanded by post-war confusion, absorbing *Human Events*. But that, for all his helpfulness, was out of line with Joe Pew's reasoning. He argued that the journal of excellence which I proposed would necessarily have a consuming overhead, while its austere appeal to reason would always hold down circulation.

---

1. On returning to Germany, Boeker rapidly rose high in the diplomatic service of the Bundesrepublik. He would become West German Ambassador to the Vatican.

Human Events, however, could be operated economically, within its modest income. In addition to Boeker, and aside from Hanighen and myself, there were only two regular employes: Evelyn Freer, and Mary Scaife, who had been my secretary on the *Post* and at Haverford. She now continued in that role while Mrs. Freer took over the office management and bookkeeping. I admired both women and at first thought the arrangement ideal. What I did not foresee was that the two would not get along well together. There was obvious jealousy, which showed itself in curious ways. Each, for instance, wanted possession of a letter from the Duke of Windsor who had become a subscriber and wrote us in complimentary fashion. In March, 1947, after nearly 14 years with me, Mary Scaife left to return to the *Post*. Other difficulties followed. Moving the printing and promotion operations to Chicago proved unsatisfactory and these were brought back to Washington, necessitating some staff enlargement.

Somewhat ironically, since both Frank and I had been called "isolationists," our little publication was for some time devoted almost exclusively to foreign affairs. At the close of its second year I wrote: "*Human Events* has continued its attempt to furnish each week an objective, intelligent and discerning examination of some facet in the seemingly kaleidoscopic international picture." I quoted Tolstoy's conviction that "the expression of the will of historical personages in the great majority of cases does not lead to any effect at all." Current illustrations had been Roosevelt's belief that he could influence Russian policy and Churchill's boast that he did not become Prime Minister in order to preside over the liquidation of the British Empire. By contrast, *Human Events* sought to identify those trends which really determine the course of history. If that could be attempted for the stock market, I told Joe Pew, it was certainly not impossible for politics.

But popularity for such an unusual venture was difficult to secure. *Human Events* made many friends, gaining subscribers in nearly every state and overseas. By 1947 the paid circulation, at $10 a year, had risen to nearly 5,000. There, however, it stuck. The little undertaking covered its expenses and paid small salaries to the editors. For me, with three children still dependent, this needed supplement. With speaking engagements and through my *Pathfinder* and *Nation's Business* articles the money was secured—at a cost. The time and energy to press on with *The Power in the People*, which I had started on leaving Haverford, was as lacking in Washington as earlier on the college campus.

In March of 1947, while struggling with this problem, I was invited by the Volker Fund to visit Switzerland, all expenses paid, for the inaugural meeting of an international group of economists and political writers aligned against the rapid drift toward socialism. I doubted whether this could be checked, given the enormous wartime extension of state controls, the popular demand for governmental intervention in one form or another and the developing military preparations against Russia. But it was a decade since I had last been in Europe, and this was an opportunity to renew contacts there. So, on short notice, I boarded a pre-jet plane for London, taking 19 hours for my first trans-Atlantic flight, including three hours for refueling stops at Gander and Shannon. London, where I stopped with old friends Vera Brittain and George Catlin, in their bomb-shaken house on Chelsea Embankment, was dismal and depressing. As a special treat two oak logs, sent parcel post from Scotland, were burned on the drawing room hearth the first evening of my visit. Paris was also bedraggled and dispirited. Switzerland, however, seemed little changed by the war and I derived much from the cosmopolitan meetings on Mont Pélerin, above Vevey on the familiar Lake of Geneva, from which the Mont Pélerin Society took its name. My former mentor William Rappard, from the University of Geneva, gave the welcoming address, emphasizing the importance of this non-governmental Euro-American conjunction of post-war liberal thinking, in the classical sense of "liberal." The moving spirit, elected president, was F. A. Hayek, Austrian-born author of *The Road to Serfdom*, which had been a lively discussion subject in my seminar at Haverford. On the whole the European representatives, including several Germans, seemed more thoughtful about the actual state of the world than the more narrowly trained American economists. Approvingly I noted Hayek's words: "Of course a political philosophy can never be built exclusively on economics, or expressed merely in economic terms. . . . Unless the breach between true liberal and religious convictions can be healed there is no hope for a revival of liberal forces."

As the conference proceeded through ten days of stimulating discussions I concluded that formal economic thinking has a definitely limited value. And the more the economists emphasize mathematical applications, developing "econometrics," the more limited the political utilization of this "dismal science" is likely to be. The outlook of man is simply too emotional to be confined within the tunnel vision of economic reasoning. Thus one may prove convincingly that a minimum wage increases unemployment, or that labor unions cannot actually raise wage rates other than temporarily. But all this will not for a moment discourage the organizer who is promoting class or ethnic solidarity. Most glaringly, war is not going to be abolished by proving that it can only be destructive of accumulated wealth, for victor and vanquished alike. For better or worse the human mind is too complex an instrument, with too many often contradictory interests, to be herded along a straight and narrow factual path. We must go back to Aristotle, I thought. He saw the "political animal" beneath the trappings of economic man.

At this and subsequent meetings of the Mont Pélerin Society I was forced to the conclusion that a large part of the American membership was politically naive. Some even thought that a valiant vanguard of pure economists, dedicated to the preservation of laissez-faire, could capture leadership in the Republican Party and make it an instrument of economic conservatism. When it came my turn I called this vision fanciful. In Europe successful conservatism had always been linked with one or more powerful elements having a privileged position to conserve—a dominant monarch, a landowning aristocracy, an established church, a military caste or a bureaucracy recruited from "the upper class." Representative government, without violent revolution, had become possible only when the directive power of the elite remained essentially unshaken.

In the United States all these preserves had been lacking, at least since the Civil War. When the franchise was limited to property owners it had been possible to have a political party—the Federalists—dedicated to their interests. But this had soon

426

melted away and the tide against privilege would set more strongly with the rising Negro demand for real equality. Nor was it meaningful to say that the GOP was traditionally the party of Free Enterprise, since it was also historically linked to monopolists. Without large-scale corruption business support would mean little at the polls, where the votes of management and substantial stockholders could always be swamped by those of organized labor. Moreover, for as long as business remained competitive, its spokesmen would be divided politically by numerous cross-currents—Free Trade vs. Protective Tariffs was only one illustration. For the United States, therefore, the ideal Presidential candidate would be one whose conservatism was strongly tinged with classical liberalism, such as Senator Robert A. Taft.

So I returned from Switzerland convinced both that *Human Events* should delve more deeply into domestic politics and that it should not align itself with those who argued that the trend toward national socialism could be reversed merely by preaching the virtues of free enterprise, and organizing a political movement behind that standard. What was necessary was a restoration of the faith in balanced government that the Founding Fathers had exhibited so resolutely. As I had explained it to some European friends, the Republicans mistrust democracy and the Democrats no longer believe in the original republic. But between the two we have kept a democratic republic functioning successfully.

Meantime, my manuscript on *The Power in the People* was making headway, though slowly. One of the admirers of *Human Events* was Jasper Crane, a retired executive of the DuPont Company. During the summer of 1946, he had invited me to join a group which planned to meet at Princeton periodically to discuss "a treatise on liberty of sound character and comprehensive scope." Others who would engage in the undertaking would be J. Howard Pew, president of Sun Oil and rather dour older brother of Joe; President Harold W. Dodds of Princeton; Donald J. Cowling, recently retired president of Carleton College; Leonard E. Read, of the Foundation for Economic Education; Ralph Robey, an economist who had earlier written for the Washington *Post*; the Rev. Norman Vincent Peale and Rose

Wilder Lane, a well-known writer who had been communistic in outlook but then reversed to become an almost anarchistic advocate of free enterprise. It was an interesting though strongly conservative group, and I was happy to attend the opening meeting at the Princeton Inn. We dined together, spent the evening in discussion under Jasper's chairmanship and continued through the following morning.

While all agreed that a book "on liberty" was desirable, none had a very clear idea as to its construction. So when I outlined *The Power in the People*, already under way, there was unanimous agreement that it should be the volume sponsored. As this was without prejudice to my individual authorship I welcomed the arrangement. It would provide a helpful impetus to writing, as draft material would have to be ready for criticism whenever the group met. This would force me to re-examine and defend all aspects of my thesis, which was philosophical rather than narrowly political in nature. Especially useful were the always pragmatic comments of Howard Pew and the individualistic enthusiasms of Rose Wilder Lane, though the loquaciousness of the latter perhaps explained why a reputed love affair between her and King Zog of Albania had lapsed in days gone by.

An incidental advantage of the Princeton arrangement was that it covered all my secretarial expenses and thereby helped *Human Events*. During my absence in Europe Frank Hanighen was of course in charge and I could see that he did not altogether welcome the policies I was developing. He was particularly critical of my belief that the Communist conquest of Eastern Europe must now be recognized by Americans as a *fait accompli*. This, in the unanimous opinion of the Germans at Mont Pélerin, was the only alternative to the unthinkable prospect of another major war, this time atomic. Frank thought that *Human Events* should emphasize attacks on what was becoming known as the "soft on Communism" school.

My tendency to juggle too many balls at once was not exhausted and helped to finesse any cleavage with Frank, for whom my feelings were most friendly. After all he had launched the little enterprise and carried most of the burden while I was still at Haverford. So I foresaw his cooperation, and a solution for

428

the financial problems of *Human Events*, in a Sun Oil radio news program in which Joe Pew, in September 1947, quite unexpectedly asked me to participate, presumably with the knowledge of brother Howard. The program was to replace one long handled successfully by Lowell Thomas, on the assumption that tossing the conversational ball among a trio would make it more lively. Ray Henle, a well-known Iowa correspondent stationed in Washington, would be the "anchor man." Ned Brooks, from Ohio, would handle domestic politics and I was asked to take over the foreign field. The undertaking, well promoted as "Three Star Extra," had prime time on NBC—6:45 to 7:00 p.m.—and of this period I had from two to three minutes, on each of the five weekday evenings, to summarize and expound upon world happenings. The task was not difficult, given a certain knack and the generous office assistance provided. Remuneration was absurdly out of proportion to the time involved, and my plan was to work Hanighen in as my alternate, lessening the load on me and the salary charges on *Human Events*. Unfortunately he lacked ability in oral presentation and suffered severely from that affliction known professionally as "mike fright." The upshot left me easily able to confront the serious inflation of 1947, but no nearer accomplishment of my long-range projects.

Our little publication, however, kept slogging along and was well known "on the Hill," where Hanighen picked up many items for his supplement titled "Not Merely Gossip." One morning, early in the summer of 1948, a phone call came from a first-term California Congressman named Richard M. Nixon. He was a member of the controversial House/Un-American Activities Committee and suggested that *Human Events* should cooperate in a probe planned by that body into alleged Communist conspiracy on the part of Alger Hiss, who had left an important post in the State Department to become president of the Carnegie Endowment for World Peace. Because of an overlapping Baltimore background I knew Hiss slightly and had heard his name mentioned as a Communist sympathizer of whom, since the early days of the New Deal, there had been a number in lower echelons of the Administration.

Consequently I accepted Nixon's invitation to call at his office, where he told me confidentially of an indictment against

429

Hiss and others which had been made to Adolf A. Berle, as Security Officer of the State Department, by an ex-Communist named Whittaker Chambers, then a senior editor of *Time* magazine. The Congressman seemed convinced that Hiss was guilty and proposed that we drive to Chambers' farm, near Westminster, Maryland, to interview him and have a look at incriminating evidence which allegedly could be obtained there. I took the matter under advisement and at Isabel's suggestion we had Nixon, with his attractive wife "Pat," to dinner to discuss the matter further. I well recall the buoyancy of the future President, who proved himself very adept at the piano and at pingpong in the basement playroom at Millstone.

For several reasons, however, I decided to keep *Human Events* clear of the suggested arrangement. While I held no brief for Alger Hiss, it seemed to me that the Congressman was planning his attack more for personal advancement than for valid reasons of national security. If Hiss had favored Soviet Russia, and cooperated with its agents, that was no more than had been done by many Roosevelt appointees, from Harry Hopkins down. Russia had been and still nominally was "our gallant ally," and after insuring a Communist victory it seemed silly to bother about the hole-and-corner machinations of a few fellow-travelers as accused by Communist turncoats. More important for *Human Events* was to concentrate on the big issues, such as the dismantling of German industry and the shipment of its war equipment to the East. A personal vendetta was not our role.

As president of *Human Events, Inc.* I made my point, though Frank Hanighen thought me mistaken. He believed that the Hiss case would prove sensational, as indeed it did, and that we could greatly increase our circulation by exploiting it, as also Senator McCarthy's sweeping charges. He was probably right, since after I left it the little publication grew rapidly by climbing aboard the anti-Communist bandwagon. In my opinion that was locking the stable door after the horse was stolen. But my interest was sufficient to bring me to the dramatic Hiss–Chambers confrontation, before the committee hearing of August 25, 1948. Alger Hiss did not emerge happily from his cross-examination there, and Nixon was fully justified in questioning his credibility. Years later, after Watergate, I would be reminded of this. So far as credibility went the wheel then came full cycle.

◐

◀I had seen little that was encouraging, from any overall viewpoint, as I looked out on the world prospect from Washington as the atomic bomb brought World War II to its cataclysmic conclusion. It is summarized in my journal for September 9, 1945. "I fear we are off on a path of power politics and world domination, and I greatly dislike it."

The European order, as it had been precariously maintained since the Congress of Vienna in 1818, was now completely destroyed. Seriously weakened by the Treaty of Versailles the whole structure had succumbed with the collapse of the Central Powers and the triumphant westward surge of Communist control. The Balance of Power carefully maintained by British diplomacy no longer existed. On the contrary, the immense British Empire itself, as well as those of France and Holland, was palpably dissolving. In the Far East, Communism was steadily moving toward the control of mainland China with the influence of Japan broken as a dominant or stabilizing factor. How to adjust these fragments into a new and stable framework was indeed a diplomatic jigsaw.

The capacity for solution clearly did not exist in Washington under President Truman, although many of my friends in the Department of State were deeply concerned as individuals. The general public reaction seemed to me light-hearted and of two equally simplistic types. On the one hand there were those who felt that the newly-organized United Nations could handle the problems, failing to realize that its potential was wholly based on improbable cooperation between the United States and the Soviet Union. The other dominant school of thought maintained that the United States should take over the Pax Britannica from failing English hands, replacing it with the undefined leadership of an "American Century." This was the line most appealing to many conservatives, who seemed shockingly unaware of the distortion of American institutions involved in such a strongly centralizing task.

431

Underlying the political dilemma were doubts as to the ability of the capitalist system to recover from the strains imposed on it by totalitarian warfare. At Haverford, confronting this problem in miniature, I had studied Joseph Schumpeter's *Capitalism, Socialism, and Democracy*. This great Viennese economist even before the war had asked himself: "Can capitalism survive?" concluding " . . . its very success undermines the social institutions which protect it and inevitably creates conditions in which it will not be able to live, and which strongly point to socialism as the heir apparent."[2]

The book is wholly anti-Marxist and rests its thesis on a three-point approach that I found difficult to refute: (1) Capitalism, though seldom operating according to text-book models, has so enormously increased material wealth that the average person living under that system now believes he has a "human right" to a secure and well-remunerated job. (2) Operating through expanding democratic processes this conviction means that the electorate will increasingly demand governmental intervention in behalf of this or that element which has come to consider itself underprivileged. (3) With the profit motive more and more under attack, there is less and less public sympathy with impersonal arguments for laissez-faire. It is no longer defended successfully by business managers who are usually not only lacking in public charisma but also timid under accusations of self-interest. Capitalism is seldom indorsed by the intellectuals, "who wield the power of the spoken and written word" and look more and more to personal incorporation in the planning machinery of the state. The system is similarly no longer supported by the remnants of an aristocracy which has in fact been effectively eliminated by the competitive conditions of capitalism. And it has little or no defense from the masses because they have no understanding of economics or finance and have been drilled by their elected leaders, and by many intellectuals, in the belief that private capitalism is not socially constructive but fundamentally rapacious.

---

2. The translated quotation is taken from a brilliant summary by Prof. Benjamin A. Rogge, delivered at Hillsdale College and reprinted in its *Imprimis*, Vol. III, No. 5, May 1974.

Schumpeter's book came to my attention shortly after Pearl Harbor, and its forceful logic was reinforced by the wartime swing to socialism, along a road already well-paved by New Deal practice. Alliance with the "liberty-loving democracy" of Soviet Russia of course helped, but probably most instrumental was the condemnation of the profit system implied by the shift to centrally organized war production. All were told, and many believed, that with the nation ostensibly endangered, free enterprise should be replaced. Production must be adapted to the demands of the military planners, with profits and wages alike controlled by the ever-willing bureaucracy. It could even be argued that the essence of communism, as an economic system, is itself merely a centrally directed arrangement for price and wage control, rigidly enforced by an all-pervasive police power. This made it logical to applaud Russia as a political ally, since the economic theories dominant in Moscow and Washington were steadily growing more similar.

It was therefore idle to expect that this new condition would be terminated merely by the unconditional surrender of the Axis powers. A generation of young men had been told that free enterprise was a fair-weather luxury. This had been reinforced by training both bombers and commando members to have no respect whatever for private property in enemy hands. The incentive to later looting, arson and vandalism among impressionable youths so indoctrinated was more obvious than remarkable.

My journal for the immediate post-war period is full of gloomy observations to this effect, and I found it difficult to follow the assertion that blame rested primarily on post-war economic instruction in the academies. My own observation was in general to the contrary. In Frank W. Fetter, Haverford had a brilliant teacher whose reputation would later rival that of Milton Friedman or von Mises. The great theoretical advantages of the free market were not ignored by the professors but the extent to which it still existed was properly questioned. The numerous violations of Adam Smith's principles—often by business leaders in such ingenious devices as administrative pricing or export incentives—were stressed. Interference with the free market by governmental subsidies, tariff barriers and even imposed quotas was not ignored. The role of unions in keeping wage increases ahead of productivity gains was perhaps under-emphasized, as was that of government in forcing inflation and sponsoring a minimum wage bound to promote unemployment. On the whole, however, accepted infringement on the theoretical "free market" seemed to me fairly presented by most of the responsible academic economists. I could not fully share the prevalent conservative view that economics should be taught, more rigorously and widely, from a "purely capitalist" viewpoint. Here the fortress had already been partially surrendered, for complex reasons in which the destructive effects of the two World Wars were at least largely responsible. I also found it disturbing when ardent disciples of Ayn Rand argued that economics should be wholly concerned with the accumulation of profits and not at all with questions of social morality. Such an approach, even when clearly reasoned, would simply fail to appeal to youthful idealism.

Consequently, at the frequent Volker Fund and other conservative seminars which I attended in the early post-war years, I generally confined my observations to the field of political government. Here I believed that college instruction was more delinquent than in economics. At Haverford, and inquiry showed the same at many other institutions, one could graduate without understanding the principles of balance and restraint on which this republic was based.

It was insufficiently emphasized that the American system of government is fundamentally dependent on individual and official morality for its operation. "Virtue," in the memorable words of John Adams, "is the *sine qua non* of the republic." Without virtue, in the old Roman sense of civil courage and sincerity, this noble experiment would gradually fall into the hands of the complacent and corrupt, with the former too materialistic and indifferent to restrain the latter. The trend toward really "democratic" government, regarded by most of the Founding Fathers with undisguised apprehension, could only hasten this deterioration and decay. Remove the sense of individual responsibility from American life and the republic would soon lose all its fragile distinction in world history. I labored this theme constantly at conferences and symposia, as well as in *The*

434

Power in the People which was published by Van Nostrand early in 1949 and followed by *Freedom and Federalism*, published by Regnery in 1953. These two books have been my major contribution to American political thought and it pleases me that both are still in print.

Nevertheless, I largely failed in my purpose of sharpening conservative thinking so as to emphasize political rather than economic theory. This I attribute in part to myopia in Republican Party leadership, which was much more interested in re-establishing a material rather than a philosophical status quo. I was already strongly committed to Senator Robert A. Taft as the potential Republican Presidential candidate in 1948. Soon after the war, I visited Ohio, Minnesota, Wisconsin and Kansas, lecturing but also making careful inquiries as to Taft's chances. In this "Middle Border" country they seemed good and in Topeka, where I was again the house guest of buoyant Alf Landon, I was pleased to find that battle-scarred veteran strongly for Bob. But the Ohioan was also much criticized for pacifist and even socialistic tendencies, and the feeble star of Governor Dewey was clearly in the ascendant. At the time few thought that Truman, bogged down in post-war problems, would be elected, and the prospect of victory made many of the GOP chieftains feel that Taft did not possess the requisite popular appeal. When Tom Dewey also failed in this respect the stage was set for Eisenhower, in the attractive guise of military hero.

Joe Pew, as already stated, was a Republican leader of whom I had great hopes. He was enthusiastic about my ambitions for *Human Events* as a vehicle to help restore the vitality of American political thinking and had been most helpful in making it possible for me to return to Washington to further this end. With "Three Star Extra," my *Nation's Business* connection, frequent lectures and other perquisites my income was soon running to more than three times what Haverford had paid me and, in spite of the mounting income tax, I was for the first time beginning to make substantial personal investments. All this was for a time without either benefit or harm to *Human Events*, which was beginning to make its way financially. There was enough surplus to pay both Frank Hanighen and me trifling salaries, though I was giving three-quarters of my time to the little publication while receiving from it less than 10 percent of my total income. This did not disturb me as long as the newsletter seemed to present an enlightened and constructive viewpoint. But a worrisome break was developing between my thinking and that of my partner.

It would ill behoove me, long after his death and at this late date, to present merely my viewpoint on these misunderstandings. Some of the causes, however, were in their way of broad significance. Hanighen thought, correctly, that to achieve financial success we must push our paid circulation well above the 5,000 mark where it had seemed to settle. To do this he wanted to exploit the popular mistrust of Russia which was daily becoming more apparent. I argued that this line could only encourage militarization and further centralization of power in Washington. It would run counter to our agreed purpose of seeking to reanimate the country's original political thought. In the Alger Hiss case Hanighen thought that we were missing a golden opportunity to gain publicity. And our disagreement rose toward crisis with the collapse of the Chiang Kai-shek regime and the easy triumph of Chinese Communism during the spring and summer of 1949.

To Hanighen this was a tocsin for rallying American strength behind the Nationalist government, in its enforced exile on Taiwan. To me the disaster was the logical result of the foreign policy blunders so shrewdly analyzed by General Stilwell, and of the widespread Communist strength which I had myself observed in China almost a quarter-century earlier. With our active assistance, Communism had now become dominant over all the great Eurasian land mass. A lengthy visit to West Germany in 1949, where we were still dismantling factories and giving their machinery to the Russian satellites, assured me that this sad development must be accepted, in Europe as well as Asia. "The moving finger writes and having writ, moves on . . . " Policy now must be defensive—to save the American way at home. So, in the over-simplified jargon of the times, I became Isolationist while Frank Hanighen moved to Interventionism.

The split thus made inevitable came early in 1950. I was president of *Human Events* but when we incorporated had agreed that the stock should be divided evenly between Hanighen, Regnery and myself. This was only fair, since the former had done most of the work during the initial stages and Regnery had provided strong support in the publication's development. But circumstances now demanded that one person should take full command of editorial policy and I called a stockholder meeting to say so. If I were chosen I would drop other work to fulfill the trust. If it were Frank I would resign my office and turn in my stock at cost. This put it up to Regnery who decided against me, telling me later that he did not think I could confine my energies to *Human Events*, while Frank would. Very likely this was a sound judgment. Anyway, in this manner, on February 14, 1950, my connection with the undertaking was terminated, though to give Frank time to reorganize I consented to keep editorial control until that summer. There was a minimum of ill-feeling, considering the fundamental difference. I know that I was happy not to be placed in a position where I would feel forced to edit sharply, or even reject, Frank's copy.

In retrospect I see this episode as symptomatic of that which has come to divide the conservative movement in the United States. Frank and Henry, in their separate ways, moved on to associate with the far Right in the Republican Party. My position remained essentially "Libertarian," though it is with great reluctance that I yield the old terminology of "liberal" to the socialists. I was, and continue to be, strongly opposed to centralization of political power, thinking that this process will eventually destroy our federal republic, if it has not already done so. The vestment of power in HEW is demonstrably bad, but its concentration in the Pentagon and CIA is worse because the authority is often concealed and covertly exercised. Failure to check either extreme means continuous deficit financing and consequent inflation which in time can be fatal to the free enterprise system. As a Federal Reserve Bulletin would later observe, with refreshing candor: "One of the primary benefits of inflation is the revenue it produces for the government."[3] In short: "Taxation without Representation."

To believe that such a nexus of problems can be confronted

3. *Bulletin*, Federal Reserve Bank of St. Louis, Nov. 1976, p. 20.

by preparation for nuclear war with Russia is close to madness. Following Korea the tragedy of our ill-judged intervention in Vietnam was a clear warning. Simply because Communism is such a primitive political system, it flourishes in the ruins caused by war. Opposition to detente therefore reveals the obscurantism of our Far Right, and presumably does not dismay the shrewd men in the Kremlin.

Furthermore, my mind remains doubtful that conservatism can successfully take political form unless there is a unified Establishment to give it focus and rallying point. In the United States, as a federal republic, only the military has ominously been able to claim authority as an elite on a national basis. Business could not do so as long as it remained decentralized, competitive and self-centered. The technicians are divided in political thinking and often, as in Russia, socialistically inclined. So there seems little prospect of building a politically potent foundation here, now that the basis of privilege has been swept away in the countries of its origin. We no longer hear the old slogan *"Noblesse Oblige,"* as contrasted with the popularity of "No Discrimination."

Consequently it is not surprising that the right-wing effort to make the Republican Party a conservative agency has not succeeded, with its leaders failing to make the grade in nation-wide electoral tests. As shown by the number of voters who jump party lines, American politics is still fundamentally mechanistic and not ideological. Within my own memory nobody expected the Democrats of Mississippi and Minnesota to have the same political principles and there was equal differentiation between the Republicans of Pennsylvania and Wisconsin. Presidential elections were only the sum of state elections at first not even held simultaneously. They gave no reliable index to national thinking on philosophic grounds, which is appropriate under a federal constitution.

Because the internal confusion of Republicanism has been so largely the fault of extremists, there is now the greater opportunity for libertarians, who are conservatives disposed to think our problems through rather than to respond emotionally. Required reading is Hayek's brilliant essay on "Why I Am Not a

Conservative,"[4] meaning of course in the narrowly political sense. "The task of the political philosopher," he says there, "can only be to influence public opinion, not to organize people for action." That was the honorable purpose of *Human Events*. Where it failed, others may succeed.

In retrospect, and in all fairness, I should add a couple of considerations to the change-over in *Human Events*, which with my withdrawal quickly became a strongly right-wing publication with greatly increased circulation. I think Hanighen was reasonably annoyed by the relative ease with which I was accumulating a handsome income while holding the newsletter to an unemotional and therefore broadly unattractive course. Among others I had argued this out with Albert J. Nock, whose *Journal of a Superfluous Man* had exerted a strong influence on me. He was a great admirer of *Human Events* in its early stages, seeing it as squarely in the tradition of the old *Freeman*, and had agreed to become a contributor. So Nock's death, early in 1946, was a blow and any substitute of his caliber was hard to find, even with the aid of regular collaborators as competent as Henry Beston or Frank Chodorov.

Furthermore I must question whether I was altogether sincere in my asserted willingness to abandon remunerative income for the sake of *Human Events*. Our large family, and lifestyle in Washington, could not be maintained on a shoestring. Added to this were prospects which were emerging as a result of my close collaboration with Bob Taft. While nothing specific was ever said on the subject he made it evident that, if nominated and elected, he would like to see me as a part of his administration. The post of Assistant Secretary of State in charge of Congressional liaison was mentioned and I could have filled this position adequately. Anyway, in this or any other official assignment, I would need all the financial backlog I was acquiring aside from poor, parsimonious *Human Events*. Henry Regnery was correct in thinking that poverty was wearing my marriage vows there a little threadbare.

---

4. Postscript to *The Constitution of Liberty*, Univ. of Chicago Press, 1960.

Another problem was the load I was carrying. With admirable secretarial assistance I was able to manage the whole involved program. But it meant exhausting and nerve-fraying labor, morning, noon and night, forcing me to become remiss in the many intangible family responsibilities. Isabel was at this time much taken with the idea of acquiring a farm, for eventual retirement, and while I knew myself wholly unfitted for this occupation, the idea of rural life attracted me. We inspected several places deep in Montgomery County, then obtainable at prices which today would seem giveaway. But there was always some deficiency, probably rooted in my negative attitude, and eventually we compromised by purchasing a 12.2 acre woodland property, on Otter Pond and the backside of Gibson Island, where we already had a hilltop summer cottage.

This was obviously a good investment at the price obtainable, offering relatively easy access to Washington with a minimum of agricultural responsibility. I asked our friend, George Englar, a seasoned islander, what it would cost to live there permanently, in modest comfort. "For you and your wife, $10,000 per annum," he replied. Ah well, that was in 1949!

◀Separation from *Human Events* had meant only a temporary contraction of my journalistic activities. Bill Grimes, the able editor of the *Wall Street Journal* had before this suggested that I should join his staff on a full-time basis. Whatever I had thought important to write in my own little publication, he said seductively, could within reason be presented to a much wider audience on that editorial page. It was an attractive offer. There was obvious opportunity, later fully achieved, in Grimes' plan to broaden the firm though narrowly financial basis of the *Journal* by expanding its coverage without lowering established standards for accuracy and objectivity. American newspapers, with a few honorable exceptions, were simply failing to probe beneath the turbulent surface of current events. The *Journal* was equipped to do this, on a national scale, without losing any of the specialized circulation already attained.

The difficulty was that I had no desire whatever to live in

New York. In sharp contrast to my brother Chris, the size and
noise and hustle of this metropolitan monstrosity had always
oppressed me. I visited New York frequently and had many
friends there. I was by no means unaware of its diverse attractions and broad cultural stimulus, but I felt strong distaste for
what seemed to me a heavy varnish of meretricious glamor and
pretense. And we were very comfortable in our Washington
home.

During several long conversations with Grimes an interesting compromise was suggested. *Barron's Weekly* was under the
same control as the *Journal* (the Dow-Jones Company) and Bill
revealed that a part of his plan was to transform this primarily
statistical publication into an American version of the famous
London *Economist*, meaning a critical weekly in the field of
politics as well as finance. With this in mind my friend John
Davenport had been installed as editor, and he would like me, as
was immediately confirmed by John, to open a bureau for *Barron's* in Washington and become its correspondent there. This, I
realized, would give me close contact with the principal administrative officers of the Presidential Establishment. It would
enable me to judge whether the burgeoning bureaucracy had
either the wisdom or the ability to direct a complicated economy,
as the Communists of course believed could be done in the case of
Russia. I had given this question some consideration as assistant to old Angus McSween in the closing stages of World
War I. Now it was possible to give more mature examination.
Currently my contacts with the federal government had been
too much limited to the field of foreign policy. Here was the
chance to get a broader perspective.

I discussed the matter with Mr. Hoover, who fully agreed
that there must be more clear exposition of political thought,
adding that Republic party leadership was deficient in this
respect. Soon, however, he complicated matters for me by
suggesting that I might like to assume directorship of the great
Huntington Library in Pasadena "if you want to get out of it all."
This, however, I did not then desire, and I went on to take
counsel with aged Bernard Baruch, an admirer of the old
Human Events, who thoroughly agreed with my contention that
many of our troubles "trace to the fact that a government estab-

lished on the principle of divided power is trying to do things demanding the utmost concentration of power." He further insisted that "political commitments must be kept in line with the economic and financial resources of the country."

So, after a further talk with Joe Pew, I decided to resign from the Three-Star radio program to accept the *Barron's* offer, even though it would mean what brother Chris called the "catharsis" of a sharp reduction of income. This would certainly be the more tolerable because over one-third of all my earnings were being confiscated by taxes—federal, state and local. More persuasive, however, was my realization that the radio contribution could only be superficial and that my forte was as an expositor and not an entertainer. It is to the latter role, even when disguised, that commentators over the airwaves are customarily doomed, though the reporting is often excellent and for "anchor men" the compensation may well be rich enough to assuage the qualms which I know some often feel.

My work for *Barron's* had barely started, however, and my new office in the National Press Building was not yet selected when, on June 25, 1950, the North Korean Army swarmed across the 38th parallel, captured Seoul and chased the South Korean forces like a rabble down the peninsula. It was asserted that this attack was prompted by an ill-advised statement from Secretary of State Acheson, placing South Korea outside the American defense perimeter. But President Truman responded with characteristic vigor, throwing our troops into action from Japan. Anyway, it could be said that we were acting as an agent of the United Nations in response to a violation of its Charter, so that no declaration of war by Congress was essential for our "police action."

In three separate respects the Korean explosion affected me profoundly. First, though most transient, was the situation of our older son, Tony. He had just reached Germany to spend the summer following his Junior year at Haverford as an "apprentice" on *Die Zeit*, the rising Hamburg weekly of which my good friend, Countess Marion Dönhoff, was then foreign editor. During my long visit to Germany in 1949 I had come to know her well and was myself doing some correspondence for *Die Zeit* until its financial situation could enable the paper to have a staff representative in Washington. The arrangement for Tony, who had natural journalistic ability, was of a reciprocal nature.

Hamburg lies only 18 miles from the zonal border with Communist East Germany. As its citizens were only too well aware, it could be overrun by Russian tanks within an hour. I thought it certain that the Russian leadership had approved the North Korean foray and, having done so, would not let it be blocked by the United States. This seemed the more probable because the Kremlin had blundered in not utilizing the UN Security Council, where its negative vote could have frustrated our ploy, defining the Korean aggression as a violation of the UN Charter. A Russian push to the west, including seizure of Hamburg with helpless Tony included, was quite likely. I used the trans-Atlantic phone to tell him to retreat to England until the dust settled which, with some tart comment on my pusillanimity, he did.

Also disconcerting, as the fighting in Korea intensified, was the question of our building plans on Gibson Island. It was clear that material shortages and restrictions might soon prevent us from constructing the permanent home envisaged there, yet I was neither ready to abandon Washington nor to take the financial plunge involved. In March, 1951, however, we closed with a satisfactory offer for our unheated summer cottage—"Compromise"—and engaged the architect for our eventual retirement home. Tax considerations now made it strongly advisable to sell "Millstone" in Washington, as "Deepwater," on Gibson Island, reached completion. It was a major wrench to abandon the beautiful home we had built on Westmoreland Circle, in 1934, but the new place promised to be equally attractive. Isabel, deprived of her farm, enjoyed the strenuous work involved in clearing the new home site, but to visualize the upkeep of two major establishments was a forbidding prospect. Accordingly, as "Deepwater" was completed, in February, 1952, we put "Millstone" on the market, selling it a month later for approximately what "Deepwater" had cost to build. We retained "Millstone" occupancy until July 1, 1952, when we had arranged to rent the "Foxhole," a quaint, tumbledown Georgetown cottage with pleasant garden on 34th Street.

The third way in which the undeclared Korean War affected

443

my plans was in its psychological effect on John Davenport, the editor of *Barron's*. Overnight, or so it seemed to me, he became super-patriotic and wedded to the formula of American military victory at any price. Probably this should not have surprised me, for I had heard John talk spaciously of "the American century" and was told that his brother, Russell, had coined the phrase. But that harmonized ill with John's acid criticism of the Washington bureaucracy and his anxiety to have me explore its many tangles, which I was happy to do. I was never able to understand how an "enlightened imperialist," as John came to call himself, could simultaneously condemn every governmental encroachment on the prerogative of "free enterprise." Imperialism is necessarily socialistic.

I had hoped to align *Barron's* with the Taft candidacy and to this end invited John to dine with the Senator at "Millstone" and spend an evening in a frank exchange of views. The meeting, on August 27, 1951, started pleasantly enough, for Davenport was always a thorough gentleman and had charming presence. But before the end it ran downhill into disastrous acrimony. Bob Taft was never one to suffer foolishness gladly. When John spoke airily of bringing "the American way" to Asiatics the Senator asked him embarrassing questions. "If you bolster these puppet rulers with American bayonets," Taft inquired, "how will you insure that our subsidies ever get beyond their immediate entourage?" For direct queries of that nature Davenport had no satisfactory answers, which deficiency did nothing to make him like the Senator. When the evening closed I knew that *Barron's* would not support Taft, while the latter openly showed surprise that I was supporting *Barron's*.

Nevertheless, I continued to do so. I knew that I had acquired some reputation for regarding my own opinions as sacrosanct and did not wish to enlarge this criticism. Equally important was my desire to probe our cumbersome administrative machinery, and examine its efficiency, personally, for which the *Barron's* position was an admirable vantage point. My old Oxford friend, Reuben Kelf-Cohen, had startled me by some revelations of what he called "the inchoate character of your bureaucracy." This was a grim indictment because Reuben, as a senior Civil Servant in the British Ministry of Fuel and Power, had come to Washington on an official mission to ascertain how we would supply their mechanized forces, if Britain followed our plea for them to become more deeply involved in Korea. "Those who make policy don't have the requisite information," complained Reuben confidentially, "while those who have the information are not connected with those who make policy." A little later the distinguished French journalist Raymond Aron also agreed with my argument that military strength alone could not establish a successful American Empire.[5] Presidential assurances of American reliability were clearly insufficient for its allies. So I continued my laborious investigations for *Barron's*, more to satisfy my own mind than for any other reason.

Certain definite conclusions emerged from these inquiries, which included many members of Congress as well as administrative officials as disparate as William McChesny Martin, Chairman of the stable Federal Reserve Board, and my old friend Alan Valentine, temporarily director of the very unstable Economic Stabilization Administration. Any attempt to streamline the bureaucracy would meet with opposition from within— from those who thought their jobs or prerogatives were jeopardized. And, less obviously, it would be resented in Congress. There the various committee members with nominal jurisdiction would resent reforms which would seem to threaten their stature. Our system of government therefore seemed to me to be slowly collapsing under the weight of centralized functions which it was not designed to carry. Any attempt at "enlightened imperialism" would only increase the overload. Many times I discussed the subject with Mr. Hoover in New York and always found him in pessimistic agreement. I was grateful to *Barron's* for helping to give me this insight.

However, after establishing its office in the National Press Building, I did not feel in any way wedded to this publication. As my salary was small I had reserved the right to continue some alternative work and, because of the Korean War, was called back to broadcast nightly for Three-Star Extra. Former Senator

---

5. In his later (1974) study of *The Imperial Republic* (Prentice-Hall, Inc.) Aron modified this viewpoint. "There is no way for the American republic to retreat from world responsibility," he wrote.

Al Hawkes, of New Jersey, had dragooned me into writing a report for his "Committee on Political Realignment," in which I concluded that any attempt to reform the Republican party in a "conservative," and the Democratic in a "liberal," image would be impractical. There was no generally accepted understanding, I asserted, of what was meant by those two terms.

More permanent in its implications was a suggestion that I should take over the Washington office of the American Enterprise Association, a New York foundation which had been organized before World War II primarily to analyze pending Congressional legislation and report to its largely business membership on the economic and political implications. While still at Haverford I had done a study on the United Nations for this organization, asserting that under its Charter the grandiose undertaking could not succeed without whole-hearted Russian-American cooperation. As the truth of this became obvious I had been invited to serve on the Advisory Board of AEA, meeting monthly in New York, with such stimulating company as Dean Roscoe Pound of Harvard, Leo Wolman, Edgar Smith of General Motors, Don Cowling, John Van Sickle, and Jim McCarthy, a "broth of a boy" from Notre Dame. In this capacity I had written another pamphlet on American Foreign Policy, conceived at Haverford, which during the summer of 1951 was enlarged into a small book, published by Knopf without any perceptible effect on our diplomacy.

The AEA offer was for a full-time and exacting job which I did not feel able to accept, still less so when it was suggested that I take full direction of the organization. But my *Barron's* connection was growing more tenuous. Differences with Davenport were ironed out by an arrangement whereby I continued to contribute but ceased to be the official Washington correspondent. This meant that I needed another office, which the AEA would supply. So I moved in there, with an agreement to see that the legislative analyses were kept up-to-date and otherwise provide supervisory service. A plus here was that Jo' Tumulty, former secretary of Woodrow Wilson, had his office in the same building, and I spent much time chatting with him about the similarities and differences between the aftermaths of World Wars I and II.

Eventually two young men from the U.S. Chamber of Commerce—Bill Baroody and Glenn Campbell—were selected to operate AEA. They were an unusual team—a Lebanese and a Scotch-Canadian—but very effective in combination. Baroody especially, smooth and suave, concealed great organizing ability beneath a modest exterior. In the course of time, and after changing the name to American Enterprise *Institute*, he improved the financial backing of the operation and greatly developed its publications program.[6] With several moves, each time to more sumptuous quarters in Washington, it became known as the Republican "Think Tank." The Brookings Institution, equally insistent on its political impartiality, had, with Ford Foundation backing, already acquired that soubriquet for the Democrats. Because of my past connection with the Brookings I found this veiled political rivalry amusing, though it strengthened my feeling that much economic research starts from an *idée fixe* and then accumulates evidence to support the preconceived viewpoint.

My relations with the AEI, to use its revised abbreviation, were for a long time close and companionable. "The boys," as I called Baroody and Campbell to myself, took my advice in several respects, notably in broadening the outlook of the Institute to the fields of governmental theory and international relations. I continued as a member of the Advisory Council, now meeting in Washington, and formed a pleasant association with Tom Johnson, the able Director of Research. Twice I flew to California with Baroody to assist in his fund-raising missions. And for a time I edited the organization's pamphlets, easing, for instance, the heavy Germanic phraseology of outstanding contributors like Dr. Gottfried Haberler, of Harvard. I was also able to arrange the transfer of Evelyn Freer, my extremely competent secretary who had come from *Human Events* to work for me at *Barron's*, to the AEI payroll as Comptroller. Without Evelyn's assistance I could never have accomplished, or even attempted, so much. To tell her that I wanted an interview with some major government official was to have the appointment made, often on

---

6. On July 1, 1978, Baroody was succeeded as president of AEI by his son, William J. Baroody, Jr.

the same day. She could copy, and even edit, my draft reports and articles with almost lightning speed.

Much of this, however, was subsequent to the shattering domestic tragedy which hit us on July 5, 1952. I had gone out to the Republican Nominating Convention, in Chicago, to do all that I could in the Taft interest. There, on the evening of my first day, came word that "your son has been killed in an accident." The grim tidings did not say which son, whether Tony, who was in Vienna or thereabouts on a Fulbright Scholarship, or Woody, who had completed his Freshman year at Western Maryland College and had a summer job on a Sun Oil tanker, running between Beaumont, Texas, and Marcus Hook, just below Philadelphia.

It was Woody who, on the completion of his first sea voyage, had holiday leave to spend at his beloved Gibson Island. There he had gone with a group to water ski, in a borrowed speedboat driven by a friend who himself was killed in an automobile accident a few years later. Skylarking around, as told by a nearby fishing party, the speedboat passed too close to a spar buoy marking the channel. It swung in a semi-circle, striking Woody, who was sitting on the stern with a girl, on the back of the head. He was knocked unconscious into 20 feet of water and half an hour passed before the body could be surfaced. The end was ironic, because he was an expert and powerful swimmer.

I flew back to Washington immediately and then taxied to Gibson Island in the early morning, finding Isabel heartbroken by the disaster and inclined to blame herself for letting the boy go on an expedition of which she had known very little. I pointed out that at nearly 20 years of age he could no longer be treated as a child, and that it was just as logical to blame me, for playing politics when I could better have spent the holiday as a responsible father at home. But such personal recriminations availed nothing and with the aid of our two daughters we had to try and put the shattered pattern together, facing as best we could the sense of irreparable loss which would always tug at our heartstrings. It was some comfort to ascertain, from the flood of condolences we received, how many of our friends had been forced to face up to comparable disasters.

One effect, perhaps paradoxical, was to make both of us

more anxious to settle permanently at Gibson Island. Here Woody had always been happy. Here he had assisted in construction of the year-round home which had been finished only shortly before his death. Here he had worked valiantly in clearing the woods where later, under a beautiful dogwood tree, we would inter his ashes. He had thoroughly approved "Deepwater" and his presence there seemed to linger for both of us, even though we would no longer hear the merry chant from his favorite poet, A. E. Housman: "Say, lad, is there nought to do?"

This fatality, together with the collapse of the Taft candidacy before the Eisenhower blitz, affected me deeply. There was no longer reason to remain in Washington in anticipation of a government position. There was the more reason to retire to Gibson Island, cooperate in working the land with my equally bereaved wife and reconsider the meaning of my life, if any. I had achieved "a country of my own." But I had also shown myself indifferent to organizational cooperation. I felt about equally alienated from the Republican swing toward imperialism, soon to be dramatized by the ghastly tragedy of Vietnam, and in the Democratic acceptance of centralized power, from which some good Senatorial friends, like Bill Fulbright, Harry Byrd, Sr. and Mike Mansfield, were outspokenly immune.

I was inclined to attempt a book on the U.S. Senate, as the last stronghold of our traditional political thinking, but was disturbed by the evidence of local corruption in state governments, not least that of my own state of Maryland. Republican Governor Theodore R. McKeldin, whom I had endeavored to align for Bob Taft, urged me to get into Maryland politics. While I told him that my role was that of critic, not participant, he had some influence in making me wish to resume residence in the so-called "Free State." I felt lonely, with only nominal Republican affiliation and somewhat suspect by leadership in both political camps. Yet I knew, with Aristotle, that I was "a political animal" and I wanted time, in the woods and by the water, to sort my problems out. Also I was cooperating closely in the work of two local educational institutions—Washington College and the new Community College of Anne Arundel county.

Humdrum considerations made immediate abandonment of our Georgetown base impractical. In Washington there were

449

sources of income which it was wise to maintain until my financial reserves seemed solid. Long-range investments had to be made carefully, with the advice of my brokerage friend, Lloyd Fisher. And there were many attractions—the theater, concerts, the Literary Society, stimulating associates like Huntington Cairns and the informal salons conducted by two *grandes dames* (Edith Hamilton and Alice Longworth)—with which I did not wish to break "just to vegetate" as I told Isabel. In fact it was nearly six years after Woody's death before we finally left the capital.

In the spring of 1953 the United States Information Agency invited me to make an extensive study of the "America Houses" established throughout Western Germany, reporting critically on their operation and management to Ambassador Conant in Bonn. This I accepted, thinking it would be good for both Isabel and me to be far away from Gibson Island on the first anniversary of our boy's death. Moreover, while I had revisited Europe in 1947 and 1949, it would be my wife's first trip there since our return from Geneva in 1931. We rented "Deepwater" and had a thoroughly successful four months' stay, mostly in Germany but with a preliminary stop in England and later a two-weeks' break to visit Edmund and Marga Stinnes in their beautiful Ascona home overlooking Lake Maggiore; then to attend the annual Mount Pélerin conference meeting at Seelisberg, near Luzerne. Here I became better acquainted with "Fritz" Hayek, whose luminous and philosophic mind seemed to me to rise far above the narrowly economic thinking of most of the American contingent. And I also had good talks with Ludwig Erhardt, as Minister of Economics a principal architect of West Germany's remarkable recovery.

With a State Department car and chauffeur at our disposal we traveled to some 20 West German cities where "America Houses" were in operation, including West Berlin, to which I went alone, leaving Isabel with friends in Munich. A bonus was three days of the Wagner Festival in Bayreuth where we were fortunate in meeting our Hungarian friend, Eugene Havas, a music lover to his fingertips, and going with him to the famous *Euler*, where Wagner's sons and members of the company were entertaining. I was the happier for this opportunity because on their honeymoon, in 1889, my mother and father had visited Bayreuth and had met Frau Wagner (Liszt's daughter), then still very much alive.

My trip to Berlin, in a different way, was also very interesting. Twice I went over to the East Zone, on long and lonely visits, wandering around to note changes since we had resided in that area shortly after World War I. My impressions of Communist control were less lugubrious than those of some American reporters and in an article for *Nation's Business* I mentioned that while there were queues at food stalls in the great Alexander Platz market, there were also crowds making purchases in the big section offering flowers and potted plants. By interesting coincidence, when this article appeared in print, I was immediately restored to the invitation list of the Soviet Embassy in Washington.

I had prepared three lectures, one on the U.S. Presidency, one on the Congress and the third entitled "Is There an American Civilization?" This last, viewed doubtfully by my State Department advisors, proved easily the most popular of the trio. Germans had been so lectured on our alleged supremacy in every field that they were delighted to have our "Kultur" called in question, even though my answer was affirmative. Being now quite expert in public speaking I was able to deliver these talks, translated for me into perfect German, as though I did not need my manuscript. In Mannheim, where the small hall was very hot and crowded, this led to an unexpected *dénouement*. Half way through the lecture my glasses became so clouded with perspiration that rapid glances at my paper were fruitless. I removed the glasses, but the type was then equally blurred. Desperately I completed the talk, without benefit of text, in my own adequate but far from proficient German. At the *causerie* afterwards a charming girl asked me if I were very tired. "Impossible in present company," I replied. "I only ask," she said bluntly, "because you started your speech in excellent German and then it suddenly became rather ungrammatical, as it is now!"

On the whole, however, my tour was regarded as successful and most of the suggestions which I made in my report to Dr. Conant were put into effect. Beyond that, on returning to this country the State Department offered me the post of Cultural Attaché at our Vienna Embassy. This was intriguing and I might well have accepted except that we were both anxious to settle at home, after this long and adventurous absence, which incidentally had seen Bob Taft's untimely death. There were several more trips to Europe, ranging from Iceland to the Isles of Greece, as well as a couple of Caribbean cruises. In 1969, after our final European visit, I could say that I had visited every country there except Hungary and Rumania. A long weekend in Leningrad, during a swing around the Baltic, gave us a glimpse of Soviet Russia. Lira, our very lovely Intourist guide, doubtless did something to create a favorable impression. She was evasive in answering some questions but, as earlier in East Berlin, I found nothing to suggest that Communist rule was not a permanency.

Our definitive remove to Gibson Island had been delayed until the early spring of 1958. Most of February, in that year, was devoted to a Chamber of Commerce "Aircade" in which a group from national headquarters, plus myself, flew nearly 10,000 miles in a chartered DC 3, criss-cross the continent. The itinerary was Washington-Boston-New York-Cleveland-Chicago-Milwaukee-Omaha-Denver-Boise-Portland (Oregon)-Bakersfield-Las Vegas-Phoenix-Long Beach-El Paso-New Orleans-Jacksonville-Charlotte-Washington, with speeches and conferences called by the local chambers at almost every stop. Rivaling my European record I had now been in every state except Alaska and South Dakota. Under the able leadership of Arch Booth the "Aircade" was a fascinating though sometimes bumpy tour. It gave me a strong impression of the geographical diversity of this continental nation and consequently the essential case for its federal structure. As some English stateman put it: "You cannot legislate simultaneously for Hottentots and Eskimos." And my many conversations with local leaders also convinced me that business alone would never produce the elite demanded by a unified conservative movement. The commercial element was too divided by differing parochial interests and by the competitive instinct happily inseparable from the free enterprise system.

At the end of March, 1958, following a snowy farewell party

452

at our second Georgetown holdout, we removed our goods and chattels there to "Deepwater" where we have been, as I write, consolidated for over 20 years. It was a wise move, giving us what my friend Dos Passos used to call "Elbow Room" yet not divorcing us from the wider, though sharply diverging, social circles of Washington, Baltimore and Annapolis. Gibson Island provides a very pleasant seclusion, of which I later drew a somewhat distorted picture in a science-fiction fantasy entitled *Gumption Island*. Faithful Ella Boone has greatly helped to make this comfortable retirement possible. Physical indolence has been enforced by a degenerative arthritis induced by the trauma of an automobile accident early in 1957. This gradually forced curtailment of travel, including attendance at the uninhibited Volker Fund conferences arranged by two then young men, Ivan Bierly and Ken Templeton, active in the management of this unique and stimulating foundation. Their viewpoints were diverse but both have encouraged me to probe for meaning in the experiences here chronicled. A Gibson Island discussion group, scathingly called "The Uplift," has also kept argument alive.

In March of 1957 my brother Chris died, after a lingering paralysis which first sadly destroyed his remarkable conversational ability. He was, I thought, about the last of the naturally romantic school of American writers and as such will be remembered. In another vein of composition Isabel was developing a talent for impressionistic painting, using our sun-dappled woodland vistas for that purpose. The unsubsidized "Morley Valley Authority" cleared and dyked a tiny stream bed, constructing miniature waterfalls and planting wildflowers along its banks. Grandchildren and old friends of various nationalities come to enjoy these innocent accomplishments, for swimming in the big pond on which our property borders, or for winter discussions warmed by our inexhaustible supply of firewood. If ever bored, we draw closer together in reading aloud. Hardy and Trollope are favorites but so also is Willa Cather and other native authors sensitive to this country's rich and varied background. Partly from our children we have learned to enjoy a good collection of classical records, and we seldom miss the often excellent English programs on non-commercial television. My wife and I have had the customary assortment of ups and downs but happily celebrated our diamond jubilee in 1977. An old friend phoned from California that she too had been married sixty years, to three successive husbands.

Shadows naturally lengthen as the sun sinks low. Nevertheless it has seemed to me that a more ominous twilight was descending during the early years of my retirement. In the opinion of Chief Justice Vinson there were no longer any absolutes. On that disintegrating assumption all sense of proportion was being lost. National security was defined in terms that meant the loss of individual freedom. "Human rights" were acclaimed without mention of the stern conditions on which such rights depend. Morality declined as its religious basis was derided and removed from education. Like the black clouds of a Chesapeake "line squall" the background grew rapidly darker. Difficult problems were side-stepped or evaded until they burst into painful boils like Vietnam, Watergate or runaway inflation.

Sitting on our point of land, where artifacts show that there was once an Indian encampment, it occurred to me that I was witnessing one of the great transition periods of human history. It has been precipitated by the devastating wars, but more than that seemed to be involved. Many historians, notably Arnold J. Toynbee, had found a sequence in the widespread upheavals when rising European nationalisms replaced the feudalism that had in its turn risen from the ruins of the Roman Empire. Now nationalism itself seemed outmoded, though proud young countries—perhaps especially Americans—would not admit that willingly. Could mankind readjust the many social and political dislocations thoughtfully? Or was a final, super-nationalistic, war the easier, as well as the most comprehensively disastrous, alternative?

I thought of the old Greek legend, telling us that originally Chaos was dominant on earth. Then Chaos fathered Time, under whom Order was slowly developed among mankind. If Time were now displaced, would it not be logical for Chaos again to resume control?

Through a glass darkly, and to the limit of my poor capacities, I pondered this.

◑

◀Long since, in the course of my occasional philosophic browsing, I turned up an ancient assertion that still intrigues me: *Non in tempore sed cum tempore finxit Deus mundum.*

I had thought that Aquinas made this perplexing declaration but have been unable to locate it in his *Summa Theologica.* Possibly it was Augustine who, as Roman civilization collapsed around him, was much concerned with the meaning and significance of time. Who said it, however, is less important than what was said: "God did not fasten the world in time but with time."

Stripped of metaphysical coverage, what does this mean? In the first place, I think, that men can "unfasten" time, but not yet completely nor without remarkable cooperative effort. It means, for instance, that currently you can travel from London to Rome by supersonic plane in just one hour, whereas in the era of Napoleon, as also that of Julius Caesar, this journey took at least a month. It means that in the course of a single morning you can go from mid-winter in New York to mid-summer in Buenos Aires. It even means that you can reach Washington, from London or Paris, an hour or more *before* you start. It does not mean that one makes personal readjustments to the altered environment automatically or intelligently.

As denizens of earth, this epigram also suggests, we are all caught in a stream of currently fast-moving action on a huge stage where the props can be shifted quickly but the setting remains at least relatively permanent in structure and design. Man is more ephemeral than his habitat. Some day this planet will quite conceivably fall into our sun and be consumed. Alternatively, this sun may exhaust its heat leaving earth as lifeless as other satellites in our rather inconsequential solar system. But with such eventualities we need not concern ourselves. Our brief individual lives are played out against what we like to think of as a timeless backdrop. *Non in tempore . . . finxit Deus mundum.*

This setting would seem to justify us in being as heedless of the future as is the case with all the lower animals. Why should we alone seek to escape the network of time? The instinct of self-preservation will usually force exertion to acquire sustenance and shelter. But beyond these requisites, and such fringe benefits as comforts and conveniences, no durable selfish advantage can be obtained by insistent effort. Therefore, when the necessary chores are done, most of us are quite content to "pass the time" in banal amusements. Yet we are careful to call our bridge, or golf, or cocktail parties, "recreation," though usually hard-put to explain just what is recreated.

In spite of many exceptions, however, the fact is that mankind is not content to accept habitual indolence. We know that it is not easy to escape the temporal trap and that the individual's chance of making any real alteration in circumstance, during his short lifetime, is negligible. Yet in a million ways, over millenial years, men and women have been striving to lessen the fetters of their mortality. And in so doing they have demonstrably begun to unfetter the race from the clutch of time, thus modifying the work of God Himself. This can scarcely be unwelcome to the Creator since He gave to us, and to no other earthly creature, ability to accomplish this amazing alteration.

I do not pretend to grasp the full relationship between space and time. But even an ignoramus can see the connection and vaguely understand what is meant by the "time-space continuum." Everyone knows that in long-distance telephoning—even so commonplace a call as New York to San Francisco—allowance for zonal time difference must be made. These cities are "fastened" differently with time. Yet instantaneous communication makes that difference unimportant. So ordinary men, to say nothing of trained astronauts, can fly around the earth, losing or gaining a day in each rapid circuit. As happens in a dream, or fairy tale, neither time nor space is any longer a barrier to communication. This achievement has had more influence on our lives than is readily realized. In our partial escape from the tyranny of space and time we have become more subject to distant yet contemporaneous events which formerly were completely ignored. The consequence is a current human interdependence requiring more than theoretical recognition.

And communication by wire was only an early step in contracting space and thereby lessening controls originally exercized by time. Now it is not only possible for men to reach a designated area of the moon, but also for all to sit at home watching and hearing these explorers operating there. At the speed of light we receive photographic and other radio messages from space ships tearing through the imaginary confines of our solar system. The development of the computer enables us to unlock the mysteries of the universe at an accelerating rate. Science and technology have completely altered the old relationships so that our world is no longer firmly fastened either in or with time. From New York one can now travel to Cape Town, or Hong Kong, more quickly and far more comfortably than to Philadelphia when the Constitution was written. There is every portent that this progression will continue—unless brought to a shattering conclusion by another scientific marvel of our era: the atom bomb.

It is not only the totality of these developments that is staggering, but even more their rapidity. From the dubious vantage point of an octogenarian I can recall a boyhood devoid of the automobile, the airplane, electric lighting, the telephone and of course all later derivations such as TV and above all the computer. I have no competence to describe how these inventions came but I do know how one individual life reacted to their advent, and I have noted the manner in which it adapted to a swiftly changing environment, mental and physical as well as spiritual.

In retrospect, what stands out for my generation is the failure of political wisdom to keep pace with the extension of knowledge. We were certainly "fastened with time" and did not anticipate what the loosening of that bond would imply, for good or evil. Largely because of my interest in politics I became a newspaper reporter and lived a good deal abroad, thereby observing how the winds of change were sweeping over communities different and distant from that of my upbringing. Coupled with some taste for inquiry this broad experience taught me to look for more than proximate causes in the kaleidoscopic shift of human events.

I had been reared in the Victorian tradition, but without inclination toward that semi-feudal form of social stability which Anglo-Saxon predominance sought to impress on a malleable world. The First World War forced realization that this era was ending. The rise of Communism seemed a not unnatural reaction. Together with the collapse of Germany as a so-called Great Power, the upheaval clearly presaged the passing of Western European supremacies. There was no promise in the vain effort to piece the broken fragments together, for fancied Anglo-French advantage, by the unworkable Treaty of Versailles.

What therefore seemed clear to me, as early as 1919, was that ardent nationalism must necessarily impede, and might conceivably destroy, the war-damaged yet essentially international free enterprise system. For capitalism it was of vital importance to escape arbitrary governmental controls, restore monetary stability and resume world trade with the least possible nationalistic impediment. But the tendency was to promote those doctrines of national socialism which Hitler would eventually bring to fullest flower. The dictated peace doomed the well-intended League of Nations and paved the way for a second European war which was, historically, a completion of the first. Here, major participation by the United States served to exaggerate an archaic form of patriotism. The first men on the moon were even ordered to stretch their flag for photography against the barren lunar landscape. By minimizing our state boundaries, the airplane has weakened federalism. Illogically, it has not yet had the same effect on nationalism.

On the contrary, nationalistic exhibitionism, in one form or another, is now apparent almost everywhere. Perhaps it is most rational in the new African nations, where old tribal loyalties are thus subordinated to more effective arrangements. In the more firmly established societies, however, patriotic fervor suggests that people are largely unaware of the political integration made necessary by technological advance. Moreover, the enthronement of nationalistic sentiment has helped to diminish the respect for Higher Authority which was so strongly present, in this country at least, when it declared its independence. Being no longer "fastened with time," Americans are not unnaturally less attached to the principles of government laid down by the Founding Fathers. The latter felt a sense of duty to posterity that has been largely lost.

If this transition has made the state "the divine on earth," as many who never heard of Hegel have come to believe, then loyalty to it will inevitably obscure the worship of any less tangible authority. Thus, the quality of reverence is diminished and it becomes more important to stand, or cheer, or march in unison than to practise as individuals the ancient Christian characteristics of humility, patience, charity, self-denial and modesty. These were the attributes which the old Romans summed up in the word "virtue"—what makes a man worthy of admiration and respect. And when Rome grew corrupt and failed politically, the virtue of the early Church enabled men to build on the imperial ruins. A similar renaissance is overdue today.

But what has been reborn, with the wars of this century, is a disposition toward depravity and violence which in my youth was certainly exceptional. To some extent the current propensity for murder, rape and vandalism may be attributed to the romanticization of "saturation bombing," of espionage and of guerilla warfare. Commando tactics have been made to seem heroic to teen-age gangsters. These vicious and often drug-stimulated outcroppings, however, are also found in carefully-planned bank robberies, kidnappings and airplane hijackings; in venomous racial confrontations and in ostensibly religious vendettas as bitter as any that blood-stained history can recall. Clearly something has happened to dissipate that decent respect for authority which once was inculcated, on the whole successfully, by home and school and church.

What we seem slow to realize is that in losing respect for authority, the capacity for self-government is also lost. As a preferable alternative to anarchy or nihilism, lawless people must, of course, be governed by external force. Today that external force is provided, not very happily, by the State. Where the overburdened police are inadequate, the National Guard or even the regular army has with us been called upon to fill a role not altogether distinct from that of the Cossacks in Czarist Russia. Proponents of "Law and Order," finally, have not infrequently been selective about the laws they would enforce, showing a willingness to cut corners if the assumed prerogatives of those in power are affected. From this partiality, coupled with official ineptitude and worse, has spread that pronounced political cynicism symbolized by the name of Watergate.

That episode has historic significance not only because its ramifications destroyed an Administration but even more because the revelations injured a faith in self-government which had been more strongly nurtured in the United States than in any other nation. We "rest all our political experiments," wrote James Madison in *The Federalist* (No. 39), "on the capacity of mankind for self-government." So when that capacity is in effect denied, by an American President, the effect is the more traumatic on those who, like myself, voted him into office. As Sir Henry Maine emphasized in his classic essays on *Popular Government*, first published in 1855, it was the Constitution of the United States that gave universal repute to the term "republic," signifying "a government resting on a widely extended suffrage." Only the relative political success of this country, Maine continues, could counter "the fact that, whenever government by the Many had been tried, it had ultimately produced monstrous and morbid forms of government by the One, or of government by the Few."[7] Morbid government by the Few is a precise characterization of the technique that Watergate disclosed, fortunately before it had become too deeply entrenched.

An underlying problem, in this distasteful concentration of power, is the desirability—perhaps better the avoidability—of imperial domination by the United States. Since the promulgation of the Monroe Doctrine, American foreign policy has evinced a trend in that direction, even though it demanded a centralization which in the Civil War was opposed to the point of secession. Curiously, Alexander Hamilton was the only one, among the Founding Fathers, who unquestionably anticipated and favored imperial development. To this end he urged that all state governors should be appointed by, and therefore directly subordinate to, "His Majesty, the President of the United States." But this was an exceptional desire during the framing of the Constitution. As Charles Pinckney of South Carolina told the Philadelphia Convention: "We mistake the object of our Government if we hope or wish that it is to make us respectable

---

7. Sir Henry Sumner Maine, *Popular Government*, Henry Holt & Co., New York, 1886, pp. 198 and 202.

abroad. Conquest or superiority among other Powers is not, or ought not ever to be, the object of republican systems."[8]

In 1787, such self-imposed restraint was readily accepted, doubtless because few could foresee the astonishing material growth of the thirteen still uncoordinated former colonies. Recent Presidents, however, have laid great stress on the alleged necessity of American military superiority, using the "adversary" strength of Soviet Russia as argument. Whatever the reality of this threat, it clearly demands continuous centralization of power, as is also the case with para-military organizations like the CIA and F.B.I. This often surreptitious attrition of popular control runs counter to the carefully planned decentralization of our political institutions and in such basic opposition either post-war policies or traditional institutions must give way. So far the latter have surrendered ground, but not without deeply disturbing the harmony of national thinking. Some think that we should intervene to block any sizable Communist penetration anywhere. Others, especially since Vietnam, believe that this simplistic formula can only strengthen the ideology that we oppose.

It is apparent that current political division corresponds very poorly with the cleavage in popular anxieties. Crude terminology, itself reflective of confused thinking, divides election reactions into Conservative and Liberal, the first-named allegedly favoring a dynamic and assertive foreign policy; the second characterized as more passive and defensive in this respect. The former position obviously requires centralization of power; the latter would permit its diffusion and some restoration of the traditional checks and balance. Therefore, with only two major political parties, we would expect one to favor and the other as clearly to oppose centralization—one to support a strong and daring President, the other to favor a Congress able and willing to keep the Executive constantly under control. We do not have that clear-cut division, which shows that our politics are still mechanistic and localized, rather than ideological and national. Unfortunately, this seems to mean diminishing popular interest. In the 1976 Presidential Election, in spite of all the

---

8. James Madison, *Debates In The Federal Convention*, June 25, 1787.

hoopla, barely 50 percent of the eligible voters bothered to go to the polls. This indifference points to a significant change in the nature of American politics. While parties have become national they no longer represent issues fundamental to the Republic.

Currently, both old parties have come to show that they favor dictatorial centralization, though by different approaches. Many Republicans, certainly those of the dominant right wing, favor almost unrestrained military expenditure. The "military-industrial complex" thus created, to use President Eisenhower's telling phrase, is a continuously centralizing force. So is the insistent Democratic demand that every sort of social need be sponsored, liberally financed and supervised from Washington. Most Republicans would willingly economize on Welfare, as would many Democrats on what is euphemistically called Defense. But the log-rolling resulting from this controversy, as shown by the ever-ballooning budget, has meant no serious economy in either field. There is no meaningful philosophic conflict between so-called Conservatives and Liberals, but rather tacit agreement to be equally spendthrift in different ways. Yet one unquestionable economic law is that no nation can continuously outspend income without debauching its currency. There is small consolation in the fact that other nations have let inflation get still more out of hand.

Seeking the fundamental cause of this degeneracy, I conclude that it is at least partially due to a shattering of that time-scheme in which the admittedly imperfect social stability of my youth was framed. Tragically, this breakage was made almost irreparable by the nationalistic hostilities that flamed up just as the need for unemotional international cooperation became imperative. This need is still obscured by the vicarious hostility between capitalistic and communistic thinking, with the former apparently believing that unfettered "free enterprise" can be restored; the latter maintaining that it must be eliminated in favor of the dictatorial power of the State. Both viewpoints are necessarily being modified, by the sheer pressure of human events. We no longer hear the old assertions that communist systems will not work. And we cannot be at all sure that their penetration will be blunted by the crude reaction of military defense. That serves to stimulate, rather than offset, the socialistic trend.

Revision of the time-scheme has had a psychological effect as momentous and chaotic as the derivative political disturbances. Much of our thinking has become thoroughly illogical. If there are no absolute values there can be no such thing as established human rights. Yet a denial of the former by the Supreme Court is followed by an affirmation of the latter by a President. Similar confusion reigns in many fields, with absence of self-control a common characteristic.

Nothing is more admirable than the gallant effort that has been made in the United States to combine two contradictory concepts in a harmonious whole of public education. On the one hand it has been argued that every American child should, *ipso facto*, be entitled to subsidized training comparable to that provided by the more aristocratic schools of Europe. On the other hand it was recognized, by all intelligent schoolmen, that education is an intensely competitive undertaking, in which the competent must be encouraged to advance over the incompetent, regardless of the individual pupil's race, color, creed or social background.

Many are inclined to think that the deterioration in public education was touched off by the Supreme Court decision, of 1954, on racial integration, but this is far from being the case. In World War II, no fewer than 716,000 young Americans were rejected by Selective Service "on grounds of mental deficiency, not mental disease."[9] The insidious theory of "Life Adjustment" as a substitute for disciplined learning was also well entrenched before the decision on *Brown* v. *Board of Education*. Undoubtedly, much of the functional illiteracy among public school pupils was concentrated in the Negro schools, but the misfortune was in trying to force the solution of an educational problem by arbitrary sociological mandate. Broadly speaking, the effect of compulsory integration was for some years not to raise the level of Black education but rather to lower it for Whites.

Education, both public and private, both school and college,

---

9. Mortimer Smith, *The Diminished Mind*, Henry Regnery Co., Chicago, 1954, p. 18.

is still a demoralized area, although there has been obvious recovery since the riotous fifties and sixties. There has been a notable improvement in facilities and teaching has been made a reasonably well-remunerated profession. Music, both appreciation and individual participation, is far better taught than in my youth, as I note when my granddaughter Caroline plays her flute. But certain inescapable problems remain unsolved and indeed largely unconsidered. One is the question of whether a large proportion of the population, increasing with medical progress, governmental paternalism and a loosened moral code, is really educable in any real sense of the word. The number of unemployable drop-outs, the lowering of graduation standards, the senseless student vandalism, argue to the contrary. So, more convincingly, does the disturbing population increase caused by the profligacy of Nature when unrestrained by impediments. In a single watermelon produced in my garden I have counted around 200 robust seeds. If they were all nursed into development, and all their reproductive potential similarly, we would soon be unable to walk without stumbling over the fruit.

The ambition of public education is to accept every human seed that has taken form and train it into acceptable citizenship. But procedures clearly indicate that this can be done only by lowering standards and by providing work which does not require reasoning power, nor even a knowledge of the alphabet or multiplication table according to some "educationists." It is highly improbable that a democracy so adulterated will long endure. A steady increase in centralized direction and discipline is indicated, if only to handle those who are incompetent and cannot be trained otherwise. Vague inspirational reference to "human rights" will never solve the problem, which also tends to involve the intellectual degradation of the more competent.

A part of this problem is its tendency to turn American education, private as well as public, toward a narrow vocationalism which is not acceptable for the people of a free society. As the military are prone to concentrate on the battles that are past, so the vocationalists become bemused by facets of a civilization they often have no ability to assess. It is assumed that as things were so they will, or at least should, be. But if the world is no longer "fixed with time" this could be a very serious

464

mistake. The ability to recognize that which is individually and socially promising, and therefore of permanent concern, could be as essential as mastery of technological processes, whether simple or complex. Of course the latter is important, but far from all-important. Classical education, with strong emphasis on development of the critical faculty, still has its place. And in a country that has ambitions for world leadership it is as necessary as it is with us generally neglected.

From the beginning shrewd observers have warned that nemesis for the republic would lie in unrestricted democracy. That was the attested anxiety of the Founding Fathers and the chief reason for adding a "Bill of Rights" designed to safeguard individual liberty from governmental encroachment, no matter how well-intentioned. The pages of de Tocqueville are rife with references to "the mutability and the ignorance of democracy" as the Achilles heel of the American experiment. Sir Henry Maine, in the enduring study of *Popular Government* already mentioned, says in his Preface that American political success "appears to me to have arisen rather from skillfully applying the curb to popular impulses than from giving them the rein."

Where the "American way" has failed, more than in any other respect, is in the fallacious belief that ideals springing from our distinctive background can be enforced on other peoples. To this end many catch phrases, as meaningless as "manifest destiny," have been elevated to the level of maxims. Many wise warnings, none more completely than that of George Washington "to guard against the imposture of pretended patriotism,"[10] have been completely ignored. The concept of an "American century," sustained by accepted corruption as a part of our "defensive" arsenal, has done far more to destroy than to elevate the once admirable influence of the United States abroad.

Along with this distortion has gone a sad transformation of our original political philosophy. In the metropolitan ganglia, local self-government has been virtually abandoned. A mystical faith in unattainable executive competence has developed. The subjection of an independent Congress to the well-organized

---

10. *Farewell Address.*

pressures of special interests and even "ethnic groups" has been accepted. There is no longer understanding, let alone belief, in the basic federal principle of divided and balanced powers. In all this general decay self-styled "conservative" thinking has often been as culpable as that of the most socialistic. And mutual recrimination has largely replaced debate between these warring camps.

"On the edge of the grave," suggested Henry Adams, men are sometimes granted a measure of foresight. Forgetfulness of the names of friends and flowers seems to me a more general characteristic of old age. Yet, as my long and not unobservant life draws to its close, I detect what seems to me a fortunate reaction against all the ephemeral fan-dancing of the immediate post-war years. This trend I believe will strengthen as Americans are forced to see less individual promise in materialistic objectives and more in the original spiritual conceptions which alone laid foundations for our over-rated prosperity. Already the elasticity of time is finding serious consideration in popular literature. We can no longer "kill time" with a clear conscience. Posterity has too strong an interest.

So change in outlook is indicated by the revolutionary change in the time-scheme which we have all been witnessing. The one advantage of old age is that the effects of this transition can be considered without fear or favor, with deference neither to pride nor prejudice. But youth also should accept the invitation from Walt Whitman, himself a timeless poet.

> Stop this day and night with me and you shall possess the
>   origin of all poems,
> You shall possess the good of the earth and sun, (there are
>   millions of suns left,)
> You shall no longer take things at second or third hand,
>   nor look through the eyes of the dead, nor feed on
>   the spectres in books,
> You shall not look through my eyes either, nor take things
>   from me,
> You shall listen to all sides and filter them from your self.

Index of Names

Fosdick, Raymond, 255
Foster, William Z., 139
Fotitch, Constantin, 345n, 423
Franco, Gen. Francisco, 283
Freeman, Douglas Southall, 304, 330
Freer, Evelyn L., 243*ff*, 417*ff*, 447*ff*
Frey, William, 388*ff*
Fulbright, Sen. J. William, 449

Gallie, Col. J. Stuart, 69
Gallup, Dr. George, 257, 351
Garey, Enoch B., 156
Garvin, James L., 308
George VI, 339
George, Sen. Walter, 395
Geraud, André (a.k.a. Pertinax), 150
Gerig, Ben, 236, 354, 378
Getts, Clark, 302
Gibson, Hugh, 233, 376, 408
Gilbert, Prentiss, 227
Gilman, Dr. Daniel Coit, 7
Gilman, Elisabeth, 155*ff*
Ginsberg, Mark (a.k.a. Gayne), 301
Goerdeler, Dr. Karl, 342
Goethe, Johann Wolfgang von, 86, 134
Goette, John, 184*ff*, 209
Gompers, Samuel, 109
Gonne, Maude, 127
Goto, Viscount, 171*ff*
Groat, Carl, 97
Grasty, Charles H., 146
Grew, Joseph C., 240
Griffith, Sanford, 139
Grimes, William, 440*ff*
Gummere, Dr. Francis B., 58

Haberler, Dr. Gottfried, 447
Haggard, "Bill," 284*ff*
Halifax, Lord, 406
Hamilton, Alexander, 299, 460
Hamilton, Edith, 156, 450
Hanighen, Frank C., 393*ff*, 401*ff*, 423*ff*, 435*ff*
Hanna, Paul, 113
Harada, Ken, 221, 344
Harden, Maximilian, 133
Harding, Warren Gamaliel, 50, 146*ff*, 357
Hardy, Charles O., 244
Harkness, James, 20
Harrell, Samuel, 378
Harrison, Cyril A., 71
Haushofer, Dr. Karl, 313

Havas, Eugene, 265, 450
Hawkes, Sen. Al, 446
Hayek, Dr. F.A. "Fritz," 425, 438, 450
Haywood, Frank and Rosalind, 290*ff*
Hearn, Lafcadio, 162, 174*ff*
Hearst, William Randolph, 296, 305
Hedges, Frank, 172
Hegel, G. Wilhelm Friedrich, 138, 170, 354, 458
Henderson, Arthur, 123*ff*, 226, 292
Henderson, Will, 292
Henle, Ray, 429
Herndon, John and Grace, 225, 239
Hewes, Clarence B. "Buzzy," 182, 393
Hiss, Alger, 429*ff*, 436
Hitler, Adolph, 116*ff*, 153, 201, 231*ff*, 253*ff*, 264*ff*, 274*ff*, 289*ff*, 312*ff*, 332*ff*, 342*ff*, 359, 408*ff*, 458
Holcombe, Dr. Arthur N., 258
Hooper, Bett, 266
Hoover, Herbert, 93, 214*ff*, 227, 231n, 234, 242n, 247*ff*, 274*ff*, 328, 353*ff*, 376*ff*, 401, 416, 441*ff*
Hopper, Bruce, 258
Hornbeck, Dr. Stanley, 326
Hotson, Dr. Leslie, 356*ff*
Hsia, David, 412
Hull, Cordell, 275*ff*, 297, 326*ff*, 343, 359*ff*, 406
Huntington, Emily, 143
Hurley, Lawrence, 421
Huston, Jay, 192*ff*

Jefferson, Thomas, 299
Jones, Alexander F. "Casey," 285*ff*, 328
Jones, Dr. Rufus, 60*ff*, 170, 239, 347, 389, 406
Johnson, Nelson T., 207
Johnson, Robert, 380*ff*
Johnson, Dr. "Tom," 447
Jordan, Joe, 418

Karakhan, Lev Mikhilovitch, 181*ff*
Kato, Prime Minister, 169
Kauffman, Reginald Wright, 222, 267, 302
Kawakami, Kyoshi K., 162, 246*ff*, 282, 344, 369*ff*, 423
Kelf-Cohen, Reuben, 444*ff*
Kelly, "Mike," 90*ff*
Kennedy, Joseph P., 266
Kennerly, Morley, 294

469

DATE DUE

GAYLORD			PRINTED IN U.S.A.